Daoist Resonances in Heidegger

Daoism and the Human Experience

Series Editor: David Chai
Associate Professor of Philosophy, Chinese University of Hong Kong

Editorial Advisory Board
Lisa Raphals, University of California, Riverside (USA)
Robin Wang, Loyola Marymount University (USA)
Franklin Perkins, University of Hawaii (USA)
Eric S. Nelson, Hong Kong University of Science and Technology (Hong Kong)
Thomas Michael, Beijing Normal University (China)
James Sellmann, University of Guam (USA)
Chris Fraser, University of Toronto (Canada)
Bret Davis, Loyola University Maryland (USA)
Zongqi Cai, University of Illinois Urbana-Champaign (USA)
Zhihua Yao, Chinese University of Hong Kong (Hong Kong)

Daoism and the Human Experience creates a platform to explore, question, and learn about the ways Daoist thought elucidates the human experience in its philosophical, literary, aesthetic, and spiritual manifestations. We welcome contributions focusing on Daoist thought itself, as well as those that explore it within the broader context of China, East Asia, continental Europe, India, Africa, the Americas, and the Islamic world.

Daoist Resonances in Heidegger

Exploring a Forgotten Debt

Edited by
David Chai

BLOOMSBURY ACADEMIC
LONDON · NEW YORK · OXFORD · NEW DELHI · SYDNEY

BLOOMSBURY ACADEMIC
Bloomsbury Publishing Plc
50 Bedford Square, London, WC1B 3DP, UK
1385 Broadway, New York, NY 10018, USA
29 Earlsfort Terrace, Dublin 2, Ireland

BLOOMSBURY, BLOOMSBURY ACADEMIC and the Diana logo are trademarks of Bloomsbury Publishing Plc

First published in Great Britain 2022
This paperback edition published 2023

Copyright © David Chai and Contributors, 2022

David Chai has asserted his right under the Copyright, Designs and Patents Act, 1988, to be identified as Editor of this work.

For legal purposes the Acknowledgments on p. xii constitute an extension of this copyright page.

Cover design by Louise Dugdale
Cover images: Pattern: CaoChunhai / Getty Images,
Texture: Gusak Olena / Shutterstock.

All rights reserved. No part of this publication may be reproduced or transmitted in any form or by any means, electronic or mechanical, including photocopying, recording, or any information storage or retrieval system, without prior permission in writing from the publishers.

Bloomsbury Publishing Plc does not have any control over, or responsibility for, any third-party websites referred to or in this book. All internet addresses given in this book were correct at the time of going to press. The author and publisher regret any inconvenience caused if addresses have changed or sites have ceased to exist, but can accept no responsibility for any such changes.

A catalogue record for this book is available from the British Library.

A catalog record for this book is available from the Library of Congress.

Names: Chai, David, 1971- editor.
Title: Daoist resonances in Heidegger: exploring a forgotten debt / edited by David Chai.
Description: London; New York: Bloomsbury Academic, 2022. |
Series: Daoism and the human experience |
Includes bibliographical references and index.
Identifiers: LCCN 2022003847 (print) | LCCN 2022003848 (ebook) |
ISBN 9781350201071 (hardback) | ISBN 9781350203525 (paperback) |
ISBN 9781350201088 (pdf) | ISBN 9781350201095 (epub)
Subjects: LCSH: Heidegger, Martin, 1889-1976. | Taoism–Influence.
Classification: LCC B3279.H49 D327 2022 (print) |
LCC B3279.H49 (ebook) | DDC 193–dc23/eng/20220323
LC record available at https://lccn.loc.gov/2022003847
LC ebook record available at https://lccn.loc.gov/2022003848

ISBN: HB: 978-1-3502-0107-1
PB: 978-1-3502-0352-5
ePDF: 978-1-3502-0108-8
eBook: 978-1-3502-0109-5

Typeset by Integra Software Services Pvt. Ltd.

To find out more about our authors and books visit www.bloomsbury.com and sign up for our newsletters.

In memory of Martin Schönfeld (1963–2020)

Contents

Figures and Tables · viii
Contributors · ix
Acknowledgments · xii

Editor's Introduction · 1

Part One   Revisiting Heidegger and Daoism

1 Thoughts on the Way: *Being and Time* via Laozi and Zhuangzi
   Graham Parkes · 11
2 Heidegger's Daoist Phenomenology *Jay Goulding* · 47
3 The Simple Onefold of Dao and Being: Reading Laozi, Zhuangzi, and Heidegger in Light of Interality *Geling Shang* · 103

Part Two   Existence and the Arts

4 Dao of Death *Jason M. Wirth* · 127
5 Thing and World in Laozi and Heidegger *Eric S. Nelson* · 141
6 Zhuangzi, Heidegger, and the Self-Revealing Being of Sculpture
   David Chai · 163

Part Three   Language and Identity

7 Rivers to the East: Heidegger's Lectures on Hölderlin as Prolegomena for Daoist Engagements *Daniel Fried* · 183
8 Thinking through Silence: (Non-) Language in Heidegger and Classical Daoism *Steven Burik* · 203
9 The Politics of Uselessness: On Heidegger's Reading of the *Zhuangzi* *Fabian Heubel* · 225
10 "We Have Been Schooled by the Cabin Haven't We?" Heidegger and Daoism in the Provinces *Mario Wenning* · 243

Index · 259

List of Figures

1.1	*Taiji* symbol	37
2.1	Heidegger's fourfold	55
2.2	Daoism's fourfold	56
2.3	Waying and Dao	57

List of Tables

2.1	Three Essentials of Socrates, Schelling, Heidegger, and Dao	64

Contributors

Steven Burik is currently Assistant Professor of Philosophy at Singapore Management University. His research interests are mainly in comparative philosophy, continental philosophy (Heidegger, Derrida), Chinese philosophy (Daoism), and critical thinking. His works include *The End of Comparative Philosophy and the Task of Comparative Thinking* (2009), a co-authored textbook on critical thinking, and articles in various journals and books. His most recent work is an edited volume (with Ralph Weber and Robert Smid) titled: *Comparative Philosophy and Method: Contemporary Practices and Future Possibilities* (2022).

David Chai is Associate Professor of Philosophy at the Chinese University of Hong Kong. He is the author of *Reading Ji Kang's Essays: Xuanxue in Early Medieval China* (2022) and *Zhuangzi and the Becoming of Nothingness* (2019). He is editor of *Daoist Encounters with Phenomenology: Thinking Interculturally about Human Existence* (2020) and *Dao Companion to Xuanxue [Neo-Daoism]* (2020). His research covers the fields of ancient and medieval Chinese philosophy, aesthetics, metaphysics, phenomenology, and comparative philosophy.

Daniel Fried is Associate Professor at the University of Alberta, where he specializes in comparative approaches to the intellectual history of China and Europe. His latest book *Dao and Sign in History* (2018) was an examination of Daoist semiotics in early and medieval China; he is currently working on the print culture of the Northern Song dynasty. He is a past president of the Association of Chinese and Comparative Literature and is co-editor of *Routledge Studies in Comparative Chinese Literature and Culture*.

Jay Goulding is Professor in the Department of Social Science at York University. His expertise lies in classical Chinese and Japanese philosophy, hermeneutics and phenomenology. Among his many publications, he participated in celebrations of the ninetieth anniversary of the Department of Philosophy at Beijing University, edited *China-West Interculture: Toward the Philosophy of World Integration, Essays on Wu Kuang-Ming's Thinking*, and contributed a paper to the fortieth-anniversary volume of the *Journal of Chinese Philosophy*. His most recent work includes a special festschrift paper for the *Journal of Chinese Philosophy* on Cheng Chung-Ying and Hans-Georg Gadamer entitled "Cheng and Gadamer: Daoist Phenomenology."

Fabian Heubel has been a member of the Institute of Chinese Literature and Philosophy at Academia Sinica since 2001 and a Research Fellow there since 2013.

He also teaches at the Institute of Philosophy at Goethe-University in Frankfurt. His main research interests center on critical theory, contemporary German and French thought, interpretations of Chinese philosophy in Western sinology, and classical and contemporary Chinese philosophy. His most recent books include *Gewundene Wege nach China: Heidegger-Daoismus-Adorno* (2020), *Was ist chinesische Philosophie? Kritische Perspektiven* (2021), and *Self-cultivation and Critique: A Transcultural Perspective on the Late Foucault* (in Chinese, 2021).

Eric S. Nelson is Professor of Humanities at the Hong Kong University of Science and Technology. He works on Chinese, German, and Jewish philosophy. His latest books include *Levinas, Adorno, and the Ethics of the Material Other* (2020), *Daoism and Environmental Philosophy: Nourishing Life* (2020), *Levinas, Adorno, and the Ethics of the Material Other* (2019), and *Chinese and Buddhist Philosophy in Early Twentieth-Century German Thought* (2017). He is also the editor of *Interpreting Dilthey: Critical Essays* (2019) and co-editor with François Raffoul of the *Bloomsbury Companion to Heidegger* (2016).

Graham Parkes was born and raised in Glasgow and educated at Oxford and the University of California Berkeley. He taught Asian and comparative philosophy at the University of Hawaii for twenty-five years, punctuated by three years as a visiting scholar and fellow at Harvard. He is now a Professorial Research Fellow at the Institute of Philosophy, University of Vienna. He has published extensively in the fields of Chinese, German, Japanese, and environmental philosophies. His most recent book is *How to Think about the Climate Crisis: A Philosophical Guide to Saner Ways of Living* (2020), and he is the editor of the critically acclaimed *Heidegger and Asian Thought* (1987).

Geling Shang is Associate Professor of Philosophy at Grand Valley State University. The author of *Liberation as Affirmation: The Religiosity of Zhuangzi and Nietzsche* (2006), his main areas of research are Chinese and comparative philosophy, particularly the concepts of "throughness" (*tong* 通) and "interality" (*jian* 間), resulting in a philosophical territory he calls "interalogy."

Mario Wenning is Professor Titular at the Loyola University Andalusia and Vice President of the Karl Jaspers Society of North America. His work focuses primarily on social and political philosophy as well as aesthetics from an intercultural perspective. His work has appeared in a wide variety of journals, including *Comparative Philosophy, Journal of Chinese Philosophy, Philosophy East and West, Confluence,* and *Studies in Philosophy and Education*. He is currently completing a book manuscript on natural agency East and West.

Jason M. Wirth is Professor of Philosophy at Seattle University, and works and teaches in the areas of Buddhist philosophy, aesthetics, continental philosophy, environmental philosophy, and Africana philosophy. His recent books include *Nietzsche and Other*

Buddhas: Philosophy after Comparative Philosophy (2019), *Mountains, Rivers, and the Great Earth: Reading Gary Snyder and Dōgen in an Age of Ecological Crisis* (2017), *Commiserating with Devastated Things: Milan Kundera and the Entitlements of Thinking* (2015), and *Schelling's Practice of the Wild: Time, Art, Imagination* (2015). He is the associate editor and book review editor of the journal *Comparative and Continental Philosophy*.

Acknowledgments

My thanks to Graham, Jay, Eric, Jason, Daniel, Steven, Geling, Mario, and Fabian, for helping me amplify the echoes of Daoism permeating Heidegger's thought. Thanks also to Colleen Coalter and Suzie Nash at Bloomsbury, and the University of Hawaii Press for permission to reprint Graham Parkes' chapter "Thoughts on the Way: Being and Time via Lao-Chuang," which originally appeared in his *Heidegger and Asian Thought* (1987: 105–44).

Editor's Introduction

The question of Martin Heidegger's (1889–1976) relationship with East Asia is as important as it is misinformed. The studies by Graham Parkes (1987), Reinhard May (1996), and Lin Ma (2008) have helped dispel the cloud of mischaracterization surrounding Heidegger's interaction with the texts and persons from China and Japan. From the East Asian side of the story, the reception of Heidegger has been uneven. For example, the first scholar from East Asia to visit Germany and study with Heidegger was Tanabe Hajime in 1922, the first article to be written about Heidegger was also by Tanabe Hajime in 1924, while the first translation of *Being and Time* appeared in Japanese in 1939 (the first English translation only appeared in 1962). The situation in China was very different. Although Chinese students and scholars visited Heidegger in Germany, studying his works in China proved untenable during the 1950s and 1960s. Despite the eagerness of the Japanese to engage Heidegger, it would be fair to say Heidegger was not as drawn to their thought as he was to ancient Chinese Daoism (i.e., the *Daodejing* 道德經 and *Zhuangzi* 莊子), despite a few remarks of his that might indicate otherwise.

According to Otto Pöggeler, in December of 1945 "Heidegger suffered a breakdown and had to be taken to a sanatorium for three weeks" during which time he began translating Laozi's *Daodejing*.[1] Andrew Mitchell, however, states Heidegger's health crisis occurred many months later. The source of this crisis was the result of being "brought before a commission of university professors assembled by the French authorities then occupying Germany for the purpose of establishing political accountability during the war … [in July of 1946] shortly after meeting with the de-nazification committee Heidegger suffered a nervous breakdown."[2] What is more, under the care of Dr. Viktor Emil Freiherr von Gebsattel (1883–1976), "Heidegger's letters of the time show the effect that Gebsattel had upon him, giving the lie to the standard account reported by Heinrich-Wiegand Petzet and confirming Hugo Ott's contention that Heidegger's stay with Gebsattel lasted three to six months, not three weeks as Heidegger reported: 'Heidegger's sojourn in Badenweiler lasted from February to the end of May 1946. After that time, the psychotherapeutic treatment continued with Gebsasttel.'"[3]

Heidegger's encounter with Daoism began well before his breakdown: the 1930 Bremen lecture "On the Essence of Truth" (*Vom Wesen der Wahrheit*, published in 1943) to be precise. It was after this lecture, during the discussion session, that Heidegger asked for a copy of the *Zhuangzi*, and upon being presented with Martin Buber's edition, he launched into a discussion of the famous story in chapter 17 on the joy of fish.[4] Buber's partial translation of the *Zhuangzi* into German was first published in 1910 and was appropriately entitled *Speeches and Parables of Tschuang-Tse* (*Reden und Gleichnisse des Tschuang Tse*). Buber's Zhuangzi text would go through several revisions, once in 1918 and again in 1951; however, Buber based his translation on the English translation carried out by Herbert Giles in 1889.[5] According to Irene Eber, Buber gave a series of private lectures on the *Daodejing* in 1924, yet they were never published and remain a typewritten manuscript entitled "Talks with Martin Buber in Ascona, August 1924, about Lao-tzu's *Tao Te Ching*."[6]

Heidegger would publicly refer to Buber's *Zhuangzi* translation several more times after his 1930 lecture. In his 1960 Bremen seminar entitled "Word and Image" (*Bild und Wort*), he discussed Zhuangzi's story of the bell-stand maker from chapter 19,[7] and the text came up in conversation with Chang Chung-Yuan when he visited Heidegger in Freiburg in 1972.[8] Besides these stories, others include the 1962 lecture "Traditional Language and Technological Language" (*Uberlieferte Sprache und Technische Sprache*)[9] wherein Heidegger talked about the theme of uselessness, a theme that arose during a conversation between Zhuangzi and his friend Huizi in chapter 1 of the *Zhuangzi*. Another story, from chapter 26 of the text in which Huizi declares Zhuangzi's words to be useless, finds its way into Heidegger's "Evening Conversation in a Russian War Camp between a Young and Old Man" from 1944 to 1945.[10] The import of these references to Daoist uselessness, according to Eric Nelson, is that they serve as "a response to the crisis conditions of National Socialism and German defeat and the technocratic regime of the necessity of the useful ... [hence they] opened up new possibilities and retrievals of his own thinking for Heidegger in the Post-war period."[11]

Of course, Daoism is not limited to the *Zhuangzi*; there is also Laozi's *Daodejing*. Of the eight lectures Heidegger gave in Bremen during the 1950s, his lecture "The Thing" (*Das Ding*) is well-known amongst Daoist scholars insofar as it borrows the analogy of the clay jug from chapter 11 of the *Daodejing*.[12] Later, in 1958, in his contribution to the Festschrift for Dr. Gebsattel, Heidegger referred to chapter 28 of Laozi's text.[13] Indeed, Heidegger would have been constantly reminded of the *Daodejing* while looking at the calligraphy written by Paul Shih-Yi Hsiao hanging on his study wall since it was couplet taken from chapter 15 of the *Daodejing*.[14] Whereas Buber's German translation of the *Zhuangzi* would have been the only one available to Heidegger, the *Daodejing* was readily accessible through the translations by Victor von Strauss (1874), Alexander Ular (1903), Richard Wilhelm (1911), and Jan Ulenbrook (1962).[15]

We know Heidegger was familiar with Wilhelm's edition of the *Daodejing* by way of the following remark from Petzet: "He [Heidegger] himself holds to Lao-tzu, but he knows Lao-tzu only through the German mediators—for example, Richard Wilhelm."[16] We also know, again via Petzet, that Heidegger was no stranger to Ulenbrook's translation:

> I knew how highly Heidegger esteemed Lao-tzu. But only after he died did I learn that at one point he began translating the *Tao Te Ching*. When Ernst Junger was about to start his trip to East Asia in 1966, Heidegger included a saying of the old sage in his letter to Junger. I am grateful to Junger for being able to quote that saying at the end of this chapter devoted to Heidegger's relationship to the

Far East ... It is the forty-seventh chapter of the *Tao Te Ching* and reads, in the translation by Jan Ulenbrook.[17]

Roughly twenty years earlier, in a letter dated October 9, 1947, to Paul Shih-Yi Hsiao, Heidegger paraphrases Hsiao's translation of chapter 15 of the *Daodejing*.[18] These lines would become the famous calligraphic scrolls hanging on Heidegger's study wall. Chapters 7, 18, and 76 would also be discussed with Hsiao and demonstrate Heidegger's acquaintance with this text.[19] In total, Heidegger mentions Laozi in the following volumes of his *Complete Works* (i.e., *Gesamtausgabe*): page 138 of Band 11 (*Identität und Differenz* (1955–1957), page 181 of Band 12 (*Unterwegs zur Sprache* (1950–1959), pages 617 and 618 of Band 16 (*Reden und andere Zeugnisse eines Lebensweges* (1910–1976), page 43 of Band 75 (*Zu Hölderlin: Griechenlandreisen*), and pages 93 and 146 of Band 79 (*Bremer und Freiburger Vorträge*).[20]

In light of the above evidence, is this enough to prove beyond a shadow of a doubt that Heidegger's comportment toward Daoist philosophy was anything but fleeting? Is it fair to say the resonance Heidegger felt with Daoism was genuine? This book will answer in the affirmative with the condition that we do not presume the entirety of Heidegger's corpus bears the stamp of Daoist philosophy. Indeed, since Elisabeth Hirsch published her paper in 1970 on Heidegger and East Asian thought,[21] scholars have consistently pointed to the explicit and unacknowledged influence of Daoism on Heidegger's later thought. As Heidegger himself said, "it has seemed urgent to me that a dialogue take place with the thinkers of what is to us the Eastern world."[22] What is more, "by thinking the clearing and characterizing it adequately, we reach a realm that can perhaps make it possible to bring a transformed European thinking into a *fruitful engagement* with East Asian 'thinking.'"[23]

And yet, when Heidegger says he was skeptical about "what his Japanese friends made out of his philosophy" and that "he has difficulty believing blindly that thoughts in a language so foreign would mean the same,"[24] one has to question his sincerity in having a dialogue with the Eastern world. Such being the case, Petzet rightly points out it "would be a mistake to want (as some have) to construct, overzealously though with good intentions, a kind of thought-harmony that would span the peoples and to attempt a direct equation of [Japanese] Zen with Heidegger's many paths of thinking."[25] Heidegger is partly to blame for the confusion surrounding his comportment to the East when he states, as he did in his interview for *Der Spiegel* in 1966, that there is no point in turning "to Zen or other Eastern experiences of the world"[26] if the West is to free itself of the chains of technology preventing it from thinking the question of Being. Just three years earlier, in 1963, Heidegger met with Bhikku Maha Mani, a Buddhist monk from Thailand, in Freiburg, after which they recorded an interview to be broadcast on television. In their pre-interview conversation, the monk asked Heidegger what he thinks needs to be done "to overcome the pre-disposition and the prejudice so that unity is restored beyond the dichotomy? Heidegger answers that the way can be opened only through releasement toward things and openness to the mystery."[27] This resulted in the following:

[Heidegger asked the monk:] What does meditation mean for Eastern humanity? The monk's response is quite simple: Meditation means 'to gather oneself.' The more humanity succeeds in gathering itself and concentrating, without exertion of the will, the more it lets go of itself. The 'I' dissolves, until in the end only one thing remains: the Nothing. But this Nothing is not nothing; it is just the opposite-fullness. No one can name this. But it is nothing and everything-fullness. Heidegger understands this and says, 'This is what I have been saying throughout my whole life.'[28]

In the words of Stanley Rosen: "In conformity with Heidegger's own characterization of his thought as a 'being under way,' Being is itself the ways in which beings come to be and pass away, or the 'way of ways': it is not the Greek physis, but the Chinese Tao."[29] The issue for Heidegger, therefore, was not the difficulty of Eastern thought but the forbidding nature of its languages. Two important pieces of evidence for this statement are offered by Lin Ma: the first is in a letter from June 30, 1955, to the Swiss psychiatrist Medard Boss in which Heidegger opines: "Today I am amazed that years ago I dared to give the lecture on language. The greatest omission belongs to the fact that the possibility for a sufficient discussion about the East Asian languages is lacking."[30] The second instance in which Heidegger admits his Eastern language handicap was in a letter from November 1969 to the organizers of a conference at the University of Hawaii devoted to his relationship with East Asian thought:

> Again and again it has seemed urgent to me that a dialogue take place with the thinkers of what is to us the Eastern world. The greatest difficulty in this enterprise always lies, as far as I can see, in the fact that with few exceptions there is no command of the Eastern languages either in Europe or in the United States.[31]

Lin Ma's book is unmatched in the hermeneutic rigor it applies to Heidegger's corpus in order to uncover its textual links with Daoism. Her reason for doing so is that "in quoting what they consider to be important evidence for their highly positive judgment on Heidegger's relation with Asian thought, some authors have taken insufficient care."[32] Not only this but "some scholars have attempted to bring Heidegger's thinking to bear on the issue of intercultural dialogue or theory of comparative philosophy ... yet the majority of contributors to such discourses have ascribed a highly positive stance toward a dialogue with the East to Heidegger himself without proper qualifications."[33] These are critically valuable insights and ones the present work will bear in mind and attempt to address.

Although the works by Parkes, May, and Ma are the standard-bearers for Heidegger-East Asian studies, they are not the only ones to do so. Katrin Froese (2006) and Steven Burik (2009) have added their own substantial contributions to this small but growing topic within comparative philosophy. Like their predecessors, however, Froese and Burik did not focus their attention on Heidegger and Daoism alone—Froese includes discussion of Nietzsche while Burik adds Derrida. There has, in other words, yet to be a book-length study in English devoted to the thought of Heidegger and Daoism. The present book will not only fill this lacuna, it will do so by availing itself of recently published volumes in Heidegger's *Gesamtausgabe*, or the English translations of the said volumes, without losing sight of Daoism's core arguments. To be sure, the chapters comprising this book will lend further credence to the notion that Heidegger's turn to Daoism was partly in response to the inability of Western philosophy to offer him the answers he needed as he sought a "second beginning" from which to reexamine the question of being. By exploring themes such as interality, nationhood, the thing, language, death, identity, and art, from the groundlessness of non-being, this book will deftly illustrate how they reverberate with ontological, spiritual, and epistemological potential.

Another aspect that makes this work a worthwhile contribution is its timeliness. The recent publication of Heidegger's "black notebooks" has proven to be a turn-off for many people, yet these same people have overlooked the fact that Heidegger's disavowal of National Socialism coincided with his "energized interest" in Daoism. This book is not an apology for his political views, nor is it claiming his post-war writings were baked in a Daoist kiln; on the contrary, the objective of this book is to show how Daoism resonated with Heidegger and how he used such resonance to aid his own thinking. This is not to say that Heidegger was trying to be Daoist, far from it; rather, Daoism equipped Heidegger with a collection of images, concepts, and meanings that enabled him to continue his questioning of the nature of being by offering him a perspective no other philosophical tradition could.

There are limitations to Heidegger's philosophy, to be sure; however, using the ideas of Daoism to supplement—not overcome—the former's arguments can, potentially, allow us to see Heidegger in a more subtle, open light. This book is thus a project of comparison by way of circularity. Whereas Heidegger warmly embraced Daoism, he was nevertheless unwilling to abandon his Western philosophical roots. Herein lies another benefit of this book: it will offer readers a lesson in the art of Daoist thinking so as to avoid being consumed by the question of being.

The chapters comprising this book are wide-ranging in terms of both methodology and subject matter. While the Western side of our discourse focuses on Heidegger, in the case of Daoism, we are dealing with two figures: Laozi and Zhuangzi.[34] Daoism, not Heidegger, is the thread that binds each chapter of this book together, the ultimate purpose of which is to present readers with a sustained analysis of the Daoist worldview by way of a resonating encounter with Heidegger. This encounter is not dependent on a traditionally defined knowing self however; rather, Daoism seeks to liberate human knowing and thinking by discarding the subjective self, dogmatic norms, and non-inclusionary theories of reality. In this way, Daoism transcends the traditional definition of philosophy by shifting the plane of truth from the human to the onto-cosmological realm of the Dao. Daoist philosophy is hence simultaneously mundane and transcendental, this-worldly and non-worldly, appreciative of things as they naturally are while also being sensitive to what said things were and will become.

To quote Graham Parkes,

> the consideration of Heidegger's ideas may help to articulate some themes that are only implicit in the stylistically very different texts of the Daoist thinkers. The discovery of resonances with Daoist ideas in Heidegger's early works should make us take more seriously his assertions of the essential unity of his thought

throughout its many phases, and also his claim to be the first thinker to have overcome the Western metaphysical tradition.[35]

Given his personal relationship with Heidegger, Chung-Yuan Chang is well-placed to offer the following assessment: "Heidegger is the only Western philosopher who not only intellectually understands Dao, but has intuitively experienced the essence of it as well."[36] High praise indeed! Caution is needed, however, because

> triangulating between the sibling languages of German and English on the one hand and Chinese ... we need to take care that we remain hermeneutically attuned to both the perilous pitfalls and fecund possibilities of translation and cross-cultural dialogue. Venturing further down the path of a dialogue between Heidegger's thought and Daoism, we must take care to be neither too timid nor too rash.[37]

In line with such remarks, this book presents essays that will be informative and stimulating for readers who wish to both further their understanding of Heidegger and Daoism, and partake in the resonance between them.

Notes

1 Graham Parkes, ed., *Heidegger and Asian Thought* (Honolulu: University of Hawaii Press, 1987), 51.
2 Andrew J. Mitchell, "Heidegger's Breakdown: Health and Healing under the Care of Dr. V.E. von Gebsattel," *Research in Phenomenology*, 46.1 (2016): 70–97, at 71.
3 Ibid., 85.
4 Heinrich-Wiegand Petzet, *Encounters and Dialogues with Heidegger, 1929–1976*, trans. Parvis Emad and Kenneth Maly (Chicago: University of Chicago Press, 1993), 18.
5 Irene Eber, "Martin Buber and Taoism," *Monumenta Serica*, 42 (1994): 445–64, at 447.
6 Ibid., 448.
7 Petzet, *Encounters and Dialogues*, 59 and 169.
8 Reinhard May, *Heidegger's Hidden Sources: East Asian Influences on His Work*, trans. Graham Parkes (London: Routledge, 1996), 3.
9 Eric S. Nelson, "Heidegger's Daoist Turn," *Research in Phenomenology*, 49.3 (2019): 362–84, at 374.
10 See ibid., 369–71.
11 Ibid., 382.
12 Parkes, *Heidegger and Asian Thought*, 61.
13 Ibid., 62.
14 Petzet, *Encounters and Dialogues*, 168.
15 See Lin Ma, *Heidegger on East-West Dialogue: Anticipating the Event* (New York: Routledge, 2008), 121.
16 Petzet, *Encounters and Dialogues*, 174.
17 Ibid., 181.
18 Parkes, *Heidegger and Asian Thought*, 102.

19 For more on their relationship, see ibid., 93–100.
20 See Francois Jaran and Christophe Perrin, *The Heidegger Concordance* (London: Bloomsbury, 2013), 201. Curiously, Zhuangzi's name does not appear in Jaran and Perrin's *Concordance*.
21 Elisabeth Feist Hirsch, "Martin Heidegger and the East," *Philosophy East and West*, 20.3 (1970): 247–63.
22 Ma, *Heidegger on East-West Dialogue*, 3.
23 Lin Ma and Jaap van Brakel, "Heidegger's Comportment toward East-West Dialogue," *Philosophy East and West*, 56.4 (2006): 519–66, at 545.
24 Petzet, *Encounters and Dialogues*, 167.
25 Ibid.
26 Veronique M. Foti, "Heidegger and 'The Way of Art': The Empty Origin and Contemporary Abstraction," *Continental Philosophy Review*, 31.4 (1998): 337–51, at 337.
27 Petzet, *Encounters and Dialogues*, 179.
28 Ibid., 180.
29 Stanley Rosen, *Nihilism: A Philosophical Essay* (New Haven: Yale University Press, 1969), 126.
30 Ma, *Heidegger on East-West Dialogue*, 145.
31 Ibid., 146.
32 Ibid., 3.
33 Ibid., 4.
34 The abbreviation "Lao-Zhuang" will henceforth be used instead.
35 Graham Parkes, "Intimations of Taoist Themes in Early Heidegger," *Journal of Chinese Philosophy*, 11.4 (1984): 353–74, at 353–4.
36 Chung-Yuan Chang, *Tao: A New Way of Thinking* (London: Singing Dragon, 2014), 8.
37 Bret W. Davis, "Heidegger and Daoism: A Dialogue on the Useless Way of Unnecessary Being," in David Chai (ed.), *Daoist Encounters with Phenomenology: Thinking Interculturally about Human Existence*, 161–96 (London: Bloomsbury Academic, 2020), at 166–7.

References

Chang, Chung-Yuan. *Tao: A New Way of Thinking*. London: Singing Dragon, 2014.
Davis, Bret W. "Heidegger and Daoism: A Dialogue on the Useless Way of Unnecessary Being." In David Chai (ed.), *Daoist Encounters with Phenomenology: Thinking Interculturally about Human Existence*, 161–96. London: Bloomsbury Academic, 2020.
Eber, Irene. "Martin Buber and Taoism." *Monumenta Serica*, 42 (1994): 445–64.
Foti, Veronique M. "Heidegger and 'The Way of Art': The Empty Origin and Contemporary Abstraction." *Continental Philosophy Review*, 31.4 (1998): 337–51.
Hirsch, Elisabeth Feist. "Martin Heidegger and the East." *Philosophy East and West*, 20.3 (1970): 247–63.
Jaran, Francois and Christophe Perrin. *The Heidegger Concordance*. London: Bloomsbury, 2013.
Ma, Lin. *Heidegger on East-West Dialogue: Anticipating the Event*. New York: Routledge, 2008.

Ma, Lin and Jaap van Brakel. "Heidegger's Comportment toward East-West Dialogue." *Philosophy East and West*, 56.4 (2006): 519–66.
May, Reinhard. *Heidegger's Hidden Sources: East Asian Influences on His Work*. Translated by Graham Parkes. London: Routledge, 1996.
Mitchell, Andrew J. "Heidegger's Breakdown: Health and Healing under the Care of Dr. V.E. von Gebsattel." *Research in Phenomenology*, 46.1 (2016): 70–97.
Nelson, Eric S. "Heidegger's Daoist Turn." *Research in Phenomenology*, 49.3 (2019): 362–84.
Parkes, Graham. "Intimations of Taoist Themes in Early Heidegger." *Journal of Chinese Philosophy*, 11.4 (1984): 353–74.
Parkes, Graham, ed. *Heidegger and Asian Thought*. Honolulu: University of Hawaii Press, 1987.
Petzet, Heinrich-Wiegand. *Encounters and Dialogues with Heidegger, 1929–1976*. Translated by Parvis Emad and Kenneth Maly. Chicago: University of Chicago Press, 1993.
Rosen, Stanley. *Nihilism: A Philosophical Essay*. New Haven: Yale University Press, 1969.

Part One

Revisiting Heidegger and Daoism

1

Thoughts on the Way: *Being and Time* via Laozi and Zhuangzi

Graham Parkes

The true nature of things loves to hide.
Heraclitus

⌐ Prologue

Time: Evening of October 9, 1930; after Heidegger's public lecture "On the Essence of Truth"
Place: The house of a Mr. Kellner, in Bremen, north Germany
Topic: Whether one can truly put oneself in another's place
Occasion: An impasse in the discussion

HEIDEGGER [*turning suddenly to the host*]:
Herr Kellner—would you please bring me the *Allegories of Zhuangzi*? I should like to read something from them.

> [*Mr. Kellner leaves the room and reappears with a copy of the Martin Buber edition*[1]]

HEIDEGGER [*turning to chapter 17*]:
Zhuangzi and Huizi were standing on the bridge above the Hao river.
"Look at the minnows swimming around," said Zhuangzi. "That's how fish are happy."
"You aren't a fish," said Huizi. "So how do you know the fish are happy?"
"You aren't me, so how do you know that I don't know the fish are happy?"
"Not being you, I don't know about you. But I do know that you're not a fish, and so you can't know the fish are happy."

---

* This chapter is reprinted as it originally appeared in 1987, aside from changing Wade-Giles romanization for Chinese terms to Pinyin, inserting Chinese characters where needed, adding the volume numbers of the *Gesamtausgabe* for Heidegger's German works, and correcting the occasional error or typo.

"Let's go back to your initial question. When you said '*How* do you know the fish are happy?' you asked me the question already knowing that I knew. I knew it from my own happiness at being up above the Hao."

[*Later*]

MR. PETZET [*aside*]:
With his interpretation of this story Heidegger is unexpectedly getting through better than with his difficult lecture, which to many people still remains obscure. Whoever is still in the dark about the essence of truth, reflection on this Chinese tale will show him Heidegger's position on it.[2]

* * *

HEIDEGGER:
The essence of truth is freedom ... Freedom reveals itself as the letting-be of beings ... as letting oneself into what-is.[3]

Introduction

"*Being and Time* is a *way* and not a shelter. Whoever cannot walk should not take refuge in it. A way, not 'the' way, which never exists in philosophy."[4] Heidegger did not publish the text of his enigmatic lecture on the essence of truth until 1943. Three years later he spent the summer working with Dr. Hsiao from Taiwan on a translation of parts of the *Laozi*.[5] But it is not until the late 1950s that he makes any reference to Daoism in print. In the lecture "The Principle of Identity" he mentions "the Chinese *dao*" in the same breath as the (Presocratic) Greek *logos*.[6] Two years later, in *Underway to Language* (1959), in which he gives the first and only account of his engagement with philosophers from Japan, he offers a brief discussion of the idea of "Dao" in "the poetic thinking of Laozi."[7] Professor Chung-Yuan Chang reports that when he visited Heidegger in Freiburg in 1972, the latter produced a German translation of the *Zhuangzi* about which he was eager to ask questions and engage in discussion.[8]

What were the grounds for Heidegger's interest, stretching over almost half a century, in a philosophy as ardently alien to Western thought as Daoism? Can we find any predisposing factors, and any elements in Heidegger's thinking prior to his contact with Daoist ideas that would suggest a "pre-established harmony" between them? And what would be the point of engaging in a comparison of the two philosophies? *Harmoniē aphanēs phanerēs kreittōn*, says Heraclitus. The hidden harmony is deeper, the invisible connection stronger, the inconspicuous correspondence more interesting than the apparent. The parallels between Heidegger's later work and Daoist ideas are so striking that they have already prompted comment.[9] The concern here will be rather with *Sein und Zeit*, where the areas of similarity are obscure and—assuming that its writing antedates the author's contact with Chinese thought—where influence is unlikely.[10]

Such a comparison points up some hitherto overlooked themes in Heidegger's early work that have a remarkably Daoist tone to them, rendering comprehensible why he should soon have found Daoism and Zen so congenial. It may also bring into relief some features that are only vaguely limned in the texts of the Daoist thinkers. Counter to the tendency of some of the secondary literature to exaggerate the differences between Heidegger's early and late work, a tendency exacerbated by viewing only the later writings as poetical and in harmony with Asian ideas, the present comparison will support Heidegger's assertions of the essential unity of his thought throughout its many phases. Above all, parallels demonstrated between his early "pre-contact" work and a non- and anti-metaphysical philosophy from a totally different historical and cultural situation lend considerable weight to Heidegger's claim to have succeeded in overcoming the Western metaphysical tradition.

A reading of Heidegger's and the Daoists' texts together makes apparent the extent to which, in philosophy, the form of what is presented constitutes the content. A foundational paradigm of content being embodied in form is the Platonic dialogue. Had Plato wished to convey "his philosophy," in the sense of setting forth his ideas about the nature of reality, he would have written discursive treatises. Because he was more concerned with prompting people to question for themselves, with inducing them to follow and make the *way* of thinking (which Heidegger calls *Denkweg* and the Daoists *dao*), to undergo the experience of going over the same topics again and again, of mis-taking highways for by-ways, of losing track of the way altogether, ending up—amazed—in cul-de-sacs and blind alleys through following at the heels of that Protean guide and master of the *aporia*, Socrates: he wrote dialogues. And given that Plato consistently wrote himself out of these dialogues, the question arises: what is his position? Where do we find his own views? To say that they are expressed in the speeches of Socrates is too simplistic. Many of the views expressed by interlocutors other than Socrates are eminently reasonable for a person to hold at that stage of inquiry—and some are surely views that Plato himself once held. To the extent that there is such a thing as Plato's position on a certain topic at a certain stage of his thinking, it is to be found *between* (one of Heidegger's favorite prepositions) that of Socrates and those of the other participants in the conversation, generated out of the tension of the opposing views presented.

Although discursive prose is not entirely inappropriate for writing on the early Heidegger alone, a comparison with the writings of Lao-Zhuang calls for a somewhat different form. Some kind of dialogue would be apposite, since Heidegger published two of his most fascinating pieces in the form of dialogues—and one might have expected more, in view of his predilection for spoken dialogue as a medium of instruction.[11] Further, the perspectivism of Daoist philosophy makes the dialogue an appropriate medium of explication, especially since the *Zhuangzi* consists largely of conversations and altercations. However, dialogue need not be overtly dramatic, as in Plato. The interlocutors in what follows are not *dramatis* but rather *cogitatoris personae*, representing tendencies within a single individual—and especially within one engaged in thinking about Heidegger and comparative philosophy. Their three voices, which are distinguished typographically (standard type, italic, and sans serif), represent different perspectives on certain issues common to the Daoists and Heidegger.

二. Dialogue

Fragmentary Beginnings

> Although everything happens according to the *logos*, men behave as though they do not understand it, both before they have heard it and after hearing it.
>
> Heraclitus 1

> My words are very easy to understand and put into practice, yet no one in the world can understand or put them into practice.
>
> *Laozi* 70

It is for good reason that Heidegger mentions *dao* 道 in the same breath as the Presocratic *logos*. A major ground for his openness to Daoist ideas is his becoming attuned early on to reading comparable texts in the form of fragments from the Presocratics. Of particular relevance in this context would be the writings of Heraclitus, the Western thinker closest in spirit to Daoism and to whom Heidegger ascribes the deepest understanding of Being.[12] The texts of the two great Daoist classics, though written somewhat later than the fragments, occupy a place in the history of East Asian thinking comparable to that of Heraclitus's work in the West. The impact of Lao-Zhuang was of course initially much greater, giving rise to one of the foremost schools of Chinese philosophy, and subsequently constituting a major force in the development of Zen Buddhism. Some of Heraclitus's ideas entered the Western mainstream through Plato, though they were largely overwhelmed by the latter's grander metaphysical concerns. Heraclitus continued, however, to be a fascinating figure exerting a mysterious and appropriately intermittent and sporadic influence throughout the development of Western thought, until Hegel's treatment (of the Presocratics in general) ended a period of relative neglect. Since then, interest in him has been further reanimated by Nietzsche and Heidegger—not to mention the numerous poets who have been inspired by the fecundity of the fragments.

The form of Heraclitus' text is especially congruent with that of Laozi's, both being woven from pregnant utterances couched in an archaic language rich in allusive power and interspersed with lacunae of obscurity. Though the patchwork of the *Daodejing* may have a somewhat more cohesive unity, a greater proportion of the fragments of Heraclitus come from a single hand than the verses attributed to Laozi. But stylistically they are remarkably similar in their blending of the arcane and the oracular, the gnomic and the poetic.[13]

Granted some elective affinity between Lao-Zhuang and Heraclitus, there is nevertheless something perverse about comparing the two major classics of Daoist thought, with their inimitably terse and poetic styles, with—of all of Heidegger's works—Sein und Zeit. The prose SZ, though hardly as hard on the reading ear as the English translation, Being and Time, is somewhat ponderous and far from poetical.[14] In contrast to the "book of five thousand characters" (as the Laozi *is sometimes called), which must rank amongst the most profound of the world's short philosophical texts, and to the episodic and fragmentary texture of the* Zhuangzi, *the length and architectonic complexity of SZ are formidable.*

In the attempt to highlight "Daoist" ideas in Heidegger's masterwork, the writing of which antedates not only his contact with Asian philosophy but also his more prolonged meditations on the thought of Heraclitus and Parmenides and Anaximander, the following reading will indeed have to wrestle constantly with the book's distinctly un-Daoist style. There will be a constant tension between the effort of sober exegesis of a hard and serious text and the temptation to escape to the later Heidegger, where language is granted far freer play and the resonances with Daoist ideas are clearly audible. As the interpretation is pulled away from close textual analysis it may do occasional violence to the text. But given Heidegger's idea that ontological interpretation and the analysis of Dasein must essentially be acts of "violence" (*Gewaltsamkeit*),[15] it is remarkable how little violence SZ has elicited from interpreters in this present age of deconstruction (of which the idea of *Destruktion* in SZ is a precursor). And for a text that happens to take the hammer as a paradigm of things we encounter in our everyday dealings with the world, a wrench or two here and there won't hurt.

The first and major task is to engage in a fairly close reading of part A (secs. 14–18) of the third chapter of SZ, which establishes several themes crucial to the development of the text as a whole. The arguments of these sections also adumbrate the primary topics of our comparison: those of nature, utility, uselessness, nothing, and death—and the possibility of authentic existence. The Epilogue will entertain a few of these themes with reference to the works of the "middle period."

> Man models himself on earth, earth on heaven, heaven
> on the way, and the way on what is naturally so.[16]
>   Laozi 25

One of Heidegger's major criticisms of traditional Western ontology is that it overlooks what he calls "the worldness of the world" (*die Weltlichkeit der Welt*), what it is about worlds that makes them worlds. The task of the third chapter of SZ is to remedy this deficiency by an analysis of the phenomenon of *Welt* by way of an examination of the being of the everyday *Umwelt* (environment). Heidegger begins by remarking that traditional ontology has taken as its primary theme "things of nature" rather than "things invested with value" (63).

It is precisely Heidegger's treatment of this issue in early work that threatens to derail the comparison with Daoism. A salient feature of SZ is that it gives remarkably short shrift to the world of nature. The entire analysis of the phenomenon of "world," and the concomitant criticism of traditional ontology, is based on the notion of Zuhandenheit *("to-handness").*[17] *Heidegger's phenomenology of the ways we customarily relate to things in the world simply assumes that we treat them as "to-hand"* (zuhanden), *viewing them from the perspective of utility, and relating to them in terms of what we can do with them.*

The Daoist view—on the conventional understanding of Daoism—could be characterized by the injunction: "Be natural."[18] A central dictum in Daoism speaks to the unity of the human and nature (tian ren he yi 天人合一), *suggesting that humanity's problems stem in great measure from becoming separated from tian. To bring one's being into harmony with* dao, *one should re-align oneself with the way of heaven, the* dao *of* tian, *natural* dao. *A comparable understanding of nature is totally lacking in Heidegger— at least in the early work. Moreover, Daoism is so radically against anthropocentrism and so roundly condemns the utilitarian perspective that Zhuangzi in particular is renowned for his extolling of "the usefulness of being useless." The Daoist would consider SZ to be informed by a hopelessly utilitarian and instrumental view of human being, and would discern in the text a program justifying the violation of the earth in the name of technology. One might even say that Heidegger's misdirected zeal over certain political issues in the early thirties was prefigured by his excessive enthusiasm several years earlier concerning the possibilities of modern technology.*

From another perspective, Heidegger's ideas about the phenomenon of world can be seen as an extreme literalization of Kant's attitude toward (knowing rather than utilizing) nature as expressed in the preface to the second edition of the Critique of Pure Reason *(B xiii), where he writes that human reason*

> must not allow itself to be kept, as it were, in nature's leading strings, but must itself show the way ... constraining nature to give answer to questions of reason's own determining.... Reason ... must approach nature ... in the character of an appointed judge who compels the witnesses to answer questions he himself has formulated.

In the language of SZ: Dasein projects in advance a world, a horizon of possibility in terms of which things can make sense to us and thus appear as *things. And this is for the most part a horizon of utility.*

It is true that by the time of the essays the mid-forties Heidegger had turned things around (a consequence of the famous Kehre) *and developed a view that was less anthropocentric. In the later work, the appropriate attitude toward the "thingness of the thing" is to let it suggest to us the best mode of approach. If we refrain from protecting a human horizon of world as the context or background against which to encounter things, we realize that things in a way generate their own worlds, and it is through those atmospheres that we should approach them. That is all quite harmonious with Daoism— but the later texts can hardly be adduced to show that Heidegger was pursuing these lines of thought prior to the "turning."*

To return to the topic of nature: it is hardly discussed at all in SZ. Hildegard Feick's Index *lists only ten pages on which the term occurs.*[19] *Moreover, the section for* die Natur *is entitled: "Nature as disclosed in for-sight (als umsichtig entdeckte) or as theoretically known," which corresponds to Heidegger's characterization of being-in-the-world as concern for beings in the world as to-hand and on-hand. Even authentic Dasein, the being for whom "its own being is an issue," relates to things in terms of their utility— as indeed it must, if it is to continue being. In general, for the Heidegger of SZ, nature is merely "discovered along with" the disclosure of the world of factical Dasein, and is thereby seen as something on- or to-hand.*

If we look at the text, we see that Heidegger first broaches the topic of nature at the beginning of chapter 3, just before introducing the ideas of *Zuhanden-* and *Vorhandenheit*. The aim of the chapter is to elucidate the phenomenon of world, by considering the being of beings within the world:

> Beings within the world are things, things of nature (*Natur-dinge*) and things "invested with value" ("*wertbehaftete*" *Dinge*). The thingness (*Dinglichkeit*) of these things becomes a problem; and insofar as the thingness of the latter depends upon nature-thingness, the being of things of nature, nature as such, is the primary theme. The fundamental character of things of nature, of substances, is substantiality.
>
> (63)

This is Heidegger's account of the viewpoint of traditional ontology, and an approach which he thinks can never on its own disclose the phenomenon of world. He is critical of the tendency to interpret this phenomenon on the basis of nature as determined by the natural sciences, which is already to see things in a particular and restricted perspective: "Dasein can discover beings as nature only in a definite mode of its being-in-the-world. This knowing (*Erkennen*) has the character of a definite de-worlding (*Entweltlichung*) of the world" (65). The "definite mode" he has in mind is presumably the taking of nature as something on-hand.

From Pen to Hammer

> To-handness is the ontological-categorical definition of what-is, as it is "in itself."
>
> SZ 71

The next mention of nature occurs five pages later; but within these pages Heidegger introduces five key ideas—those of *Zeug*, *Verweisung*, *Zuhandenheit*, *Umsicht*, and *Vorhandenheit*—which are relevant to our topic. He calls what we immediately encounter in our everyday dealings with things *Zeug* (68), a word so basic in German that it is almost impossible to translate, especially since it occurs in a variety of compounds.[20] He gives as examples writing utensils (*Schreibzeug*), sewing equipment (*Nähzeug*), tools (*Werkzeug*, literally: "work-thing"), vehicles (*Fahrzeug*: "travel-thing"), and measuring instruments (*Messzeug*). *Zeug* basically means "things" or "stuff," and in Heidegger's usage more specifically "something for such-and-such an activity or use." The primary feature of *Zeug* is that there is never just one of it: "*Ein Zeug 'ist' strenggenommen nie.*" A piece of equipment can be what it is only with reference (*Verweisung*) to other equipment: "writing materials, pen, ink, paper, blotting pad, desk, lamp, furniture, windows, doors, the room." The context is primary: these items do not present themselves individually and then make up a totality; rather, the room as a whole is what we immediately experience—and not "in a geometrically spatial sense, but as a 'living-utensil' (*Wohnzeug*)" (68).

This theme corresponds to the Daoist insistence that anything is what it is only in relation to other things, that a particular is entirely dependent on its context. In fact Zhuangzi makes this point with specific reference to the idea of utility, in terms similar to those Heidegger uses to describe *Verweisung*, emphasizing that usefulness is nothing absolute but is always relative to a context. In the "Autumn Floods" chapter, Ruo of the North Sea says: "A battering ram is good for smashing down a wall, but not for stopping up a hole, which is to say that it is a tool with a special use" (ch. 17, *IC* 146–7). In the language of *SZ*, the battering ram is "something ... in order to" destroy a city wall; it has a "reference" to the entire relational matrix of sieges and fortifications. In filling a small hole the battering ram would be—because of its great mass, which suits it ideally for demolishing something firm—with respect to something fluid entirely useless.

This "relational dependence" of usefulness is made even clearer by the realization that what is useful depends for its utility on what is not being used. This point is exemplified by a passage from the Outer Chapters which invites us to contemplate our relationship to the earth, the ground on which we stand and walk. Zhuangzi is speaking to Huizi:

> "In all the immensity of heaven and earth, a man uses no more than is room for his feet. If recognizing this we were to dig away the ground around his feet all the way down to the Underworld, would it still be useful to the man?"
> "It would be useless."
> "Then it is plain that the useless does serve a use."
> (Ch. 26, *IC* 100; cf. ch. 3, *IC* 62)

A piece of ground does not *an sich* support anything (at least not anything locomotive); the abyss is, as in Nietzsche, always already "there." It provides support only in relation to something to-hand—in this case: to-foot—that is not being used, but offers the *possibility* of being used. Thus, Heidegger characterizes the "in-itselfness" (*An-sich-sein*) of the to-hand as being founded upon the phenomenon of world. An implement has its possibilities only as long as it participates in a relational matrix.

That passage from *SZ* in which Heidegger coins the neologism *Wohnzeug* is reminiscent, by the way, of one of the few discussions of "equipment" in the *Laozi* (ch. 11), which makes the point that a room can be used as a "living-utensil" only if it includes emptiness in the form of space between the walls, and within them in the form of windows and doors.

Let us not get carried away by notions of emptiness until we have understood the more prosaic reality of pens and paper. There is a danger of reading into these sections of SZ something (or nothing) that is simply not there. In characterizing the way of being tools or equipment Heidegger is doing precisely that: he is not making a universal ontological statement about the ultimate nature of things.

But he nevertheless does want us to see the thing of use as a paradigm for things in general—especially since the purpose of his discussion here is to elucidate the phenomenon of world.

And if we continue to follow this elucidation, it will lead us back to our original topic: nature. The scene changes from study to workshop, as Heidegger goes on to argue that no mere observation of a hammer, nor theoretical contemplation of it, can lead to a genuine understanding of its being.[21] Its "to-handness" can be appreciated only if we grasp the hammer in its being by picking it up and using it. "Hammering itself discovers the specific 'handiness' (*Handlichkeit*) of the hammer. The way of being of *Zeug* is *Zuhandenheit*" (69). Heidegger calls the hammer's "to-handness" its *An-sich-sein*, its "being-in-itself": we need to return to the paradox (which has generally gone unnoticed) generated by this unusual use of *An-sich-sein*. In dealing with things as to-hand we see them in the context of a network of "in-order-to's" (*Um-zu*)—the pen is something "in-order-to" make marks on paper—and so Heidegger calls this kind of vision *Umsicht*, or "for-sight."[22] Having stressed that for-sight does not grasp the being of what is to-hand explicitly in any kind of thematized understanding, and that we most fully understand its being by handling it, Heidegger then remarks on its most peculiar feature—namely, that when a thing of use is optimally fulfilling its function it *withdraws*. "What is peculiar about what is immediately to-hand is that it simultaneously withdraws in its to-handness, just in order to be properly to-hand."[23]

Heidegger goes on to remark on another feature of our dealings with things as to-hand: that our attention is directed not so much to the tool itself as to the work we are engaged in. For example: when writing, our attention is focused not on the pen but rather on the-words-appearing-on-the-page. He points out that the work always carries with it a reference to a further possible use, to other people as possible users—and also to nature. "Through using tools 'nature' is also discovered, 'nature' in the sense of natural products" (70).[24]

He goes on to distinguish three possible ways in which things of nature can be encountered.

> But nature must not be understood here as what is merely on-hand—nor as the *power of nature* (*die Naturmacht*). The wood is forest, the mountain is quarry, the river is water power, the wind is wind "in the sails" … It is possible not to see the being [of nature] as to-hand, and to discover and determine it simply in its pure on-handness (*Vorhandenheit*). This cognizance of nature misses it as something which "stirs and strives," overwhelms us, captivates us as landscape. The plants of the botanist are not the flowers of the hedgerow, the geographically determined "source" of a river is not the "spring in the ground."

It is clear from this passage that *Vorhandenheit* and *Zuhandenheit* do not refer to two set classes of things but rather to two different ways in which things can be encountered. A hammer can be to-hand or on-hand, depending on the mode of our concern with it—practical or theoretical. And the same is true of a tree, or the wind, or any other natural phenomenon, depending on whether our concern is to utilize it or investigate it scientifically. (For example: a botanist who does pull-ups from the bough of a tree on his day off is treating it as *Zeug*, as something for exercising with, taking it as something to-hand, rather than in his usual working mode as something on-hand.)

However, the passage implies that there is a third way of relating to things of nature, which is to understand them—the flowers of the hedgerow and the source in the ground—as manifestations of the "power of nature." Heidegger goes on to talk about how "environing nature" (*Umweltnatur*) is disclosed, though not explicitly as such, in our dealings with various kinds of *Zeug*, and then immediately embarks upon a discussion of *Zuhandenheit* without saying anything more about the third possible way of treating things of nature (71).

He mentions this third possible mode of being only once again, in a similarly offhand manner, at the beginning of the section entitled "Reality and Care": "The nature which 'surrounds' us ... does not, however, display the mode of being of the to-hand or the on-hand in the sense of 'the thingliness of nature'" (211). But again the theme is left undeveloped and disappears, the subsequent references to nature having to do with the traditional ontological and scientific understanding of the natural world.[25]

There is, however, a long and rather cryptic footnote in one of the 1929 essays which contains a further reference to nature. There Heidegger warns specifically against "[interpreting] being-in-the-world as commerce with things of use (*Umgang mit den Gebrauchsdingen*)"[26] and continues:

> But if in the ... analysis of Dasein nature is apparently missing—not only nature as an object of the natural sciences but also nature in an original sense (cf. *SZ* 65f)—there are reasons for this. The decisive thing is that nature lets itself be encountered neither in the surroundings of the environment (*im Umkreis der Umwelt*) nor primarily as something *to which we relate* (wozu *wir uns* verhalten). Nature is originally manifest in Dasein in as far as the latter exists as disposedattuned (*befindlich-gestimmt*) *in the midst of* what-is ... [It is only in the] full concept of *care* (*Sorge*) ... that the *basis* for the *problem* of nature can be attained.

Heidegger forgoes an investigation into "nature as an object of the natural sciences" (as something "on-hand") because his concern is on a deeper ontological plane—with that projected horizon which determines in advance whether we see a given being as a natural thing, a possible tool or resource, an object of scientific study, or whatever. "Nature in an original sense" presumably corresponds to what was called "the power of nature" in *SZ*.[27] The next couple of sentences make it clear why the scientific or instrumental perspectives cannot see nature "in the original sense"—because it manifests *inside* us as much as outside. And yet, unfortunately, the analysis in *SZ* of *Stimmung* (mood) as an "attunement" of our being-(t)here[28] that is neither internal nor external gives no examples related to nature.

Such a study of the ways in which natural (including meteorological and physiological) phenomena condition the clearing of our being-here would be well worth while. Presumably the third possible attitude toward nature, being neither practical nor theoretical, is primarily aesthetic. Whereas to deal with manufactured things as to-hand is to disclose them as they are *in themselves* (*an sich*), to relate to natural things only as on/to-hand is not to discover "nature in an original sense," is to fail to appreciate the "power of nature." It is indeed disappointing that Heidegger failed to elaborate on the third way, in view of the misinterpretations that have arisen as a result of overlooking the two cursory mentions of it in *SZ*. He does, however, describe the appropriate attitude toward things of nature (and in general) in the essay from 1935 "On the Origin of the Work of Art."[29]

Uses of the Useless

"Now this talk of yours is big but useless, dismissed by everyone alike."

Huizi to Zhuangzi[30]

This talk about utility needs to be tempered by the consideration that one of the major thrusts the Daoists' attack against anthropocentrism is a repudiation of the utilitarian view of the world. They are wary of most forms of discriminative consciousness, holding the value judgments that issue from them to be inherently one-sided and therefore distorting; but they particularly abhor the division of things into the instrumental categories of the useful and the useless. Along with the exhortation to a creative engagement with nature is their rather idiosyncratic praise of uselessness.

The theme is exemplified in the Inner Chapters *primarily in stories concerning things of nature (including human beings) which reach an advanced age precisely through not being good for anything. Of trees that are useful to human beings Zhuangzi says: "So they do not last out the years Heaven assigned them, but die in mid-journey under the axe. That is the trouble with being stuff which is good for something" (ch. 4, IC 74). In the same chapter, Carpenter Shi encounters the gigantic old oak at the earth altar and says of it: "This wood is wretched timber, useless for anything; that's why it's been able to grow so old." But shortly afterwards the holy oak appears to him in a dream and says: "Supposing that I had been useful, would I have had the opportunity to grow so big? You and I are both things ... and the good-for-nothing man who is soon to die, what does he know of the good-for-nothing tree?"[31] Even granting Heidegger a kind of mitigated instrumentalist position, Zhuangzi's emphasis on the "usefulness of being useless" is too prominent to allow a comparison on this topic to be viable.*

It is true that one doesn't find in early Heidegger a corresponding praise of usefulness *per se*, but he does appreciate the usefulness of the *unusable*—at least for the task of a phenomenology of "everydayness." And in fact we have just reached the point in the text where Heidegger takes up precisely that issue.

At the beginning of section 16 Heidegger reminds us that the point of his investigation of things to-hand was to help elucidate the phenomenon of world. He had left himself (and us) in the *aporia* of trying to grasp the being of the hammer by using it—and then experiencing its withdrawal as soon as one starts. One is reminded of the Daoist dictum (*Laozi* 64): "He who grasps, loses it." As a way out, Heidegger points our attention to three ways in which the *Weltmässigkeit* of the environment (*Umwelt*) announces itself: "conspicuousness" (*Auffälligkeit*), where a tool is unusable or a particular material unsuitable for the job; "obtrusiveness" (*Aufdringlichkeit*), in which the work is obstructed when a needed tool is missing; and "obstinacy" (*Aufsässigkeit*), where a tool is not unusable or missing but is irremovably "there" and in the way (73–4).

(There comes to mind here an example—which Heidegger, being an oenophile, would appreciate—of a situation in which all three features come together. At a picnic on a hot summer's day we take out the carefully chilled bottle of wine—only to find that we've left the corkscrew at home. The cork, having been rendered un-to-hand, announces itself as conspicuously immovable without the obtrusively absent corkscrew; while the unopenable bottle stands there as obstinately and tantalizingly un-to-hand—or, even more so, un-to-mouth. To push the cork *into* the bottle is a solution about which Heidegger would probably hesitate longer than Zhuangzi.)

Owing, then, to the peculiar tendency of what is to-hand to withdraw, for us to become aware of its being it must "in a certain way [lose] its to-handness." There has to be "a disturbance of reference (*Verweisung*)" (74), "a *breach* in the relational context disclosed by our for-sight" (75). These gaps, disturbances, and interruptions in our ongoing dealings with things serve to illuminate the context in which all this activity has been taking place—and the phenomenon of world thereby "announces itself."

To this extent the idea of unusability serves a function in Heidegger comparable to the role of uselessness in Zhuangzi, insofar as it makes us pull back and contemplate the surrounding context and thereby lets us see the perspective of utility *as* a perspective. This kind of consideration counters the tendency to exaggerate the differences between Heidegger and Zhuangzi by making the latter look overly "anti-" and the former overly "pro-instrumentalist." There are, of course, from the thing's point of view, definite disadvantages in being potential *Zeug* or "[good] for something." But for the Daoists the problem is less with the standpoint of utility *per se* than with getting stuck in any single perspective. And surely Heidegger, with his emphasis on the "multi-dimensionality" of Being, would, just as much as Zhuangzi, pray with Blake that we be kept from "single vision and Newton's sleep."

The issue is exemplified amusingly in the exchange between Zhuangzi and Huizi concerning the large gourds the latter has been given. He ends up in frustration smashing them to pieces because they are too unwieldy to be used as water containers or dippers—"because they were useless" (ch. 1, *IC* 47). Zhuangzi's response is that Huizi has been stupid in failing to see that he could have "[made] them into those big bottles swimmers tie to their waists and [gone] floating away over the Yangtse and the Lakes." The point is not that the perspective of utility is inherently pernicious; the anecdote rather points up our tendency to become fixated in calculating and utilitarian modes of relating to things, rather than conducting ourselves "with a full view of heaven." And even within the perspective of utility our vision tends, like Huizi's, to be too narrow, our "for-sight" too short: being taken in by the customary ways of understanding things we become blind to their myriad possibilities. Because Huizi was fixated on putting the gourds to their conventional use by putting water in them, he could not see his way to putting himself on them and getting into the water instead.

Finally, if we look at the language Heidegger uses to talk about our relations to things to-hand, we'll find that it's much less aggressive than our objector's neo-Kantian paraphrase (in terms of laying down in advance how things can be encountered) suggested.

The contrast between early and late Heidegger, between the supposedly aggressive instrumentality of *SZ* and the serene releasement (*Gelassenheit*) of the later writings, is indeed generally overdrawn—as we can appreciate if we go on to look at section 18. Inquiring after the worldness of the world, Heidegger asks: "How can world let things be encountered? ... What we encounter within the world has been ... freed in its being for concernful for-sight (*ist für die besorgende Umsicht ... in seinem Sein freigegeben*) ... What does this prior freeing (*Freigabe*) amount to?" (83). This freeing, or release, takes place through *bewendenlassen* (letting be involved), which he characterizes as "to let something to-hand be so-and-so (*Zuhandenes so und so sein lassen*) *as* it already is and *so that* it can be so" (84). The double *so* here is significant: for-sight lets things be what they already are *and* as they can also be. Through the prior freeing of a being for being to-hand we help it come into its own. This is not a one-sided operation in which we unilaterally impose our will on things, but rather a reciprocal interaction. In forging a piece of metal into a knife, for example, the metalworker realizes a certain potential of that metal for sharpness, a potential it could never realize on its own. But the success of the work depends in advance on certain properties of the metal itself—since no amount of working on wood could ever achieve such sharpness.

It is true that at the root of the complex network of interconnections among things to-hand there is the ultimate *Worum-willen* ("for-the-sake-of-which") which informs the entire structure—namely, our concern for our own welfare. This means that we naturally look at things in the light of our concern for our own being, and so always "let things be encountered as to-hand" (86). That, for Heidegger, is simply a fact—Wittgenstein would say "form"—of life.

A Short Handnote

> "Not too slow, not too fast; I feel it in the hand and respond from the heart, the mouth cannot put it into words, there's a knack in it somewhere which I cannot convey to my son."
>
> Zhuangzi 13

In line with the Daoist emphasis on being-in-the-world without being taken in by it, the models the *Zhuangzi* offers of people who are on to the *dao* are not sage-hermits who spend their lives meditating in isolation from the world, but are often artisans and craftsmen and others who have attained consummate mastery of certain psychophysical skills—most of whom work primarily with their hands.[32] Manual dexterity, smooth, graceful, and effortlessly responsive, is a sign that one's power (*de* 德) has become fully integrated. The idea behind many Daoist stories is that if one can disconnect discursive thought and respond from the wisdom of the body, the hands will do their own kind of thinking.

In the early forties, as he became more concerned with the idea of *Denken*, Heidegger alluded to its relations to the hand by calling genuine thinking a *Handeln*, or activity. He soon began to refer to thinking as a *Hand-Werk*, a craft—but literally a work of the hand.[33] Thinking with the hands rather than with the brain consists for Heidegger in the hand's "reaching and receiving, holding and carrying, pointing and gesturing." It is not surprising that he also mentions the hand's drawing (*zeichnen*), given his admiration for artists such as Cezanne and Klee for their thoughtful renderings of things and (their) Being.[34]

"The gestures of the hand pervade the whole of language and in fact most purely when man speaks in being silent." Heidegger surely has in mind here not only a language of gesture, but also the thinking that takes place in writing, the silent movements of the hand over the page. In writing, if one is fortunate to receive a block of inspiration, one then has to work somewhat as a carpenter works wood. From a rough draft the careful writer will make numerous passes over it as with a plane, smoothing out the rough surfaces and shaping the form of the whole.[35]

It is true that Heidegger did not develop this theme until the later work; but if one looks at *SZ* "chirologically" one sees that a thinking of the hand, though not explicitly called such, runs throughout the text—in the descriptions of our everyday dealings with things as *zuhanden*. Not that our everyday activity is on a par with the accomplished Daoist's, but perhaps authentic dealings with things, as described below, could be. In the words of Wallace Stevens, "it is a world of words to the end of it, in which nothing solid is its solid self."[36]

The exchange between Zhuangzi and Huizi about digging away the ground around where one is standing illustrated the usefulness of the unused (in Heideggerian terms, the dependence of utility on possibility). A related theme in Daoism is the interdependence of utility and emptiness, or nothing (*wu* 無).[37] Chapter 11 of the *Laozi* presents three kinds of thing: a cartwheel, a jug, and a room; and in each case the point is to show that these implements are only "to-hand" on the basis of an emptiness, a nothing, where there is a breach in the fullness of the material. "Thus what we gain is Something, yet it is by virtue of Nothing that this can be put to use." Were there no hub at the center of the wheel, there could be no rotation; were there no hollow within the jug, it could not hold anything; and were there no openings in the walls in the form of windows and a door, neither light nor occupants could enter the room.

These verses offer in a way the inverse perspective on utility from the analysis in *SZ*. There the implement can be what it is only insofar as it stands out against a surrounding horizon of World; in *Laozi* the thing can function only on the basis of an emptiness *within* the implement itself. But in both cases the realization of a particular emptiness, lack, or non-being within the world conduces to a realization of the Nothing that is the ultimate (un-)ground of everything. Heidegger was later to write of a jug in a manner reminiscent of—and probably influenced by—Laozi, in the 1950 essay "Das Ding" (The Thing).[38] In both cases the jug (or wheel, or room) is to be taken as an image for the human being: were there in us no emptiness, we would not be able to be, as human beings, here (or there). In fact Heidegger remarked on the thing's intimating its own nothingness as early as 1935:

> Beings cannot, however, throw off the question-able thing about them that whatever they are and how they are—they also could *not* be. This possibility is not something we ... merely add in thought, but the being itself announces this possibility, announces itself as the being in [the possibility].
>
> (*EM* 22, *IM* 29)

Let us go back for a moment to Heidegger's discussion of the breakdown of our dealings with things to-hand. When something to-hand is missing, there opens up "a *breach* in the relational context disclosed by our for-sight. For-sight falls into emptiness ... " (75). This is the first intimation of Nothing in *SZ*. Since in our everyday activity our concern is not with the implements themselves but with the work they are being used for, it is only when something goes wrong that the relational context which conditions and makes all such activity possible comes to light. Only through a break can we see the World—as that which conditions in advance all "what-for's," "in-order-to's," and other implemental relationships. This totality of the relational context, the world, is itself no thing: it is neither to-hand nor on-hand; but only thanks to this empty horizon can any implement, or thing, be what it is. But in "everydayness" we tend to lose ourselves in beings and fail to attend to that which lets them be—to the empty horizon of World, the background of Nothing against which every being presents itself as *not* nothing, that is, as something.

(This is the topic of the question with which *Introduction to Metaphysics* opens: "Why is there anything at all and not rather nothing?" Why? To what end? What's the use of it all? The answer, insofar as there is one, would be: No reason, no ground—simply, World. Heidegger re-reads the principle of sufficient reason with an idiosyncratic change of emphasis: *Nihil est sine ratione*—nothing is without ground.)

We don't encounter anything corresponding to the emptiness revealed through this break again until the sixth chapter of Division One, in the section that describes how *Angst* discloses "nothingness, i.e., the world as such" (187).

There is a key phenomenon in Heidegger to which nothing—or perhaps one should say, rather, "not anything"—in Daoism corresponds. Angst plays a pivotal role in SZ in the transition to authentic existence as described in Division Two. There is no trace of existential anxiety and the related phenomena of constriction and weird uncanniness (Unheimlichkeit) *in the writings of Lao-Zhuang. The abyss of* dao *and the emptiness of nothing are contemplated with a calm serenity that is far from "the terror of the abyss"* (der Schrecken des Abgrundes) *of which the later Heidegger so eloquently speaks.*[39]

There does appear to be a major discrepancy here, a difference in tone and quality of affect. But when we look to the underlying views of the self which Heidegger and the Daoists inherit from their respective traditions, it may turn out to be more a difference in degree than in the nature of the (understanding of the) self itself. Both cultures began with a sense of the self's open participation in the world, of a dynamic process of flowing and permeable boundaries. Shortly before the emergence of Daoism, the self had apparently begun to coagulate, as it were, around a core of self-interest. So that Confucius, in a spirit similar to that which moved Socrates, had to exhort his fellow men to "overcome the self" (*ke ji* 克己) by ignoring prospects of profit and gain, honor and reputation, and re-open the self, through the observant practice of sacred ritual (*li* 禮), to the matrix of relationships in which it essentially inheres. In the same vein the Daoists speak of "forgetting the self" (*wang ji* 忘己), such that "the utmost man has no self" (*Zhuangzi* 1).

While Socrates similarly abhorred self-interest and considerations of personal profit, power, and fame as motives for action, the resulting dynamics of the self were different—consisting in a gathering of the rational soul into itself so that it would not suffer dissolution after separation from the body at death. The idea of the self as substance persisted as a central tenet of the Platonic/Christian tradition, culminating in the extreme coagulation of the *res cogitans* around the center of the ego in the philosophy of Descartes—and in the absolute separation of this substance from the radically different substance (*res extensa*) comprising the world. In spite of Nietzsche's attacks on the substantial conception of the self and his attempts to crack the hardened husk of the "atomic" soul, the idea of self which Heidegger was faced with was still far harder to "destruct" and far more abysmally separated from the world than that which confronted the Daoists. Hence the *Angst* when the center fails to hold and the construct begins to fall apart.

But the degree of proneness to *Angst has to do not only with different understandings of the self but also with a concomitant difference in their understandings of the world. For the ancient Chinese the question of the possible meaninglessness of the cosmos simply never arises: the cosmos is inherently invested with meaning. There may be dispute amongst various schools as to the nature of its meaning, but—for the Daoists at least— the cosmos is an ordered whole. Not patterned from without by transcendent* archai, *nor heading purposively towards a pre-existent* telos, *but informed from within by the patterning they call* dao.

The cosmic situation in which post-Copernican Western man finds himself after "the death of God" is indeed more alienating than the situation of the Zhou dynasty Chinese. The collapse of a structure that had given meaning to existence for over two thousand years was bound to occasion considerable psychical and spiritual turmoil. However, there is another side to the picture. The passage in which Heidegger writes of the terror of the abyss reads:

> The clear courage for genuine anxiety guarantees the mysterious possibility of the experience of Being. For close by genuine anxiety as the terror of the abyss dwells awe. This clears and protects that realm of human being within which man dwells at home in the enduring.

The point he is making here is that *Angst*, as anxiety in the face of the abyss, and *Scheu*, as awe and wonder at there being *anything* at all, are two aspects of the same phenomenon. In the major discussion of *Angst* in the entire corpus (in "What Is Metaphysics?") the encounter with nothing is said to be pervaded by "a strange kind of peace" and "a spellbound calm."[40] But even though the terrifying side is not evident in Daoism, what *Angst* reveals does—as we shall see shortly—have a counterpart.

It might help to establish that point if we first take a quick look at the salient points from the discussion of *Angst* in SZ. That will also help us to appreciate better the analogy between the breakdowns described in section 16, in which breaches in the fabric of interconnections of things to-hand reveal what they are *for*, and the breakdown *par excellence* that is *Angst*, in which all our relations to things in the world are ruptured.

We learn from Heidegger's description in section 40 that "what anxiety is about is not anything within the world ... nothing of what is to- and on-hand"; and he speaks of the "obstinacy (*Aufsässigkeit*) of the Nothing and Nowhere within the world" that presses upon us in *Angst* (186), which turns out to be "the *possibility* of what is to-hand at all, that is: the world itself" (187). The "nothing of what is to-hand (*dieses Nichts des Zuhandenen*)" is grounded in "the world as such," "the world as world," or—as he puts it in the second discussion of *Angst*, in Division Two—"the nothing of the world (*das Nichts der Welt*)" (343).

In this more global breakdown, things recede from us, and the hitherto unnoticed background (the empty horizon of World) comes to the fore and lets us see what it is all for: nothing. The full realization is then that the nothing of the world is also the nothing of the self. Wallace Stevens has expressed something like this: "Until the used-to earth and sky ... these men, and earth and sky, inform each other by sharp informations ... breaches of that which held them fast."[41]

The Issue of Death

> Which of us is able to think of nothingness as the head,
> of life as the spine, of death as the rump? ... He shall
> be my friend.
>
> Zhuangzi 6

> For Hades and Dionysos are the same.
>
> Heraclitus 15

Heidegger makes the connection between *Angst* and death in the Second Division, revealing the nothingness of world to be—since "Dasein *is* its world"—the nothingness of the self. His understanding of death as a constant presence within life rather than a state beyond and opposed to life is close to the Daoists'. Just as Heidegger emphasizes that "*our sight is too short* if life is made the problem *and then also occasionally* death is considered" (316), so Laozi remarks that "it is because people set too much store by life that they treat death lightly" (ch. 75).

But at first glance the Daoist perspective on death appears quite different from Heidegger's. Death is not a major theme in the *Daodejing, and most of the references to it there have to do primarily with literal, biological death. Laozi has heard of "one who excels in safeguarding his own life ... for [whom] there is no realm of death" (ch. 50); and one gets the general impression the work that the sage has identified himself with* dao *in such a way that the encounter with death is of little moment. The issue figures more prominently in Zhuangzi, and Angus Graham has remarked upon "the ecstatic, rhapsodic tone" in which Zhuangzi writes on the topic (IC 23). As in Laozi, the prospect of death loses its terror because the individual has identified with the larger cycles of change which pattern the cosmos, and is thereby able to move into death as simply the next transformation in the endless series cycles that constitute* dao.

In SZ on the other hand, the encounter with death in Angst *and the appropriate response of total openness to that nothing of the self are crucial for both an existential and ontological understanding of our being here. The tones and the treatments are quite different: the Daoists' informed by a serenity tinged with wonder, a grave matter-of-factness tempered by traces of exultation at the prospect the next transformation; Heidegger's weighted heavily toward* Angst *and grim resoluteness in the face the abyss.*

When death is faced with equanimity, there are several possible background conditions. At one end of the spectrum, death has hardly become an issue, since the person's individuality is not yet sufficiently differentiated from the social group—as in the case of members of so-called "primitive" societies, for example. The prospect of death is terrifying only to the ego, to that part of the self which has come to experience itself as an entity separated from the world. To the extent that one is identified with the deeper layer of the self which is implicated in the procession of the generations, the prospect of individual death has less import—since there is no reason to suppose that the annihilation of whatever self there is will have any effect on the larger process in which it participates.

At the other extreme is an equanimity based on a belief in the immortality of the soul. In this case (of which the Socrates of the *Phaedo* would be a paradigm) the individual withdraws from the world of the senses, dis-identifies with the body, and identifies with the highest functions of the rational soul, which are universal and transpersonal. In the first instance there is no problem because the self is insufficiently concentred to be self-aware, and in the second because it is so powerfully concentrated that dissolution appears impossible. Since for both Heidegger and Zhuangzi there is already an awareness of the self, the question is whether either of the views involves a regression to a state of "primitive" non-self-awareness, a simple acceptance of annihilation, a belief in transcendence and individual survival, or some further alternative.

There seems to be a difference between the Laozi *and* Zhuangzi *on this point. The Daoists' emphasis on spontaneity and their praise of primordial naturalness might suggest that their ideal involves a total immersion in purely natural processes and a regression to a stage of quasi-primitive participation in the world, and some passages in* Laozi *which advocate "returning to the root" and reverting to "the uncarved block" reinforce this impression. Under these circumstances death would not be an issue, because there is not sufficient self-awareness or extension of consciousness beyond the present moment. On the other hand, the pre-dominance of Daoist imagery about wandering above and beyond the dust and grime of worldly affairs and their concern with not being bound by things (especially evident in* Zhuangzi, *ch. 6), taken together with the passages that seem to suggest that* dao *is at least in part transcendent to the world, inclines one to ascribe the Daoists' equanimity in the face of death to their having transcended the realm of life and death. Neither alternative, however, would characterize Heidegger's position.*

That is true. But even though there is a sense in which both Zhuangzi and Plato view death as a transformation, their understandings are essentially different. In Daoism the movement of transformation is the opposite of the Platonic one: rather than concentering the soul in preparation for the ascent to unity with the Absolute, one de- and ex-centers the self to allow it to merge in all directions with the formlessness of *dao*. To the extent that *dao* is "transcendent" it is transcendent to the individual as a particular, but it is wholly immanent in the world if we include in that the history of the race. And to the extent that the Daoists advocate detachment from the dust and grime of the world, this is to be understood as only a necessary stage on the way to a reintegration with it. The "true man" (*zhen ren* 真人) has gone beyond mere unconscious participation in the world and also beyond transcendent detachment from it. He has reintegrated himself with the processes of change in such a way as to become "the helper of heaven" (*xiang tian* 相天). He is one "in whom neither heaven nor man is the victor," who participates in the world-process with full awareness of its macrocosmic dimensions, "[opening] things up to the light of heaven."[42] If one insists on applying the categories of transcendence and immanence, one would have to characterize the Daoist position as one of "transcendence-*in*-immanence." There is after all something paradoxical about Zhuangzi's position on death, which Graham sums up well when he writes that Zhuangzi "seems to foresee the end of his individuality as an event which is both an obliteration and an opening out of consciousness" (*IC* 23).

Thus the Daoist attitude toward death, which helps one "forget" the self and allow it consciously to identify with the macrocosm, may not be so different from Heidegger's existential conception of death as possibility. But rather than go further into this vast topic, let us focus on what kind of transformation of our dealings with things is effected by the confrontation with death.

An obstacle remains in the course of comparison concerning the incompatibility between Heidegger's insistence that authentic existence continues to relate to things as to-hand and the Daoist idea of wuwei 無為. *This idea of "doing nothing" or "non-interfering activity" appears to involve a broadening of one's perspective(s) so that one is able to see things in "the full light of heaven," and a forgetting of the self in such a way that one is open(ed) to respond to the movements of* dao *by spontaneously realizing one's own particular* de, *or natural potential. Such a process seems quite foreign to the emphasis in* SZ *on grim resoluteness and self-assertion.*

In the account of authentic existence in *SZ* Heidegger twice speaks of "letting the ownmost self act through one (*in sich handeln lassen*)."[43] One does this by letting the self "shatter itself against death," so as to "give death the possibility of assuming power (*Macht*) over the existence of Dasein."[44] This idea corresponds to the Daoist notion that if one can "empty out" the self, then *dao* will naturally work (and play) through one in the form of "the daemonic" (*shen* 神) or, more generally, as "power" (*de* 德). Angus Graham's commentary on a passage from chapter 4 of Zhuangzi describes this phenomenon in terms remarkably similar to Heidegger's: "Then the self dissolves ... The agent of his actions is no longer the man but Heaven working through him, yet paradoxically ... in discovering a deeper self he becomes for the first time truly the agent" (*IC* 69).

One of the factors which appear to vitiate the comparison with Daoism is in fact an artifact of the English translation of *SZ*. Macquarrie and Robinson's choice of "resoluteness" for *Entschlossenheit* gives a misleadingly subjectivistic or "will-full" impression of what authentic existence is about. A better word for that essential precondition for authentic relations with things would be "openedness." Heidegger constantly plays the term off against *Erschlossenheit* (disclosedness), describing *Entschlossenheit* as the authentic mode of the disclosedness of being-(t)here.[45] He makes it clear, however, that this openedness, far from distancing us from the everyday world, rather "brings the self precisely into the current concernful being with what is to-hand" (298). The difference between such openedness and the "average" disclosedness is that the guiding *Umsicht* has a far wider temporal and spatial range. He calls such an "opened being with what is to-hand" in the current situation "the active letting-be-encountered (*das handelnde Begegnenlassen*) of what is *present* in the environment," and "the undistorted letting-be-involved of that which in acting it grasps (*dessen, was sie handelnd ergreift*)" (326).

The key term here is "undistorted" (*unverstellt*). Heidegger's view is that in general our perceptions and conceptions of things are conditioned by *das Man*, by "the way things have been publicly interpreted" (sec. 27). The culture has already set up the structures of meaningfulness and laid down in advance what and how things are. Thus, our everyday dealings with things are grounded in a *Worum-willen* (for-the-sake-of) that is inauthentic—usually in something equivalent to "for-the-sake-of-staying-alive." However, the ultimate *Worum-willen* includes our uttermost possibility—death.

In inauthentic existence our understanding "projects itself upon what we are concerned with, upon what is feasible, urgent, indispensable in the business of everyday activity" (337). Understood temporally, we "come back to ourselves" from the things (to-hand) with which we are concerned—rather than from our "ownmost, irrelatable being-able-to-be" (337), which is the nothingness of our death. Authentic being-toward things to-hand operates in the "moment" (*Augenblick*), which is deeper and broader than the present "now." "In openness the present is not only brought back from its dispersal into the immediate objects of concern, but is held in the future and past too" (338). Heidegger then uses what is in the context of *SZ* an unusual word to characterize the authentic relation to things to-hand as experienced in the moment: *Entrückung*, or "rapture." The term "moment" refers to "the opened, but held in openness, rapture of being-(t)here by the possibilities and circumstances of the situation." The idea of rapture is the more passive counterpart to the more active *ekstases* of temporality: to talk of "the raptures of future, past and present" (350) is to balance the ways in which we "stand out from" ourselves toward those horizons by pointing up the ways in which we are "transported" by them.

The closest thing we find to an explicit account in *SZ* of authentic dealings with things to-hand is in section 69(a). Heidegger begins by emphasizing again that authentic existence is still concerned with producing and using things to-hand (352). He reiterates that there is never some *one* thing to-hand but always a multiplicity of things to-hand in a context: the fact that one tool can be present and another, related one be missing underscores their belonging together.[46] This time around, in tracing the structural relationships involved in using tools Heidegger stresses the temporal aspects of "letting things be involved": that we are always "ahead of" ourselves in dealing with what is to-hand, allowing the "what-for" (*wozu*) to guide our present activity, and at the same time retaining a sense of how the work has been going up till now and also of the present context. He goes on to say that "'authentic' wholehearted dealing with things ... dwells neither with the work nor with the tool, nor with both together" (354)—presumably since our awareness at all times pervades all three horizons of temporality.

This suggests that in authentic dealings with things to-hand we see through the network of equipmental relationships to the ultimate *Worum-willen* which gives them meaning—the empty horizon of World and death. With one eye on Nothing, an ear open for the voice of stillness, and one foot always already in the grave, we let the hand be guided by the power of Being. So that when Heidegger says that "In order to be able—'lost' in the world of equipment—'really' to go to work and get busy, the self must forget itself" (354), he is speaking on two levels, referring both to the dissipation of the self into the world of its concern and to authentic dealings with things. In the latter, however, forgetting the self means opening it up to allow one's actions to be guided by the authentic self, which, itself nothing, is one with the nothing of world:

> If one takes everyday ideas as the sole measure of things, then philosophy is always something crazy (*etwas Verrücktes*) ... It constantly brings about a shifting (*Verrückung*) of standpoints and levels. In philosophy one often doesn't know for long periods of time where one's head is.[47]

Granted that authentic existence as described in SZ is less aggressively manipulative—involving more "freeing" and "letting" and "releasing"—than it might first appear, the use of technology in relation to ecology still seems to force the parallels of the comparison apart. There are numerous passages in the Daoist texts describing a primeval condition of mankind living in simple harmony with the world of nature, and advocating a return to such a condition. Chapter 80 of the Laozi *paints the (admittedly somewhat extreme) picture of a society in which people own such things as ships and carts—but make no use of them. In the first three Outer Chapters of* Zhuangzi *we find praise of a primal Utopia conjoined with a vigorous repudiation of technology and numerous denunciations of man's interference in the course of nature. And then there is the famous episode (ch. 12) concerning the old gardener who contemptuously dismisses the idea of using a well-sweep—an ecologically respectable and respectful implement if ever there was one—as a substitute for laboriously watering his garden by hand.*

The story of the well-sweep is at first puzzling, since the gardener's rejection of such a benign labor-saving device seems uncharacteristically rigid and narrow—if he represents the Daoist position. However, a careful reading of the story makes it clear that the gardener's objection is to the frame of mind that gives rise to calculating dealings with things, and which the use of technology in turn encourages, rather than to the products *per se* of this way of thinking.[48]

But the important thing to understand is that the thrust of the technological examples in these chapters is primarily metaphorical. As Angus Graham puts it: "[The Primitivist] objects to people wanting to manipulate human nature as the potter molds clay rather than to the potter himself" (*IC* 186). As long as we don't take these examples literally, the attitude of *Zhuangzi* toward technology does not appear especially negative (though its products are not treated with any great enthusiasm either).

Correspondingly, on the Heideggerian view, to take things as to-hand is not necessarily to manipulate or mis-handle them. It is quite possible to take advantage of the power of nature in a way that is quite compatible with the Daoists' *wuwei*. In making use of the wind to propel a sailboat, for example, or of water to drive a mill-wheel, we can contribute to the wind's and water's being what they are "in themselves." (The paradoxical nature of the *an sich* again.) In making responsible use of fire or in using a tree for shade, we can, by bringing forth their appropriate possibilities, reveal those elements more fully in their being.

Heidegger would no doubt want to go further and say that the felling of trees for lumber to build a cabin could still be an instance of authentic use of the wood. The question is at what point the use of a natural thing as *Zeug* in such a way as to realize its possibilities with respect to human concerns begins to impinge overly on the unfolding of its possibilities when left to itself. Clearly the deforestation of an area of beautiful trees in order to mass-produce ugly furniture is something even the most social-utility-minded Heideggerian would not condone. At the other extreme there is no doubt that Heidegger would applaud a woodworker who himself seeks and finds the perfect tree for the chair he has in mind, and then proceeds to fashion it with thoughtful hands that respond to the uniqueness of the wood, so that its hidden beauty may shine forth to the fullest. One is tempted to say not just that the woodworker has helped the tree to become more fully itself, but has actually helped it to become more than itself.

There is a story along these lines in the *Zhuangzi* about the woodworker Qing, whose bell stand was so beautiful as to be "daemonic" (ch. 19, *IC* 135). After going into the forest to "observe the nature of the wood as heaven makes it grow," he waits for "a complete vision of the bell stand" before picking his tree and going to work. He is sufficiently open to the daemonic to be able to describe his working the wood as "joining heaven's to what is heaven's"—by allowing the *de* in him, his natural ability, to respond to the *de* in the wood, its natural potential. It is characteristic, incidentally, of Daoism to prize especially a craft in which careful subtraction rather than skillful composition is the art.

The *Zhuangzi*'s view of the instrumental approach toward things can be summed up by citing a remark from one of the stories concerning Zhuangzi himself (ch. 20, *IC* 121). After commenting on the advantages to a tree of its not being good for timber, Zhuangzi, later the same day, on being asked which of two geese should be killed for dinner, replies: "The one that can't cackle." On being pressed by a disciple to say what his position really is, he responds: "I should be inclined to settle midway between being good for something and good for nothing." This corresponds to the attitude toward technology recommended later by Heidegger in *Gelassenheit*: "the simultaneous Yes and No to the world of technology."[49] However, the story finishes by suggesting that even more important than "[settling] midway between being good for something and good for nothing" is to loosen one's ties to things altogether by "[refusing] to be turned into a thing by things."

This admonition suggests a final interesting parallel between Heidegger and Zhuangzi. The latter plays on the noun "*wu* 物," for "thing," by using it as a verb, "to thing" (*IC* 185). Graham brings together a number of passages in which Zhuangzi talks of "thinging things" under the heading "Self-Alienation," and compares the idea with Hegel's notion of alienation and the tendency of people to "turn themselves into things by becoming identified with their possessions." The comparison with Hegel is illuminating, but even more so is the parallel with a major theme in *SZ*—namely, that (existentially speaking) we misunderstand ourselves by "falling into" the things in the world with which we are concerned, and (ontologically) the Western metaphysical tradition has misunderstood the nature of human being by interpreting it as a being on a par with other beings, as something *vorhanden*, or on-hand.

Zhuangzi asks: "If you treat things as things and are not made into a thing by things [literally: 'thinged by things'], how can you be tied by involvements?" (ch. 20, *IC* 121 and 185). Put in Heideggerian terms: "If you let things (to-hand) be involved in the context of the ultimate possibility of nothingness, and allow your own nothingness to keep you from understanding yourself as something either on- or to-hand, how can you be taken in (*benommen*) by things in the world?" Correspondingly, Zhuangzi's "What things things is not itself a thing" (ch. 22, *IC* 164) would elicit immediate assent from Heidegger. It is true that it is not until the later Heidegger that we hear talk of "things thinging"; but it was not long after *SZ* that he began to say that "world worlds" (*die Welt weltet*) and "nothing nothings" (*das Nichts nichtet*).[50]

三. Epilogue

The Chalk Is Flightier than the Hammer

[The scene is Lecture Room 5 at the University of Freiburg, at the start of the summer semester of 1935. The course is entitled "Introduction to Metaphysics," and the early lectures begin by considering the difference between Something and Nothing][51]

HEIDEGGER [turning from the blackboard, a piece of chalk concealed in his left hand]:
  What is needed is, without being seduced by over-hasty theories, to experience in whatever is closest things as they are. This piece of chalk here is an extended, relatively hard, gray-white thing with a definite form, and in and with all that a thing to write with.

  [*Places the chalk on the lectern*]

  Just as certainly as it belongs to this thing to be lying here, it belongs to it as much to be able to be not here and not so large. The possibility [*Möglichkeit*] of being drawn along the blackboard and being used up is nothing that we merely add to the thing in thought. It itself as this being is in this possibility, otherwise it would not be a piece of chalk as a writing instrument [*Schreibzeug*].

STUDENT B [*aside*]:
  This must correspond to the being "in-itself" [*an-sich-sein*] or what is to-hand, in the account in *SZ*.

HEIDEGGER [*goes to the board and writes the word* Möglichkeit]:
  Correspondingly, every being has in various ways this potential [*dieses Mögliche*] to it. This potential belongs to the chalk. It itself has a definite appropriateness for a definite use in itself…

  [*Holds the chalk up between forefinger and thumb*]

  Our question should now first open up what-is [*das Seiende*] in its wavering between Notbeing and Being. Insofar as what-is with stands the uttermost possibility of Notbeing, it itself stands in Being and yet has never thereby overtaken and overcome the possibility of Notbeing.

STUDENT A [*aside*]:
Didn't Laozi say that something and nothing produce one another, and that it's by virtue of nothing that something can be put to use?

* * *

[Six months later Heidegger is teaching a course on Kant's *Critique of Pure Reason*, in which this early lecture is devoted to a more general consideration of what a thing is. He is discussing space and time, since what appears to make a thing the particular thing that it is, what seems to make it "this one," is that it occupies a particular place at a particular time.]⁵²[52]

HEIDEGGER:
Initially we have the impression that space and time are in some sense "external" to things. Or is this impression deceptive?

[*Picks up a piece of chalk from the lectern*]

Let us take a closer look! This piece of chalk: Space—or rather the space of this classroom—lies around this thing … This piece of chalk, we say, takes up a particular space; the space taken up is bordered by the outer surface of the chalk. Outer surface? Surface? The piece of chalk is itself extended; there is space not only around it but at it, or even in it; only this space is occupied, filled up.

[*Places it back on the lectern*]

The chalk itself consists inside of space; we even say [in German], it takes *in* [*ein*, "up"] space, encloses it by its outer surface as its inside. Space is thus not a merely external frame for the chalk. But what does inside mean here? How does the inside of the chalk look? Let us see. We'll break the piece of chalk in two.

[*Picks it up and breaks it in half*]

STUDENT B [*aside*]:
Is this the right way to go about it, I wonder? Didn't he suggest in his lecture on the work of art the other day that any way of approaching things that perpetrates an "assault" [*Überfall*] on them is bound to fail?[53]

HEIDEGGER:
Are we now at the inside? Just as before we're outside again; nothing has changed. The pieces of chalk are somewhat smaller; but whether they're larger or smaller makes no difference now. The surfaces at the break are not as smooth as the rest of the outer surface; but that is also unimportant. The moment we wanted to open the chalk up by breaking it into pieces, it already closed itself off, and we can continue this process until the whole chalk has become a little heap of dust.

STUDENT B [*aside*]:
> So that's what he meant in the other lecture by speaking of the mere thing's "holding itself back" [*Sichzurückhalten*] and being essentially "off-putting and closed off" [*das Befremdende und Verschlossene im Wesen des Dinges.*][54]

STUDENT C [*who has been leafing through copy of* Sein und Zeit, *stops at page 69 and reads to himself*]:
> "What is peculiar about what is immediately to-hand is that it simultaneously withdraws in its to-handness, just in order to be properly to-hand." I'm beginning to understand what he means by saying that a primary feature of what is to-hand is "self-withholding non-emergence" [*das ansichhaltende Nichtheraustreten*] (*SZ* 75). But now he seems to be extending this notion to apply to *all* things.

HEIDEGGER:
> [We] were unable to find the space we were looking for inside the chalk, the space which belongs to the chalk itself. But perhaps we weren't quick enough. Let's try breaking the piece of chalk once again!
>
> [*Repeats the routine*]
>
> So where on earth does the inside of the chalk begin, and where does the outside stop?

Earth and World (from Chalk to Rock)

[The scene is a lecture hall in Frankfurt; the date: November 1936; the topic: "The Work [of Art] and Truth"][55]

HEIDEGGER:
> The Greek temple [as a work of art] opens up a world [*Welt*] and sets this back on to the earth [*Erde*] .... Through the opening up of a world, all things receive their time and place, their farness and distance, their breadth and narrowness.... The earth is the forthcoming-sheltering ... the unimpressionable tireless-indefatigable ... the essentially self-closing ... which withdraws from any attempt to open it up and holds itself constantly closed.

STUDENT A:
> Given Professor Heidegger's background, it's likely that the roots of these ideas of world and earth are in Presocratic thought and Greek myth; certainly the idea of world has become more concrete than it was in *SZ*. But I wonder whether he's been reading Wilhelm's translation of the *I Ching*, since *Welt* and *Erde* are strikingly similar to the primal powers represented by the primary trigrams of *yang* and *yin* lines respectively: *qian* 乾, "the creative," associated with the openness of heaven, and *kun* 坤, "the receptive," associated with the darkness of the earth.[56]

HEIDEGGER:
> What is the earth, that it thus attains what is unconcealed? The stone is heavy and manifests its weight. But while its weight weighs on us, it at the same time refuses any penetration into it.
>
> [*Proceeds to ponder the heaviness the stone as he did the space within the chalk in the earlier lecture*]

STUDENT C [*aside*]:
> So we have the same situation as with trying to comprehend the being of what is to-hand. Contemplate the hammer in a detached and objective manner and you'll never grasp it in its being. Pick it up and hammer with it and it withdraws. Feel the weight of the stone in your palm and its heaviness remains somehow mysterious. Try to get to the inside of it by smashing it and the fragments pose the same enigma—plus you've lost the stone. Put it on the scales and you can no longer feel the weight. Subject it to molecular analysis and you lose the stone again. There seems to be a certain "earthiness" to all things, from hammers to rocks.

HEIDEGGER:
> The earth thus lets every penetration shatter against it. It lets every merely calculative pushiness turn into a destroying.

STUDENT D:
> This reminds me of a discussion I heard recently between Werner Heisenberg and Niels Bohr on the topic of "complementarity." One of them pointed out the impossibility of determining the position of every atom in a cell without killing the cell.[57] Heisenberg's "uncertainty principle" suggests that the exclusively *yang* 陽 power of "world" is unable unequivocally to open up the secrets of the *yin* 陰 power of "earth." And it seems that Heidegger is advocating something close to what Zhuangzi calls the "ultimate *yin* [which unravels things]" approach for when the going gets tough and the inquiry deep (*Zhuangzi* ch. 3, IC 62–3).

HEIDEGGER:
> All things of the earth, and earth itself as a whole, flow together in reciprocal harmony. But this confluence is not a blurring. Here flows the stream—resting in itself—of distinguishing, which distinguishes everything present in its presence. Thus there is in each of the self-enclosing things a similar not-knowing-itself.[58]

STUDENT D:
> This is rather uncharacteristic language for Professor Heidegger. It sounds a lot like Daoism—with overtones of Chinese Buddhism—in which the oneness of all things similarly maintains distinction within non-difference. It's in chapter two, I think, that Zhuangzi says something to the effect that "The Way interchanges [apparently opposite] things and deems them one …

All things, whether forming or dissolving, in reverting interchange and are deemed to be one."

HEIDEGGER:
World and earth are essentially different from one another and yet are never separated ... The world as the self-opening tolerates no being closed off. But the earth inclines as the sheltering to envelop and encompass world within itself. The opposition of world and earth is a contention [*Streit*] ... [which is different from] discord and dispute.[59]

STUDENT F [*aside*]:
I keep being reminded of Nietzsche's distinction between the forces of the Apollinian and the Dionysian in *The Birth of Tragedy*. Taken as very general perspectives on the world, or world views, or projections which create worlds, the Apollinian attitude, with its penchant for openness and distance and light, seems analogous to the power of world, while the Dionysian, with its more feminine darkness and closeness and blurring of borders, would correspond to the power of earth.

HEIDEGGER:
The contention is not a rift [*Riss*] as in the tearing open of a mere gap, but is rather the interiority of the belonging-to-one-another of the contenders. This rift draws the opponents together into the origin of their unity from a single ground ... The *Riss* does not let the opponents burst apart, but brings the opposition of measure and border into a unitary outline [*Umriss*].

STUDENT A [*looking at the* taiji 太極 *symbol* (Figure 1.1) *he has been drawing in his notebook*]:
Since *Riss* means "line" as well as "rift," it could also refer to the line between the *yin* and *yang* in the *taiji* symbol and the outline [*Umriss*] bounding them. And since Heidegger further characterizes the *Riss* as the image of the primordial contention of truth as the opposition between revelation and concealment, it would correspond to *dao* as the "single ground" of the origin of the unity of *yin* and *yang*.[60]

Figure 1.1 *Taiji* symbol.

HEIDEGGER:
[The issue of truth could not even come up] if the unconcealment of what-is had not exposed us to that clearing into which all beings stand and from which they withdraw ...

This clearing ... this open middle is not surrounded by what-is, but the illuminating middle itself surrounds—like Nothing, which we hardly know—all that is.

Every being that is encountered maintains this strangely ambiguous presence, in that it always simultaneously holds itself back in concealment ...

In this way, self-concealing Being is illuminated.[61]

LAOZI:
>The Way is empty, yet use will not drain it.
>Deep, it is like the ancestor of the myriad things.
>Abysmal, it only seems as if it were there.
>I do not know whose son it is.
>It images the forefather of the Gods.[62]

ZHUANGZI:
>The myriad things have somewhere from which they grow but no one sees the root, somewhere from which they come forth but no one sees the gate. Men all honor what wit knows, but none knows how to know by depending on what his wits do not know; may that not be called the supreme uncertainty?[63]

STUDENT A [*waking up after having dozed off briefly*]:
>It seems as if I was just sitting at the feet of a Chinese sage. Something to do with the myriad things' entering into and withdrawing from unconcealment?
>
>[*Looks down at his notebook where someone has transcribed a few lines from the* Zhuangzi]
>
>"While we dream we do not know that we are dreaming, and in the middle of a dream interpret a dream within it; not until we wake do we know that we were dreaming. Only at the ultimate awakening shall we know that this is the ultimate dream."[64]
>
>Was I just dreaming that I was listening to Lao-Zhuang? Or is this all Professor Heidegger's dream? Or shall I wake up to find a butterfly dreaming it was in a lecture theatre? Is *this* what Zhuangzi means by "the transformations of things?"

Notes

1. Martin Buber, *Reden und Gleichnisse des Tschuang-Tse* (Leipzig: lnsel Verlag, 1921), 62.
2. The scenario is based on the account given by Heinrich Wiegand Petzet in Günther Neske (ed.), *Erinnerung an Martin Heidegger* (Pfullingen: Verlag Günther Neske, 1977), 183–4, and in his book *Auf einen Stern zugehen* (Frankfurt: Societäts-Verlag, 1983), 24.
3. "*Vom Wesen der Wahrheit*," in Martin Heidegger, *Wegmarken* [GA 9] (Frankfurt: Vittorio Klostermann, 1967), 81–3; David F. Krell (ed.), *Martin Heidegger: Basic Writings* (New York: Harper and Row, 1977), 125–7.
4. Martin Heidegger, *Schelling's Treatise on the Essence of Human Freedom*, trans. Joan Stambaugh (Athens: Ohio University Press, 1985), 64.
5. The *Daodejing*, attributed to Laozi, is the better known of the two great works of philosophical Daoism, the other being the anthology known as the *Zhuangzi*. For the former I have used D.C. Lau (trans.), *Lao Tzu: Tao Te Ching* (London: Penguin

Books, 1963), and also Guying Chen, *Lao Tzu: Text, Notes and Comments*, trans. Rhett W. Young and Roger T. Ames (San Francisco: Chinese Materials Centre, 1977). A revised translation by Professor Lau, based on the Ma Wang Tui manuscripts, has been published in a bilingual edition under the same title (Hong Kong: Chinese University Press, 1982). In quoting from the *Zhuangzi* I shall refer to the chapter number and also to the partial translation by A.C. Graham, *Chuang-tzu: The Inner Chapters* (London: George Allen and Unwin, 1981), henceforth abbreviated as *IC* followed by the page number. Professor Graham's seems to me the philosophically most insightful of the extant translations, and is furnished with an illuminating commentary. It also has the great virtue of retaining intact the crazy patchwork texture of the text, rather than distorting it by smoothing it out into a seamless whole.

Both the *Zhuangzi* and the *Laozi* are anthologies compiled by a succession of editors. The traditional view used to be that Laozi was an older contemporary of Confucius, but Professor Lau argues convincingly in appendix 1 of his translation that it is doubtful whether Laozi was in fact a historical person at all, and that the text probably dates from as late as the third century BCE. Of the thirty-three extant chapters of the *Zhuangzi*, which appear to date from the fourth, third, and second centuries BCE., the first seven, known as the "Inner Chapters," are thought to come from the same hand—that of Zhuang Zhou (Zhuangzi), who flourished probably around the end of the fourth century BCE.

6   Martin Heidegger, *Identität und Differenz* [GA 11] (Pfullingen: Verlag Günther Neske, 1957), 25; Martin Heidegger, *Identity and Difference*, trans. Joan Stambaugh (New York: Harper and Row, 1969), 36.

7   Martin Heidegger, *Unterwegs zur Sprache* [GA 12] (Pfullingen: Verlag Günther Neske, 1959), 198; Martin Heidegger, *On the Way to Language*, trans. Peter D. Hertz (New York: Harper and Row, 1971), 92.

8   Chung-Yuan Chang, "The Philosophy of Taoism according to Chuang Tzu," *Philosophy East and West*, 27.4 (1977): 409-22.

9   Chung-Yuan Chang has done the most work on the comparison with Daoism—though he focuses almost exclusively on the later Heidegger: see, in particular, *Tao: A New Way of Thinking* (New York: Harper and Row, 1975). There is, however, the danger in working exclusively with the later writings that their poetic style, because it admits of freer interpretations, also allows greater possibility of distortion in the interests of comparison.

10 Since nobody has yet looked at the work of the middle period from the comparative point of view, the epilogue will play with excerpts from works published shortly after *SZ*, up to the second book on Kant, *Die Frage nach dem Ding: Zu Kants Lehre von den Transzendentalen Grundsätzen* [GA 41] (Tübingen: Niemeyer, 1962), which is based on lectures given in the winter semester 1935-6; English translation by W.B. Barton and Vera Deutsch, *What Is a Thing?* (Chicago: Regnery, 1967). Martin Buber's edition of *Zhuangzi* was published in 1910, so Heidegger may well have read it before authoring *SZ*. However, given how wary he was of assimilating philosophical influences—and especially in the case of a philosophy couched in a language so alien to his mother tongue—any comparable themes discovered in the works of the few years following his first exposure to Asian thought will still be of significance.

11 "Zur Erörterung der Gelassenheit: Aus einem Feldweggspräch über das Denken" (1945), in Martin Heidegger, *Gelassenheit* (Pfullingen: Verlag Günther Neske, 1959), and "Aus einem Gespräch von der Sprache" (1954) in Martin Heidegger, *Unterwegs zur Sprache*; English translations in John M. Anderson and E. Hans Freund (trans.),

Discourse on Thinking (New York: Harper and Row, 1966), and *On the Way to Language*. Both dialogues were based on actual conversations, but were considerably re-worked by Heidegger. The Heraclitus seminars conducted with Eugen Fink (*Heraklit*) were published in the form of a dialogue but are closer to transcripts than something written by Heidegger himself. In the *Vorbemerkung* to *Einführung in die Metaphysik* Heidegger writes (presumably without having said it): "What has been spoken no longer speaks in what has been printed." Martin Heidegger, *Einführung in die Metaphysik* (Tübingen: Niemeyer, 1953); English translation by Ralph Manheim, *An Introduction to Metaphysics* (New Haven: Yale University Press, 1959)—hereafter abbreviated as *EM* and *IM* respectively.

12   A comparison of the ideas of Heraclitus and Lao-Zhuang would be a fascinating study in its own right. For a sketch of fruitful areas of comparison between Daoism and a late Western scion of Heraclitus, Nietzsche, see Graham Parkes, "The Wandering Dance: *Chuang Tzu* and *Zarathustra*," *Philosophy East and West*, 33.3 (1983): 235–50.

13   Heidegger's intuition that the *logos* of Heraclitus and the *dao* are comparable is on the mark—and to examine the similarities between the two ideas could be an illuminating instance of explicating *obscurum per obscurius*. The fragments concerning the cyclical transformations of the cosmic elements have obvious counterparts in Daoist cosmology, and Heraclitus' understanding of the mutual interdependence of opposites and the relativity of all perspectives harmonizes closely with the thought of *Zhuangzi*. A thorough comparison would examine the deeper implications of such comparable utterances as the following (the numbers of Heraclitus' fragments are preceded by H, and the chapters of *Zhuangzi* and *Laozi* by C and L respectively): H50, C1; H102, C2; H111, L2; H88, C6; H61, C18; H103, C17/27; H40, L81; L40.

14   The language of *SZ* is undeniably innovative, though few of the neologisms are elegant. The text is characterized by a multitude of subtle interconnections and word plays, some but by no means all of which have been pointed out by Macquarrie and Robinson in their footnotes. The language also has powerful "body" which has gone largely unnoticed by commentators.

15   *Sein und Zeit* [GA 2] (Tübingen: Niemeyer, 1967), 311; *Being and Time*, trans. John Macquarrie and Edward Robinson (New York: Harper and Row, 1962), 359. Cf. also *SZ* 327: "Acts of violence are in this field not capriciousness but rather a necessity grounded in the issue itself." References to *SZ* will be given hereafter in the body of the text simply by way of the page number (the pagination of the German edition is given in the margins of the Macquarrie and Robinson translation). All translations from the German are mine.

16   In *SZ* (65) Heidegger writes: "Even the phenomenon of 'Nature' in the sense of the Romantic conception of nature can be grasped ontologically only from the conception of world."

17   The terms *das Zuhandene* and *das Vorhandene* defy elegant translation. In an attempt to preserve something of the simple similarity of these terms they will be rendered as "[what is] to-hand" and "on-hand" respectively. Heidegger emphasizes in his use of *das Vorhandene*, which is a common word in German, the connotation of "objective" or "neutral presence," whereas he uses *das Zuhandene* so much as a technical term that it comes close to being a neologism. In both cases it is important to retain the "hand" of the original German in view of the philosophical import of the somatic metaphors in *SZ*.

18 The problem of the natural in Daoism is compounded by the fact that there is no single term in Daoist vocabulary that corresponds exactly to our word "nature" in the sense of the natural world. The one that comes closest is *tian*, or "heaven"—especially when it occurs in the compound *tiandi* 天地, meaning "heaven-and-earth." Two relevant terms that are distinctively Daoist are *zhen* 真, meaning "genuine, authentic, true," and *ziran* 自然, meaning "spontaneous activity" or, more literally, "self so-ing."

19 Hildegard Feick, *Index zu Heideggers "Sein und Zeit"* (Tübingen: Niemeyer, 1968), 63. (Omits one of the more important references—SZ 362.)

20 Macquarrie and Robinson opt for "equipment," which has the advantage that it catches the primary feature of *Zeug* which is that there is no such thing as "a" single, isolated "equipment."

21 It is not clear why Heidegger changes his example from writing utensils to hammers, since he could make all the same points about handiness, and make them more vividly, with reference to his immediate activity of using a pen to write the text of SZ. Perhaps Nietzsche's enterprise (made explicit in the preface to *Twilight of the Idols*) of "philosophizing with a hammer" is a subliminal influence here—though his penchant for percussing idols with a hammer "as with a tuning fork" is exercised in the workshop of traditional philosophical ideas and ideals.

22 Heidegger repeatedly remarks that most of our everyday activities are carried out without any theoretical reflection or thematized understanding, but rather in the light of a "pre-ontological understanding" based on *Umsicht*. While Macquarrie and Robinson's choice of "circumspection" for *Umsicht* has the virtue of being a straightforward translation of the German word, it fails to reflect the distinctive meaning Heidegger gives to the term. They are right to note that "Heidegger is taking advantage of the fact that the prefix '*um*' may mean 'around' or 'in order to'" (footnote 2 on page 98 of *Being and Time*). Heidegger does want to emphasize that *Umsicht* involves peripheral rather than sharply focused vision (and in this sense it corresponds to the "soft focus" and global appreciation of the entire situation that is the precondition for Daoist spontaneity). But, especially when talking about inauthentic everydayness, he lays much more stress on the meaning "in order to"—to emphasize that in the light of *Umsicht* we see and understand things in terms of what they are "for." For this reason "for-sight" would be an appropriate translation (even though the German word is not a neologism), especially if we can hear in it an overtone of the understanding of future possibilities. Far from conveying a sense of circumspection, the term suggests a certain confidence in dealing with things that is grounded in our pre-ontological familiarity with how they work. As long as the hammering is going well, one's hand can pick up more nails without one's having to look over at the can in which they are stored.

23 *Das Eigentümliche des zunächst Zuhandenen ist es, in seiner Zuhandenheit sich gleichsam zurückzuziehen, um gerade eigentlich zuhanden zu sein* (SZ 69). This is reminiscent of Zhuangzi's remark that "When one has the proper shoes one forgets one's feet" (ch. 19).

24 Compare with SZ 63: "Nature is itself a being which we encounter within the world and is discoverable in various ways and on various levels."

25 Toward the end of the book Heidegger takes up the topic (in the passage overlooked by Feick) of the *a priori* "mathematical projection of nature" that is the prerequisite for modern scientific discovery—a theme he was to develop fully in the second book on Kant in 1935–6.

26 "Vom Wesen des Grundes," in *Wegmarken*, 51; English translation in Terrence Malik (trans.), *The Essence of Reasons* (Evanston: Northwestern University Press, 1969), 80–3.

27 The particular passage Heidegger is referring to on *SZ* 65 says that even the "Romantic conception of nature" must be understood on the basis of the concept of world. Be that as it may, it is nevertheless strange—in view of the traditional interest in nature on the part of German philosophers from Kant through the *Naturphilosophen* and up to Schopenhauer and Nietzsche—that Heidegger discusses it so little in *SZ*. This would have been more understandable had he been an insensitive city-dweller, but his love of living close to the land is well known—and evident from the content of his later essays.

28 There is a danger in the common (and well-justified) practice of leaving the term *Dasein* untranslated, that the reader may simply mouth the German term, forgetting that Dasein is always mine, yours, ours. While *Dasein* is an ordinary word for "existence," Heidegger made it into such a special term that there is some justification for rendering it by the written neologism "being-(t)here." While not a particularly attractive word to look at (and difficult to pronounce), it has the advantage of conveying the ambiguity of the German primal syllable *da*, which means both "here" and "there." To write "being-(t)here" and say "being here and there" invite us to hear the "here" and "there" both spatially and temporally: "here/now" (anywhere) and "there/then" (any other time future or past).

29 Martin Heidegger, "*Der Ursprung des Kunstwerkes*," in *Holzwege* [GA 5] (Frankfurt: Vittorio Klostermann, 1972)—subsequent references will be abbreviated *UK* and followed by the page number in *Holzwege*; English translation in Albert Hofstadter (trans.), "The Origin of the Work of Art," in *Poetry, Language, Thought* (New York: Harper and Row, 1975)—hereafter *OWA*. Any impression that the proper attitude toward things is merely technological is quickly dispelled by this essay, a major concern of which is to describe a way of relating to things that is quite different from taking them as to- or on-hand. The work of art, whose essential nature cannot be appreciated if it is taken as an implement or an object of scientific investigation, is to be seen here as a paradigm of things in general. The "Epilogue" will point up the distinctly Daoist tone to what, for Heidegger, is the appropriate attitude to the work and the thing.

30 Heidegger would add: "Philosophy is not knowledge which one ... could apply and calculate the usefulness of. However, what is useless can still be a true power." Heidegger, *EM* 7, *IM* 10.

31 *IC* 73. There are four passages about useless trees in chapter 4 (*IC* 72–5), one at the end of ch. 1 (*IC* 47), and another in ch. 20 (*IC* 121).

32 Aside from the well-known story of Cook Ding, the adept carver of oxes, in the Inner Chapters (ch. 3, *IC* 63), there is the wheelwright Pian of chapter 13 (*IC* 139–40), the buckle forger in chapter 22 (*IC* 139), and the stories of numerous woodworkers and other artisans collected in chapter 19 (*IC* 135–8). Several consummate swimmers the human counterpart to the many fish that swim through the *Zhuangzi*—play roles as models for our behavior. (Heidegger would no doubt want to include skillful skiers.)

33 "Nachwort zu: 'Was Ist Metaphysik?'" in Heidegger, *Wegmarken*, 106; Martin Heidegger, *Was Heisst Denken?* [GA 8] (Tübingen: Niemeyer, 1954), 51; English translation in J. Glenn Gray (trans.), *What Is Called Thinking?* (New York: Harper and Row, 1968), 16. This is *besinnendes* as opposed to *rechnendes Denken*, sensitive and meditative rather than calculative thinking. This is comparable to the distinction

in *Zhuangzi* between *lun* 論, a kind of "sorting" which "evens things out" rather than ranks, and *bian* 辯, which denotes the kind of thinking that discriminates between opposites and weighs alternative courses of action. (See Graham's discussion of these two in *IC* 12.)

34 See Otto Pöggeler's discussion of Heidegger's interest in these artists, *supra*; and see also his book, *Die Frage nach der Kunst: von Hegel zu Heidegger* (München: Alber, 1984).
35 This suggestion may appear to contradict Heidegger's saying in almost the next breath, then writing on the next page, that "Socrates is the purest thinker of the West. Therefore he wrote nothing" (*Was Heisst Denken?* 51–2; *What Is Called Thinking?* 16–17).
36 Wallace Stevens. *The Collected Poems of Wallace Stevens* (New York: Alfred A. Knopf, 1954), 345. Stevens apparently knew little about Heidegger and less about Daoism. However, sometimes he simply seems to say it better than anybody else.
37 Emptiness—whether of things, the self, or of *dao*—is a major theme in Daoism; see Graham Parkes, "Intimations of Taoist Themes in Early Heidegger," *Journal of Chinese Philosophy*, 11.4 (1984): 353–74.
38 "Das Ding," in Martin Heidegger, *Vorträge und Aufsätze* [GA 7] (Pfullingen: Verlag Günther Neske, 1967); "The Thing," in *Poetry, Language, Thought*—hereafter *PLT*.
39 "Nachwort zu: 'Was Ist Metaphysik?'" in *Wegmarken*, 103. While there are no extended discussions of death in later Heidegger, the topic retains a central position: as "the shrine of nothingness" death is still our sole access to Being itself (*VA* 177; *PLT* 200). The only substantial treatment in the later work is in the essay on Rilke, "Wozu Dichter?" where Heidegger elaborates a position aligned with Rilke's, regarding "Death and the realm of the dead [as belonging] to the totality of beings as its other side" (*Holzwege*, 279; *PLT* 124).
40 Heidegger, "*Was Ist Metaphysik?*" in *Wegmarken*, 32–4; *Basic Writings*, 102–5.
41 Stevens, *Collected Poems*, 441.
42 Ch.19, *IC* 182; ch. 6, *IC* 85; ch. 2, *IC* 52.
43 *SZ* 288 and 295. It is significant that the word Heidegger chooses for the operation of the authentic self (*handeln*) has "hand" as its root.
44 *SZ* 385 and 310. The only mention of "joy" (*Freude*) in *SZ* occurs, significantly, in this context of giving death power over one's existence (310). Heidegger speaks later of the necessity of letting death become powerful in one's being (*den Tod in sich mächtig werden [lassen]*) so that one can experience one's fate historically (384).
45 *SZ* 297. At the same time he characterizes the disclosedness of world as "the release (*Freigabe*) of the current involvement-totality of what is to-hand."
46 This time Heidegger presses the point home by playing on the word *zu*, "[in order] to": "This simply shows that what is to-hand belongs to something else to-hand (*Darin aber bekundet sich Zugehörigkeit des gerade Zuhandenen zu einem anderen*)" (353).
47 Heidegger, *The Question about the Thing*, 1.
48 As Angus Graham remarks: "The 'Primitivist' writer is unrepresentative, as we imply by giving him that name" (*IC* 185). Cf. his comments on the well-sweep story (*IC* 186).
49 This "simultaneous Yes and No" actually constitutes "releasement towards things (*Gelassenheit zu den Dingen*)" (*Gelassenheit*, 23; *Discourse on Thinking*, 54).
50 In "The Origin of the Work of Art" and "What Is Metaphysics?" respectively.
51 The year 1935–6 was a particularly productive one for Heidegger. The lecture notes from two courses from that year were published as two of his best books, *Einführung in die Metaphysik* and *Die Frage nach dem Ding*, and lectures given outside the

university during that period were published as his most extended meditation on the work of art, "Der Ursprung des Kunstwerkes." Heidegger's words are taken from *EM* 23, *IM* 30.

52   For the rest of this section, Heidegger's words are taken from *FD* 14–16.
53   *UK* 14–21, *OWA* 25–32.
54   *UK* 21, *OWA* 32.
55   All Heidegger's words from here on are taken from the second and third sections of *UK*.
56   Richard Wilhelm, trans., *I Ching: Das Buch der Wandlungen* (Düsseldorf: Diederichs, 1970). Wilhelm's translation of the *I Ching* with commentary was first published in 1923. The translation of his translation by Cary F. Baynes, *I Ching: The Book of Changes* (Princeton: Bollingen Series, 1967), then became the definitive edition in English. The distinction between *Erde* and *Welt* also corresponds to Schelling's distinction between *Grund* and *Existenz* (ground and existence) as articulated in his essay on Human Freedom (1809). Heidegger devoted a semester's course to lectures on this text in 1936, which have been published as *Schellings Abhandlung über das Wesen der menschlichen Freiheit* [GA 42] (Tübingen: Niemeyer, 1971). The reciprocal relationship between *Grund* and *Existenz* together with a number of related ideas in Schelling's essay has a remarkably Daoist tone to them, independently of Heidegger's interpretation. An interesting comparison of Schelling's thought with Daoism and Tian-tai Buddhism can be found in Bruno Petzold, *Die Quintessenz der T'ien-T'ai (Tendai) Lehre*, ed. Horst Hammitzsch (Wiesbaden: Harrassowitz, 1982).
57   Heisenberg recounts a conversation from the early thirties in which Bohr says, "In principle, we could probably measure the position of every atom in a cell, though hardly without killing the living cell in the process. What we would know in the end would be the arrangement of the atoms in a dead cell, not a living one" (Werner Heisenberg, *Physics and Beyond* (New York: Harper and Row, 1972), 111). It is interesting that in another conversation with Bohr the following year Heisenberg mentions the Chinese idea of *dao* (see page 136).
58   *So ist in jedem der sich verschliessenden Dinge das gleiche Sich-nicht-Kennen* (*UK* 36, *OWA* 47). The final phrase is ambiguous. Albert Hofstadter takes the *Sich* as plural rather than singular, and so translates it: "the same not-knowing-of-one-another." While this reading is grammatically possible, it seems to go against the sense of "reciprocal harmony" just mentioned. Things have sufficient self-enclosing tendencies to keep them from merging into total undifferentiation—but presumably could not flow together in reciprocal harmony if they did not know each other at all.
59   *Streit* is difficult to translate here, since Heidegger specifically dispels connotations of "strife" and "struggle." He probably has in mind Heraclitus' notion of *polemos*—since he mentions fragment 53 earlier in the essay (*UK* 32, *OWA* 43) which has in any case a very Daoist ring to it.
60   The comparison *Welt/Erde* and *yang/yin* prompts a further reflection. Just as the latter are so primordial that they operate as powers in the human psyche as well as in the cosmos as a whole, so world and earth might also be thought of in regard to the distinction between consciousness and the unconscious in depth psychology.
61   *Dergestalt ist das sichverbergende Sein gelichtet* (*UK* 44, *OWA* 56).
62   *Daodejing*, ch. 4.
63   *Zhuangzi* 25, *IC* 102.
64   *Zhuangzi* 2, *IC* 59–60.

References

Baynes, Cary F., trans. *I Ching: The Book of Changes*. Princeton: Bollingen Series, 1967.
Buber, Martin. *Reden und Gleichnisse des Tschuang-Tse*. Leipzig: Insel Verlag, 1921.
Chang, Chung-Yuan. *Creativity and Taoism*. New York: Harper and Row, 1970.
Chang, Chung-Yuan. *Tao: A New Way of Thinking*. New York: Harper and Row, 1975.
Chang, Chung-Yuan. "The Philosophy of Taoism according to Chuang Tzu." *Philosophy East and West*, 27.4 (1977): 409–22.
Chen, Guying. *Lao Tzu: Text, Notes and Comments*. Translated by Rhett W. Young and Roger T. Ames. San Francisco: Chinese Materials Centre, 1977.
Feick, Hildegard. *Index zu Heideggers "Sein und Zeit."* Tübingen: Niemeyer, 1968.
Graham, A.C., trans. *Chuang-tzu: The Inner Chapters*. London: George Allen and Unwin, 1981.
Heidegger, Martin. *Einführung in die Metaphysik*. Tübingen: Niemeyer, 1953.
Heidegger, Martin. *Was Heisst Denken?* [GA 8]. Tübingen: Niemeyer, 1954.
Heidegger, Martin. *Identität und Differenz* [GA 11]. Pfullingen: Verlag Günther Neske, 1957.
Heidegger, Martin. *Gelassenheit*. Pfullingen: Neske, 1959.
Heidegger, Martin. *An Introduction to Metaphysics*. Translated by Ralph Manheim. New Haven: Yale University Press, 1959.
Heidegger, Martin. *Unterwegs zur Sprache* [GA 12]. Pfullingen: Verlag Günther Neske, 1959.
Heidegger, Martin. *Being and Time*. Translated by John Macquarrie and Edward Robinson. New York: Harper and Row, 1962.
Heidegger, Martin. *Die Frage nach dem Ding: Zu Kants Lehre von den Transzendentalen Grundsätzen* [GA 41]. Tübingen: Niemeyer, 1962.
Heidegger, Martin. *Discourse on Thinking*. Translated by John M. Anderson and E. Hans Freund. New York: Harper and Row, 1966.
Heidegger, Martin. *Sein und Zeit* [GA 2]. Tübingen: Max Niemeyer Verlag, 1967.
Heidegger, Martin. *Vorträge und Aufsätze* [GA 7]. Pfullingen: Verlag Günther Neske, 1967.
Heidegger, Martin. *Wegmarken* [GA 9]. Frankfurt: Vittorio Klostermann, 1967.
Heidegger, Martin. *What Is a Thing?* Translated by W. B. Barton and Vera Deutsch. Chicago: Regnery, 1967.
Heidegger, Martin. *What Is Called Thinking?* Translated by J. Glenn Gray. New York: Harper and Row, 1968.
Heidegger, Martin. *The Essence of Reasons*. Translated by Terrence Malik. Evanston: Northwestern University Press, 1969.
Heidegger, Martin. *Identity and Difference*. Translated by Joan Stambaugh. New York: Harper and Row, 1969.
Heidegger, Martin. *On the Way to Language*. Translated by Peter D. Hertz. New York: Harper and Row, 1971.
Heidegger, Martin. *Schellings Abhandlung über das Wesen der menschlichen Freiheit* [GA 42]. Tübingen: Niemeyer, 1971.
Heidegger, Martin. *Holzwege* [GA 5]. Frankfurt: Vittorio Klostermann, 1972.
Heidegger, Martin. *Poetry, Language, Thought*. Translated by Albert Hofstadter. New York: Harper and Row, 1975.
Heidegger, Martin. *Martin Heidegger: Basic Writings*. Edited by David F. Krell. New York: Harper and Row, 1977.

Heidegger, Martin. *Schelling's Treatise on the Essence of Human Freedom*. Translated by Joan Stambaugh. Athens: Ohio University Press, 1985.

Heisenberg, Werner. *Physics and Beyond*. New York: Harper and Row, 1972.

Lau, D.C., trans. *Lao Tzu: Tao Te Ching*. London: Penguin Books, 1963.

Neske, Günther, ed. *Erinnerung an Martin Heidegger*. Pfullingen: Neske, 1977.

Parkes, Graham. "The Wandering Dance: *Chuang Tzu* and *Zarathustra*." *Philosophy East and West*, 33.3 (1983): 235–50.

Parkes, Graham. "Intimations of Taoist Themes in Early Heidegger." *Journal of Chinese Philosophy*, 11.4 (1984): 353–74.

Petzet, Heinrich Wiegand. *Auf einen Stern zugehen: Begegnungen und Gespräche mit Martin Heidegger*. Frankfurt: Societäts-Verlag, 1983.

Petzold, Bruno. *Die Quintessenz der T'ien-T'ai (Tendai) Lehre*. Edited by Horst Hammitzsch. Wiesbaden: Harrassowitz, 1982.

Pöggeler, Otto. *Die Frage nach der Kunst: von Hegel zu Heidegger*. München: Alber, 1984.

Stevens, Wallace. *The Collected Poems of Wallace Stevens*. New York: Alfred A. Knopf, 1954.

Wilhelm, Richard, trans. *I Ching: Das Buch der Wandlungen*. Düsseldorf: Diederichs, 1970.

2

Heidegger's Daoist Phenomenology

Jay Goulding

Introduction

Indispensable to Martin Heidegger's understanding of Daoism is the provocative reading initiated by Friedrich Schelling (1775–1854) in the 1842 Berlin Lectures. Schelling's early, unique, and pinpoint inquiry into the essence of Dao directly connects to Heidegger's later interpretation. This chapter will begin with this relatively unknown interconnection followed by intriguing instances of Daoist imagery in Heidegger's *Contributions* (1936), *Parmenides* (1942–3), and *Heraclitus* (1943). Utilizing a full range of Heidegger's writings, the chapter examines the Void (*Leere*) in relation with the non-being/nothingness of Daoism. The valley, the cup, and Vincent van Gogh's shoes reverberate with Daoist inklings of the hollow. Over a fifty-year engagement with East Asian thinkers, Heidegger arrives at four counter-positions to the Western spatialized, materialized world as he crosses paths, from time to time, with Dao: 1) *Da-sein* (there-being—non-Cartesian subjectivity as a collection of beings searching for primordial there); 2) *Das Ding* (the thing—non-Euclidean space as four-dimensionality); 3) *Die Kehre* (the turn—non-Aristotelian time as a reversibility); 4) *Vernehmen* (ap-prehension—non-representational and non-conceptual thought). Dao resonates throughout Heidegger's forest of fourfolds leaving a trace (*Spur*) similar to Zhuangzi's *ji* 跡 (footprint/trace) where the sage disappears in the midst of time's passing while vanishing into things around him, reminiscent of Laozi.

Dao as *Die Pforte* (the Portal)

There is important scholarship on the philosophical interactions of Heidegger and Schelling[1] that opens a floodgate of studies on God, metaphysics, freedom, and mythology. Many commentaries focus on *Er-eignis, Da-sein, Seyn, Gelassenheit*, "the last God," "the abyss," and more.[2] There is, however, little scholarship on Schelling's analysis of Daoism;[3] and even less on tracing seminal linkages from Schelling's observations to Heidegger's own contemplations on Daoism. *Schelling gazes at Dao's portal of nothingness*; *Heidegger steps back (Schritt züruck) and descends into its Void*

(*Leere*).⁴ For the longest day that Schelling lives, he is not an expert on the philosophy, history, or religion of Daoism nor does he spend much time examining East Asia. However, his deep, pinpoint contemplations on Dao 道 are valuable to professional scholars of Chinese philosophy, and to novices looking to feel their way from the Western world to the Far East. This section highlights Schelling's understanding of Daoism as a preamble influence on Heidegger's longtime interlocution with Chinese thinkers. Schelling initiates a deep introspection on Dao, and Heidegger carries it forward in his own fashion. At Heidegger's humble hut of the Black Forest village Todtnauberg in Baden-Württemberg, two portraits hang on the wall: one of the Alemannic poet Johann Peter Hebel (1760–1826) (commemorating the prize that Heidegger won in 1960),⁵ and the other of Schelling "the truly creative and boldest thinker of this whole age of German philosophy."⁶ On the wall of Heidegger's study at his house in Freiburg hang two calligraphic pieces from chapter 15 of the *Daodejing*⁷ alongside an original Hishikawa Moronobu 菱川師宣 (1618–94) wood block engraving of a Buddhist monastery—artefacts that indicate his continuously high esteem for East Asian philosophy and culture.⁸ Schelling is known for a rigorous analysis of ancient Greece and Rome. He attends Bebenhausen's monastic school near Tübingen where the chaplain, his father Joseph Friedrich Schelling (1737–1812) teaches philology and philosophical theology. Concentrating on the Near East, Joseph himself studies Arabic, Syriac, and Hebrew languages. These formative years might encourage the young Friedrich to also learn about the Far East. Friedrich masters six languages by the age of thirteen (including four ancient languages), entering university at fifteen.

In the 1842 Berlin lectures, Schelling explains Dao and the unique monosyllabic character of Chinese language:⁹

> Tao [Dao] is not called [*heisst*, named] Reason, as people have translated it until now, Tao doctrine is not called doctrine of Reason. Tao is called gateway [*Pforte*, passageway, door, entrance, portal], Tao doctrine is the doctrine of the great gateway in Being [*Seyn*], from the Non-beings [*Nichtseyenden*], the merely able to be [*seyn Könnenden*] through which every finite Being goes into the actual Being [*wirkliche Seyn*]. (You remember the very similar expressions which we have used for the first Potency). The great art or wisdom of life consists precisely in preserving this pure potential [*lauter Können*], which is nothing and yet at the same time all. Hence, the entire Tao-te-King [*Daodejing*] solely shifts itself [*bewegt sich*, moves, makes way] and appears [*zu zeigen*, points toward] through a great turning [*Abwechslung*, rotation] of profound twists [*sinnreichsten Wendungen*, ingenious windings, clever utterances], the great and insurmountable power of non-Being [*nicht Seyenden*].¹⁰

The expression *sinnreichsten Wendungen* (artfully translated by Kwok-Kui Wong as "most pregnant tropes")¹¹ appears one way or another throughout Schelling's work. Schelling likes to use the term "*sinnvoll*" more often than not for pregnant. However, language might speak behind Schelling's back and hint prophetically at something deeper, specifically in respect to Dao.

With the nearness of the preceding term *Abwechslung* (turning, rotation, alternation), we might retain *Wendungen*'s sense of wending your way or winding, twisting, and changing direction. This insight comes to fruition with *Wendung*, *Kehrung*, and *Drehung* that are seminal expressions for Heidegger who speaks likewise of *Wendungsmitte* as a "turning-midpoint" or a pivot.[12]

Perhaps Schelling is alluding to the twisting, turning torque of life-energy in the middle of Laozi's Daoist wheel from chapter 11 (another one of Heidegger's favorites).[13] The Daoist storyteller Zhuangzi (late fourth-century BCE) calls this the Dao Pivot (*dao shu* 道樞) in chapter 2: "Where none of that or this obtains its counterpart—people call it the Tao [Dao] Pivot. Then the Pivot begins to obtain its middle point of the circle, and—with it, it responds till there-is-no end."[14]

As an expert on the reception of Dao in Western philosophy, Wong provides a fascinating commentary on the above Schelling quote:

> When Schelling says that *dao* is the portal of being, he might be referring to *Daodejing* chapter 6: "The spirit of the valley never dies. This is called the mysterious female. The gateway of the mysterious female is called the root of heaven and earth. Dimly visible, it seems as if it were there, yet use will never drain it." Here Laozi describes how things come to be from the mysterious portal. This metaphor has already been used in the last sentence of the famous chapter 1, "Mystery upon mystery—The gateway of the manifold secrets." However, in chapter 1 we are looking at the portal from an opposite direction: when we look at things in the real world and then speculate about the *dao* behind the myriad things, we come across a portal which leads to the mystery behind these things, whereas in chapter 6 the portal is the origin from which the myriad things are born. In both cases Stanislas Julien [1797–1873] uses the French word *porte* for *men* 門 (portal), thus Schelling's *Pforte*. Therefore, this portal is also the threshold of language: within this threshold is the realm of beings, names, concepts, the nonconstant *dao*, where things can be named but their names are not constant, *dao* can be spoken but this *dao* is not eternal. Beyond that portal is the ever moving, mysterious *wu* [無], the origin of all things, which can hardly be described by names. Therefore, Schelling points out that Laozi sees this portal as the origin of the universe.[15]

Wong explains that Hegel, during his Berlin Lectures of 1825–6, has available Abel-Rémusat's (1788–1832) French translation of *Daodejing* (with five chapters), whereas Schelling has the new Julien translation with wider selections.[16] To underscore Wong's point, we might mention several other Laozi chapters regarding *men* 門 (gateway, gate, portal) that would spark Schelling's interest, including chapter 10's opening and shutting of the gates of heaven, and chapters 52 and 56 in which there is an opening and shutting of the portals of the nostrils.[17]

In the 1840s, Schelling delivers the Berlin Lectures on the *Philosophy of Mythology*, two of which are dedicated to China. Schelling is on intellectual display as the supreme thinker of the time. An all-star cast of scholars attend Schelling's initial lectures. While many of Schelling's lectures have gained considerable attention, little effort in the Western world goes to exploring his two lectures (number 23 and number 24) on China. Since Gottfried Wilhelm von Leibniz's *Novissima Sinica* (1697), many European philosophers became fascinated with Chinese thought including Johann Gottfried von Herder (1744–1803). In Schelling's posthumous 1857 *Philosophie der Mythologie* (Philosophy of Mythology), the section "China" offers an essential sketch of Daoism. As Professor of theology, canon law, and Chinese thought from the University of Nijmegen, Knut Walf (1936–) proclaims: "Although Schelling had at his disposal only a few original texts in translation, he discerned and tried to describe the essence of *Dao* in a way that is hard to excel." He continues:

> Herman Schell (1850–1906) passed the judgement: Of all known Scriptures, outside the Old and New Testament, which are an inheritance to the future, there can scarcely be found one to challenge the primacy of Laozi's little book ... Julius Grill (1840–1930), Professor at Tübingen, claimed to have discovered about 80 parallels between the New Testament and the book of Laozi [1910].[18]

In line with Walf's judgment on Schelling's "discerning and describing" of "the essence of *Dao* in a way that is hard to excel," Eric S. Nelson elaborates:

> In contrast to the dismissive evaluation of Daoism of his predecessors, such as Kant and Hegel, and his own negative assessment of Confucius as anti-Socrates ... the mature Schelling has a brief but thought-provoking account of Laozi in his *Philosophy of Mythology*. He rejected the previous elucidation of *dao* as reason (*Vernunft*), which Hegel had also used. Schelling interpreted *dao* instead as gateway (*Pforte*), a gateway between the unknowing of finite being and the genuine knowing of actual being (*das wirkliche Seyn*). Dao, construed as real being as potency (*Können, erste Potenz*), which comprises both all and nothing, requires an art or wisdom of practical knowing and living through the play of polarities, of not-being and being. The *Daodejing* is for Schelling "purely philosophical," rather than mythological, and of the "highest interest." It does not develop a systematic account of nature, but rather exhibits the confrontation of a principle (*Auseinandersetzung eines Princips*) with myriad forms. In the second half of the nineteenth century, a number of authors inside and outside Germany would compare Laozi's thinking with that of Schelling as examples of speculative or transcendental systems of reason and the absolute in nature.[19]

Contributing a finely tuned historical analysis to Schelling's era, Nelson describes the European reception of Daoism:

> The early European interpretations of Daoism advanced diverse and contradictory views of Laozi and his teaching. A 1769 edition of collections of travel descriptions translated into German depicted Laozi as an atheistic materialist and leader of a sect consisting of "nothing but a confused fabric of all sorts of excuses and godlessness." The philosopher, historian, and geographer Karl Hammerdorfer, interpreting *dao* as God, portrayed Laozi in a popular book on world history from

1789 as a complete religious dreamer or enthusiast ("vollendeter Schwarmer"), whose teaching was incompatible with rational religion and pure Deism. Laozi was interpreted in the early European reception of Daoism as a religious fanatic, an otherworldly mystic, a cosmic metaphysician of *dao* construed as reason or the absolute, a personal political advisor and strategist to kings, or as a materialist philosopher of private tranquility akin to Epicurus.[20]

The lectures themselves encourage intriguing responses. The philologist and master of fairy tale and fable Jacob Grimm (1785–1863) takes up Schelling's challenge to update, rethink. and outdo Johann Gottfried von Herder's (1744–1803) work on language written eighty years prior. Herder, Humboldt, and Abel-Rémusat have fairly somber views of ancient Chinese language and philosophy. Overall, Schelling is somewhat enthusiastic, especially regarding Dao. In Lecture 24 of the Berlin Lectures, he writes: "If Confucius seeks to trace back all teaching and wisdom to the ancient foundations of the Chinese State, so Laozi penetrates totally, into the unbethinged [unconditioned, *unbedingt*] and universally into the deepest Ground of Seyn [*in den tiefsten Grund des Seyns*]."[21] The "Ground of Being" is often used in Schelling. This last *exact* expression "the deepest Ground of Being" appears rarely and perhaps only once—as far as I see—in the entire corpus of Schelling's work, and in proximity to one of the few places where he names Laozi directly. The expression itself "*in den tiefsten Grund des Seyns*" is important to Heidegger as later explained and opens a double convergence on Heidegger's reception of both Schelling, and his dabbling in Daoism over a five-decade period. Although Schelling chooses not to go this way in respect to Dao, Bruce Matthews opens up a possibility for commentators to return to previous incarnations of Schelling's thought when he writes:

> Schelling's negative philosophy begins with the affirmation of a negation, or better, the affirmation of a *void*. The starting point of his negative science is a wanting [*ein Wollen*], since according to Schelling only the dynamic of desire and wanting can account for the initial conditions of a real beginning. As he much more eloquently phrases the matter, "all beginning lies in an absence, [and] the deepest potency, which holds fast to everything, is nonbeing [*das Nichtseyende*] and its hunger for being."[22] In the wanting of desire, Schelling discovers a way of conceptualizing a beginning that is robust enough to encompass the presence and absence of being and nonbeing as one. And as the hunger of desire, this beginning satisfies his requirement that the highest speculative concepts also be ethical, for if freedom is going to be the determining principle of his entire architectonic, then even the necessary science of reason itself must be initiated in a free act of desire.[23]

As quoted above, we highlight Matthews' translation of Schelling's expression: "all beginning lies in an absence, [and] the deepest potency, which holds fast to everything, is nonbeing and its hunger for being." As in the quote from Laozi, it would appear that Schelling senses the non-being [*das Nichtseyende*] of the Daoist Void as a creative opening that shifts and turns and winds within itself. Here, we might find the inkling of a deeper reading of the Chinese *wu* 無 as nothingness or the void.

Although Schelling does not do so, we might engage the Daoist Void with his views on magnetism and polarity. Schelling writes: "Granted this identity of sensibility and of magnetism with respect to their cause, magnetism must be the determining factor of all dynamical forces, just as sensibility is the determining factor of all organic forces."[24] And further:

> One cannot doubt on the grounds of experience that in an infinite heap of matter a common constitution of all parts to infinity is at all possible ... for the magnet demonstrates polarity to infinity, e.g., as in the newly discovered magnetic serpentine stone [possessing powers of healing in energy balance]. It cannot be denied that the magnetism of our globe penetrates down to the smallest particle.[25]

In his lectures on the *Philosophy of Mythology*, Schelling writes:

> But how many treasures of poetry lie hidden in language itself, treasures that the poet has not placed in it, that he only puts into relief so to speak, or retrieves out of it as from a treasure house, or that he merely induces the language to reveal. Is not, however, every name-giving already a personification; and if all languages conceive as sexually differentiated those things that admit of an antithesis, or expressly designate them in this way—when German says: the masculine [*der*] sky, the feminine [*die*] earth; the masculine [*der*] space, the feminine [*die*] time—then how far is it really from there to the expression of spiritual concepts through masculine and feminine deities. One is almost tempted to say: language itself is only faded mythology [*die verblichene Mythologie*; faded, faint, dim]; what mythology still preserves in living and concrete differences is preserved in language only in abstract and formal differences.[26]

Recognizing hints of Yin 陰 and Yang 陽 from Schelling's reading of the *Yijing* in the above descriptions of feminine and masculine entities, Schelling's adjective *verblichene*[27] as faded, faint, or dim might equally find the murky waters of Dao.

Schelling insists that the contents of the mythological process begin with *the thing itself*: "with the pure creating potencies whose original product is consciousness itself. Thus it is here where the explanation fully breaks through into the objective realm, becomes fully *objective*."[28] As humanity moves from monotheism to di-theism to polytheism, languages follow "from original monosyllabism, via di-syllabism, to an entirely unfettered polysyllabism."[29] Schelling rejects the notion that Chinese language is monosyllabic and "nothing but root, pure substance." In effect, the Chinese language is "polysyllabic in principle" since monosyllabism and di-syllabism both have "lost their meaning as principle."[30] As Wong explains, Schelling observes that within the theogonic process, China was "atheistic," and "one of its kind" as "nonmythological, nonreligious, antimythological" (*unmythologisch, unreligiös, antimythologisch*).[31] Not the matter but only the principle of the primordial language (*Ursprache*) is preserved in the Chinese language. Schelling concludes that first "the Chinese script is so unique in its kind as is the Chinese language,"[32] and that second "China alone is a great and unique exception"[33] to his philosophy of languages.

Heidegger, Schelling, and the Dao Pivot

As a time-tested and astute commentator, Edward Allen Beach notes that Schelling sees ancient Chinese language as "the closest descendant in historical times from this primitive *Ursprache*."[34] Beach provides a powerful overview on Potencies:

> Schelling conceives of an era prior to the beginning of worldly time, during which the generative Potencies would subsist in a state of quiescence. During this primordial, first "time" within eternity (or "proto-time," as we might rather say, in order to distinguish it from worldly time), motion and change would not yet exist, for there would be no physical matter or energy present to serve as the bearers of change. Instead, there would only be the pure dialectical relations of the Potencies in their original condition, a condition marked by total harmony and a mutual codetermination by each of the others' essential natures.[35]

Following Beach, a short detour into the philosophy of Potencies underscores how thought-provoking Schelling proves to be in his discussion of Dao. Schelling is quite consistent over a forty-year exploration of Potencies. In his earlier work, *First Outline of a System of the Philosophy of Nature* (1799), Schelling writes:

> That which, in the dynamical process, is perceived in the product, takes place *beyond* the product with the simple factors of all duality. The first inception of original production is the limitation of productivity through the primitive antithesis, which, *as* antithesis (and as the condition of all construction), is distinguished only in *magnetism*; the second stage of production is the *alternation* [*Wechsel*] of contraction and expansion, and *as* such becomes visible only in *electricity*; finally, the third stage is the transition of this change into indifference, a change [*Wechsel*] which is recognized as such only in *chemical* phenomena. Magnetism, electricity, and chemical process are the *categories* of the original construction of Nature—the latter escapes us and lies outside of intuition, the former are what of it remains behind, what stands firm, what is fixed—the general schemata for the construction of matter.[36]

From Schelling's later works, Beach artfully and succinctly lays out the three Potencies of God. The first Potency, as -A or as A^1 is "the sheer, unlimited possibility of being, *das sein Könnende*." As "pure subjectivity," it is undifferentiated "in itself" (*an sich*) as the primordial "being-in-itself" (*an-sich-Seiende*). As indefinite, it is devoid of objective being, since objectivity requires definite structure. Schelling describes the first Potency as "the infinite lack of being" (*der unendliche Mangel an Sein*).[37] Beach explains that the second Potency as +A or A^2 is "the principle of order" as "the pure being" (*das rein Seiende*), contra to A^1 as the pure possibility of being, a "pure act" (*actus purus*) or "pure being" as the "being-in-itself" (*an-sich-Seiende*). Schelling calls A^2 as the "being-outside-itself" (*das ausser-sich-Seiende*) as "being-that-must-be" (*das sein Müssende*).[38] Finally, the third Potency is "the ideal fulfillment and balance of the first two Potencies." A^3 as "being-with-itself" (*das bei-sich-Seiende*) lifts itself above the other two. As the "subject-object" (*Subjekt-Objekt*), A³ is the highest Potencies. Beach summarizes:

> In order to clarify its relation to the first Potency, *das sein Könnende*, and to the second, *das sein Müssende*, Schelling defines the third Potency as *das sein Sollende* ... The essential function of A³ in terms of this dialectical analysis is to furnish the pattern for an ultimate ontological synthesis of selfhood (as foreshadowed by A¹) and an objective world (presaged by A²).³⁹

As a culminating symbol of the above, Schelling describes the Roman Janus-head as the Chaos of primal unity. From whence we get "January," Janus is the Roman god with two heads facing opposite directions; the Latin word *janua* is itself connected with door. The mythological lexographer William Smith (1813–93) explains that: "Janus was the god of the beginning of everything: he protected the beginning of all occupations and actions as well as of human life ... we find at a later period, when Janus was regarded as the god of all entrances and gates."⁴⁰ Schelling writes of the primacy of Hesiod's Chaos followed by Heraclitus' Πόλεμος πάντων μὲν πατήρ ἐστι [war is the father of all things].⁴¹ Coinciding with his views on Dao, Schelling emphasizes the connection between the Potencies and the gate (*Pforte*, passageway). Janus is the key: "Especially here those religious customs of Rome hearken to the age of war when the gates of Janus stand open where in peace they were closed."⁴² Schelling is fascinated with a Roman coin of the Janus head crowned by a crescent moon. Schelling explains: "And so we had in the Janus Head, the most perfect symbol of the three primordial potencies, according to the earlier explicated concepts, as Seynkönnendes, Seynmüssendes und Seynsollendes, the symbol of these potencies appearing in their divergencies, but nevertheless at the same time in their inseparabilities."⁴³ Schelling continues with Janus:

> The mythological Urpotenzen B and A² appear in the result of the processes as male and female. However, there were only two potencies. But now located between the two heads on a Roman coin is a symbol that does appear to mark the third potency. This symbol between the two heads that turn away from one another is the waxing [emerging, *wachsende*] moon.⁴⁴

The waxing moon is often a symbol of pagan occultation. Although the original Roman coin of which Schelling speaks seems to be lost, it would look something like the ones from 84 BCE.⁴⁵ For Schelling, Dao's portal as a gate of the first Potency anticipates Janus' gate of the three Potencies.

Heidegger refers to Janus in a citation from *Zur Sache des Denkens* that reads:

> Between the epochal figures of Being and the transformation of Being into the event stands the Ge-stell. This is, as one might say, a stopover, putting forward a double glimpse—a Janus-head. It can name then the same as a continuation of the Will to Will, therefore as the extreme expression of Being that can be obtained. At the same time, however, it is a precursor of the event itself.⁴⁶

From the compiled notes of participants in 1969's *Vier Seminare* at Le Thor in France, Heidegger further explains: "An extraordinary way of drawing near to Ereignis [the event] would be to gaze into the essence of Ge-stell [the enframing], insofar as it is a passage through [*Durchgang*, passageway, crossing] from metaphysics to another thinking—Gestell is, so to speak, the photographic negative of Ereignis."[47] For Heidegger, I would maintain that "the passage through" to "another thinking" involves Dao. As commentator and translator of the *Zhuangzi*, Kuang-Ming Wu (1935–), colleague of John Wild (1902–72) at Yale University, garnishes much thought for convergences between Schelling's Janus-face and Zhuangzi's Dao Pivot (*dao shu* 道樞) of chapter 2:

> All are various earthenware freely turned forth from the potter's wheel, the heavenly wheel, the Pivot of the Way of things; Such a turning is neither moving nor stopping, but both … This condition is called the "pivot of the way" of things; when the pivot is fitted into the "ring" of the ceaseless "yes" and ceaseless "no," we can then respond to them ceaselessly. The … [Roman] gate-god Janus faced both ways, in opposite directions. Chuang Tzu wants us to be a Janus of the universe, or perhaps the pivots at the center of the circles of things co-arising. Soon he would propose to walk both ways, formation and breakdown, as the ways of nature swing to and fro.[48]

For Heidegger, October is a big month for Daoism as he quotes for the very first time from Daoist classics: initially, from Laozi's chapter 28 at the Bremen Philosophy Club lecture on October 8, 1930, and secondly, from Zhuangzi's chapter 17 at the home of the book merchant Mr. Kellner on October 9, 1930. Heidegger reads from the story about Zhuangzi and Huizi above the Hao River contemplating whether the fish are happy. The images of wandering free and easy by means of the Dao Pivot would lead Heidegger's audience into the boundary of the boundless while dispelling the necessity of physically being in someone else's place.[49] In 1936, Heidegger writes: "Da-sein is the happening of the Encleavage of the turning-middle of the turn of the Event … Dasein is the turning-point in the turn of the Event, the self-opening middle of the counter-play of acclamation and belonging."[50] The pivot is the fulcrum and progenitor of Heidegger's fourfold (Figure 2.1). I explain:

In 1936, Heidegger's fourfold or quadrate (*Geviert*) appears in *Contributions to Philosophy: (From Enowning)*, which can be visualized as such:

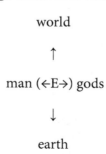

Figure 2.1 Heidegger's fourfold.

We see the "E" for encleavage (*Erklüftung*) as the midpoint of the world-earth and man-gods axes as the "truth-ground" of the event (*Ereignis*). *Da-sein* unfolds at this central midpoint. An encleavage is an enfolding unto itself. The ontological difference is a "scission" between Being and beings that link each to the other by "cleaving" them into two. *Da-sein* is "the truth of being." On advice from William J. Richardson (1920–2016)—Heidegger's first English speaking student—I embrace a later version of the fourfold—*sky-earth and mortals-gods*. In a 2004 conversation with Richardson in Boston, and hinted at in his writing, he professes that Heidegger took inspiration from Laozi for the very idea of the fourfold. I elaborate: Heidegger's metaphor of the fourfold might owe something to pre-Socratic cosmology or to Aristotle but also to Daoism. Heidegger's 'fourfold oneness' might reflect the 'four greatnesses' (*si da* 四大) of the *Daodejing*'s chapter 25: "the Way is great, Heaven is great, Earth is great, the King too is great."[51]

Wu's *Zhuangzi* commentary recalls *two wheels* in chapter 11 of the *Laozi*: the explicit wheel with thirty spokes, and the implicit potter's wheel of the next line that Heidegger addresses in "The Thing," from a lecture delivered at the *Bayerischen Akademie der Schönen Künste*, on June 6, 1950.[52] In light of Heidegger's "The Thing," an imaginary Daoist fourfold (Figure 2.2) might look like:[53]

Figure 2.2 Daoism's fourfold.

Erklüftung (encleavage) is replaced by *Leere* (the empty nothingness) from 1943's chapter 11. This encleavage shows itself in the 1950 interpretation of the valley, the jug, and Van Gogh's shoes. The temple does not reside within the valley but the openness of the valley arises by means of the temple; the jug is not only a retainer but the clay on its outside "shapes the void [*Leere*]."[54] The openings of the valley, the cup, and the shoes connect to Laozi's chapters 11, 15, and 28. Heidegger observes three of Van Gogh's paintings by spectating *all sides* of the shoes, the temple, and the cup. I explain: "The *dunklen Öffnung* (dark opening, cleft, aperture, cave, hollow) of the shoes, the openness of the temple, and the gap of the cup generate the potential of the *schwingt* [hovering, reverberation] as a resonating, oscillating, vibrating Void. Heidegger's Void is not the passive Greek Void of emptiness but more akin to an active Chinese Daoist Void of creation."[55] Recalling Zhuangzi's Dao Pivot that "responds till there-is-no end," Schelling also highlights the interactions of an eternal pivot at the midst of the Potencies in *Ages of the World* (1915): "There is only an unremitting wheel, a rotatory movement that never comes to a stand-still and in which there is no differentiation."[56]

Heidegger and Schelling: Deepest Ground of Being

A virtually neglected but provocative intersection between Schelling and Heidegger manifests through Dao. In *On the Way to Language* (1959), Heidegger explains:

> The word "way" probably is an ancient primary word [*Urwort der Sprach*] that speaks to the reflective mind of man. The key word in Laotse's poetic thinking is *Tao*, which "properly speaking" means way. But because we are prone to think of "way" superficially, as a stretch connecting two places, our word "way" has all too rashly been considered unfit to name what *Tao* says. *Tao* is then translated as reason [*Vernunft*], mind, *raison*, meaning, *logos* [λόγος]. Yet *Tao* could be the way that gives all ways, the very source of our power to think what reason, mind, meaning, *logos* properly means to say—properly, by their proper nature. Perhaps the mystery of mysteries of thoughtful Saying conceals itself in the word "way," *Tao*, if only we will let these names return to what they leave unspoken ... All is way.[57]

Whereas Schelling moves away from *Vernunft* as a translation for Dao—breaking the spell of "reason" coupled with λόγος—Heidegger deconstructs both words. *Vernunft* opens into *Vernehmen lassen* (letting be apprehended), and λόγος from λέγειν opens into saying and laying.[58] We can include the idea of waying as follows (Figure 2.3):[59]

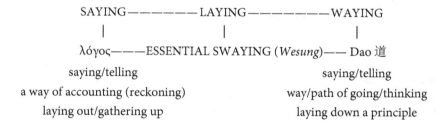

Figure 2.3 Waying and Dao.

There are many differences between Schelling and Heidegger. Although each goes their own way, there are unique convergences. Examining Dao greatly enhances readers' abilities to understand the directions of both thinkers. Schelling's approach to Dao emerges from the challenge to account for a civilization that does not seem to fit into his system. Schelling sees China as straddling the edge of an eternally timeless time: "The absolutely prehistoric time [*Die absolut vorgeschichtliche Zeit*], the time before the emergence of peoples was also the relatively unmythological time, because mythology only came into being with the peoples."[60] In *Historical-Critical Introduction to the Philosophy of Mythology*, Schelling postulates:

> The ultimately pre-historical time is, *according to its nature*, the indivisible, absolutely identical time; and for this reason, whatever duration one ascribes it, it is to be considered only as a *moment*—that is, as time in which the end is as the beginning and the beginning is as the end, a type of eternity, because it itself is not a series of times but rather is only *one* time, which in itself is not an actual time, that is, a series of times, but rather only becomes time (namely, the past) relative to that time following it ... A true succession [*Aufeinanderfolge*] is not formed by events that disappear without trace and leave the *whole* in the condition in which it was before. Thus, for the reason that in the absolutely pre-historical time the whole is, at the end, as it was in the beginning, thus because in this time itself there is no longer a succession of times [*in dieser Zeit selbst keine Folge von Zeiten mehr ist*], because it (also in this sense) is only One time [*nur Eine*], namely (as we expressed ourselves), the *simply identical* and thus basically *timeless* time.[61]

The above passage introduces a "timeless time" as non-Aristotelian (no longer a succession of nows). As itself a timeless time, Dao is an opening wherefore Schelling incorporates his own philosophy of positivity while pondering *the case that does not fit*. Heidegger clearly utilizes this opening to develop his own method of hermeneutic phenomenology. Both philosophers are attracted to Dao—even for the blink of an eye—because it starts with nothing, and then generates something from nothing.

Schelling sees that "all beginning lies in an absence" as that absence "hungers for Being." First distilled from the pre-Socratic Parmenides as the cliché nothing out of nothing,[62] and later popularized by followers of the Epicurean Lucretius (99 BCE–55 BCE) as *ex nihilo nihil fit*, the expression is adapted by a theologically inspired Schelling as *creatio ex nihilo* and metamorphized by an existentially inclined Heidegger as *ex nihilo omne ens qua ens fit*. In *What Is Metaphysics* (1929), Heidegger outlines movements from nothing to something with resonance from Schelling and Dao:

> Since ancient times metaphysics has expressed itself on the subject of Nothing in the highly ambiguous proposition: *ex nihilo nihil fit* nothing comes from nothing. Even though the proposition as argued never made Nothing itself the real problem, it nevertheless brought out very explicitly, from the prevailing notions about Nothing, the over-riding fundamental concept of what-is. Classical metaphysics conceives Nothing as signifying Not-being (*Nichtseiendes*), that is to say, unformed matter which is powerless to form itself into "being" and cannot therefore present an appearance (*eidos*) ... Christian dogma, on the other hand, denies the truth of the proposition *ex nihilo nihil fit* and gives a twist to the meaning of Nothing, so that it now comes to mean the absolute absence of all "being" outside God: *ex nihilo fit—ens creatum*: the created being is made out of nothing. "Nothing"

is now the conceptual opposite of what truly and authentically [*eigentlich*] "is;" it becomes the *summum ens*, God as *ens increatum* [supreme Being] ... But at the same time the question of Nothing pervades the whole of metaphysics only because it forces us to face the problem of the origin of negation, that is to say, forces a decision about the legitimacy of the rule of "logic" in metaphysics. The old proposition *ex nihilo nihil fit* will then acquire a different meaning, and one appropriate to the problem of Being itself, so as to run: *ex nihilo omne ens qua ens fit*: [every being, so far as it is a being, is made out of nothing]. Only in the Nothingness of *Da-sein* can what-is-in-totality—and this in accordance with its peculiar possibilities, i.e., in a finite manner—come to itself.[63]

Heidegger's expression "*ex nihilo omne ens qua ens fit*" is accompanied with an inserted translation by R.F.C. Hull and Alan Crick. They leave a clue to connections between Heidegger and Dao. In footnote 30, they write: "Cf. 'Tao Te Ching' XL: for though all creatures under heaven are the products of Being, Being itself is the product of Not-being [Nothing]."[64] They refer to Heidegger's text:

Only in the clear night of dread's Nothingness is what-is as such revealed in all its original overtness (*Offenheit*): that it "is" and is not Nothing. This verbal appendix "and not Nothing" is, however, not an *a posteriori* explanation but an *a priori* which alone makes possible any revelation of what-is. The essence of Nothing as original nihilation lies in this: that it alone brings *Da-sein* face to face with what-is as such. Only on the basis of the original manifestness of Nothing can our human *Dasein* advance towards and enter into what-is. But insofar as *Dasein* naturally relates to what-is, as that which it is not and which itself is, Da-sein *qua Dasein* always proceeds from Nothing as manifest.[65]

Heidegger's *Auseinandersetzung* (con-versation, confrontation) with East Asian philosophy and with Daoism spans several decades from the early 1920s to the 1970s.[66] Schelling dips his toes deeply into Daoism albeit for only a moment. Having spent several decades charting Heidegger's twentieth-century encounters with East Asian philosophy,[67] especially Dao (and in recent years its distant Japanese cousin Zen 禪),[68] I shall not rehearse these arguments but explain what Heidegger does with such engagements, especially in relation to intersections with Schelling. Recalling Schelling's expression that "Laozi penetrates totally into the unbethinged [*unbedingt*] and universally into the deepest Ground of Beyng [*in den tiefsten Grund des Seyns*]," we see resonances with Heidegger on several levels. "Laozi," "the unbethinged,"[69] and "deepest ground of Being" are together in one place. Unpacking them takes us into Heidegger's dearest regions. Schelling's *unbedingt* as un-bethinged points to both Zhuangzi and Heidegger's coincident "the thingness of a thing is not itself a thing."[70] For Heidegger, this might direct him to concentrating on the thing (*Das Ding*),[71] and reading Laozi's Daoist successors such as Zhuangzi and his redactor Guo Xiang 郭象 (d. 312 CE)[72] who leave the traceless trace of a step-back (*Schritt zurück*) through to the deepest ground of Being.[73] At the same time as his work on Schelling in 1936 to 1938, Heidegger writes in *Beiträge zur Philosophie* (*zum Ereignis*): "But why this de-cision

[*Entscheidung*]? Because a *salvation* of beings is possible only out of the deepest ground of Being itself."[74] Heidegger's *Entscheidung* appears in three forms as Michael Inwood explains:

> 1. The separation involved in the event of being, separation between earth, world, men and gods [*das Geviert*, the fourfold, quadrate] and between beyng and beings ... 2. Momentous decisions about human life that determine whether a new beginning, a new event of being, will happen ... 3. Ordinary human decisions, whether individual or collective, about whether to marry, to go to war.[75]

For Heidegger, *Entscheidung* is a *de-cision* or *scission* that splits being-in-the-world (*das Seiende*) from Being (*Das Sein*) as its essence. Schelling utilizes the expression *Unvordenkliche Entscheidung* (un-pre-thinkable decision) in a commentary on the nature of God and non-Being (*Nichtseyenden*).[76]

In *Philosophical Investigations into the Essence of Human Freedom* (1809), Schelling elaborates on *Entscheidung*:

> Man is in the initial creation, as shown, an undecided being [*ein unentschiedenes Wesen*]—(which may be portrayed mythically as a condition of innocence that precedes this life and as an initial blessedness)—only man himself can decide. But this decision [*Entscheidung*] cannot occur within time; it occurs outside of all time and, hence, together with the first creation (though as a deed distinct from creation).[77]

Schelling describes China as "un-pre-thinkable": "China, as it is, through an un-pre-thinkable event, essentially unaltered since its origin, has always been the same."[78] For his time, Schelling's understanding of Dao is poignant and insightful. For him, "such a purely philosophical appearance as the Dao doctrine would also be of the highest interest."[79] Concurring with Gottfried Wilhelm Leibniz (1646–1716),[80] Schelling sees a fundamental mystery within Chinese characters:

> Namely in the system of Chinese writing one searches for the greatest scientific mysteries ... But even [Étienne] Fourmont [1683–1745, published grammars of Arabic, Hebrew, Chinese] was bewitched by the Chinese script concerning the latter 214 so-called ciphers [radicals, *sogenannten Schlüsseln*] of the Chinese characters ... The hieroglyphic or representative characters were believed to contain all human fundamental ideas but it is especially not easy to say why it is just 214.[81]

Four Cornerstones

Schelling's penetrating understanding of Dao—as a portal—finds renewed life and new possibilities in Heidegger. Through my personal experience of Chinese philosophy, religion, medicine, and internal martial arts, I summarize to date, my lifetime engagement with Heidegger's hermeneutic phenomenology and East Asia. I generate *four cornerstones* of East Asian thinking—primarily emanating from my understanding of Dao—which manifest through one thinker in the contemporary Western world: Heidegger. Those cornerstones I dub:[82]

1. non-Cartesian subjectivity (there is no "I" but a person as temporally/dimensionally "in-between" as *renjian* 人間).[83]
2. non-Euclidean space (fractal geometry, Chinese chaos theory;[84] no vanishing point).
3. non-Aristotelean time (reversibility of time; every moment an instance of a different time).[85]
4. non-representational thinking (thing as itself, that which things a thing is not itself a thing) imbedded equally within Heidegger's thought as within Daoist cosmology.

Remarkably, Heidegger arrives at these four cornerstones on his own—as counter-positions to traditional Western spatialized and materialized thinking, calling them respectively:

1. *Dasein* (*there-being*, non-Cartesian subjectivity as a collection of beings searching for primordial there).[86]
2. *Das Ding* (*the thing*, non-Euclidean space as four-dimensionality within essential spirit).[87]
3. *Die Kehre* (*the turn*, non-Aristotelian time as a reversibility).[88]
4. *Vernehmen* (*ap-prehension, approception, proception*) as alternative to *Vorstellung* (representation).[89]

The material West contrasts to the spiritual East through reversibilities including time and space. Western *binaries* such as center and periphery, shape and shadow, interior and exterior, stillness and motion give way to East Asian *dipolarities* that do not culminate or overcome each other as in dialectical practices but are mutually conditioned linked opposites that are necessary for each other as co-constitutive, co-resonating, and equiprimordial.[90]

As a preamble to Heidegger's own philosophical development, Schelling might have a hand in the understanding of the above cornerstones. "On the Nature of Philosophy as a Science," Schelling's 1821 Erlangen lectures explains: "The idea or the endeavor of finding a system of human knowledge ... within a form of coexistence, presupposes ... that originally and of itself it does not exist in a system, hence that it is an ἀσύστατον [*asystaton*]—something whose elements do not coexist, but rather something that is in inner conflict."[91] Schelling continues:

> We could use the term ecstasy for this relation. Our ego, namely, is placed *outside* itself, i.e., outside its role. Its role is to be subject. Confronted with the absolute subject, it cannot remain a subject, for the absolute subject cannot behave like an object. It must, then, give up its place, it must be placed outside itself, as something

that no longer exists. Only in this state of having abandoned itself can the absolute subject appear to it in its state of self-abandonment, and so we also behold it in amazement.[92]

As *non-Cartesian*, Schelling's subject that steps out of itself, disentangles with an object and emerges as an ecstasy:

> Ἔκστασις [*ekstasis*; ecstasy] is a *vox anceps* [an ambivalent expression, from Ovid's Janus headed incantation] ... Namely, there is ecstasy whenever something is removed or dislodged from its place. What matters, though, is whether something is removed from a place that it merits or from a place that it does not merit. In the latter case, we have a beneficial ecstasy which brings us back to our senses, while the former leads us into senselessness.[93]

As a non-Cartesian maneuver, Schelling's disjoining of subject and object anticipates both the Daoist absence of the I as *renjian* 人間 (temporally/dimensionally "in-between") and complements Heidegger's *Da-sein* as a collectivity of beings searching for the *Da* through abandonment (*Verlassenheit*) and releasement (*Gelassenheit*). This pre-shadows Heidegger's own ecstasis as a standing forward of *Da-sein* or a timeliness in stepping outside of itself.[94] Complementing the "horizontal" phenomenology of everyday life, I write:

> What Kuki [Shūzo 九鬼周造, 1888–1941] adds is a second level, the notion of a 'vertical' phenomenology which is no longer simply an existential reality but a 'mystical ecstasis:' 'each instant, each present, is an identical moment of different times ... Each present has identical moments, in the future as well as in the past ... time is in this sense reversible.'[95]

A retrograde temporality as a reversibility of time flows back upon itself to its source.[96] Kuki's time is a καιρός (*Kairos*), a revelatory moment of eternal nows or what Heidegger calls *Augenblick*, the blink of an eye or an instance. Being and time are not separate but are linked as "being-time." Being itself is a "time-word."

In the 1943 Heraclitus seminar, Heidegger explains:

> The word 'Being,' as the primordial word of all words, is the 'time-word' purely and absolutely. The time-word 'Being,' as the word of all words, names 'the time of all times.' Being and time primordially fit together [belong together]. Erstwhile, thinking must think this togetherness of 'being and time;' otherwise, it comes into the danger of forgetting, what remains, for the thinking of the thinkers, the to-be-thought.[97]

In *Ages of the World* (1815), Schelling reminds us of the above with a *non-Euclidean space* of multiple time-lines (every moment an instance of a different time) accompanying a *non-Aristotelian time* that refutes a succession of nows (through the vanishing point). In the *Philosophy of Mythology*, these are exemplified in the absolutely pre-historical time of China that seems to anticipate Heidegger's thingness of a thing in relation to Zhuangzi.[98]

Schelling guides Heidegger in moving to an alternative—*Vernehmen* as body phenomenology.[99] Schelling's *Beschlossenheit* appears as a family precursor of Heidegger's *Erschlossenheit* (open up, un-concealment, disclosure) and *Entschlossenheit* (un-close, resolution, determination) and possibly an early trace of Heidegger's seminal *Ge-stell*.

As Heidegger states in *Being and Time*: "Resoluteness [*Entschlossenheit*] is a distinctive mode of Dasein's disclosedness [*Erschlossenheit*]."[100] Although Schelling does not allot himself time to do so, Heidegger carries these thoughts deeply into an engagement with East Asian philosophy. The Western containment of "being in time" becomes "being and time" followed by "time and being"[101] and finally "time in being" or perhaps "time as being" which I suggest are Daoist-inspired reversals.[102] Along these lines, Markus Gabriel writes:

> for positive philosophy ... a future which is to take place *within* being itself ... not as eternity. On the basis of the logical concept of being ... history can at best be grasped as a caricature of 'eternal being (ἀεὶ ὄν)' [Plato, *Timaeus*, 27d6f.], as the tradition of Platonism ... Unlike this tradition, Schelling thinks *being as time*: with this move he comes into direct contact with Heidegger.[103]

With help from Schelling, Heidegger continues to proclaim: "Perhaps the mystery of mysteries of thoughtful Saying conceals itself in the word 'way,' Tao [Dao], if only we will let these names return to what they leave unspoken ... All is way."[104]

The "Rule" of Three

Complementing the preceding discussion, Table 2.1 below lays out the strategy of Schelling's three Potencies against Heidegger's three approaches to phenomenology (as I see it), and what I dub Dao's three "rules" for long life. For contrast's sake, I add Socrates' (470–399 BCE) tripartite methodology of argumentation. All positions deal with the contradictions of impasse. Socrates is instrumental in moving Schelling and Heidegger in a step back through the portal of the Void. Both Schelling and Heidegger are immensely influenced by Socrates but do not end with him. Schelling sees Socrates' *maieutics* (μαιευτικός, helping interlocutors give birth to their own ideas) as a "midwifery" or philosophical obstetrics that stands outside the I—"against a subjective=logical pseudoknowledge."[105] Socrates' language of the marketplace and his judgement of poets as interpreters of the gods stimulate Heidegger to employ his own unique vocabulary while re-inaugurating the power of the human muses as half-gods (*Halbgötter*) by a return to the Void. In the 1930s, Heidegger writes: "Halbgötter denken heisst: aus der ursprünglichen Mitte auf die Erde zu und auf die Götter hin denken [What is called the thinking of the demi-gods (poets on the way to the gods) is to think out from the primordial middle toward the Earth, and up toward the gods]."[106]

Table 2.1 Three Essentials of Socrates, Schelling, Heidegger, and Dao

Socrates	Schelling	Heidegger	Dao
ἀπορία [aporia] Impasse, no way out	das sein Könnende (able to be) as "being-in-itself" (an-sich-Seiende) as the "infinite lack of being" (der unendliche Mangel an Sein)	ἔχειν [echein] originary "holding ground"	forget, bracket, suspend, put out of play
ἔλεγχος [elenchus] Interrogation/refutation	das sein Müssende (must be) as "being-outside-itself" (das ausser-sich-Seiende)	ἐπέχειν [epechein] "withholding" or suspension of thought since pre-Socratics but still a freshness in the air like a storm long past*	return to origin (turn back into the polarity of nothingness as the Void) Daodejing chapter 28 follow the Way
ἀνάμνησις [anamnesis] Not not knowing, re-membering	das sein Sollende (out to be) as "being-with-itself" (das bei-sich-Seiende) ultimate ontological, synthesis of selfhood	θεωρεῖν [theorein] a beholding or theorizing of a life-world	

*Heidegger relates: "The *ek-sistence* of man sustains what is ecstatic and so preserves what is epochal in Being, to whose essence the *Da*, and thereby *Da-sein*, belongs … whether in our knowledge of the past only the faintest glimmers of a storm long flown cast a pale semblance of light." Martin Heidegger, *Early Greek Thinking*, trans. David F. Krell and Frank A. Capuzzi (San Francisco: Harper and Row, 1975), 26.

Heidegger's own creative Void is reminiscent of the Daoist cosmology of *wu* 無 and the Chinese elements[107] as illustrated in chapter 28 of the *Daodejing*'s return to origin, *fugui yu wuji* 復歸於無極 (turn back into the polarity of nothingness as the Void). I suggest:

> In "A Dialogue on Language, between a Japanese and an Inquirer" Heidegger's inquirer speaks: "Then, man, as the message-bearer of the message of the twofold's unconcealment, would also be he who walks the boundary of the boundless [*Grenzgänger des Grenzenlosen*. See *Zhuangzi* ch. 22: 'The Boundary of the Boundless is the Boundless of the Boundary' (不際之際，際之不際者也)]." The Japanese speaker responds: "And on this path he seeks the boundary's mystery." This dialogue seems to draw much strength from Zhuangzi's 'borders that are yet to be.' Heidegger's insistence on an East/West dialogue would ultimately wish to achieve a global 'clearing' where boundaries were boundless, that is, where 'borders are yet to be.' Although Chung-Yuan Chang focuses on *ming* 明 as the luminosity of Being/Nothingness, we might also open this up into the Chinese characters for 'glade' or 'clearing:' *linjian kongdi* 林間空地. The characters are self-illuminating. 'The empty inbetweenness of forest and earth' is similar to Heidegger's explanation for *Lichtung* in *On Time and Being*: "The clearing is the open for everything that is present and absent." Reinhard May is persuasive in arguing that [Father] Leon Wieger's 1915 description of the Chinese character for 'nothing,' *wu* as a 'wood clearing' was influential in Heidegger's formulation of 'the clearing.' May then

juxtaposes two descriptions, the first from Wieger's lexicon and the second from Heidegger's "The End of Philosophy and the Task of Thinking": "A multitude ... of men, acting upon a forest, felling the trees, clearing of wood, a tract of land. In the old form [the graph] stated that the wood had vanished. Hence ... the general abstract notions of vanishing, defect, want, negation." A passage of Heidegger's from the 1960's reads correspondingly as follows: "To clear [*Lichten*] something means: to make something light, free and open; for example, to make a place in the woods free of trees. The open space that results is the clearing [*Lichtung*]." From the above, it is evident that Heidegger's complex intertwinings with Eastern thought influenced his understanding of the relations between being and Being, between subject and object, between visible and invisible. The move from logical, textual-style analyses to poetry affords him a phenomenal body which allows the East to converse with the West.[108]

Parmenides

Beyond his sketch of the *Wendungsmitte* (pivot) in *Contributions* (1936), Heidegger continues with the 1943 lectures on *Parmenides*. Heidegger recalls that Shih-Yi Hsiao attends the Parmenides and Heraclitus lectures of 1943–4. These interactions prompt Heidegger to work on translating eight chapters from *Daodejing* with Hsiao later in 1946.[109] A letter exchange between Heidegger and existential philosopher Karl Jaspers (1883–1969) from August 6 to 12, 1949, chronicles these events. Jaspers writes:

I have read the letter on humanism just now ... I was enthralled. Your defense against misunderstanding is impressive. Your interpretations of the ancients are always surprising ... I help myself a little with memories of things from Asia, where I liked to go over the years, knowing full well that I do not actually penetrate into it, but from there I am awakened in a wonderful way. Your being, the clearing of being, your reversal of our relation to being into the relation of being to us, the leaving-over of being itself—I believe I have perceived something of this in Asia. That you push in that direction—and, as your interpretation of *Being and Time* asserts, you have always pushed in that direction—is extraordinary ... What you have produced up to now is for my comprehension still essentially a promise ... I am anxious to see what will still come of this and how you fulfill your promise.[110]

Heidegger responds to Jaspers' letter:

What you say about Asian [ideas] is exciting [*aufregend*, thrilling]; a Chinese [Shih-Yi Hsiao] who heard my lectures on Heraclitus and Parmenides in the years 1943–44 ... also found resonances [*Anklänge*, intimations, echoes] of Eastern thinking. Where I am not native to the language, I remain skeptical [*skeptisch* as Graham Parkes might say in the ancient Greek connotation of close investigation]; I became even more so when the Chinese, who is himself a Christian theologian and philosopher, translated a few verses from Laozi with me; I only found out through questions how strange the whole language system is to us; we then gave up trying. Nevertheless, there is something exciting here and, I believe, essential for the future, if centuries of devastation are to be overcome. The resonances may have a completely different root; Eckhardt [Meister Eckhart, 1260–1328], the reading master and life master, has accompanied me since 1910; this and constantly trying to think through Parmenides [fragment 5] *to gar auto noein estin te kai einai* [τὸ γὰρ αὐτὸ νοεῖν ἐστίν τε καὶ εἶναι, "for thinking and being are the same"] the constant question about the *auto* [αὐτὸ] which is neither *noein* [νοεῖν] nor *einai* [εἶναι]; the absence [*Fehlen*, lack] of the subject-object relationship in Greek brought me, in addition to my own thinking, to what looks like a reversal [*Umkehrung*, inversion, turn-around], but is something other and prior.[111]

The letter exchange illustrates Heidegger's continuing curiosity with both Daoist thought and Eckhart's mystical tradition in respect to non-Cartesian and non-binary relations as the absence of a subject-object disclosed through Parmenides. The trajectory of Eckhart, Parmenides, Laozi, and Daoism is close to Schelling's embrace of *Gelassenheit*,[112] and stimulus for Heidegger's own work on releasement. Jason M. Wirth comments on *Gelassenheit*:

> Schelling would call the relationship of the intellect to sensibility *die gelassene Vernunft*, reason that lets be … It is the mortification of the ego whose death is the birth of the life of reason. 'Reason is not a faculty [*Vermögen*], not a tool, nor can it be used. Anyhow there is no reason at all which we could have, but only a reason which has us.'[113]

Gelassenheit as taking leave or releasement and *Verlassenheit* as abandonment to freedom excite both Schelling and Heidegger. Saitya Brata Das suggests that Heidegger, "following Meister Eckhart's *Gelazenheit*, is the gesture of withdrawal from the metaphysical determination of being as potentiality."[114] Accompanying Schelling's dismantling of the ego in freedom, Heidegger's later work on Parmenides (*Identity and Difference*)[115] deconstructs the identity principle. As Heidegger comes to grips with Schelling's "eternal becoming, the not-yet remains," he writes:

> There remains in God the eternal past of himself in his ground. The 'afterwards' and 'soon' are to be understood here in an eternal sense. The whole boldness of Schelling's thinking comes into play here. But it is not the vacuous play of thoughts of a manic hermit, it is only the continuation of an attitude of thinking which begins with Meister Eckhart and is uniquely developed in Jacob Boehme [1575–1624].[116]

In *Parmenides*, Heidegger employs a passage that engages *Gelassenheit* ("that first releases") while shining back both to Dao as do by not doing ("free of"), and forward to Schelling's Potencies ("free for"):

> Yet the open in the sense of the essence of ἀλήθεια [*Aletheia*, unconcealment] does not mean either space or time as usually intended, nor their unity, space-time,

because all that already had to borrow its openness from the openness holding sway in the essence of disclosedness. Similarly, everywhere that something is 'free of ... ' in the sense of 'exempt from ... ' or is 'free for ... ' in the sense of 'ready to ... ' a freedom already comes to presence out of the freedom that first releases even space-time as an 'open,' traversable, extention and spread. The 'free of' and the 'free for' already require a clearing in which a detachment and a donation constitute a more original freedom that cannot be grounded on the freedom of human comportment.[117]

Lao-Zhuang's Daoist abandonment as doing by not doing (*wei wuwei* 爲無爲) seems to divest from the world in a similar fashion as Schelling, Eckhart, and Heidegger's releasement to the mystery. In the letter to Jaspers, Heidegger teases us with Laozi ("something exciting" [*etwas Erregendes*] and "essential" [*Wesentliches*]) coupled with Eckhart ("since 1910"). Heidegger's immediate "resonances" (*Anklange*) look to Parmenides' αὐτὸ not as "the same" or equal to "the identical" but as a collecting together of difference.[118] In *Was Heisst Denken?* (*What Is Called Thinking*) Heidegger proclaims that νοεῖν "governs" *Vernehmen* (apprehension) not simply as "thinking" but as "scenting" (*Wittern*) that gathers through εἶναι (*Sein*).[119] Although he does not mention it, the word Heidegger might conjure up here is νεύειν (to scent, to nod, to beckon, to bow). The words νόος and νοῦς are probably back-formed from νεύειν rather than νοεῖν.[120] Heidegger hints at a connection between the mystery of Laozi, Eckhart, and Parmenides in respect to a reversal "something other and prior" like Schelling's view of China as *Unvordenkliche Entscheidung* (un-pre-thinkable decision). Heidegger explains further the idea of a πολος (pivot) as he launches into his patent παρονομασία (*paronomasia*, "spectating the name beside") as a method or homonymic style of etymological analysis that puns upon words that stand nearby and sound alike. Phenomenologically, Heidegger opens hidden worlds of the past through non-representationality, reminiscent of the torque of the Daoist wheel—as a turning effect of alternating energy fields—from Laozi's chapter 11 that he translates and comments upon in 1943. The sharp turning around of our thought (from being to time, then time to being; from the *sein* of *Da-sein* to the *da* of *Da-sein*) as twisting free—*Umkehrung*—requires a pivot:

> What is the πόλις [city]? The word itself puts us on the right course, provided we bring to it the all-illuminating Greek experience of the essence of Being and of truth. Πόλις is the πολος [pivot, axis], the pole [*Der Pol*], the place around which everything appearing to the Greeks as a being turns in a peculiar way. The pole is the place around which all beings turn and precisely in such a way that in the domain of this place beings show their turning and their condition. The pole, as this place lets beings appear in their Being and show the totality of their condition. The pole does not produce and does not create beings in their Being, but as pole it is the abode of the concealedness of beings as a whole. The πόλις is the essence of the place [*Ort*], or as we say, it is the settlement [*Ort-schaft*] of the historical dwelling of Greek humanity. Because the πόλις lets the totality of beings come in this or that way into the unconcealedness of its condition, the πόλις is

therefore essentially related to the Being of beings. Between πόλις and Being there is a primordial relation. This word πόλις is in its root identical with the ancient Greek word for "to be," πέλειν: "to emerge, to rise up into the unconcealed" … Hence the πόλις is not the notorious "city-state" but is rather the settling of the place of the history of Greek humanity neither city nor state but indeed the abode of the essence of this humanity. This essential abode gathers originally the unity of everything which as the unconcealed comes to man and is dispensed to him as that to which he is assigned in his Being. The πόλις is the abode gathered into itself of the unconcealedness of beings.[121]

In Heidegger's etymological unfolding of πόλις (the city) into πολος (pole, pivot, axis) and then into πέλειν ("to emerge, to rise up into the unconcealed," to come into existence, to be), he opens up new possibilities. We extrapolate Heidegger's argument to see πολέω (πέλω) (go about, range, haunt, turn over as in ploughing). The double edge of πόλεμος (war) as "over-turning" and farming as "turning over" later exemplifies "polemics" and the *auseinandersetzen* (con-frontation, con-versation) as they coincide with λόγος as the laying, saying, and waying that gather.[122] Equiprimordially, we envision Heidegger's originary Greek city pivot interpolating into ancient China with the "pivot of the four quarters" (*si fang zhi ji* 四方之極), a turn of phrase referring to a city of cosmic order. Praising "the cosmo-magical role of the ancient Chinese city," the geographer Paul Wheatley (1921–99) translates the poem "Yin Wu 殷武" from *Shijing* 詩經 (*Book of Odes*): "The capital of Shang was a city of cosmic order, the pivot of the four quarters. Glorious was its renown purifying its divine powers, manifested in longevity and tranquility and the protection of us who come after."[123]

Der Anklang

A sustained commentary on *Der Anklang* appears in Heidegger's *Contributions*. The word *Anklang* encompasses a variety of connotations including echo, resonance, reverberation, a sounding, an assonance or alliteration amongst others. In Heidegger's vocabulary, *Anklang* is a key to non-representational thinking, supported by *Vernehmen* as ap-prehension. It is the abandonment of Being (*Seinsverlassenheit*). Heidegger writes of the origin of language: "When gods call the earth and a world resonates in the call and thus the call echoes [*anklingt*] as Da-sein of man, then language is as historical, as history grounding word. Language and enowning [event]. Fleeting shimmer of earth, resonance of world. Strife, the originary sheltering of the cleavage, because the innermost rift. The open place."[124] In terms of Heidegger's six jointures (1) echo, (2) the leap,[125] and (3) the ones to come entail "the other beginning," while (4) playing-forth, (5) grounding, and (6) the last god constitute "the first beginning."[126] In *Schelling's Treatise*, Heidegger comments on the necessity of "the second beginning": "For us that means that a second beginning becomes necessary through the first, but is possible only in the complete transformation of the first beginning, never by just letting it stand."[127] The leap into Being grounds its truth in the truth of Being and makes way for the ones to come and the last god. The truth of Being is the Being of truth.

Anklang stands outside of "comparison" that itself resides at the center of identity-principled inquiry. If we wish to talk about inter-cultural texts, a crucial question arises: How is comparison possible? In professional academics, many disciplines wish to raise to apotheotic level, the idea of comparison: comparative philosophy, comparative religion, comparative sociology, comparative social science, comparative ideas, comparative cultures, comparative linguistics, comparative governments, comparative political theory, and global comparative thought.[128] Few of these areas have addressed the *idea* of comparison itself. The Latin word verb *comparāre* means "to liken, to compare," from *com* "with, together" + *par* "equal." It is often assumed that little compares with the Roman Empire—what is above it is *superstitio* as supernatural (standing aloof and thus not relevant), and what is below it is *falsum* (false and fallen); what is true to it is *certum* (certitude) or *veritas* (rectitude)—complete reconfigurations and often misconstructions of early Greek pre-Socratic terms.[129] Ironically, the phrase "without compare" (from the 1530s) revised by folk etymology from *compeer* as competitor meaning "rival" (*with-outen compere* from 1400) is more aptly stated as "without rival." "Without compare" means "without rival." For centuries, it was the default for a person to be "without compare." Only in the contemporary world do we seem to value "compare" as the goal of various intellectual fields. The Chinese expression *duizhao* 對照 means both *compare/contrast* as a noun (attributing to its ambiguity) and *juxtapose/contradistinguish* as a verb. Respectively, Heidegger, Schelling, and Lao-Zhuang are *incomparable*. They can be understood only on *their own accounts* or in terms of their *own nature* and their *own environments*, such as it is. We understand *such as it is* as the Daoist *ziran* 自然 as self so; so of its own; so of itself and naturally; spontaneously; freely; in the course of events. In *Being and Time* (1927), Heidegger explains the shortfall of comparison:

> No matter how easy it may be to show how ontological problematics differ formally from ontical research there are still difficulties in carrying out an existential analytic, especially in making a start ... The rich store of information now available as to the most exotic and manifold cultures and forms of Dasein seems favorable to our setting about this task in a fruitful way. But this is merely a semblance. At bottom this plethora of information can seduce us into failing to recognize the real problem. We shall not get a genuine knowledge of essences simply by the syncretistic activity of *universal comparison* [my emphasis] and classification. Subjecting the manifold to tabulation does not ensure any actual understanding of what lies there before us as thus set in order. If an ordering principle is genuine, it has its own content as a thing (*Sachgehalt*), which is never to be found by means of such ordering but is already presupposed in it.[130]

Part of Heidegger's alternative to identity-principled "comparison" (itself at the epicenter of the representational repertoire) is *Anklang* as "Echo." Here, I follow the renderings of Parvis Emad and Kenneth Maly.[131] Emad says it brilliantly:

> The significance of the first joining [*Fügung*] *Der Anklang*/The Echo, consists in revealing the relation to being that comes to the fore in beings' being abandoned by

> being and in the forgetfulness of being, as a relation that must be thought through and opened up as *das Zu-denkende* [what is to be thought]. The significance of *Der Anklang* will be missed if it is seen as consisting in a body of doctrine that has thought the echo of being *completely*—or neatly wrapped it up. More specifically, the significance of the first joining consists in revealing the relation to being as *Enteignis* ["expropriation" contrasts to "*Ereignis*" as "appropriation"], which comes to the fore as question and must be thought through as a task. Seeing the structure of *Beiträge zur Philosophie* as a whole, *Der Anklang*, the echo of being, is the first *Zu-denkendes* and not the final *Fertig-gedachtes* [something completely thought through]. This echo, *Anklang*, marks the historical moment (*geschichtlicher Augenblick*) of an other epoch of thinking which is no longer metaphysical.[132]

Heidegger's "the other beginning" or what Emad calls "an other epoch of thinking" sets out to strip thought of its representational clothing.

As a verse at the commencement of section 50 of *Contributions*, Heidegger writes: "Echo of the essential swaying of Beyng out of the abandonment of being [*Seinsverlassenheit*] through the distressing distress of the forgetfulness of Beyng [*Seynsvergessenheit*]."[133] Fusing Laozi's chapter 28 from Bremen in 1930, and *Anklang* of 1936, we stretch Heidegger forward to "The End of Philosophy and the Task of Thinking" of 1964: "the clearing, the opening, is not only free for brightness and darkness, but also for resonance and echo, for sounding and diminishing of sound. The clearing is the open for everything that is present and absent."[134] In the winter of 1931–2, still contemplating the freshness of the Bremen lectures on Dao, Heidegger explains:

> 'Brightness' [*Helle*] comes from 'reverberate' or 'echo' [*hallen*] and is originally a character of tone or *sound*, that is, the opposite of 'dull'. Brightness, therefore, is not at all originally a character of the visible, but was transferred over in language *to* the visible, to the field where light plays a role. So we speak of a 'bright sunny day.' But such linguistic transferences from the realm of the audible to that of the visible are never accidental, and generally indicate an early power and wisdom of language—although we freely admit that we have only a very inadequate and superficial knowledge of the essence of language. If the meaning of 'bright' is transferred to the visible and made equivalent to 'lit up,' 'brightness' made equivalent to 'light,' this can only happen on the basis of an essential kinship between the two phenomena, such that brightness as reverberation has something essential in common with light as illumination. The bright tone or sound, which is further intensified in shrillness (e.g., the nightingale) is what *penetrates*: it not only spreads itself out, but it forces itself through. What is dull or sluggish stays back as it were, is not able to force itself through. Brightness has the character of going-through. The same thing is shown in a different way with light and the 'light of day.' Light also has the character of going-through, and it is this character, as distinct from the staying-back of darkness, which allows the meaning of 'brightness' to be transferred from the audible to the visible. Brightness is that *through which* we see. More precisely, light is not only what penetrates through, but is what *permits* penetration, namely

in seeing and viewing. Light is the *transparent* [*das Durchsichtige*] that spreads out, opens, lets through. The *essence* of light and brightness is to be transparent.[135]

In relation to Heidegger's text, we find *the other beginning* in another Daoist, Liezi 列子 (fifth century BCE), who comments: "The Book of the Yellow Emperor says, 'When a shape moves, it produces a shadow, not another shape. When a sound resonates, it produces an echo, not another sound.' Stillness does not generate stillness but movement."[136] The final line can also be read: "When Non-Being becomes active, it does not produce Non-Being but Being," recalling Laozi's chapter 40. In *Contributions*, Heidegger's interpretation of "Echo" resonates with Laozi's chapter 28 of the 1930 Bremen lectures. In this context, Heidegger's "Echo" is not altogether Greek or Western nor is his χάος (Chaos). Both are possibly shaped by Dao:

> Heidegger's Void is not the passive Greco-Roman Void of the dull emptiness of the Underworld but more akin to an active Chinese Daoist Void of creation. The Greek Void appears in Hesiod's eighth century BCE creation myth as χάος (Chaos), a rift ripped between heaven and earth where from everything must naturally arise, but nothing wishes to ever return. Generally, the early ancient Greeks avoid the Void as a dark, abysmal dankness. Heraclitus' most enigmatic fragment displays an alchemical rotation of the elements that moves around but not within the Void.[137]

We recall Heidegger's expression: "To think demigods means to think toward the Earth and out to the gods, from out of the originary middle."[138] In *Contributions to Philosophy*, Heidegger explains why his Void is *not* Hesiod's χάος. Being needs the Void ("Ground needs ab-ground"). The Void is not χάος (Hesiod's "mere gaping and yawning open") but an essential "tuning enjoining" (*stimmende Erfügen*).[139]

Heraclitus

In regard to "tuning enjoining," Graham Parkes entwines Heraclitus and Laozi through Heidegger:

> It is for good reason that Heidegger mentions the *tao* [Dao] in the same breath as the Presocratic *logos* [λόγος]. A major ground for his openness to Taoist ideas is his becoming attuned early on to reading comparable texts in the form of fragments from the Presocratics. Of particular relevance in this context would be the writings of Heraclitus, the Western thinker closest in spirit to Taoism, and to whom Heidegger ascribes the deepest understanding of Being. The texts of the two great Taoist classics, though written somewhat later than the fragments, occupy a place in the history of East Asian thinking comparable to that of Heraclitus's work in the West. The impact of Lao-Chuang was of course initially much greater, giving rise to one of the foremost schools of Chinese philosophy, and subsequently constituting a major force in the development of Zen Buddhism.

> Some of Heraclitus's ideas entered the Western mainstream through Plato, though they were largely overwhelmed by the latter's grander metaphysical concerns. Heraclitus continued, however, to be a fascinating figure exerting a mysterious and appropriately intermittent Thoughts on the Way and sporadic influence throughout the development of Western thought, until Hegel's treatment (of the Presocratics in general) ended a period of relative neglect. Since then, interest in him has been further reanimated by Nietzsche and Heidegger—not to mention the numerous poets who have been inspired by the fecundity of the fragments. The form of Heraclitus' text is especially congruent with that of Lao-tzu's, both being woven from pregnant utterances couched in an archaic language rich in allusive power and interspersed with lacunae of obscurity. Though the patchwork of the *Tao Te Ching* may have a somewhat more cohesive unity, a greater proportion of the fragments of Heraclitus come from a single hand than the verses attributed to Lao-tzu. But stylistically they are remarkably similar in their blending of the arcane and the oracular, the gnomic and the poetic.[140]

Parkes discerns that Heidegger seeks to assemble deeper implications from the two thinkers best exemplifying distinct civilizations: Laozi and Heraclitus.[141] Parkes cites Heraclitus' fragment 54: "*Harmoniē aphanēs phanerēs kreittēn* [ἁρμονίη ἀφανὴς φανερῆς κρείττων (The unapparent jointure [fitting together] is stronger than the manifest)], says Heraclitus. The hidden harmony is deeper, the invisible connection stronger, the inconspicuous correspondence more interesting, than the apparent."[142]

Heidegger's sameness is a collectivity of difference but a difference at an ontological and cosmological level. Heidegger translates fragment 54:

> [The not clearly visible jointure is more precious (noble) than the conjuncture pressing to bring to appearance (manifest)].[143]

Recalling Schelling's sound as the resonance of God's eternal affirmation in nature, Heidegger writes:

> When we measure the nobility of the word in terms of what remains to be said in it, what could be more joined to what is to be said than a saying of Heraclitus'? Where, after all, does a higher concern for the word speak? To be sure, the reason or the inceptual nobility of this thoughtful speaking lies not in a special linguistic ability belonging to the thinker, but rather in the essence of what is thought in this thinking and what remains the to-be-thought, and which, *is* the to-be-thought, calls forth the word in such a way that the thinker is merely summoned to echo [*nachzusagen*] this call.[144]

Heidegger underscores the above:

> The Greek word for 'jointure' is ἁρμονία [*Fügung*]. When we hear this word, we think immediately of the joining of sounds, and take 'harmony' to mean that which is in 'uni-son [*Ein-klang*].' However, the substance of ἁρμονία does not lie

in the realm of sounds and tones. Rather, it lies in ἁρμός [*Füge*]: i.e., in the joint, that whereby one thing fits into another, where both join themselves [*sich fügt*] into the joint in such a way that that the jointure is.[145]

In effect, ἁρμός is a technical term for a joint in masonry or metal working, and the front and back faces of blocks or fastenings for doors.[146] We can contrast these fittings to the Anaximander fragment on δίκη (*Fug*) as the ordering jointure of *thinking fit*.[147] Φύσις (initially *Aufgehen* as "emerging" and eventually ἁρμονίη ἀφανὴς as "unapparent fitting") is contained within ἁρμονία (*Fügung*) as a hidden fitting. Hence δίκη is *a thinking fit* whereas ἁρμός is *a physical fit*. Whereas ἁρμονία is the jointure between φύσις and δίκη in Heraclitus, ἁρμονία is the jointure between νοεῖν and εἶναι in Parmenides. Heidegger summarizes: "However, in Greek, σοφόν [*wissen*] is also always an echo of σαφές [*Helle*], which means luminous—manifest—radiant."[148]

Helle (brightness) emerges from *hallen* (to echo). Reminiscent of Dao, we have co-constitutive, co-resonating, and equiprimordial interactions.[149] In Heraclitus, σοφόν (*wissen*) is "always" an *Anklang* (echo, reverberation, resonation) of σαφές (lucid, clear, radiant). *Anklang* as the first jointure tasks itself with the abandonment of Being; it escorts in *the other beginning* that is neither metaphysical nor representational. Non-Being begets Being, and sound begets echo as we hear reverberations through Schelling, Heidegger, and Lao-Zhuang.

In the summer of 1960, Heidegger returns to Bremen where he brings together Heraclitus and Zhuangzi as distinct components of the jointure, enacting a unity through diversity. Otto Pöggeler recalls:

> Heidegger sought with Hölderlin, and thereby from a dialogue with the Greeks or a differentiation from them, to achieve a different future. But in contrast with Hölderlin he not only distinguished the Greek from the oriental, but also related the origin of the occidental to the origin that the East Asian world has in Taoism ... He was thus able to take into account the Taoist conception of art when he gave a lecture in Bremen in 1960 entitled "Image and Word [*Bild und Wort*]." The introduction to this talk focused on five texts: "a quotation from Augustine Confessions X (7 and 8), fragment 112 of Heraclitus, Chuang-tzu's story of the bell-stand (ch. 19), Paul Klee's Jena lecture 'On modern art'—and Heidegger's own couplet, 'Nur Gebild wahrt Gesicht/Doch Gesicht ruht im Gedicht' (Only images guard the face/yet the face rests in the poem) ... This connection between Being, which with its truth belongs to time or the event of appropriation (*Ereignis*), and the word, Heidegger sees addressed in Heraclitus's fragment 112. Heidegger believes that he has found in the word *phusis* [φύσις] a central term of Heraclitus and that this word is to be understood as "arising holding-sway" (*das aufgehende Walten* [emerging, blossoming, prevailing, presiding]). Thus, he can say with fragment 112 that genuine wisdom consists in saying and doing what is true or unconcealed, and moreover from hearkening to that which arising from itself shows itself (*phusis*) ... He was able to introduce this theme into the Bremen discussion through Chuang-tzu's story of the bell-stand: through long fasting and through concentration and meditation the woodworker becomes able to find in

the forest that one tree which is already the bell-stand yet to be made, in such a way that matter and form in this consummate work of art can be completely one. In this Bremen seminar, however, Heidegger wanted to do more than just break through the traditional religio-metaphysical ideas to choose beginnings which he found for the Western tradition in Heraclitus and for the Far East in Taoism. He wanted to follow the trace of this primordial thinking in such a way that it would lead our own time to a new beginning.[150]

In 1943, Heidegger creatively utilizes Ioannes Stobaeus' (fifth century) compilation, rendering Heraclitus' fragment 112 as such: Τὸ φρονεῖν ἀρετὴ μεγίστη, καὶ σοφίη ἀληθέα λέγειν καὶ ποιεῖν κατὰ φύσιν ἐπαΐοντας (τοῦ Λόγου).[151]

> Meditative thinking is the highest nobility, and it is this, because knowledge is: The unconcealing (out of the concealing in the unconcealment) gathers in the wisdom of bringing-forth [spawning, *Hervor-bringens*] in what is produced and set up with regard to the swelling up (all of this indeed) in the drawing-out and drawing-in relation to the primordial fore-gathering.[152]

Heidegger links Heraclitus' fragment 112 with the bell stand from the *Zhuangzi* chapter 19, quoting Buber's text, informed by Herbert Giles' (1845–1935) and James Legge's (1815–97) English translations.[153] Buber entitles his story "Der Glockenspielständer"—the bell stand.[154]

As a pioneer in bringing Heraclitus and Zhuangzi together, Heidegger speaks of an ontological resonance in "Bild und Wort": "However, the threads [*fäden*, strings, strands] named are so strangely intertwined that therein a fabric [*Gewebe*] is visible that points into a gathering of the *An-Wesen* [*Gewese* as 'collected presence'] of which we would otherwise not catch sight [bring into view or en-vision]."[155] What Heidegger sees as the "fleeting pursuit" (*flüchtige Verfolg*) of the five "guiding threads" (*fünf Leitfäden*) emerges in the following task: "To contemplate the fabric, that is the fabric of a veil, that unveils [uncovers, reveals], by covering up [veiling, concealing], namely the imageless of the wordless."[156] Heidegger continues:

> The essential alternating change of images and words—and that of human relation to both—does not spring up from today's helplessness and the consequent consumption of images and words; the change mentioned is carried out specifically by drives, from the essential origin of which one looks away. That is why, in the course of the conversation, we are led to clear the realm into which both names speak, if not a definition of image and word. However, this requires an approximate clue [tip, hint] of the direction of the way that the conversation wants to take.[157]

In the above passages, the non-representational reversals alongside the tapestry metaphor are echoes of *the other beginning* of a post-metaphysical thinking of both Zhuangzi and the *Chinese web that has no weaver*.[158] In respect to Zhuangzi's words and images, Kuang-Ming Wu observes: "Those seemingly stray fragments can be seen to refer one to another, mutually dovetailing into a surprising theme."[159] Zhuangzi's "goblet words" (*zhiyan* 卮言) "incite a tuning-in of mutual resonance"[160] by tipping over when full and standing upright when empty, pouring out endless changes. Wu explains:

> They are at the deep recesses of actuality and can only be captured with faltering speech (with a paradoxical ring) or simple silence (of which these words are echoes). What words say echoes what they do not say, that to which they call our attention, their "intention" ... what is by nature unsayably actual. Then the listener realizes that this echo is itself part of the actual, which envelops the effort at reaching it; otherwise actuality is not real. The *Chuang Tzu* is actuality expressing itself through the reader's effort to capture it, or rather, to be captured by it and become it.[161]

Heidegger's jointure of Heraclitus and Zhuangzi as *the other beginning* through the *abandonment* of Being (*Seinsverlassenheit*) is reinforced by *the leap*, and *the ones to come*. Whereas Schelling pre-sages Heidegger *then*, Heidegger makes Schelling possible *now*. Through an exploration of Dao, both are heard in an echo of a living futures past. A new Heidegger together with a new Schelling is part of the ones to come. Michael Inwood explains:

> Stones, trees and animals are affected by their past, but they have only a *Vergangenheit* ['dead' past], not a *Gewesenheit* ['living' past] that they can go 'back to' ... Later, Heidegger associates historiology with the dead rather than the living past: *Historie* is the 'determining and explanation of the past [*Vergangenen*] from the viewpoint [horizon, *Gesichtskreis*] of the calculative preoccupations of the present.'[162]

Heidegger expounds further: "Only because care is based on the character of 'having been,' can Dasein exist as the thrown entity which it is. 'As long as' Dasein factically exists, it is never past [*vergangen*], but it always is indeed as already having been [*gewesen*], in the sense of the 'I am-as-having been.'"[163] We do not move toward the future but wait for it to come to us (*zu-kommen*). A non-representational past will stand before us as a new future. Heidegger's concealing/revealing withdrawal into the echo is quite reminiscent of the Daoist sage who disappears in the midst of time's passing as he vanishes into things around him while the world dims down into the oblivion of nothing.[164] Heidegger's "guiding threads" (*Leitfäden*) that point to the fabric of a veil that unveils as it covers up is reminiscent of what I call "visceral manifestation." I explain:

> The 'visceral manifestations' (藏象) of *Huangdi Neijing* 黃帝內經 (Yellow Emperor's Classic of Internal Medicine) find complements in phenomenological writings. The Chinese body is a matrix of energy lines, something like Merleau-Ponty's chiasm come *chora*, the crossings of experience between subject and object. The physical organ is a token which serves an energy field, known as a meridian, which eternally links the stars to the body to society to writing. The

Chinese character for meridian, *jing* (經) also means scroll or book, as in the Daoist *Yijing*. The old Chinese character represents a skein of silk guided by the banks of a river. Writing is confluent with the way of the water. This concept is crucial for understanding an East Asian communicative body. The old Chinese character for Tibet, *zang* (藏), also means scrolls or holy writings which also means repository, reservoir or treasury. Tibet is a country hidden in the mountains and in the middle of it we find scrolls hidden in vaults and in the middle of the scrolls are hidden truths. When the Chinese for elephant, *xiang* (象) slides to meaning 'manifestation' and an extra moon (*yue* 月 piece of flesh, meat, the body) is added in the modern text (臟) we no longer have a 'Tibetan Elephant' [*Xizang da xiang* 西藏大象] but 'the icon of the viscera' [*zang xiang* 藏象], the sacred body of life-force into which the stars write our fate. In traditional Chinese medicine, pulse diagnosis manifests the unseen orbs that are crossings of energy mapped into organs. The body and the body of philosophy are matrices of energy lines floating between Heaven and Earth and between East and West.[165]

Heidegger's deconstruction of both physical "image" and "word" into "imageless" and "wordless" resonates with Wang Bi 王弼 (226–249 CE), Laozi's redactor. Heidegger might be familiar with Wang Bi's version of *Laozi* through Richard Wilhelm's translation.[166] As I outline:

Wang Bi sees an opposite strategy based on *wang* 忘 (to forget) from the *Zhuangzi*: "The Image is that by which a meaning is arrested. Once the meaning is reached, the image is forgotten." This would be a type of deconstruction. As Wang Bi summarizes 'Getting the meaning consists in forgetting the image; getting the image consists in forgetting the words ... All this leads to the scholarly explication of the dark."[167]

As parallel to the above, John Sallis explains echo as an "irreversible shift after Heidegger": "a shift to speech, to the voice, to a voice detached from intuition, from the preservation and recovery of presence, from the dream of presence. Not the voice, then, of transcendental philosophy, which could never echo but in whose interiority the echo-effect would be utterly reduced." Sallis continues: "a voice as detached from subjectivity and from origin as the disembodied echoes returned to it across the open enclosure in the mountains. A voice listening beyond itself, ecstatically [reminiscent of Schelling]. A shift also from the condition of vision, light, to that of an echoing voice, namely, the open enclosure, what Heidegger will call clearing (*Lichtung*)."[168]

Heraclitus' "unapparent jointure" of fragment 54 combined with the meditative thinking of fragment 112 fits well with Zhuangzi's carpenter Qing who meditatively composes his self in order to quell the heart-mind. For Heidegger, the deeper underlying affinities of these fragments decloak as an ontic "attunement" (*Gestimmtheit*) of an ontological "already-having-found-itself-there-ness" (*Befindlichkeit*).[169] In *Being and Time*, Heidegger writes: "Dasein's openness to the world is constituted existentially by the attunement of an already-having-found-itself-there-ness."[170] In reference to fragment 112, we recall Pöggeler's observation that Heidegger discovers an "arising holding-sway" (*das aufgehende Walten*) as prevailing or presiding, and that "genuine wisdom" emerges together with φύσις as an "hearkening" to that which arises from itself as it shows itself. Likewise, carpenter Qing's *Befindlichkeit* leads him to the perfect tree. Both Heraclitus and Zhuangzi listen to the pipings of heaven rather than simply those of humans or earth. As Pöggeler announces, the gathering of these deep soundings might uncover "the trace" of an originary thinking that points our own era to "a new beginning."

Conclusion

Heidegger's multi-decade engagement with Daoism finds a welcome ally in the rich beginnings from Schelling in the 1800s. Schelling understands Dao as an opening to nothingness with Laozi penetrating into the territory of the unbethinged (*unbedingt*) and to the deepest Ground of Being (*in den tiefsten Grund des Seyns*). For both Schelling and Heidegger, Dao is not "reason" but the way as a portal or gateway to nothingness. Schelling stimulates Heidegger's going under (*untergehen*) and deconstruction (*abbau*, dismantling) of the Cartesian subject, Euclidean space, and Aristotelian time that collect together as representational thinking (*Vorstellung*). Heidegger's *Da-sein* (there-being), *Das Ding* (the thing), *Die Kehre* (the turn), and *Vernehmen* (ap-prehension) leave traces similar to Zhuangzi's *ji* 跡 (footprint) where the sage fades into the mists of time past. The opening of the valley, the void of the cup, and the hollow of the shoes conjure up Laozi's chapter 11 and connect to chapters 15 and 28. The *dunklen Öffnung* (dark opening, cleft, aperture, cave, hollow) of the shoes, the temple, and the cup generate an oscillating, vibrating Void. Heidegger's Void is not the passive Greek Void of emptiness but is similar to an active Daoist Void of creation. For Heidegger, the mystery of mysteries of *saying* conceals itself through *waying* of a primordial Dao. Drawing upon Graham Parkes' insightful intertwining of Heraclitus and Laozi, the chapter explores Heidegger's ontological resonances or threads stretching from the 1930 to the 1960 Bremen lectures. Heraclitus and Laozi together are so uncannily intertwined that their fabric reveals a gathering which would otherwise be invisible. For Heidegger, the imageless of the wordless suggests *the echo* of a new beginning somewhere in the midst of the essential swaying between *logos* and Dao.

Notes

1 This commences with the *habilitationschrift* of Walter Schulz (1912–2000) under the supervision of Hans-Georg Gadamer (1900–2002), *Die Vollendung des Deutschen Idealismus in der Spätphilosophie Schellings* (Stuttgart: Neske, 1955).
2 Lore Hühn, "A Philosophical Dialogue between Heidegger and Schelling," *Comparative and Contemporary Philosophy*, 6.1 (2014): 16–34. See George J. Seidel, "Heidegger's Last God and the Schelling Connection," *Laval Theologique et Philosophique*, 55.1 (1999): 85–98.

3 See Kui-Wong Kwok, "Hegel, Schelling and Laozi on Nothingness," *Frontiers of Philosophy in China*, 13.4 (2018): 574–84. See also Kui-Wong Kwok, "Schelling's Understanding of Laozi," *Dao: A Journal of Comparative Philosophy*, 16.4 (2017): 503–20.

4 See Jay Goulding, "'Visceral Manifestation 藏象:' Chinese Philosophy and Western Phenomenology 現象學," in Keli Fang (ed.), *Chinese Philosophy and the Trends of the 21st Century Civilization* 中国哲學和二十一世紀文明走向, volume 4, 360–417 (Beijing: Commercial Press Inc., 2003). See the section "Heidegger's Lichtung and the Daoist Ming 明," 362–72.

5 Heidegger implies that there is no Hegel without Hebel, and no dialectic without dialect. See Martin Heidegger, "Hebel: Friend of the House," in Darrel E. Christensen, Manfred Riedel, Robert Spaemann, Reiner Wiehl, and Wolfgang Wieland (eds.), *Contemporary German Philosophy*, volume 3, 87–101 (University Park: Penn State University Press, 1983).

6 Martin Heidegger, *Schelling's Treatise on the Essence of Human Freedom*, trans. Joan Stambaugh (Athens: Ohio University Press, 1985), 4. Appearing and disappearing at different times, the portrait of Schelling seems to move around Heidegger's hut. During the 1966 *Der Spiegel* interviews, Heinrich Petzet emphasizes the "austerity" of Heidegger's study: "Not even the picture of the aged Schelling hung on the wall." Heinrich Petzet, *Encounters and Dialogues with Martin Heidegger, 1929–1976*, trans. John Sallis and Kenneth Maly (Chicago: University of Chicago Press, 1993), 97. An unpublished photograph of Heidegger sitting with a portrait of Schelling on the table-top in front of him confirms a continuing reverence. The architects Adam Sharr and Simon Unwin incorporate interviews with Heidegger's granddaughter, Gertrud Heidegger (1955–) who remembers the hut of old and describes one of the "sacred" places: "Eating took place at a corner table, presided over by a portrait of Friedrich von Schelling rather than an icon, set for particular, almost ritual, configurations of meals." Adam Sharr with Simon Unwin, "Heidegger's Hut," *arq: Architectural Research Quarterly*, 5.1 (2001): 60. "The table at the hut, presided over by the portrait of Hebel rather than a Catholic icon [crucifix], can be seen as marking the rites of hut life." Adam Sharr, *Heidegger's Hut* (Cambridge: MIT Press, 2006), 68. Schelling's portrait stands as a *Zier*, more than simply an ornament or adornment. It is a holy rood, a portal, a cosmology, a lighting that brings the present as present. See Martin Heidegger, *Sojourns: The Journey to Greece* (Albany: State University of New York Press, 2005), 27. Through Dao, Schelling's work becomes a primordial crossing for Heidegger.

7 I quote from my own reflections in an essay commemorating the 2001 *official return of philosophy to China*—opening the doors of interaction with world scholars—sponsored by Chung-Ying Cheng's *International Society for Chinese Philosophy* and the *12th International Conference on Chinese Philosophy* held in Beijing, July 21–24: "[Paul Shih-Yi Hsiao (1911–1986)] translates 'literally' from the Chinese: 'Who can, settling the muddy, gradually make it clear? Who can, stirring the tranquil, gradually bring it to life?' See Paul Shih-Yi Hsiao, "Heidegger and Our Translation of the *Tao Te Ching*," in Graham Parkes (ed.), *Heidegger and Asian Thought*, 93–104 (Honolulu: University of Hawaii Press, 1987), 100. But Heidegger carried the thought further, in suggesting that 'clarifying finally brings something to light, and subtle motion in the tranquil and still can bring something into being' (Hsiao, 'Heidegger,' 100). Looking at the German in Heidegger's letter of October 9, 1947, we find: 'Wer kann still sein und aus der Stille durch sie auf den Weg bringen (bewegen) etwas so, das es zum Erscheinen kommt?' [Wer vermag es, stillend etwas so ins Sein zu bringen? Des Himmels Tao] (Ibid., 103).

Parkes translates this as: 'Who can be still and out of stillness and through it move something on to the Way so that it comes to shine forth?' [Who is able through making still to bring something into Being? The tao of heaven] (Ibid., 103). Taking this in order, we see some interesting possibilities regarding *Lichtung* ('the clearing'). Hsiao's translation of the two lines are literal, but the Dao that can be told is not the eternal Dao; the name that can be named is not the eternal name. Heidegger takes the opening lines from chapter 1 of *Daodejing* sincerely, and thus liberally adds intervening text. Parkes' translation of the German better indicates the extent of Heidegger's understanding. Cultivating stillness at the center of motion is a Daoist strategy for meditation. Heidegger equates this with the 'clearing.' ... Looking at the Chinese text for Laozi's two lines from chapter 15, we see rich and delightfully ambiguous terms that Heidegger is struggling to bring to language. With the help of Hsiao, Heidegger consulted the 1937 Shanghai edition of Xi-Chang Jiang's *Laozi* [*Daodejing*] which compiled over eighty ancient texts (Ibid., 97) ... [Heidegger's] gentle invitation to Hsiao in 1947 to return to the translation was, alas, met in silence. Almost twenty-five years later, Heidegger picked up some of the excitement/revelation of translating Laozi with Chung-Yuan Chang (1907–88). In his view: 'Who is able to gradually reach purity from impurity through quiescence? Who is able to gradually grow lively from motion through motionless?' (Chung-Yuan Chang, *Tao: A New Way of Thinking*. London: New York: Harper and Row, 1975, 45). The remaining lines of Chang's translation are also telling ones: 'One who abides in Tao never desires to reach an extreme. Because he never desires to reach an extreme, He can remain in the old, yet become the new' (Ibid., 45–6). Chang's commentary not only illuminates Laozi but explains something of the turning in Heidegger's lifelong project: "The qualities mentioned in this chapter, that is, prudence, calmness, respectfulness, fluidity, solidity, vacancy, lacking clear discriminations, all reflect the center of being of the man of *Tao*. According to Lao Tzu, one achieves these aspects through quiescence and motionlessness. When one reaches quiescence, one's impurity is pure. When one reaches motionlessness, one's motion is more lively. Purity and liveliness are products of the form of the formless and the action of non-action. In order to reach the form of the formless and the action of non-action, Lao Tzu advises one to be free from extremes. When one is free from extremes, one abides with the middle way or the identity of opposites. Thus, the last words of this chapter are: 'He can remain in the old, yet become the new'" (Ibid., 46) ... After interaction with Asian thinkers, Heidegger did not attempt to 'reach out,' rather, his *ek-stasis* reached inward to the 'clearing' between subject and object, the *jian* (間) between Heaven and Earth." See Goulding, "Visceral Manifestation," 363–8. ... The expression "Des Himmels Tao" as the "Dao of Heaven" (*Tiandao* 天道) is added by Hsiao to the two Laozi lines to perhaps segue into chapter 47 which is invoked in a letter by Heidegger (with creative modifications) on May 29, 1965, to Ernest Jünger (1895–1998) (former soldier, author and friend) on occasion of his journey to the Far East: "Do not go out the door and come to know the world. Do not throw open the window and see the path of heaven [*und den Himmel ganz sehen*]; the farther away one goes, the less one knows. Thus, the wise: He makes no journey, yet he knows; he does not look, yet he offers praise; he does not act, but he accomplishes." Martin Heidegger and Ernst Jünger, *Correspondence 1949–1975*, trans. Timothy Sean Quinn (New York: Rowman and Littlefield, 2016), 32.

8 See Petzet, *Encounters and Dialogues*, 68–9. For a detailed account of Heidegger's Chinese students, see Jay Goulding, "Xiong Wei 熊偉: Chinese Philosophy and Hermeneutic Phenomenology," *Gate of Philosophy, Beijing University's Journal of Philosophy*, 5 (2004): 116–30.

9   See F.W.J. Schelling, *Sämmtliche Werke* (Berlin: E. Hahn, 1997), II.2, 548.
10 Schelling, *Sämmtliche Werke*, II.2, 564.
11 Wong, "Hegel, Schelling and Laozi," 577.
12 Martin Heidegger, *Contributions to Philosophy (From Enowning)*, trans. Parvis Emad and Kenneth Maly (Bloomington: Indiana University Press, 1999), 218.
13 See Jay Goulding, "Cheng and Gadamer: Daoist Phenomenology," special issue on "Gadamer and Chung-Ying Cheng: Hermeneutics and Onto-Generative Hermeneutics," *Journal of Chinese Philosophy*, 48.4 (2021): 368–382. In 1943, Heidegger creatively renders Laozi's chapter 11: "Thirty spokes meet the hub; but the Void between them gives shelter to the Being of the Wheel. From the Clay e-merges the vessels; but the Void within them gives shelter to the Being of the container. Walls and windows and doors make the house; but the Void between them gives shelter to the Being of the house, Be-ing arises from workability. Non-Being gives shelter to Being." Martin Heidegger, *Zu Hölderlin: Griechenlandreisen* [GA 75], ed. Curd Ochwadt (Frankfurt: Vittorio Klostermann, 2000), 43. Heidegger translates the Chinese character *wu* 無 with the German *Leere* (Void, empty nothingness). *Leere* intrigues Heidegger in its relationship to Dao. As Xianglong Zhang argues, Heidegger's handwritten lecture notes, "Vom Wesen der Wahrheit" (On the Essence of Truth), presumably delivered at the Bremen Philosophy Club on October 8, 1930, illustrates the earliest use of Laozi's philosophy of Yin-Yang polarity. See Xianglong Zhang, "The Coming Time 'between' Being and Daoist Emptiness: An Analysis of Heidegger's Article Inquiring into the Uniqueness of the Poet via the *Lao Zi*," *Philosophy East and West*, 59.1 (2009): 71–87. Heidegger quotes a line from chapter 28 of the *Daodejing*: "Freedom as the disclosing Letting-be (of being as itself) unveils itself as the essence of truth. Now it shows itself: freedom as the essence of truth is in itself the authentic open-mindedness to the mystery. 'Whoever knows its brightness, shrouds himself in its darkness' (Laozi)." See Xianglong Zhang, *Heidegger Biography* (Beijing: Beijing University Press, 2008). In 1957 at Freiburg, Heidegger publishes a revised version of the 1930 lecture and writes of the Laozi quote: "To do this, we join in the truth that everyone knows but few are able to make possible: mortal thinking must lower itself into the darkness of the well to see the star by day. It remains more difficult to maintain the purely lucid integrity of the dark than to provide a brightness that only wants to appear as such. What only seems to shine shines not." Martin Heidegger, *Bremer und Freiburger Vorträge* [GA 79], ed. Petra Jaeger (Frankfurt: Vittorio Klostermann, 1994), 93. Cf. "Lao Tzu says, 'Whoever knows its brightness, cloaks himself in its darkness,'" in Martin Heidegger, *Bremen and Freiburg Lectures: Insight into That Which Is and Basic Principles of Thinking*, trans. Andrew J. Benjamin (Bloomington: Indiana University Press, 2012), 89. Recalling October 9, 1930, in Bremen when Heidegger reads from Zhuangzi's chapter 17 regarding the fish, we note the supplementary story of the frog and the turtle whereby the frog cannot see the ocean from a caved-in well. Heidegger's "purely lucid integrity of the dark" (*Lauterkeit des Dunklen*) echoes Schelling's "primordially lucid purity" (*der uranfängliche Lauterkeit*). See F.W.J. Schelling, *The Ages of the World (1811)*, trans. Joseph P. Lawrence (Albany: State University of New York Press, 2019), 127 and 134. In "Notes and Fragments to the First Book" transcribed by Manfred Shröter (1880–1973) just before the 1944 destruction of the Munich archive, Schelling discusses "originary lucid purity" (*die Urlauterkeit*). See Schelling, *Ages of the World*, 197. Schelling relates: "We are attempting now, in a preliminary fashion, [to heighten awareness] of the unprethinkable [*Unvordenklich*] (ἀνυπόθετον [absolute, without

foundation]) as such. We strive toward the unprethinkable in the hope of elevating ourselves. Instead of holding lucid purity for something real and essential, we recognize in it only a basis (*Unterlage*), something that we might use as an aid and, as it were, a support, in order {with its help} to attain to what is truly essential, the beginning of all things." Ibid., 198. Schelling states "the stars are the spawn of the primordially dark," a premonition of Heidegger's link with Laozi. Ibid., 242. Dainian Zhang (1909–2004) interprets the above Laozi line from chapter 28 in relation to chapter 15: "Know honor but keep to what is despised; then you will be a valley for under-heaven. For one who is a valley for under-heaven, constant virtue is enough, and one will go back to the uncarved block." Dainian Zhang, *Key Concepts in Chinese Philosophy*, trans. Edmund Ryden (New Haven: Yale University Press, 2002), 71–2. Chung-Yuan Chang says "'to be aware of the white, yet to abide in the dark' indicates the balance of opposites. To achieve this balance is to remain in the state of original non-differentiation [recall Schelling's pivot]." Chang, *Tao: A New Way of Thinking*, 75. Heidegger's fascination with chapter 15's primordial nothingness includes the valley before the mountain, and the uncarved block before the statue which bears out equally in chapter 28. See Goulding, "Gadamer and Cheng," 368–382.

14 Kuang-Ming Wu, *The Butterfly as Companion: Meditations on the First Three Chapters of the Chuang-Tzu* (Albany: State University of New York Press, 1990), 140–1.
15 Wong, "Schelling's Understanding of Laozi," 508–9.
16 Ibid., 506. See Jean-Pierre Abel-Rémusat, *Memoire sur la Vie et les Opinions de Lao-Tseu* (Paris: De L'imprimerie Royale, 1823); Stanislas Julien, *Le Livre de la Voie et de la Vertu, composé dans le VIe siècle avant l'ère chrétienne, par le philosophe Lao-Tseu* (Paris: De L'imprimerie Royale, 1842).
17 See Chang, *Tao: A New Way of Thinking*. With a Heideggerian flavor, Chang is a pioneer in translating Daoist and Buddhist classics in the West. See Goulding, "Xiong Wei"; see also Goulding, "Cheng and Gadamer," 368–382.
18 Knut Walf, "Fascination and Misunderstanding: The Ambivalent Western Reception of Daoism," *Monumenta Serica*, 53 (2005): 277.
19 Eric S. Nelson, *Chinese and Buddhist Philosophy in Early Twentieth-Century German Thought* (London: Bloomsbury Academic, 2017), 113. Nelson adds: "Compare Gustav A. C. Frantz, *Schelling's Positive Philosophie, nach ihrem Inhalt, wie nach ihrer Bedeutung fur den allgemeinen Umschwung der bis jetzt noch herrschenden Denkweise* (Cöthen: P. Schettler, 1880), 97; Thomas Watters, *Lao-tzu: A Study in Chinese Philosophy* (Hong Kong: China Mail Office, 1870), 35, 40, and 55; Alexander Winchell, *Reconciliation of Science and Religion* (New York: Harper, 1877), 49." See Nelson, Chinese and Buddhist Philosophy, 279–80.
20 Nelson, *Chinese and Buddhist Philosophy*, 113. See Jay Goulding, "Unity through Diversity: Inter-world, Family Resemblance, Intertextuality," *Journal of World Philosophies*, 3.1 (2018): 142–50. I review three splendidly, well-researched books on East-West philosophy: Kwok-Ying Lau, *Phenomenology and Intercultural Understanding: Toward a New Cultural Flesh* (Cham: Springer, 2016); Lin Ma and Jaap van Brakel, *Fundamentals of Comparative and Intercultural Philosophy* (Albany: State University of New York Press, 2016); and Nelson, *Chinese and Buddhist Philosophy*.
21 Schelling, *Sämmtliche Werke*, II.2, 562.
22 Schelling, *Sämmtliche Werke*, II.1, 294.
23 Bruce Matthews, trans. *F.W.J. Schelling, The Grounding of Positive Philosophy: The Berlin Lectures* (Albany: State University of New York Press, 2007), 33.

24 F.W.J. Schelling, *First Outline of a System of the Philosophy of Nature*, trans. Keith R. Peterson (Albany: State University of New York Press, 2004), 181.
25 Ibid., 83.
26 F.W.J. Schelling, *Historical-Critical Introduction to the Philosophy of Mythology*, trans. Mason Richey and Markus Zisselsberger (Albany: State University of New York Press, 2007), 40.
27 Schelling, *Sämmtliche Werke*, II.1, 52.
28 Ibid., 144.
29 Ibid., 95.
30 Ibid., 96.
31 Wong, "Schelling's Understanding of Laozi," 505.
32 Schelling, *Sämmtliche Werke*, II.2, 550.
33 Ibid., 521.
34 Edward Allen Beach, *The Potencies of God(s): Schelling's Philosophy of Mythology* (Albany: State University of New York Press, 1994), 284.
35 Ibid., 116.
36 Schelling, *First Outline*, 228.
37 Beach, *Potencies of God(s)*, 117.
38 Ibid., 122.
39 Ibid., 126.
40 William Smith, ed., *Dictionary of Greek and Roman Biography and Mythology* (London: Taylor, Walton and Maberly, 1849), volume 2, 551.
41 Schelling, *Sämmtliche Werke*, II.2, 608. Heidegger writes: "Heraclitus says (Fragment 53); Confrontation [setting one against the other] is indeed for all (that comes to presence), the progenitors (who let rise) but (also) for all the guardians that holds sway. For it lets some appear as gods, others as human beings, some it lets stand as slaves but others as the free. The Πόλεμος named here is above all gods and humans, a quarrel that holds sway not as war in the human way. As Heraclitus thinks it, struggle first and foremost allows what essentially unfolds to step apart against each other, allowing position and status and rank to establish themselves in coming to presence. In such a stepping apart, gaps, intervals, distances, and jointures open up. In con-frontation, the world becomes. (Confrontation neither separates nor destroys. It even builds Oneness [Unity]; it is the gathering [λόγος]. Πόλεμος and λόγος are the same thing)." See Martin Heidegger, *Einführung in der Metaphysik* [GA 40], ed. Petra Jaeger (Frankfurt: Vittorio Klostermann, 1983), 66.
42 Schelling, *Sämmtliche Werke*, II.2, 607. Roman armies march through the Janus gates of the Forum to acquire magical powers; hence, the gates remain open in time of war. See Betty Radice, *Who's Who in the Ancient World* (London: Penguin, 1971), 144.
43 Schelling, *Sämmtliche Werke*, II.2, 603–4.
44 Ibid., 602.
45 David R. Sear, *Roman Coins and Their Values* (London: Spink and Son, 2000), volume 1, 205.
46 Martin Heidegger, *Zur Sache des Denkens* [GA 14], ed. Friedrich-Wilhelm von Herrmann (Frankfurt: Vittorio Klostermann, 2007), 63.
47 Martin Heidegger, *Seminare* [GA 15], ed. Curd Ochwadt (Frankfurt: Vittorio Klostermann, 1986), 366.
48 Wu, *Butterfly as Companion*, 180 and 194. What Schelling sees in Dao and Janus, Wu sees in the pivot of Zhuangzi's "heavenly potter's wheel" (*tian jun* 天鈞) or windlass

(lu lu 轆轤), and Heidegger sees in *Leere* as the empty Void of nothingness in the cartwheel (*che* 車) of *Daodejing* chapter 11.

49 See the opening page of Part 1 (i.e., "Prologue") of Graham Parkes' chapter in this volume. Coincidently, on October 9, 1947—some seventeen years to the day—Heidegger writes a letter to Hsiao reminiscing about their translations of the *Daodejing* and hoping to "resume" or "take up" (*aufnehmen können*) their project together by quoting two lines from chapter 15. See Paul Shih-Yi Hsiao, "Heidegger and Our Translation," 103. In the 1960s when Paul Hsiao brings a friend for a mountain visit, Heidegger jokes that it was Hsiao who did not wish to continue the translations. See Paul Shih-Yi Hsiao, "Heidegger and Our Translation," 98.

50 Martin Heidegger, *Beiträge zur Philosophie (zum Ereignis)* [GA 65], ed. Friedrich-Wilhelm von Herrmann (Frankfurt: Vittorio Klostermann, 1989), 310–11.

51 Goulding, "Gadamer and Cheng," 368–382.

52 On June 10, 1950, Heidegger discusses "The Thing" and the fourfold (*das Geviert*) in relation to Laozi in a seminar at Icking, a municipality in the district of Bad Tölz-Wolfratshausen in Bavaria (D.H. Lawrence's 1927 home). See Petzet, *Encounters and Dialogues*, 73.

53 Goulding, "Cheng and Gadamer," 368–382.

54 Martin Heidegger, "The Thing." In *Poetry, Language and Thought*, trans. Albert Hofstadter (New York: Harper Collins, 1971), 169.

55 Goulding, "Cheng and Gadamer," 368–382. Heidegger's description of the woman's old shoes and the *Feldweg* resound here: "From the dark opening (cleft, aperture, cave, hollow) of the beaten-up interior of the rugged (motley) shoes, the hardship of the worker's step gazes forth (stares with eyes wide open). In the abrasively sturdy heaviness of the motley shoes is gathered the toughness (tenacity) of the tardy gait (course) through the far reaching and ever uniform corrugations (furrows) of the farmland, withstanding the harsh (raw) wind (breeze). Upon the leather is the moistness and richness of the earth (ground, soil). Under the soles, the loneliness of the field-path slides itself through the falling, sinking evening. Within the rugged shoes resonates (oscillates, vibrates, brandishes) the concealed (secluded, untold) call of the earth, its silence (stillness) gives way to the ripening grain and its unexplained breakdown in the barren fallowness (unplowedness) of the wintry fields." Martin Heidegger, *Holzwege* [GA 5], ed. Friedrich-Wilhelm von Herrmann (Frankfurt: Vittorio Klostermann, 1977), 19.

56 F.W.J. Schelling, *The Ages of the World, (Fragment) from the Handwritten Remains Third Version (c. 1815)*, trans. Jason M. Wirth (Albany: State University of New York Press, 2000), 20.

57 Martin Heidegger, *Unterwegs zur Sprache*, [GA 12], ed. Friedrich-Wilhelm von Herrmann (Frankfurt: Vittorio Klostermann, 1985), 187. See Martin Heidegger, "The Nature of Language," in Martin Heidegger (ed.), *On the Way to Language*, trans. Peter D. Hertz (New York: Harper and Row, 1971), 92.

58 Heidegger states: "And because the function of the λόγος lies in merely letting something be seen, in letting entities be *perceived* [im *Vernehmenlassen* des Seienden], λόγος can signify the *reason* [*Vernunft*]." Martin Heidegger, *Being and Time*, trans. John McQuarrie and Edward Robinson (Oxford: Blackwell, 1962), 58.

59 Goulding, "Cheng and Gadamer," 368–382.

60 Schelling, *Sämmtliche Werke*, II.2, 522.

61 Schelling, *Historical-Critical Introduction*, 127 and 163.

62 Heidegger's Parmenides Fragment 4 explores paths of Being and Nonbeing: "[ἡ μὲν ὅπως ἔστιν τε καὶ ὡς οὐκ ἔστι μὴ εἶναι] The one: how it is (what it, Being, is) and how also Nonbeing (is) impossible" and "[ἡ δ' ὡς οὐκ ἔστιν τε καὶ ὡς χρεών ἐστι μὴ εἶναι] But the other: that it is not and also that Nonbeing (is) necessary." Heidegger, *Einführung in der Metaphysik*, [GA 40] 118. Also Fragment 8: "τοῦ μηδενὸς ἀρξάμενον, φῦν; οὕτως ἢ πάμπαν πελέναι χρεών ἐστιν ἢ οὐχί [if it began from nothing? Thus (it) must be completely or not at all]." See Parmenides, *Parmenides of Elea Fragments*, trans. David Gallop (Toronto: University of Toronto, 1984), 54–5, 64–5.

63 See Martin Heidegger, "What Is Metaphysics," trans. R.F.C. Hull and Alan Crick, in Martin Heidegger, *Existence and Being*, With an introduction by Werner Brock (Chicago: Henry Regnery Company, 1949), 375–7.

64 R.F.C. Hull and Alan Crick, "Notes," in Martin Heidegger, *Existence and Being*, With an introduction by Werner Brock (Chicago: Henry Regnery Company, 1949), 399.

65 Martin Heidegger, "What Is Metaphysics," 369–70. Cf. Martin Heidegger, *Wegmarken* [GA 9], ed. Friedrich-Wilhelm von Herrmann (Frankfurt: Vittorio Klostermann, 1976), 114–15.

66 Rolf Elberfeld (1964–) writes: "Heidegger is the first great European thinker who was not only first received in East Asia, but whose whole path of thinking was accompanied by conversations with Asian philosophers." Rolf Elberfeld, "Heidegger und das ostasiatische Denken: Annäherungen zwischen fremden Welten," in Dieter Thomä (ed.), *Heidegger Handbuch: Leben-Werk-Wirkung*, 469–74 (Stuttgart: Metzler, 2003), at 469.

67 In the early 1970s at McMaster University in Hamilton, I encounter Hans-Georg Gadamer (1900–2002) through his nephew who teaches engineering mathematics. Gadamer, who spends several terms in Canada, tells me that Heidegger needs my help as he is most fascinated with Chinese philosophy. As such, I study Greek, study Chinese, and connect with philosophers in Hawaii, principally Chung-Ying Cheng. Chang-Chung Yuan teaches in Hawaii from the early 1960s to the late 1980s with Wing-Tsit Chan (1901–94) preceding him from the 1930s. Along the way, I assemble Heidegger students from John Wild's (1902–72) first graduate class of phenomenology taught in the United States at Yale University in the 1960s, including Kuang-Ming Wu, a leading scholar of Daoism, Hwa Yol Jung (1931–2017), a leading scholar of Buddhism, and Chung-Ying Cheng, a leading scholar of Confucianism. See Goulding, "Cheng and Gadamer," 368–382; Goulding, "Beginnings: The Global Crossings of Classical Daoism," in Kuang-Ming Wu (ed.), *Globalization Dynamics: Psychological, Economic, Technological, and Cultural Intercourses*, 118–32 (New York: Nova Science Publishers, 2012); Goulding, "Hwa Yol Jung's East Asian Philosophy and Phenomenology," in Jin Young Park (ed.), *Comparative Political Theory and Cross-Cultural Philosophy: Essays in Honor of Hwa Yol Jung*, 119–36 (Lanham, MD: Lexington Books, 2009); Jay Goulding (ed.), *China-West Interculture, Toward the Philosophy of World Integration: Essays on Wu Kuang-Ming's Thinking* (New York: Global Scholarly Publications, 2008); Goulding, "Cheng Chung-Ying's Onto-Cosmology: Chinese Philosophy and Hermeneutic Phenomenology," in On-cho Ng (ed.), *The Imperative of Understanding: Chinese Philosophy, Comparative Philosophy, and Onto-Hermeneutics: A Tribute Volume Dedicated to Professor Chung-Ying Cheng*, 135–55 (New York: Global Scholarly Publications, 2008); Goulding, "New Ways toward Sino-Western Philosophical Dialogues," *Journal of Chinese Philosophy*, 34.1 (2007): 99–125; Goulding, "Rorty, Heidegger, Cheng: Pragmatism, Phenomenology, Onto-Cosmology," in Derong Pan (ed.), *Ontology and Interpretation: A Special Collection of Treatises Honoring Cheng Chung-Ying's 70th Birthday* 本體與詮釋:賀成

中英先生70壽誕論文專輯, 263-97 (Shanghai: Shanghai Academy of Social Sciences Press, 2005).

68   See Jay Goulding, "Japan-West Interculture: Time's Step Back—Dōgen, Watsuji, Kuki and Heidegger," in Aya Fujiwara and James White (eds.), *Conference Proceedings of the 31st Japanese Studies Association of Canada Annual Conference, Japan's World and the World's Japan: Images, Perceptions and Reactions* (Edmonton: Princess Takamado Japan Centre for Teaching and Research at the University of Alberta, 2019), 1–26.

69   Schelling writes: "Thus the word I have used casually thus far, the word *bedingen*, is an eminently striking term of which one can say that it contains almost the entire treasure of philosophical truth. *Bedingen* means the action by which anything becomes a *thing* (Ding). *Bedingt* (*determined*) is what has been turned into a thing. Thus, it is clear at once that nothing can posit itself as a thing, and that an unconditioned thing is a contradiction in terms. *Unbedingt* (unconditioned) is what has not been turned into a thing, and what cannot at all become a thing." See F.W.J. Schelling, *The Unconditional in Human Knowledge: Four Early Essays 1794–1796*, trans. Fritz Marti (Lewisburg: Bucknell University Press, 1980), 74.

70   Chapter 22 of the *Zhuangzi* reads: "that which things a thing is not itself a thing." Cf. "[Die] Dingheit des Dinges ... kann selbst nicht wieder ein Ding sein." Martin Heidegger, *Die Frage nach dem Ding: Zu Kants Lehre von den Transzendentalen Grundsätzen* [GA 41], ed. Petra Jaeger (Frankfurt: Vittorio Klostermann, 1984), 8.

71   Heidegger, "The Thing," in *Poetry, Language, Thought*, 161–84.

72   "Both Zhuangzi and Guo Xiang discuss the trace (*ji* 跡), a crucial idea resonating throughout Heidegger's writings. According to Guo, the Daoist sage has 'no deliberate mind or purpose of his own.' Instead, he acts spontaneously. People who follow the actions or words of the sages are mistaken. What counts is the spontaneous action of the sage or *ziran* 自然 as that which leaves the traces. Traces are places where the sage has left the world. For Heidegger, you find your own place to leave the world, and what he calls the turn back or bend back (*Kehre*) as it relates to the trace (*Spur*) is a 'wending your way' (*wenden*) ... The proper walker of Laozi's *Daodejing* chapter 27 leaves no trace (tracks, wagon tracks, footprints). Traces of the past as what has been, and traces of the future as not yet weigh on the duel meaning of *Spur*. Parallel to Guo Xiang, Heidegger reflects in 1938–1939: 'The There (Da). A trace of the There in the ἀλήθεια of φύσις. But the trace has long since been extinguished—it can never simply be followed again but must be found from one's own trail.'" Goulding, "Japan-West Interculture," 22–3. Chung-Yuan Chang writes: "Heidegger's thinking, in contrast [to Hegel], no longer has the character of elevation, but is the 'step back.' The thinking of the step back leads to the realm of the 'event of Appropriation,' which 'until now has been skipped over, and from which the essence of truth first of all becomes worthy of thought.' The entry of thinking into Appropriation constitutes 'an awakening from the oblivion of Being—an awakening which must be understood as a recollection of something which has never been thought.' According to Heidegger, 'metaphysics is the oblivion of Being.' Thus, the thinking which awakens from the oblivion of Being and enters into Appropriation is thinking which steps back 'out of metaphysics into the active essence of metaphysics.' In Taoist terms, the step back is the method of reducing, through which one attains Tao. As Lao Tzu says in chapter 48 of the *Tao Te Ching*: To learn, one accumulates day by day. To study Tao, one reduces day by day. By reducing and further reducing, one reaches the state of non-interference and spontaneity, through which nothing is left undone." Chang, *Tao: A New Way of Thinking*, x–xi.

73   Heidegger is familiar with Zhuangzi, *The True Book on the Southern Land of Blossoms*, a compilation of texts most likely drawn from the 1919 *Song Edition of the True Classic of Southern Florescence*. See Martin Heidegger, "Traditional Language and Technological Language," *Journal of Philosophical Research*, 23 (1998): 129–45; *Dschuang Dsi, Das wahre Buch vom südlichen Blütenland: Nan Hua Dschen Ging*, trans. Richard Wilhelm (Jena: Eugen Diederichs, 1923); Zhuangzi, *Song Edition of the True Classic of Southern Florescence* 宋刻南華真經, in Yuanji Zhang (ed.), *Continuation of a Collection of Lost Ancient Writings* (Nanjing: Jiangsu Guji Chubanshe, 1919), volume 3, 81–227.
74   Heidegger, *Beiträge zur Philosophie* [GA 65], 100.
75   Michael Inwood, *A Heidegger Dictionary* (London: Blackwell, 1999), 188–9.
76   Schelling, *Sämmtliche Werke*, I.8, 197.
77   F.W.J. Schelling, *Philosophical Investigations into the Essence of Human Freedom*, trans. Jeff Love and Johannes Schmidt (Albany: State University of New York Press, 2006), 51.
78   Schelling, *Sämmtliche Werke*, II.2, 549.
79   Ibid., 564.
80   "Leibniz also corresponded with the Berlin scholar Andreas Müller [1630?–1694] who claimed to have found a *clavis sinica* or a 'key' to the Chinese language that would 'decode' it. Any such creation of a 'universal characteristic' intrigued Leibniz. Since Müller insisted on money for his secret, it seemed to die with him since no one was willing to pay." Jay Goulding, "Franklin Perkins' *Leibniz and China: A Commerce of Light*," *Dao: A Journal of Comparative Philosophy*, 5.1 (2005): 183–7, at 185–6.
81   Schelling, *Sämmtliche Werke*, II.2, 553.
82   Goulding, "Japan-West Interculture," 9–10.
83   "The Chinese idea of 'person' (between heaven and hell [different realms of death and reincarnation]) is often rendered *ren jian* 人間, that is between heaven and earth, between one and another, between outside and inside. Perhaps the Chinese idea of person dwells in Heidegger's clearing or Laozi's concealed luminosity ['clearing luminosity' (*qingming* 清明) with the Void]." Goulding, "Visceral Manifestation," 400.
84   Jay Goulding, *China-West Interculture*, 183–206. The section "Mirrors, Shadows, Ladders, Echoes" explores Daoism and phenomenology, highlighting traces of Chinese body thinking and chaos theory, 193–8.
85   Shūzo Kuki, "The Notion of Time and Repetition in Oriental Time," in Stephen Light (ed.), *Shūzo Kuki and Jean-Paul Sartre: Influence and Counter-influence in the Early History of Existential Phenomenology*, 43–50 (Carbondale: Southern Illinois University Press, 1987), at 45–6.
86   Heidegger, *Being and Time*, 27, 46–58.
87   Heidegger, *Poetry, Language and Thought*, 163–87; Martin Heidegger, *On Time and Being*, trans. Joan Stambaugh (New York: Harper and Row, 1972), 15.
88   Martin Heidegger, *Concept of Time*, trans. William McNeill (London: Blackwell, 1992), 18E.
89   Martin Heidegger, *The Question Concerning Technology and Other Essays*, trans. William Lovett (New York: Harper Collins, 1977), 15–19, 130–2. William Lovitt explains: "The noun *Vernehmer* is related to the verb *vernehmen* (to hear, to perceive, to understand). *Vernehmen* speaks of an immediate receiving in contrast to the setting-forth (*vor-stellen*) that arrests and objectifies." Ibid., 131.
90   Goulding, "New Ways toward Sino-Western," 100.

91 F.W.J. Schelling, "On the Nature of Philosophy as Science," in Rüdiger Bubner (ed.), *German Idealist Philosophy*, 209–53 (London: Penguin, 1997), at 210. Although Heidegger does not address ἀσύστατον directly, he would be fascinated by Schelling's response to the metaphysical "system." Heidegger's *Fug* as "jointure" or "enjoining" might find sympathy from Schelling's thought-provoking reversals. Heidegger lectures on Schelling's system in the 1936 summer semester. See Martin Heidegger, *Schelling: Vom Wesen der menschlichen Freiheit* [GA 42], ed. Ingrid Schüssler (Frankfurt: Vittorio Klostermann, 1988), 86. Joan Stambaugh translates: "We can already see here the sameness of Being and jointure shining through. Insofar as we understand 'Being' at all, we mean something like jointure and joining. The oldest saying of Western philosophy handed down to us, that of Anaximander, already speaks of *dike* [Δίκη, *Fug*] and *adikia* [Ἀδικία, *Unfug*], of the jointure and disjointure of Being." See Heidegger, *Schelling's Treatise*, 50. In 1936, Heidegger explains: "*Hier liegen die Blöcke eines Steinbruchs, in dem Urgestein gebrochen wird* [here the blocks of a quarry lie, in which the primordial stone is broken]." Heidegger, *Beiträge zur Philosophie* [GA 65], 421 and 509. These blocks—yet to be excavated—include thinking (*Das Denken*), history (*Die Geschichte*), Dasein, and the essential holding sway or prevailing of Being (*Die Wesung des Seyns*).
92 Schelling, "On the Nature of Philosophy as Science," 228.
93 Ibid., 229.
94 Heidegger, *Being and Time*, 377–9.
95 Jay Goulding, "Kuki Shūzo and Martin Heidegger: Iki (いき) and Hermeneutic Phenomenology," in Joseph F. Kess and Helen Lansdowne (eds.), *Why Japan Matters!*, volume 2, 677–90 (Victoria: Centre for Asia Pacific-Initiatives, University of Victoria, 2005), at 682.
96 In respect to Hölderlin, Heidegger observes: "The rambling journey goes from the Indus, that is from the East, across Greece, here to the upper Donau to the West. The Danube is now actually streaming in exactly the opposite direction. So, if the river itself were and should be the wandering from the land of morning (the East) to the land of evening (the West), and were able to be this, then the Ister would have to run counter to its own actual current." Martin Heidegger, *Hölderlins Hymne Der Ister* [GA 53], ed. Walter Biemel (Frankfurt: Klostermann, 1984), 42.
97 Martin Heidegger, *Heraklit* [GA 55], ed. Manfred S. Frings (Frankfurt: Vittorio Klostermann, 1979), 58–9.
98 See Goulding, "Japan-West Interculture," 11.
99 See Kuang-Ming Wu, *Chinese Body Thinking* (Leiden: Brill, 1997). See Jay Goulding, "Wu Kuang-Ming's *Chinese Body Thinking*: A Cultural Hermeneutic," *Dao: A Journal of Comparative Philosophy*, 2.2 (2003): 350–3. See Jay Goulding, "Wu Kuang-Ming's *China Wisdom Alive: Vignettes of Life-Thinking*; *Story-Thinking: Cultural Meditations*; *Nonsense: Cultural Meditations on the Beyond*," *Journal of Chinese Philosophy*, 40.2 (2013): 355–9.
100 Heidegger, *Being and Time*, 343. Cf. Martin Heidegger, *Sein und Zeit* [GA 2], ed. Friedrich-Wilhelm von Herrmann (Frankfurt: Vittorio Klostermann, 1977), 297.
101 Goulding, "Cheng and Gadamer," 368–382.
102 Goulding, "Japan-West Interculture," 19. See Goulding, "Kuki Shūzo and Martin Heidegger," 688–9.
103 Markus Gabriel, *Transcendental Ontology: Essays in German Idealism* (New York: Continuum, 2011), 73.
104 Heidegger, *Unterwegs zur Sprache*, 187; Heidegger, *On the Way to Language*, 92.

105 F.W.J. Schelling, *The Grounding of Positive Philosophy*, trans. Bruce Matthews (Albany: State University of New York Press, 2007), 157.

106 Martin Heidegger, *Hölderlins Hymnen "Germanien" und "Der Rhein"* [GA 39], ed. Susanne Ziegler (Frankfurt: Vittorio Klostermann, 1980), 226.

107 Goulding, "Cheng and Gadamer," 368–382.

108 Goulding, "Visceral Manifestation," 384–385.

109 "Concurrently through Gadamer, I take up Heidegger's fascination with a 'stratum' (*Schicht*, layer) of 'subterranean philosophizing in antiquity' (*unterirdischen antiken philosophierens*) … Given Friedrich Wilhelm Schelling's … mystical influence upon Heidegger, I suggest that the term 'subterranean' might ultimately enter the Heidegger vocabulary through him. In respect to Greco-Roman mythology, Schelling is fond of the expression as in '*unterirdische Gott*' (subterranean god), '*unterirdische Feuer*' (subterranean fire), '*unterirdischen Kammern*' (subterranean store-rooms of Mycenae), '*unterirdischen Grottwerke*' (subterranean grotto works and labyrinth of Daedelus' Crete) and '*unterirdischen Gemächern*' (subterranean chambers as catacombs) to name a few … Going where Plato could not, Heidegger's book entitled *Parmenides* is itself a *subterranean philosophy*—a descent into the Underworld. Since Cumae is the first Greek settlement in Italy dating from eighth century BCE, and Parmenides resides within travelling distance, we might extend [Alexander G.] McKay's intriguing question regarding Vergil's adventures: did Parmenides visit the *actual* Underworld? Heidegger fashions Parmenides *himself* as travelling with a team of steeds to the home of Ἀλήθεια in the House of Night (δώματα Νυκτός, *das Haus der Nacht*) and out into the light, where accompanied by the Sun-maids (Ἡλιάδες κοῦραι, *Sonnenmädchen*), he gazes upon the Gate or Portal (πύλαι, *das Tor*) of the Way of Night and Day (Νυκτός τε καὶ Ἥματός εἰσι κελεύθων, *der Wege der Nacht und des Tages*) … If Ἀλήθεια (*Aletheia*) *is* the Cumaean Sibyl (devotee of Apollo) and Hades *is* the House of Night, then Vergil and Parmenides in their respective times might *physically* pass through the Gates of Hell (Gates of Night and Day) by entering the Oracle of the Great Antrum at the Bay of Baiae. This re-enforces Heidegger's judgment on Ἀλήθεια not as simply 'truth' but as un-concealment. Heidegger writes [in *Parmenides*]: 'The Iliad, XXIII, 244, speaks of Ἄϊδι κεύθωμαι, being ensconced [*geborgenwerden*, secretly hidden] in Hades. Here the earth itself and the subterranean [*das Untererdige*] come into relation with sheltering and concealing … The earth is the in-between, namely between the concealment of the subterranean and the luminosity, the disclosiveness, of the supraterranean (the span of heaven, οὐρανός).' … Perhaps stimulated by the presence of Hsiao, Heidegger's seemingly Yin-Yang polarity of the in-between resonates with chapter 5 of the *Daodejing*. Is not the hollow (the in-between Void) of heaven and earth (*tiandi zhijian* 天地之間) like the bellows (*tuo yue* 橐籥)? When empty, they do not yield (*xu er buqu* 虛而不屈) and when full they move out more air (*dong er yu chu* 動而愈出). Not as good as guarding the middle (*buru shou zhong* 不如守中)." See Goulding, "Cheng and Gadamer," 368–382.

110 Walter Biemel and Hans Saner (eds.), *Martin Heidegger/Karl Jaspers: Briefwechsel 1920–1963* (Frankfurt: Vittorio Klostermann, 1990), 178. Cf. Walter Biemel and Hans Saner (eds.), *Heidegger-Jaspers Correspondence, 1920–1963*, trans. Gary Aylesworth (New York: Humanities Press, 2003), 170. Hsiao teaches Chinese language and philosophy at Freiburg between 1955 and 1969.

111 Biemel and Saner, *Heidegger/Jaspers Briefwechsel*, 180; Cf. Biemel and Saner, *Heidegger-Jaspers Correspondence*, 172.

112 Schelling writes: "die stille, nach der Tiefe dringende Gelassenheit des Geistes [(the still, the silent), according to the deeply penetrating releasement of the spirit]." Schelling, *Sämmtliche Werke*, I.7, 62. As I suggest: "Similar to the Daoists, Heidegger's idea of *Gelassenheit* (letting-be) 'resonates' with *wuwei* 無爲 (do by not doing) insofar as it offers an opening for other beings through one's actions. A pot must be shaped in accord to what it will hold by being attentive to its hollow space." Jay Goulding, "Katrin Froese's *Nietzsche, Heidegger, and Daoist Thought: Crossing Paths In-Between*," *Journal of Chinese Philosophy*, 38.4 (2011): 670. Heidegger's *Gelassenheit* is letting things be in their releasement to the mystery. With *kudos* to Schelling, Bret W. Davis says: "Schelling's intimations ... of an originary letting-operate, and of a freedom of 'willing nothing' as the proper end of—or as the recovery from—all willing, were among the influential provocations behind Heidegger's own attempt to think a non-willing freedom of *Seinlassen* [letting-be] and *Gelassenheit* [releasement] ... Human freedom must be rethought, according to Heidegger, from within the clearing of being as *das Freie*. Human freedom is an ecstatic engagement in this clearing, this *Da* of *Sein* that lets beings be (see GA 9: 188). Human freedom is most properly an engaged *Gelassenheit* that corresponds to the *Seinlassen* of being." Bret W. Davis, *Heidegger and the Will: On the Way to Gelassenheit* (Evanston: Northwestern University Press, 2007), 120–1. Joan Stambaugh writes: "Thus, to sense, or, in Heidegger's special use of the term, to think, means precisely to be on the way. In answer to our previous question whether the fact that the way was a way of thinking meant that the way was something produced by us, and thus totally subjective, we can now say that thinking, sensing, being on the way is about as far removed from subjectivity as you can get. The change from all subjectivistic reifying representational thinking to the kind of thinking or sensing Heidegger is trying to convey occurs through releasement (*Gelassenheit*). The Taoist equivalent for releasement is, of course, *wu wei* (at times perhaps best rendered as 'non-interference'). Now, *Gelassenheit*, or releasement, is, of course, not a term originating with Heidegger, but is, for example, a central term in Meister Eckhart. It even has a kind of precursor in the Stoic conception of *apatheia* [ἀπάθεια], a term designating freedom from strong and turbulent emotions." Joan Stambaugh, "Heidegger, Taoism, and the Question of Metaphysics," in Graham Parkes (ed.), *Heidegger and Asian Thought*, 79–92 (Honolulu: University of Hawaii Press, 1987), at 85. In translating Zhuangzi's chapter 11, Hyun Höchsmann and Guorong Yang write: "Heidegger also affirmed that 'the essence of truth is freedom' and that 'freedom discloses itself as the letting be of beings.'" [Martin Heidegger, *Basic Writings*, ed. David F. Krell (London: Harper Perennial, 1993), 127]. Hyun Höchsmann and Guorong Yang, trans., *Zhuangzi* (New York: Pearson, 2007), 146.

113 Jason M. Wirth, *The Conspiracy of Life: Meditations on Schelling and His Time* (Albany: State University of New York Press, 2003), 62.

114 Saitya Brata Das, *The Political Theology of Schelling* (Edinburgh: Edinburgh University Press, 2016), 4.

115 Ibid., 160.

116 Heidegger, *Schelling's Treatise*, 117.

117 Martin Heidegger, *Parmenides*, trans. Andre Schuwer and Richard Rojcewicz (Bloomington: Indiana University Press, 1992), 149.

118 Martin Heidegger, *What Is Called Thinking*, trans. Fred D. Wieck and J. Glenn Gray (New York: Harper and Row, 1968), 240. Heidegger translates Parmenides'

Fragment 5: "The same, namely, is Apprehension [Apperception, Proception] (Thinking), as well as Being." Martin Heidegger, *Identität und Differenz* [GA 11], ed. Friedrich-Wilhelm von Herrmann (Frankfurt: Vittorio Klostermann, 2006), 36. Cf. Heidegger, "For the Same Perceiving (thinking) as Well as Being," in Martin Heidegger, *Identity and Difference*, trans. Joan Stambaugh (New York: Harper and Row, 1969), 27.

119   Heidegger writes: "Νοεῖν governs an Ap-perception (Ap-prehension, Proception) which never was nor is a mere accepting of something. The νοεῖν per-ceives beforehand by taking care (heed). Care is the watchtower, safeguarding what lies before us, though this custody itself needs that safekeeping which is carried out in the λέγειν as gathering. Νόος and νοῦς therefore, do not originally signify what later emerges as Reason. Νόος signifies the minding that has something in mind and takes it to heart. Thus, νοεῖν also means what we understand as scent and the scenting—though we use the word mostly of beasts in the wild. Humanity's scenting is divination (prophecy, foretelling)." Martin Heidegger, *Was Heisst Denken?* [GA 8], ed. Paola-Ludovika Coriando (Frankfurt: Vittorio Klostermann, 2002), 210. In *The Beginning of Western Philosophy: Interpretation of Anaximander and Parmenides* (1934), Heidegger illustrates Parmenides' fragment 5 while further unpacking νοεῖν as: "'Ap-prehend' [*Vernehmen*] is supposed to render the Greek word νοεῖν, which means to take into *sight*, specifically: a) to look at and to *take away* what is looked at; b) *to take* into sight, to look something over, take it in, consider it, *take it into consideration* ... ap-prehension (a taking up that takes away), rendered as *understanding*." Martin Heidegger, *The Beginning of Western Philosophy: Interpretation of Anaximander and Parmenides*, trans. Richard Rojcewicz (Bloomington: Indiana University Press, 2015), 89. Cf. Martin Heidegger, *Der Anfang der abendländischen Philosophie Auslegung des Anaximander und Parmenides* [GA 35], ed. Peter Trawny (Frankfurt: Vittorio Klostermann, 2012), 117.

120   Kurt von Fritz, writes: "There are, as far as I can see, only two etymologies of the word [νοεῖν] which deserve serious consideration—one from νεύειν, 'to nod' (Lat. nuere; Ger. nicken); the other from a root *snu*, 'to sniff' (MHG snöuwen; Ger. schnuppern, schnüffeln), which pre-supposes, of course, that the original form of νόος was σνόϝος [*snówos*]. The connection between the noun and the original verb ... might be found in a comparison of those many passages in which Zeus expresses his will by a nod ... an animal raises its head with a jerk when it senses or 'smells' danger, there is just a faint possibility that the roots of the words for 'to nod' and for 'to sniff' were originally identical." Kurt von Fritz, "ΝΟΟΣ and Noein in the Homeric Poems," *Classical Philology*, 38.2 (1943): 79–93, at 92–3.

121   Heidegger, *Parmenides*, 89–90.
122   Goulding, "Cheng and Gadamer," 368–382.
123   Paul Wheatley, *The Pivot of the Four Quarters: A Preliminary Enquiry into the Origins and Character of the Ancient Chinese City* (Edinburgh: Edinburgh University Press, 1971), 450.
124   Heidegger, *Contributions to Philosophy*, 358. Cf. Heidegger, *Beiträge zur Philosophie* [GA 65], 510. Cf. Schelling, *Sämmtliche Werke*, I.6, 454 and I.4, 17. Schelling addresses the Daoist divination text *Yijing* in *Sämmtliche Werke*, II.2, 537. Similar to Heidegger, Schelling's *Streit* (strife) assumes cosmic and cataclysmic meaning. Chung-Ying Cheng writes: "There is, of course, no inconsistency between Heideggerian temporality and the primary ontological 'time as timing' in the *I Ching*

[*Yijing*]. Heideggerian temporality reflects the movement of time inside the Being of Dasein, which in a primary ontological perspective reveals the fundamental time as timing. Or to use a later Heideggerian expression, temporality reveals time as a feature of fundamental Being, hence it transcends the finitude of Dasein and encloses both Dasein and the Void as parts of its comprehensive movement. This aspect of time is called 'transformation' (*hua* [化]) in the *I Ching* and 'appropriation' (*Ereignis*) in the later Heidegger." Chung-Ying Cheng, "Confucius, Heidegger, and the Philosophy of the *I Ching*: A Comparative Inquiry into the Truth of Human Being," *Philosophy East and West*, 37.1 (1987): 51–70, at 62.

125 Heidegger is influenced by Schelling's "auf dem Sprung in das Seyn" as a "leaping toward Being." See Heidegger, *Beiträge zur Philosophie* [GA 65], 7. Cf. Heidegger, *Contributions to Philosophy*, 6.

126 See Graham Harman, *Heidegger Explained: From Phenomenon to Thing* (Chicago: Open Court, 2006), 119–20.

127 Heidegger, *Schelling's Treatise*, 161. Cf. Heidegger, *Schelling: Vom Wesen der menschlichen Freiheit*, 279.

128 With Cary J. Nederman of the Department of Political Science at Texas A and M, I inaugurate a field of "Comparative Political Thought" with chapters for *New Dictionary of the History of Ideas*, editor-in-chief Maryanne Cline Horowitz (New York: Charles Scribner's Sons, 2005): "Barbarism and Civilization," volume 1, 195–7; "Globalization: Asia," volume 3, 941–7; "Religion: East and Southeast Asia," volume 5, 2060–4; "Society," volume 5, 2238–41; and "Zen," volume 6, 2513–14.

129 Heidegger, *Parmenides*, 35–48.

130 Heidegger, *Being and Time*, 76–7.

131 Heidegger, *Contributions to Philosophy*, 48–50, and 75–114.

132 Parvis Emad, "The Echo of Being in *Beiträge zur Philosophie—Der Anklang*: Directives for its Interpretation," *Heidegger Studies*, 7 (1991): 15–35, at 35.

133 Heidegger, *Beiträge zur Philosophie* [GA 65], 107.

134 Heidegger, *On Time and Being*, 65. Cf. Heidegger, *Zur Sache des Denkens*, 81.

135 Martin Heidegger, *The Essence of Truth: On Plato's Cave Allegory and Theaetetus*, trans. Ted Sadler (London: Continuum, 2002), 40–1. Cf. Martin Heidegger, *Vom Wesen der Wahrheit: Zu Platons Höhlengleichnis und Theatet* [GA 34], ed. Hermann Mörchen (Frankfurt: Vittorio Klostermann, 1988), 54–5.

136 Eva Wong, *Lieh-tzu: a Taoist Guide to Practical Living* (Boston: Shambhalah Publications, 1995), 5. Liezi utilizes *xiang* 響 for echo as in *huixiang* 迴響 (reverberate, ring). In chapter 2, Zhuangzi says: "(Thus) the mutual depending of those changing sounds is like they are not mutual depending at all; (rather), Harmonizing them with heavenly equality, following-on them with their own flows which spread-far-and-wide—This is that with which to live to the end of our years of life." Wu, *Butterfly as Companion*, 152. Wu comments: "*Hua sheng* [化聲] is 'changing voices,' perhaps referring to earthly and human pipings … The heavenly piping is now seen to be the echoes of changes (*hua sheng* 化聲) in which we dwell and are. To be awakened to this fact is self-lessly to overhear the heavenly piping." Wu, *Butterfly as Companion*, 169, 216. Zhuangzi's piping is unique in that a sound "as invisible as nothing" is inspired by an invisible breath of wind: "Furthermore, piping can mean echo and resonance, sounding back and forth that is as individual as it is mutual … All of these are symbolic of heavenly piping, that mysterious dark power of enablement that is itself a non-being." Wu, *Butterfly Companion*, 188. In chapter 33, Zhuangzi employs the echo: "The Barrier Keeper Yin said, 'When a

man does not dwell in self, then things will of themselves reveal their forms to him. His movement is like that of water, his stillness like that of a mirror, his responses like those of an echo. Blank eyed, he seems to be lost; motionless, he has the limpidity of water. Because he is one with it, he achieves harmony; should he reach out for it, he would lose it. Never does he go ahead of other men, but always follows in their wake.'" Burton Watson, trans. *The Complete Works of Zhuangzi* (New York: Columbia University Press, 2013), 295.

137 Jay Goulding, "Cheng and Gadamer," 368–382.

138 Martin Heidegger, *Hölderlin's Hymns "Germania" and "The Rhine,"* trans. William McNeill and Julia Ireland (Bloomington: Indiana University Press, 2014), 206.

139 Heidegger writes: "'Staying away' as (hesitating) self-refusal of ground is essential swaying of ground as ab-ground. Ground needs ab-ground. And the lightening [*das Lichten*] that occurs in self-refusing is not a mere gaping and yawning open (χάος vis-à-vis φύσις) but the tuning enjoining [*stimmende Erfügen*] of the essential *displacings* of merely *what* is lit up, which lets self-sheltering enter into it." Heidegger, *Contributions to Philosophy*, 266; Cf. Heidegger, *Beiträge zur Philosophie* [GA 65], 381.

140 See the opening pages of Part 2 (i.e., "Dialogue") of Graham Parkes' chapter in this volume.

141 Parkes suggests: "The fragments concerning the cyclical transformations of the cosmic elements have obvious counterparts in Taoist cosmology, and Heraclitus' understanding of the mutual interdependence of opposites and the relativity of all perspectives harmonizes closely with the thought of Chuang-tzu. A thorough comparison would examine the deeper implications of such comparable utterances as the following (the numbers of Heraclitus' fragments are preceded by H, and the chapters of Chuang-tzu and Lao-tzu by C and L respectively): H50, C1; H102, C2; H111, L2; H88, C6; H61, C18; H103, C17/27; H40, L81; L40." See note 13 of Graham Parkes' chapter in this volume. On cosmic elements, see Goulding, "Cheng and Gadamer," forthcoming, 368–82.

142 See p. 12 of Graham Parkes' chapter in this volume.

143 Heidegger, *Heraklit*, 142. Cf. "Inconspicuous jointure, more precious than the conjoined that insistently pushes toward appearance." Martin Heidegger, *Heraclitus, The Inception of Occidental Thinking Logic; Heraclitus's Doctrine of the Logos*, trans. Julia Goesser Assaiante and S. Montgomery Ewegen (London: Bloomsbury Academic, 2018), 108.

144 Ibid., 23. Cf. Heidegger, *Heraklit*, 28.

145 Ibid., 141.

146 Henry George Liddell and Robert Scott, *Greek-English Lexicon* (Oxford: Clarendon Press, 1996), 244.

147 "Whenever injustice prevails, Heidegger says, then 'there is something not right with things. This means, something is out of joint.' He plays here on two words '*die Fuge*' and '*der Fug*,' which sound very similar, but have quite different meanings. '*Die Fuge*' means joint; '*der Fug*' means order. Heidegger wishes to show that the situation of injustice, which he describes using the idiom 'something is out of joint,' corresponds to the state of disorder." W. Julian Korab-Karpowicz, *Presocratics in the Thought of Martin Heidegger* (Frankfurt: Peter Lang, 2016), 92.

148 "Im griechischen ist aber auch stets der Anklang an das σοφόν, das bedeutet leuchtend—offenbar—hell." Heidegger, *Heraklit*, 247.

149 "All are mutually conditioning elements that have unity through diversity. They are co-constitutive, co-resonating, and equiprimordial. As co-constitutive, not

one is acceptable without the other; they stand together in a web of experiences. As co-resonating, one points to the next and the next points to another. As equiprimordial, it does not matter where one begins; all three positions cross paths through the flux of East–West experiences." Goulding, "News Ways Towards Sino-Western," 100.

150 Otto Pöggeler, "West-East Dialogue: Heidegger and Lao-tzu," in Graham Parkes (ed.), *Heidegger and Asian Thought*, 47–78 (Honolulu: University of Hawaii Press, 1987), at 55–6. Heidegger's *aufgehende Walten* recalls Schelling's 1809 *nie aufgehende Rest* (never emerging remnant, remains or relic), the lingering non-Being of Being from the outbound preceding primordial darkness (*vorausgehende Dunkel*)—a harbinger of the 1842 Dao lectures. Schelling, *Sämmtliche Werke*, I.7, 360.

151 Heidegger, *Heraklit* [GA 55], 375. Heidegger appends τοῦ Λόγου to fragment 112 to parallel fragment 50, Ibid., 376. Assaiante and Ewegen translate fragment 50: "οὐκ ἐμοῦ, ἀλλὰ λόγου ἀκούσαντας ὁμολογεῖν σοφόν ἐστιν ἓν πάντα εἶναι. If you have not listened merely to me, but have listened compliantly to the Λόγος (i.e., the originary forgathering), then the essential [authentic] knowledge that subsists therein is (while gathered in itself) to gather the presencing of what, as the sole-One, unites all (i.e., the presence of the originary forgathering)." Heidegger, *Heraclitus*, 280. In 1951, Heidegger translates Fragment 50 as such: "Hearken (attune) not to me but to the Laying that gathers: let the Same lie: the fateful essentially holds sway (*west*) (the Laying gathers): One is All." Martin Heidegger, *Vorträge und Aufsätze* [GA 7], ed. Friedrich-Wilhelm von Herrmann (Frankfurt: Vittorio Klostermann, 2000), 231.

152 Assaiante and Ewegen translate: "Reflective thinking is (the) nobility, because knowing is to gather the unconcealed (from out of concealment into unconcealment) in the manner of bringing-forth into the set-forth and set-up in view of emerging (and all this, nevertheless) within the drawing-out drawing-in relation toward the originary foregathering." Heidegger, *Heraclitus*, 279.

153 See Martin Buber, *Reden und Gleichnisse des Tschuang-tse* (Zürich: Manesse Verlag, 1951), 140–1. Heidegger quotes from Buber's version of chapter 17 at Bremen thirty years prior.

154 Buber translators render *ju* 鐻 either "The Chimepost" [Jonathan R. Herman, *I and Tao: Martin Buber's Encounter with Chuang Tzu* (Albany: State University of New York Press, 1996), 59] or "The Stand for Chimes" (Martin Buber, *Chinese Tales: Zhuangzi, Sayings and Parables and Chinese Ghost and Love Stories*, trans. Alex Page (London: Humanities Press International, 1991), 67). As an astute observation, David Chai remarks: "The character *zhai* 齋 appears in the story of bellstand maker Qing but without the *xin* 心 element, thereby changing the meaning from 'composing the heart-mind' to 'composing the self.' The text reads: 'When I am preparing to make a bell stand, I do not let it wear out my energy [*qi* 氣] but compose myself in order to still my heart-mind.'" David Chai, *Zhuangzi and the Becoming of Nothingness* (Albany: State University of New York Press, 2019), 189.

155 Martin Heidegger, *Zum Wesen der Sprache; Zur Frage nach Der Kunst* [GA 74], ed. Thomas Regehly (Frankfurt: Vittorio Klostermann, 2010), 185. In reference to Heraclitus' Fragment 50, Heidegger explains *Gewese*: "λέγειν is to speak—not from speaking out loud, but from the corresponding gathering of the primordially open assembly; from the relation to the presencing of the present—(hither from the still unthought and primordially unthinkable care). The collected presence—as the gathering of the pre-sences." Ibid., 170.

156 Ibid., 186.
157 Heidegger, *Zum Wesen der Sprache*, 187.
158 Joseph Needham characterizes Chinese cosmology as "this Web woven by no weaver." See Joseph Needham, *Science and Civilization in China* (Cambridge: Cambridge University Press, 1956), volume 2, 556. Heaven's "net" or "web" or "net of nature" (*tian wang* 天網) from Laozi's chapter 73 refers to the endless crisscross of cosmic and worldly action and non-action. See Chang, *Tao: A New Way of Thinking*, 179.
159 Wu, *Butterfly as Companion*, 306.
160 Ibid., 392.
161 Ibid., 263.
162 Inwood, *Heidegger Dictionary*, 155. Heidegger writes: "Das feststellende Erklären des Vergangenen aus dem Gesichtskreis der berechnenden Betreibungen der Gegenwart [The ascertaining (scientific) explanation of the past within the horizon of the calculating activities of the present]." Heidegger, *Beiträge zur Philosophie* [GA 65], 493.
163 Heidegger, *Being and Time*, 376. Cf. Heidegger, *Sein und Zeit*, 434.
164 Goulding, "Japan-West Interculture," 15. I suggest: "A page of writing is not spatial but temporal, unfolding time as you read. The Western world thinks of vanishing into nothing and appearing into things; the Chinese world vanishes into things. As *xuanxue* 玄學 (studies of the dark or mysterious), Dao 道 is not about getting the meaning; it is about getting rid of the meaning; it is not about remembering; it is about forgetting … The Daoist sage disappears into the midst of time's passing while vanishing into things around him … the pivotal Zhuangzi commentator Guo Xiang's (252–312 CE) term *ming* 冥, meaning 'to vanish into' rather than the conventional 'dark, obscure, distant, or hard to see' … The character *ming* 冥 is composed of several radicals: *mi* 冖 (a cover), *ri* 日 (the sun), and *liu* 六 (six). Collectively, the sun recedes under cover into the six hours of night's darkness. Although *ming* as 'vanishing' does not encompass the word 'thing,' the etymological aspect of its character is also worth inspecting. 'Thing' is *wu* 物, composed of these radicals: 牛 *niu* (ox) and *wu* 勿 (do not, without), the latter broken originally into *dao* 刀 (knife) with *pie* 丿 (drops of blood). Together, the undoing of the ox is the cutting away into nothing. The ox which is everything of usefulness in classical China becomes nothing. The character's etymology is key to Zhuangzi's story. For nineteen years, Cook Ding carves the oxen yet rarely sharpens his knife because he reaches the hollows at the center of things, and the animals falls away into naturally constitutive parts. The thing things and un-things itself, such as it is. The knife moves him to the self-so. Like the sage, Cook Ding and his knife follow the endless Dao pivot (*dao shu* 道樞)." Jay Goulding, "Barry Allen's *Vanishing into Things: Knowledge in Chinese Tradition*," *Journal of Chinese Philosophy*, 44.1–2 (2018): 113–16, at 113–14. The world dimming down, diminishing, and disappearing into nothing is captured by Heidegger's description of the woman's old shoes.
165 Goulding, "Visceral Manifestation," 394–5. I write: "The entire cosmogony of Chinese life from Heaven to Earth, from city to country, from society to the individual is connected through meridians of vapor that 'manifest' through writing. The ancient Chinese 'icon' (*xiang* 象) as an 'imaging,' 'figuring' or 'shaping' finds life in a type of visceral iconography (*zang xiang* 藏象). Nathan Sivin explains: 'orbisiconography,' is not the counterpart of Western anatomy

but its antithesis. Anatomy is concerned with the organism as a structure of parts, and orbisiconography (*tsang-hsiang* [藏象]) with the dynamic interplay of what is best described as a number of functional systems. Any normal Chinese-English dictionary, for instance, will define *kan* [肝] simply as 'liver.' In medicine (as opposed to, say, cooking) this word seldom refers to the physical organ, but rather to the energetic sphere ('orb') which the organ serves as a material substratum." Goulding, "Kuang-Ming Wu and Maurice Merleau-Ponty," 190–1.

166 Reinhard May, *Heidegger's Hidden Sources: East Asian Influences on His Work*, trans. Graham Parkes (London: Routledge, 1996), 3–4.

167 Jay Goulding, "Rudolf G. Wagner's The Craft of a Chinese Commentator: Wang Bi on the Laozi; A Chinese Reading of the Daodejing: Wang Bi's Commentary on the Laozi with Critical Text and Translation; Language, Ontology, and Political Philosophy in China: Wang Bi's Scholarly Exploration of the Dark," *China Review International*, 14.1 (2007): 61–7, at 63.

168 John Sallis, *Echoes: After Heidegger* (Bloomington: Indiana University Press, 1990), 13.

169 William J. Richardson, *Through Phenomenology to Thought* (New York: Fordham University Press, 2003), 64.

170 Heidegger, *Being and Time*, 176. Cf. Heidegger, *Sein und Zeit*, 183.

References

Abel-Rémusat, Jean-Pierre. *Mémoire sur la Vie et les Opinions de Lao-Tseu*. Paris: De L'imprimerie Royale, 1823.

Beach, Edward Allen. *The Potencies of God(s): Schelling's Philosophy of Mythology*. Albany: State University of New York Press, 1994.

Biemel, Walter and Hans Saner, eds. *Martin Heidegger/Karl Jaspers: Briefwechsel 1920–1963*. Frankfurt: Vittorio Klostermann, 1990.

Biemel, Walter and Hans Saner, eds. *Heidegger-Jaspers Correspondence, 1920–1963*. Translated by Gary Aylesworth. New York: Humanities Press, 2003.

Buber, Martin. *Reden und Gleichnisse des Tschuang-tse*. Zürich: Manesse Verlag, 1951.

Buber, Martin. *Chinese Tales: Zhuangzi, Sayings and Parables and Chinese Ghost and Love Stories*. Translated by Alex Page. London: Humanities Press International, 1991.

Buber, Martin. *Werkausgabe 2.3, Schriften zur chinesischen Philosophie und Literatur*. Edited by Irene Eber. München: Gütersloher Verlagshaus in der Verlagsgruppe Random House, 2013.

Chai, David. *Zhuangzi and the Becoming of Nothingness*. Albany: State University of New York Press, 2019.

Chang, Chung-Yuan. *Tao: A New Way of Thinking*. New York: Harper and Row, 1975.

Cheng, Chung-Ying. "Confucius, Heidegger, and the Philosophy of the *I Ching*: A Comparative Inquiry into the Truth of Human Being." *Philosophy East and West*, 37.1 (1987): 51–70.

Das, Saitya Brata. *The Political Theology of Schelling*. Edinburgh: Edinburgh University Press, 2016.

Davis, Bret. W. *Heidegger and the Will: On the Way to Gelassenheit*. Evanston: Northwestern University Press, 2007.

Elberfeld, Rolf. "Heidegger und das ostasiatische Denken: Annäherungen zwischen fremden Welten." In Dieter Thomä (ed.), *Heidegger-Handbuch: Leben-Werk-Wirkung*, 469–74. Stuttgart: Metzler, 2003.

Emad, Parvis. "The Echo of Being in *Beiträge zur Philosophie—Der Anklang*: Directives for Its Interpretation." *Heidegger Studies*, 7 (1991): 15–35.

Frantz, Gustav A.C. *Schelling's Positive Philosophie, nach ihrem Inhalt, wie nach ihrer Bedeutung fur den allgemeinen Umschwung der bis jetzt noch herrschenden Denkweise*. Cöthen: P. Schettler, 1880.

Fritz, Kurt von. "ΝΟΟΣ and Noein in the Homeric Poems." *Classical Philology*, 38.2 (1943): 79–93.

Gabriel, Markus. *Transcendental Ontology: Essays in German Idealism*. New York: Continuum, 2011.

Goulding, Jay. "'Visceral Manifestation 藏象:' Chinese Philosophy and Western Phenomenology." In Fang Keli 方克立 (ed.), *Chinese Philosophy and the Trends of the 21st Century Civilization* 中国哲學和二十一世紀文明走向, volume 4, 360–417. Beijing: Commercial Press Inc., 2003.

Goulding, Jay. "Wu Kuang-Ming's *Chinese Body Thinking*: A Cultural Hermeneutic." *Dao: A Journal of Comparative Philosophy*, 2.2 (2003): 350–3.

Goulding, Jay. "Xiong Wei 熊偉: Chinese Philosophy and Hermeneutic Phenomenology." *Gate of Philosophy: Beijing University's Journal of Philosophy*, 5 (2004): 116–30.

Goulding, Jay. "Barbarism and Civilization." In Maryanne Cline Horowitz (editor-in-chief), *New Dictionary of the History of Ideas*, volume 1, 195–7. New York: Charles Scribner's Sons, 2005.

Goulding, Jay. "Franklin Perkins' *Leibniz and China: A Commerce of Light*." *Dao: A Journal of Comparative Philosophy*, 5.1 (2005): 183–7.

Goulding, Jay. "Globalization: Asia." In Maryanne Cline Horowitz (editor-in-chief), *New Dictionary of the History of Ideas*, volume 3, 941–7. New York: Charles Scribner's Sons, 2005.

Goulding, Jay. "Kuki Shūzo and Martin Heidegger: Iki and Hermeneutic Phenomenology." In Joseph F. Kess and Helen Lansdowne (eds.), *Why Japan Matters!*, volume 2, 677–90. Victoria: Centre for Asia Pacific-Initiatives, University of Victoria, 2005.

Goulding, Jay. "Religion: East and Southeast Asia." In Maryanne Cline Horowitz (editor-in-chief), *New Dictionary of the History of Ideas*, volume 5, 2060–4. New York: Charles Scribner's Sons, 2005.

Goulding, Jay. "Rorty, Heidegger, Cheng: Pragmatism, Phenomenology, Onto-Cosmology." In Pan Derong (ed.), *Ontology and Interpretation: A Special Collection of Treatises Honoring Cheng Chung-Ying's 70th Birthday*, 263–97. Shanghai: Shanghai Academy of Social Sciences Press, 2005.

Goulding, Jay. "Society." In Maryanne Cline Horowitz (editor-in-chief), *New Dictionary of the History of Ideas*, volume 5, 2238–41. New York: Charles Scribner's Sons, 2005.

Goulding, Jay. "Zen." In Maryanne Cline Horowitz (editor-in-chief), *New Dictionary of the History of Ideas*, volume 6, 2513–14. New York: Charles Scribner's Sons, 2005.

Goulding, Jay. "New Ways Toward Sino-Western Philosophical Dialogues." *Journal of Chinese Philosophy*, 34.1 (2007): 99–125.

Goulding, Jay. "Rudolf G. Wagner's *The Craft of a Chinese Commentator: Wang Bi on the Laozi*; *A Chinese Reading of the Daodejing: Wang Bi's Commentary on the Laozi with Critical Text and Translation*; *Language, Ontology, and Political Philosophy in China: Wang Bi's Scholarly Exploration of the Dark*." *China Review International*, 14.1 (2007): 61–7.

Goulding, Jay. "Cheng Chung-Ying's Onto-Cosmology: Chinese Philosophy and Hermeneutic Phenomenology." In On-cho Ng (ed.), *The Imperative of Understanding: Chinese Philosophy, Comparative Philosophy, and Onto-Hermeneutics: A Tribute Volume Dedicated to Professor Chung-Ying Cheng*, 135–55. New York: Global Scholarly Publications, 2008.

Goulding, Jay. "Wu Kuang-Ming and Maurice Merleau-Ponty: Daoism and Phenomenology." In Jay Goulding (ed.), Jay *China-West Interculture, Toward the Philosophy of World Integration: Essays on Wu Kuang-Ming's Thinking*, 183–206. New York: Global Scholarly Publications, 2008.

Goulding, Jay. "Hwa Yol Jung's *East Asian Philosophy and Phenomenology*." In Jin Young Park (ed.), *Comparative Political Theory and Cross-Cultural Philosophy: Essays in Honor of Hwa Yol Jung*, 119–36. Lanham: Lexington Books, 2009.

Goulding, Jay. "Katrin Froese's *Nietzsche, Heidegger, and Daoist Thought: Crossing Paths In-Between*." *Journal of Chinese Philosophy*, 38.4 (2011): 669–72.

Goulding, Jay. "Beginnings: The Global Crossings of Classical Daoism." In Kuang-Ming Wu (ed.), *Globalization Dynamics: Psychological, Economic, Technological, and Cultural Intercourses*, 118–32. New York: Nova Science Publishers, 2012.

Goulding, Jay. "Wu Kuang-Ming's *China Wisdom Alive: Vignettes of Life-Thinking*; *Story-Thinking: Cultural Meditations*; *Nonsense: Cultural Meditations on the Beyond*." *Journal of Chinese Philosophy*, 48.4 (2021): 368–82.

Goulding, Jay. "Barry Allen's *Vanishing into Things: Knowledge in Chinese Tradition*." *Journal of Chinese Philosophy*, 44.1–2 (2018): 113–16.

Goulding, Jay. "Unity through Diversity: Inter-World, Family Resemblance, Intertextuality." *Journal of World Philosophies*, 3.1 (2018): 142–50.

Goulding, Jay. "Japan-West Interculture: Time's Step Back—Dōgen, Watsuji, Kuki and Heidegger." In Aya Fujiwara and James White (eds.), *Conference Proceedings of the 31st Japanese Studies Association of Canada Annual Conference, Japan's World and the World's Japan: Images, Perceptions and Reactions*, 1–26. Edmonton: Princess Takamado Japan Centre for Teaching and Research at the University of Alberta, 2019.

Goulding, Jay. "Cheng and Gadamer: Daoist Phenomenology," special issue on "Gadamer and Chung-Ying Cheng: Hermeneutics and Onto-Generative Hermeneutics." *Journal of Chinese Philosophy*, 48.4 (2021): 368–382.

Harman, Graham. *Heidegger Explained: From Phenomenon to Thing*. Chicago: Open Court, 2006.

Heidegger, Martin. "What Is Metaphysics." Translated by R.F.C. Hull and Alan Crick. In Martin Heidegger, *Existence and Being*. With an introduction by Werner Brock, 353–392. Chicago: Henry Regnery Company, 1949.

Heidegger, Martin. *Being and Time*. Translated by John McQuarrie and Edward Robinson. Oxford: Blackwell, 1962.

Heidegger, Martin. *Identity and Difference*. Translated by Joan Stambaugh. New York: Harper and Row, 1969.

Heidegger, Martin. *What Is Called Thinking*. Translated by Fred D. Wieck and J. Glenn Gray. New York: Harper and Row, 1968.

Heidegger, Martin. *Poetry, Language and Thought*. Translated by Albert Hofstadter. New York: Harper Collins, 1971.

Heidegger, Martin. *On the Way to Language*. Translated by Peter D. Hertz. New York: Harper and Row, 1971.

Heidegger, Martin. *On Time and Being*. Translated by Joan Stambaugh. New York: Harper and Row, 1972.

Heidegger, Martin. *Early Greek Thinking*. Translated by David F. Krell and Frank A. Capuzzi. San Francisco: Harper and Row, 1975.
Heidegger, Martin. *Wegmarken* [GA 9]. Edited by Friedrich-Wilhelm von Herrmann. Frankfurt: Vittorio Klostermann, 1976.
Heidegger, Martin. *Holzwege* [GA 5]. Edited by Friedrich-Wilhelm von Herrmann. Frankfurt: Vittorio Klostermann, 1977.
Heidegger, Martin. *Sein und Zeit* [GA 2]. Edited by Friedrich-Wilhelm von Herrmann. Frankfurt: Vittorio Klostermann, 1977.
Heidegger, Martin. *The Question Concerning Technology and Other Essays*. Translated by William Lovett. New York: Harper Collins, 1977.
Heidegger, Martin. *Heraklit*. [GA 55]. Edited by Manfred S. Frings. Frankfurt: Vittorio Klostermann, 1979.
Heidegger, Martin. *Hölderlins Hymnen "Germanien" und "Der Rhein"* [GA 39]. Edited by Susanne Ziegler. Frankfurt: Vittorio Klostermann, 1980.
Heidegger, Martin. *Einführung in der Metaphysik* [GA 40]. Edited by Petra Jaeger. Frankfurt: Vittorio Klostermann, 1983.
Heidegger, Martin. "Hebel: Friend of the House." In Darrel E. Christensen, Manfred Riedel, Robert Spaemann, Reiner Wiehl and Wolfgang Wieland (eds.), *Contemporary German Philosophy*, volume 3, 87–101. University Park: Pennsylvania State University Press, 1983.
Heidegger, Martin. *Die Frage nach dem Ding: Zu Kants Lehre von den Transzendentalen Grundsätzen* [GA 41]. Edited by Petra Jaeger. Frankfurt: Vittorio Klostermann, 1984.
Heidegger, Martin. *Hölderlins Hymne "Der Ister"* [GA 53]. Edited by Walter Biemel. Frankfurt: Klostermann, 1984.
Heidegger, Martin. *Unterwegs zur Sprache* [GA 12]. Edited by Friedrich-Wilhelm von Herrmann. Frankfurt: Vittorio Klostermann, 1985.
Heidegger, Martin. *Schelling's Treatise on the Essence of Human Freedom*. Translated by Joan Stambaugh. Athens: Ohio University Press, 1985.
Heidegger, Martin. *Seminare* [GA 15]. Edited by Curd Ochwadt. Frankfurt: Vittorio Klostermann, 1986.
Heidegger, Martin. *Schelling: Vom Wesen der menschlichen Freiheit* [GA 42]. Edited by Ingrid Schüssler. Frankfurt: Vittorio Klostermann, 1988.
Heidegger, Martin. *Vom Wesen der Wahrheit: Zu Platons Höhlengleichnis und Theatet* [GA 34]. Edited by Hermann Mörchen. Frankfurt: Vittorio Klostermann, 1988.
Heidegger, Martin. *Beiträge zur Philosophie (zum Ereignis)* [GA 65]. Edited by Friedrich-Wilhelm von Herrmann. Frankfurt: Vittorio Klostermann, 1989.
Heidegger, Martin. *Concept of Time*. Translated by William McNeill. London: Blackwell, 1992.
Heidegger, Martin. *Parmenides*. Translated by Andre Schuwer and Richard Rojcewicz. Bloomington: Indiana University Press, 1992.
Heidegger, Martin. *Basic Writings*. Translated by John Sallis. London: Harper Perennial, 1993.
Heidegger, Martin. *Bremer und Freiburger Vorträge* [GA 79]. Edited by Petra Jaeger. Frankfurt: Vittorio Klostermann, 1994.
Heidegger, Martin. "Traditional Language and Technological Language." *Journal of Philosophical Research*, 23 (1998): 129–45.
Heidegger, Martin. *Contributions to Philosophy (From Enowning)*. Translated by Parvis Emad and Kenneth Maly. Bloomington: Indiana University Press, 1999.
Heidegger, Martin. *Vorträge und Aufsätze* [GA 7]. Edited by Friedrich-Wilhelm von Herrmann. Frankfurt: Vittorio Klostermann, 2000.

Heidegger, Martin. *Zu Hölderlin: Griechenlandreisen* [GA 75]. Edited by Curd Ochwadt. Frankfurt: Vittorio Klostermann, 2000.
Heidegger, Martin. *The Essence of Truth: On Plato's Cave Allegory and Theaetetus.* Translated by Ted Sadler. London: Continuum, 2002.
Heidegger, Martin. *Was Heisst Denken?* [GA 8]. Edited by Paola-Ludovika Coriando. Frankfurt: Vittorio Klostermann, 2002.
Heidegger, Martin. *Identität und Differenz* [GA 11]. Edited by Friedrich-Wilhelm von Herrmann. Frankfurt: Vittorio Klostermann, 2006.
Heidegger, Martin. *Zur Sache des Denkens* [GA 14]. Edited by Friedrich-Wilhelm von Herrmann. Frankfurt: Vittorio Klostermann, 2007.
Heidegger, Martin. *Zum Wesen der Sprache; Zur Frage nach Der Kunst* [GA 74]. Edited by Thomas Regehly. Frankfurt: Vittorio Klostermann, 2010.
Heidegger, Martin. *Bremen and Freiburg Lectures: Insight into That Which Is and Basic Principles of Thinking.* Translated by Andrew J. Benjamin. Bloomington: Indiana University Press, 2012.
Heidegger, Martin. *Der Anfang der abendländischen Philosophie; Auslegung des Anaximander und Parmenides* [GA 35]. Edited by Peter Trawny. Frankfurt: Vittorio Klostermann, 2012.
Heidegger, Martin. *Hölderlin's Hymns "Germania" and "The Rhine."* Translated by William McNeill and Julia Ireland. Bloomington: Indiana University Press, 2014.
Heidegger, Martin. *The Beginning of Western Philosophy: Interpretation of Anaximander and Parmenides.* Translated by Richard Rojcewicz. Bloomington: Indiana University Press, 2015.
Heidegger, Martin and Ernst Jünger. *Correspondence, 1949–1975.* Translated by Timothy Sean Quinn. New York: Rowman and Littlefield, 2016.
Heidegger, Martin. *Heraclitus, The Inception of Occidental Thinking Logic; Heraclitus's Doctrine of the Logos.* Translated by Julia G. Assaiante and S. Montgomery Ewegen. London: Bloomsbury Academic, 2018.
Herman, Jonathan R. *I and Tao: Martin Buber's Encounter with Chuang Tzu.* Albany: State University of New York Press, 1996.
Höchsmann, Hyun and Guorong Yang, trans. *Zhuangzi.* New York: Pearson, 2007.
Hsiao, Paul Shih-Yi. "Heidegger and Our Translation of the *Tao Te Ching*." In Graham Parkes (ed.), *Heidegger and Asian Thought*, 93–104. Honolulu: University of Hawaii Press, 1987.
Hühn, Lore. "A Philosophical Dialogue between Heidegger and Schelling." *Comparative and Contemporary Philosophy*, 6.1 (2014): 16–34.
Hull, R.F.C. and Alan Crick. "Notes." In Martin Heidegger, *Existence and Being.* With an introduction by Werner Brock, 394–399. Chicago: Henry Regnery Company, 1949.
Inwood, Michael. *A Heidegger Dictionary.* London: Blackwell, 1999.
Julien, Stanislas. *Le Livre de la Voie et de la Vertu, composé dans le VIe siècle avant l'ère chrétienne, par le philosophe Lao-Tseu.* Paris: De L'imprimerie Royale, 1842.
Korab-Karpowicz, W. Julian. *Presocratics in the Thought of Martin Heidegger.* Frankfurt: Peter Lang, 2016.
Kuki, Shūzo. "The Notion of Time and Repetition in Oriental Time." In Stephen Light (ed.), *Shūzo Kuki and Jean-Paul Sartre: Influence and Counter-influence in the Early History of Existential Phenomenology*, 43–50. Carbondale: Southern Illinois University Press, 1987.
Lau, Kwok-Ying. *Phenomenology and Intercultural Understanding: Toward a New Cultural Flesh.* Cham: Springer, 2016.
Liddell, H.G. and R. Scott. *Greek–English Lexicon.* Oxford: Clarendon Press, 1996.

Ma, Lin and Jaap van Brakel. *Fundamentals of Comparative and Intercultural Philosophy.* Albany: State University of New York Press, 2016.
Matthews, Bruce, trans. *F.W.J. Schelling, The Grounding of Positive Philosophy: The Berlin Lectures.* Albany: State University of New York Press, 2007.
May, Reinhard. *Heidegger's Hidden Sources: East Asian Influences on His Work.* Translated by Graham Parkes. London: Routledge, 1996.
Needham, Joseph. *Science and Civilization in China*, volume 2. Cambridge: Cambridge University Press, 1956.
Nelson, Eric S. *Chinese and Buddhist Philosophy in Early Twentieth-Century German Thought.* London: Bloomsbury Academic, 2017.
Parmenides. *Parmenides of Elea Fragments.* Translated by David Gallop. Toronto: University of Toronto Press, 1984.
Petzet, Heinrich. *Encounters and Dialogues with Martin Heidegger, 1929–1976.* Translated by John Sallis and Kenneth Maly. Chicago: University of Chicago Press, 1993.
Pöggeler, Otto. "West-East Dialogue: Heidegger and Lao-tzu." In Graham Parkes (ed.), *Heidegger and Asian Thought*, 47–78. Honolulu: University of Hawaii Press, 1987.
Radice, Betty. *Who's Who in the Ancient World.* London: Penguin, 1971.
Richardson, William J. *Through Phenomenology to Thought.* New York: Fordham University Press, 2003.
Sallis, John. *Echoes: After Heidegger.* Bloomington: Indiana University Press, 1990.
Schelling, F.W.J. *The Unconditional in Human Knowledge: Four Early Essays 1794–1796.* Translated by Fritz Marti. Lewisburg: Bucknell University Press, 1980.
Schelling, F.W.J. *Urfassung der Philosophie der Offenbarung*, Teilband 1. Edited by Walter E. Ehrhardt. Hamburg: Felix Meiner Verlag, 1992.
Schelling, F.W.J. "On the Nature of Philosophy as Science." In Rüdiger Bubner (ed.), *German Idealist Philosophy*, 209–53. London: Penguin, 1997.
Schelling, F.W.J. *Sämmtliche Werke.* Berlin: E. Hahn, 1997.
Schelling, F.W.J. *The Ages of the World, (Fragment) from the Handwritten Remains, Third Version (c. 1815).* Translated by Jason M. Wirth. Albany: State University of New York Press, 2000.
Schelling, F.W.J. *First Outline of a System of the Philosophy of Nature.* Translated by Keith R. Peterson. Albany: State University of New York Press, 2004.
Schelling, F.W.J. *Philosophical Investigations into the Essence of Human Freedom.* Translated by Jeff Love and Johannes Schmidt. Albany: State University of New York Press, 2006.
Schelling, F.W.J. *Historical-Critical Introduction to the Philosophy of Mythology.* Translated by Mason Richey and Markus Zisselsberger. Albany: State University of New York Press, 2007.
Schelling, F.W.J. *The Ages of the World (1811).* Translated by Joseph P. Lawrence. Albany: State University of New York Press, 2019.
Schulz, Walter. *Die Vollendung des Deutschen Idealismus in der Spätphilosophie Schellings.* Stuttgart: Neske, 1955.
Sear, David R. *Roman Coins and Their Values.* London: Spink and Son, 2000.
Seidel, George J. "Heidegger's Last God and the Schelling Connection." *Laval Theologique et Philosophique*, 55.1 (1999): 85–98.
Sharr, Adam. *Heidegger's Hut.* Cambridge: MIT Press, 2006.
Sharr, Adam and Simon Unwin. "Heidegger's Hut." *arq: Architectural Research Quarterly*, 5.1 (2001): 53–61.

Smith, William, ed. *Dictionary of Greek and Roman Biography and Mythology*, volume 2. London: Taylor, Walton and Maberly, 1849.
Stambaugh, Joan. "Heidegger, Taoism, and the Question of Metaphysics." In Graham Parkes (ed.), *Heidegger and Asian Thought*, 79–92. Honolulu: University of Hawaii Press, 1987.
Walf, Knut. "Fascination and Misunderstanding: The Ambivalent Western Reception of Daoism." *Monumenta Serica*, 53 (2005): 273–86.
Watson, Burton, trans. *The Complete Works of Zhuangzi*. New York: Columbia University Press, 2013.
Watters, Thomas. *Lao-tzu: A Study in Chinese Philosophy*. Hong Kong: China Mail Office, 1870.
Wheatley, Paul. *The Pivot of the Four Quarters: A Preliminary Enquiry into the Origins and Character of the Ancient Chinese City*. Edinburgh: Edinburgh University Press, 1971.
Wilhelm, Richard, trans. *Dschuang Dsi: Das wahre Buch vom südlichen Blütenland*. Jena: Eugen Diederichs, 1923.
Winchell, Alexander. *Reconciliation of Science and Religion*. New York: Harper, 1877.
Wirth, Jason M. *The Conspiracy of Life: Meditations on Schelling and His Time*. Albany: State University of New York Press, 2003.
Wong, Eva. *Lieh-tzu: A Taoist Guide to Practical Living*. Boston: Shambhalah Publications, 1995.
Wong, Kwok-Kui. "Schelling's Understanding of Laozi." *Dao: A Journal of Comparative Philosophy*, 16.4 (2017): 503–20.
Wong, Kwok-Kui. "Hegel, Schelling and Laozi on Nothingness." *Frontiers of Philosophy in China*, 13.4 (2018): 574–84.
Wu, Kuang-Ming. *The Butterfly as Companion: Meditations on the First Three Chapters of the Chuang-Tzu*. Albany: State University of New York Press, 1990.
Wu, Kuang-Ming. *Chinese Body Thinking*. Leiden: Brill, 1997.
Zhang, Dainian. *Key Concepts in Chinese Philosophy*. Translated by Edmund Ryden. New Haven: Yale University Press, 2002.
Zhang, Xianglong. *Heidegger Biography* 海德格爾傳. Beijing: Beijing University Press, 2008.
Zhang, Xianglong. "The Coming Time 'between' Being and Daoist Emptiness: An Analysis of Heidegger's Article Inquiring into the Uniqueness of the Poet via the Lao Zi." *Philosophy East and West*, 59.1 (2009): 71–87.
Zhuangzi. *Song Edition of the True Classic of Southern Florescence* 宋刻南華真經. In Yuanji Zhang (ed.), *Continuation of a Collection of Lost Ancient Writings* 續古逸叢書, volume 3, 81–227. Nanjing: Jiangsu Guji Chubanshe, 1919.

3

The Simple Onefold of Dao and Being: Reading Laozi, Zhuangzi, and Heidegger in Light of Interality

Geling Shang

The thesis of this chapter arises from questions in a comparative study of Martin Heidegger, Laozi, and Zhuangzi: What is that which remains, in Heidegger's word, *unthought* in the history of Western metaphysics? From his early search for the meaning of Being, then the truth of Being and later the place of Being, Heidegger has ventured an "other beginning" (*der andere Anfang*) as opposed to a "first beginning" (metaphysics) in the thinking of Being (*seindenken*). Where does such a beginning possibly take place? Is it the "step back/forth" away from and over the "first beginning"? Can Lao-Zhuang's notion of the Dao 道, grounded in the perspective of "interality" (*jian* 間), be a legitimate candidate for this "other beginning"? By exploring what Heidegger meant by Being in light of Lao-Zhuang's utterance of *Dao*, this chapter presents a conviction that Heidegger's meditation on Being is more in tune with Lao-Zhuang's notion of Dao than it is with the views of the ancient Greeks.

The Concept of Interality (*jian* 間)

In an attempt to "twist free" from Western metaphysical dogma in my comparative studies, I was often puzzled by such questions: What makes Lao-Zhuang's thinking of *Dao* different from ontology qua the study of being? On which ground does early Chinese thought lay its foundation other than being? Put simply, where is the beginning of Chinese philosophy? Having experimented with various possible answers, I have come to the conclusion that the Chinese word *jian* 間 offers the best solution.

The graphic image *jian*, which is the ancient form of the modern character *jian* 間, displays a crack or opening *on* the door (*men* 門) through which the light of the moon (*yue* 月) or sun (*ri* 日) shines and makes its presence known. Contrary to a proper name, *jian* does not denote any substantial entity (being); instead, it refers to those incorporeal aspects of reality such as between, middle, interval, void, surrounding, or whatever happens inconspicuously in the midst of entities. These aspects do not appear or exist as things do; rather, they can be experienced or illuminated only when our intentionality moves away from the body of things into the encircling *rift* (i.e., *jian*) to access a holistic *draft* of reality. In other words, reality consists of at least two parts: thing/being and no-thing/non-being, or there-is and there-is-not. The latter corresponds to what functions as relationality, possibility, spatial-temporality, interactivity, compositionality, and so on. *Jian*, or what I call "interality," is thus understood philosophically as the ensemble of all those other-than-being phenomena of reality.[1] The summation of my investigations has led me to the realization that *jian* is an *ur-word* that has, in fact, contributed a point of departure to most, if not all, fundamental inquiries in ancient China.

At the outset of Chinese thought, as early as the appearance of the *Yijing* 易經 (*Book of Changes*), attention to *jian* was emphatically directed toward the field of pre-philosophical concern. Although the *Yijing* was originally a book of divination, it contains rich insight into how we can see the world as an ever-changing process (*yi* 易). The idea of Yin 陰 and Yang 陽 as complementary forces joining together to form what is called *taiji* 太極 (the Ultimate One) reveals how all things are in a state of change and transformation, becoming and ceasing to be, such that they are either in an auspicious or unfortunate state of being. Changes of the two primary lines in placement and combination, the broken and unbroken lines that symbolize Yin and Yang forces and which provide the framework of the *Yijing*'s sixty-four hexagrams, determine the changes of their meaning and function circumstantially. Divergent from early Greek thinkers, Chinese sages were not interested in seeking a transcendental being (neither universal nor highest); rather, what they were anxious to know was how the situation, time-space, order, relation, and arrangement essentially and ecstatically impact the state of things in the *interality* of heaven and earth (*tiandi zhi jian* 天地之間).[2] Obviously, this mode of thinking prioritizes the inquiry of interality (interalogy) over that of things (ontology).[3] After the *Yijing*, interalogical thinking became an essential characteristic of Chinese thought such that other terms (i.e., Yin-Yang, heaven and earth, the ultimate one and non-ultimate one, humaneness and righteousness) were established and obtained their proper signification.

In what follows we will see that Lao-Zhuang developed their philosophies on the ground of interality. Perhaps they were the earliest, after the *Yijing*, to thematize terms such as Dao, no-thing, naturalness, and throughness with regard to interalogical interrogation. If Lao-Zhuang's account of the Dao was founded on the bases of *jian*, what about Heidegger's Being? If Heidegger were an ontologist, comparing him to Lao-Zhuang would make very little sense.

Heidegger is not an ontological thinker in the traditional sense. From the outset of his career, he explicitly claims in his exposition of ontological difference that Being itself is not a being. In *Being and Time*, he already prepared himself for a "destructuring" or "destruction" of "traditional content of ontology."[4] Later he explains that he takes the word "ontology" in the "broadest sense," "without reference to ontological direction and tendencies":

> In this case "ontology" signifies the endeavor to make being manifest itself, and to do so by way of the question "how does it stand with being?" (and not only

with the essent as such). But since thus far this question has not even been heard, let alone echoed; since it has been expressly rejected by the various schools of academic philosophy, which strive for an "ontology" in the traditional sense, it may be preferable to dispense in the future with the terms "ontology" and "ontological." Two modes of questioning which, as we now see clearly, are worlds apart, should not bear the same name.[5]

With a series of turns, Heidegger no longer uses "ontology" for his distinct way of *Seindenken*.

From the word Being we might assume that Heidegger was proposing another kind of being ontologically. But when we carefully examine the names he gives to Being—clearing, open, near, belonging together, *aletheia*, letting, giving, *Ereignis*, *topos* or place, Way, and so forth—none of them would make sense in traditional ontology. However, they make perfect sense in Lao-Zhuang's interalogical discourse. Heidegger insists that Being must not be thought of as a being, but as "Being without beings," which means "without regard to metaphysics."[6] Given this, we ought to think differently, from an "other beginning."

The Meaning of Dao and the Truth of Being: Dao as Being or Being as Dao?

On the surface, Dao and Being do not have anything in common and neither designates the same *matter* (*Sacht*) in their respective philosophical tradition. The "first beginning" of Western philosophy began with the question of being that places ontology at the forefront, as the "first philosophy." If we closely scrutinize Heidegger, we will notice his use of "ontology" and Being is different from that seen in antiquity. First, he distinguishes Being from being by the concept of "ontological difference," disclosing the fact that Being has been misplaced by ontic being or beingness, hence the oblivion of Being. Being is not one of the beings. He subsequently opens another ground and realm for understanding the meaning of Being, and as his thinking of Being unfolds, the terms he selects to characterize Being move closer and closer to Lao-Zhuang's Dao.

In early Chinese history, the central or ultimate concern is "Dao" (even cook Ding in the *Zhuangzi* seeks the Dao over the mere skill of butchery).[7] Coincidently, Heidegger has much to say about *weg* (way) and *bewegung* (waying or way-making) in his later works to indicate the truth/unconcealment of Being, even referencing Laozi's Dao.[8] How could the two, Dao and Being, thinking/saying of Being and of Dao, reconcile and inter-appropriate with one another? Is the saying of Dao saying something more original (pre-metaphysical) than the onto-theological concept of being?

Lao-Zhuang never speak about being and beings. The *matter* of their thinking is the Dao, not with regard to *what* being is but *how* things come into existence and *how* they live in the world. Dao simply refers to Way as such, through which one is free to walk and reach their potential destination and become their own.

Laozi's *Daodejing* opens by saying: "The Dao that can be *dao*-ed is not the constant Dao." A supplementary interpretation may be helpful: "Dao can be *dao*-ed (said of) as the extra-ordinary Dao-ing." The next stanza of chapter 1 can be treated in the same way: "The name that can be named is not primordial naming (or primordial way of naming)," or "the name can be named as the extra-ordinary naming (or saying)." Looking at the last three characters of the opening line of the *Daodejing* (*fei chang dao* 非常道), if we take "*fei chang*" separately, they mean "is-not" and "constant"; however, if we read them together, they mean "extra-ordinary" or "not-constant." Thus, the "constant Dao" (*chang dao* 常道) can be interpreted as the "extraordinary Dao" that cannot be *dao*-ed and said of "ordinarily."[9] Both share the same meaning of Dao: it is both waying and saying, neither *dao*-ed nor named. Reading it in both ways not only makes apparent the Oneness of Dao and Name, waying and naming (saying), but also the togetherness between *dao*-ing and *dao*-ed, naming and named. They interact, inter-transform and thus give birth to each another.[10]

Dao resides only in the realm of *jian* and functions as part of it. As Laozi said in chapter 21:

> The all-inclusiveness of the virtuosity of emptiness is always associated with Dao. Dao appears ever so obscure and indefinite. Indefinite and obscure, it contains images; obscure and indefinite, it encircles things. Broad and profound, it encapsulates essence, which is very authentic. Within the essence there is truthfulness. From the present moment back into antiquity, [Dao] so named never goes away, through which we are able to trace the origin of all [things]. This is how I get to know the origin of all things.[11]

The first sentence addresses the all-inclusiveness and pervasiveness of interality (*kongde zhi rong* 孔德之容) and its intrinsic relation to Dao. "*Kongde zhi rong*" has been misinterpreted as great virtuous person or power. According to Wang Bi's 王弼 (226–249 CE) commentary on the *Daodejing*, *kong* 孔 means *kong* 空 (emptiness); conversely, He Shanggong's 河上公 (fl. second or third century CE) commentary takes *kong* to mean *da* 大 (big) which accords with the name Laozi forcefully gave to Dao.[12] *Da* depicts the nature of Dao in terms of interality rather than some higher beings. *Rong* 容 signifies Dao's enormous capacity of containing and encompassing. Laozi describes Dao in the image of a container in reference to *rong* in chapter 4: "Dao is like an empty container which never overflows (no matter how much it receives). It is bottomless as the origin of ten thousand things."[13]

A second thought follows on the heels of the first: Dao does not pertain to the realm of things but to interality. Dao is not a thing, and it does not appear as a thing; hence as an interalogical factor, Dao is void of form and body and does not appear as a thing but inconspicuously unfolds in the realm of interality or *jian*. The third point Laozi makes is that the inconspicuous Dao is the primordial and fundamental origin of all things, even before the separation of heaven and earth.[14] A further implication of this passage is the following: it is from the perspective of interality that we are able to know the origin of all things. This is quite representative of Lao-Zhuang's thinking of Dao.

Within the void interality, Dao moves itself to create possibilities and conditions for what comes into being. From the movement of Dao there emerges one, the undifferentiated one or totality of the world of becoming. From one there emerges two, as the difference or opposite of one itself. The undifferentiated Dao keeps differentiating, resulting in the two. The two could be conceived of as the Yin-Yang forces representative of all opposites, the fundamental relation of all relations. The interaction between the two as the unity of opposites becomes three, from which the ten thousand things come into being.[15]

Some readers misconstrue Laozi's Dao as the originator or demiurge of the cosmos or physical world and assign it theo-ontological meaning. This is what Heidegger called the "calculative thinking" mode characteristic of the age of technology. The "sequence" enumerated here should not be understood as a mathematical formula to represent creation but a dynamic process of becoming. Dao, namely waying and saying, is in the midst of 0, 1, 2, 3, etc., and of all things; it connects, proceeds, directs, changes, and unifies all to constitute a world.

Going a step further, Zhuangzi clarified Dao directly in the sense of *tong* 通 or *throughness*, which somehow resembles Heidegger's notion of clearing. In chapter 2 of his text, Zhuangzi states, "Dao and throughness are the same" or "Dao throughs (all different) as One (same)."[16] The Chinese character for Dao, in its original sense, refers to walking and passing through. To be able to walk, there needs to be an open space or passage that is through or clear. It is the throughness of Dao that gives the condition and possibility of becoming. Dao is no-thing but *throughness* that allows things to have presence and humans to go through and become their own (*ziran* 自然 *par excellence*). Dao interpreted as throughness eschews any possible misconception of it as a higher being. For Zhuangzi, *tong* is the ideal state of interality. It gives open, free, and clear access for everything to breath, dwell, grow, relate, and flourish. In the meantime, it also frees the human heart-mind from being stuck and fixed by partial opinions and doctrines that often perpetrate serious conflicts in the human world.

The notion of *tong* suggests a new way of looking at the world focusing on no-thing: "Only Dao gathers what is void."[17] The real art of Dao lies in cultivating the mind-heart into a state of *tong* and making the void useful for one's life. For example, cook Ding effortlessly cuts up oxen by letting his knife play *through* the space between their bones and joints.[18] Likewise, Yanhui (a disciple of Confucius) becomes one with the Great Throughness by practicing mind-fasting and sitting-forgetting.[19] By staying in a place of interality, people can liberate themselves from being captivated by things and opinions; in being one with thoroughness, people can reach the ultimate freedom that Zhuangzi calls "floating near and far at ease" or "dancing with the flow" (*xiaoyaoyou* 逍遥游).

Heidegger's utterance about Way with respect to Being looks quite similar to Lao-Zhuang's understanding of Dao. He says in *On the Way to Language*:

> The word "way" probably is a primary word of language that speaks to the reflective mind of man. The key word in Laozi's poetic thinking is *Tao*, which "properly speaking" means way. But we are prone to think of "way" superficially, as a stretch connecting two places, our word "way" has all too rashly been considered as reason, mind, *raisin*, meaning, *logos*.[20]

Way (*weg*) makes it possible to think how reason, meaning, and method reveal their proper nature or essence. Even today's reign of method is derived from the hidden stream that "moves all things along and makes way for everything." Hence, "all is way."[21] Heidegger has made it clear that the original and essential meaning of Dao is Way, waying/Saying itself. He has also released the word "Dao" from the traditional ontological interpretation as reason, mind, *logos*, as well as creator or lord. Dao is simply way and "all is way." This means Dao throughs, flows, and opens thereby as the constant movement of gathering, conjoining, and unifying.

Through ways we reach somewhere and settle down there. Dao enables and allows things to reach something or some place to become what they are. Dao is not itself one of these things (beings) but is there as the empty interality that is without form, substance, or body before the appearance of things. In Laozi's words, "isn't interality between heaven and earth like a bellows! It is empty but persistent, and the more it moves the more [air] comes out."[22] For Heidegger, Dao, as "world-moving Saying … is the relation of all relations. It relates, maintains, proffers, and enriches the face-to-face encounter of the world's regions, holds and keeps them, in that it holds itself-Saying-in reverse."[23]

In *Country Path Conversations*, Heidegger tells us how:

> In thinking there is neither method nor theme, but rather the region, so called because it gives its realm and free reign to what thinking is given to think. Thinking abides in that of country, walking the ways of that country. Here the way is part of the country and belongs to it … We are even now walking in that region, the realm that concerns us.[24]

What he tries to stress is that ways are in the region of interality that concerns humans who are dwelling and walking in-the-world. By using modern Western terms Heidegger concedes that Dao must not be conceived as an ontological entity but a topological field cross-country. In sum, Being is more like an interalogical concept of Dao than any ontological being.

Being and Nothing Are the Same: The Groundless Ground of Dao and Manifestation of Being

Unlike the Western ontological exclusion of non-being, Laozi is perhaps the first person to suggest that *wu* 無 (no-thing, there-is-not) is the primary source and groundless ground in the name of Dao. According to Lao-Zhuang, Dao unfolds in and as no-thing (e.g., field, forest, sky) so it cannot be named and willed as a thing. *Wu* is hence the opposite and absence of *you* 有 (there-is). In combination with other words such as "name," "will/desire," "use," "action," and "self," *wu* designates not only their opposite and absence, but also the human comportment of negating and overcoming them. In addition, *wu* may connote the sense of absolute nihility, but there is no textual evidence which shows Laozi or Zhuangzi used the term in this sense.

For Lao-Zhuang, *wu*'s existence (paradoxically) precedes everything that *is*, and *wu* is that wherein all things are born. What it gives is not the property of a thing or the proposition of an idea but vacancy, emptiness, and void—in other words, interality in and between things. No-thing pre-exists and then co-exists with things (elements, energy, matter thus formed), and continues to exist (inapparently) after the passing and perishing of things. Everything comes from *wu* and returns to it. Things perish while no-thing does not, it is eternity, constancy, and infinity like the "godlike valley" that dies not.[25] Why? Because it is not self-born.

Not only does *wu* encompass all events and things, presences and absences, it also locates and places them into various positions of their own and in relation to others. The relation itself precedes things/beings. Before things become things there are relations in the midst of the realm of no-thing. As the godlike empty valley, no-thing shapes the appearance of mountains, high and low, near and far, big and small, sky and vegetation, in a single *draft*. It brings and gathers all things and events together and lets them relate to one another in various modes. The variation of relations, interweaved and led by Dao, determines how things become and what they actually are. And the primordial relation is the correlation and interaction between *wu* and *you*, which constitutes the becoming of the world.

With regard to relation or relatedness, *wu* tends to differentiate itself as the undifferentiated one (neither identity nor difference) and is why Laozi said: "Dao manifests as one; one produces two; two becomes three and three gives birth to ten-thousand-things."[26] Dao moves (*daos*) in the realm of no-thing that constantly differentiates the undifferentiated as the essential movement of reversal.[27] Inside this "dialectically" reversed movement, *you* presupposes *wu* and *wu* posits *you* to be its own opposite companion. Hereafter, "*you* and *wu* give birth to each other,"[28] while "the two spring out of the same well though different in name. Both can be called abysmal uncanny (*xuan* 玄). One uncanny over another, opens the gateway to the wonders of wondrous (*miao* 妙)."[29] Inasmuch as the two spring out of the same well, they belong together within an uncanny identity (*xuantong* 玄同).[30]

The *Zhuangzi* recommended a further idea of no-no-thing (*wuwu* 無無) to obtain a more comprehensive understanding of *wu* as such and to divulge Dao as the state of throughness.[31] In chapter 12 of the *Zhuangzi*, we read: "In the ultimate beginning, there is no-no-thing and there is nameless"; chapter 22 says: "Guang Yao (Light Glamorous) told Wu You (No-there-is), 'I have heard there-is-not, but have not yet reached no-there-is-not. When there-is-not is reached it has already turned itself into a thing. How difficult this (no-no-thing) is!'"[32] Thus, even *wu* can be fossilized (ontologized) and in need of overcoming by returning to *wuwu*, the un-differentiated flux of throughness.

A few insights might be drawn from the utterance of *wuwu*: first, *wu* is *you* and *you* is *wu*, together forming reality as a whole. When one is attached to *wu* as absolute truth or principle, it turns into *you* and becomes a thing. Second, *wu* moves in processes without any fixation and halting, *wu wus* if you like, or nothing *no-things*, as a constant flow of self-negating and self-affirming with things. Third, the understanding of *wuwu* releases a person from attachment to *wu* in order to attain the ultimate state of enlightenment, that is, having a heart-mind with throughness and "clearing," which stays and sways *through* between *you* and *wu*.

Furthermore, *wu* is the space between and around things that gives room and passage to things for their functionality and vitality. In other words, *wu* has no substance but plays an indispensable role for all that comes into being. Dao itself not a thing but "*things* things."[33] The significant way of letting things become and exist is to provide an empty space around and within them. In chapter 11, which was once quoted by Heidegger, Laozi writes:

> A wheel is composed of thirty spokes but the function of a wheel depends on the No-thing in between. A vessel is made of clay but the function of a vessel comes from the No-thing inside. A house is pieced together with doors and windows but the use of a house is indeed its Noth-ing (*space*). Therefore, things (*you*) bring about benefits whereas no-thing (*wu*) makes them functional and move free.[34]

Overall, *wu* and *you* are two orders (visible and invisible) of reality. They belong and interact together to form the world. Therefore "*wu* and *you* give birth to each other" as "the beginning of heaven-earth and the mother of all things."[35] "Everything comes from *you* and *you* comes from *wu*" for Laozi because *wu* is more original and fundamental than *you*. Ultimately speaking, *wu* is what binds *you* and *wu* together as one.[36]

In Heidegger's writings we read a series of questions regarding Nothing: "Why are there beings rather than nothing?"[37] "Why does metaphysics and science never have a question of Nothing?"[38] "We are seeking Nothing: where shall we seek the nothing? Where will we find the nothing? In order to find something must we not already know in general that it is there?"[39] "How is it with the nothing?"[40] The exposure of "ontological difference" is where Heidegger started his enterprise of thinking about Being. One of the points he made is that Being is not a being, nor the beingness of beings thought by traditional ontology; rather, Being is something "other than being."[41] Being and the nothing belong together or more precisely, "pure Being and pure Nothing are the same."[42] Why?

First, as the negation of beings, the nothing or the "nihilation of the nothing" is the condition in human thinking of beings as a whole. Every time we say "this is" or "that is" we are in the process of differentiating or identifying what a being *is* from what it *is not*. As the negation of beings, thinking cannot think anything without its *other*: nothing or non-being. Second, by the time we call for a being in the face of form, substance, essence, or idea, it becomes an empty word and swings into its opposite of non-being. "Can it now surprise us that 'being' should be so empty a word when the very word form is based on an emptying and an apparent stabilization of emptiness?"[43] Third, once we question the meaning of being, we, the questioning Dasein, are held out into nothing. "Human existence can relate to beings only if it holds itself out into the Nothing. Going beyond beings occurs in the essence of Dasein."[44] Nothing reveals and manifests itself in Dasein's anxiety; it brings Dasein before beings belong essentially to Dasein. "Dasein means: being held out into the nothing."[45] Finally, this "holding out" into nothingness transcends the relation of Dasein to beings into that of Being itself. In traditional metaphysics everything is concerned with the Being of beings. "The origins, legitimacy, and limits of this conception of Being are as little discussed as the nothing itself."[46] Therefore, thinking of the nothing can now be understood as the same as thinking of Being, because the nothing, beyond being and remaining the "indeterminate opposite of beings," reveals itself as "belonging to Being of beings."[47] This is the whole sense of the question "Why are there beings rather than nothing?"

Being and nothing belong together and are the same or "Being: Nothing: the Same" posted in Heidegger's *Four Seminars*. Being and nothing together make thinking-saying possible, and let the essence of Dasein reveal and go beyond to reach its individuality (mineness or selfhood) and creativity (freedom).[48] More profoundly, "Nothing is a characteristic of Being,"[49] the revelation of which belongs "especially to Dasein."[50] By turning away from beings, Nothing characterizes Being in a way that exhibits and unfolds a "determinate activity of Being" "as conditions for the arrival of beings; Being lets beings presence."[51] Heidegger's seeking of the nothing stands forth toward Lao-Zhuang's *wu* and *wuwu* which rest and reveal themselves on the abysmal ground of interality.

Dao Follows Its Own Nature: The Emerging and Arising Nature of Self-So-ing

Laozi said, "Dao follows its own nature."[52] In other words, the mode (truth) of Dao is its nature which shines through as such in the realm of interality. *Ziran* 自然 has been translated as "nature," "naturalness," "spontaneity," or simply "self-so," all of which perfectly demonstrate a naturalistic respect of the term but overlook its interalogical meaning.

Etymologically, the closest sense of *ziran* is self-so. The character *zi* connotes multiple meanings: 1. Self or itself as opposed to the "other" in a sense that is close to immanence or spontaneity. "Horses and oxen have four feet" is called self-so (naturally-so) while "horses with halts and oxen with pierced noses" is not.[53] There are quite a few words associated with *zi* in Lao-Zhuang's usage: self or self-transformation, self-rectification, self-tranquility,[54] and self-withholding.[55] The implications of *ziran* include self-reliance, self-sufficiency, autonomy, thusness, and spontaneity, with no help of any other power to show its own becoming. 2. "From" (*cong* 从), indicating a place in time-space in which the motion of appearing originates. This sense of "from" also implies that *ziran* is an active movement of Dao. 3. As "letting" (*you* 由), self-so has the meaning of letting-be or letting appear from and by what is its "ownmost" (origin). 4. "Guiding" or "leading" (*shuai* 率), which shows the way of becoming its own. Lao-Zhuang's application of *ziran* thus clearly designates a natural web[56] within which Dao acts as the connective or joint lines constituting or fabricating the web/world as a whole. Thus, *ziran* labels "self-so-ing" or "thus-so-ness" of becoming/appearing-by/as-one's own, which is the primal meaning or essence of what is meant by "natural."

Based on the above, *ziran* can be taken to mean nature in the following senses: First of all, what is natural amounts to what is primary/original, like the state of uncarved wood (*pu* 樸) which genuinely shows itself as such.[57] Everything springs from *pu* and returns to it in the end. A thing becomes as such due to the dispersion (dissemination) of the *pu* as an undifferentiated unity. For this reason, sages only use things according to their intrinsic functionalities because *ziran* does not carve (differentiate) itself.[58] By the same token, *ziran* has very little to say in words.[59] As the original state and primary source of all appearances, *ziran* shows itself with no additional work for improvement. For Lao-Zhuang, humans are obsessed with the desire to make things *better* and put extra work into developing their nature. This results in the destruction of *ziran* and creates only more unsatisfactory feelings than before. A sage, however, lets things *thing* by their self-so nature and dares not act [to alter their course].[60]

Second, self-so-ing as presencing, showing, appearing, revealing [of/from concealment], clearing, lighting, etc., is the movement of Dao. It does not appear as what is apparent; instead, it appears as appearing itself which admits and accepts the appearance of what is apparent. Moreover, *ziran* is fundamentally the vital force of life generated from the chaotic interactions among opposite or different potencies. When some of them reach a certain level of equilibrium, a thing emerges into appearance and becomes a thing as such. The connotation of *ziran* immediately accords with what Heidegger says about Nature (*physis*), which originally means "the emerging and arising, the spontaneous unfolding that lingers."[61] Similar to *ziran*, Heidegger thinks of Nature (*physis*) "in the broad and essential sense." "It means the Being of beings." Being occurs as "the incipient power gathering everything to itself, which in this manner releases every being to its own self."[62] The power of this *physis* is the "overpowering presence that is not yet mastered in thought." "But this power first issues from concealment" as *aletheia* or unconcealment "when the power accomplishes itself as a world." "It is through the world that the being first becomes a being."[63] The original meaning of *aletheia*, letting, and giving, which were favored and re-interpreted by Heidegger for Being, is adequately harnessed with the Chinese word *ziran*.

The Dao for Lao-Zhuang is *ziran*, and stands in opposition to the Confucian *dao* of human endeavor or moral discipline. The Dao does not will something and act but simply lets-be by and for itself, in virtue of which nothing is left undone.[64] In Heideggerian language, it is "showing itself from itself."[65]

Opening Openness: The Essence of Dao-Being

Though the word "open" (*kai* 開) is rarely used in Lao-Zhuang's writings, its meaning was implied and discussed in their teaching of Dao. One of the central characters of Dao, for both thinkers, is its openness. First, Dao lies and unfolds in interality, which is itself the open space-time among heaven and earth and humans and things. Second, *wu* and *wuwu* imply that Dao is that which opens up the open and makes possible the birth of heaven, earth, and all things. Third, the openness of Dao leads the way toward the opening of possible destinations in which a thing becomes and finds itself of its own accord. Moreover, the aforementioned terms of *jian*, void, throughness, etc., can all be interpreted as open or opening.

On the ground of openness, Dao is itself the opening. What *is* depends on the availability of opening space-time. Though it seems devoid or empty, the open abounds with indeterminate forces, relations, movements, and the constant flow of life. Dao opens itself as the interality between heaven and earth—amidst things and humans—to create void intervals and valleys that give everything free room and throughness for breathing, moving, and interacting with others. To be one with such openness is the highest state of spiritual awareness a person can attain in Daoism.

Heidegger has made the meaning of the open even more explicit than either Laozi or Zhuangzi: "Only this openness grants to the movement of speculative thinking the passage ... We call this openness which grants a possible letting-appear and show 'opening.'"[66] According to Heidegger, the word "opening" comes from the translation of the French *clairiere* in terms of foresting and fielding:

> The forest clearing (opening) is experienced in contrast to dense forest, called 'density' (*Dickung*) in older language. The substantive 'opening' goes back to the verb 'to open.' The adjective *licht* 'open' is the same word as 'light.' To open something means: to make something light, free and open, e.g., to make the forest free of trees as one place. The openness thus originating is the clearing ... light can stream into clearing, into its openness, and let brightness play with darkness in it. But light never first creates openness. Rather, light presupposes openness ... (also sound, resonance and echo) ... The clearing is the open for everything that is present and absent.[67]

The many meanings of the open are spread throughout his works: 1) clearing (*lichtung*) of space-time, like foresting, to make room for light to shine and trees to grow. In a broader sense, openness is what allows beings to be, bids them to dwell, and brought together as a whole. 2) The open region without boundary: "In Rilke's language, open means something that does not block off. It does not block off because it does not set bounds."[68] This resonates with Zhuangzi's notion of throughness and Laozi's nothing as "not blocking off" what flows unfoundedly. 3) The open admits, as the "including attraction." Beings are admitted into the open. They are "in the world."[69] 4) The open is nothing itself that has no substance as pure sphere, well-rounded circling stillness of a heart that has no preference or prejudice.[70] Dao, as openness, lets things be shown and exist:

> The way is appropriating ... To clear a way, for instance across a snow-covered field, is ... called *wesen* even today ... means to form a way ... way-making understood in this sense no longer means to move something up and down a path that is already there. It means to bring the way ... forth first of all and thus to be the way.[71]

5) As clearing, the open is Being itself, which promises all dwellings, in their places, sites, times, and paths. It is through such clearing and opening that Being un-conceals (*aletheia*) or truths itself. 6) Openness is also the essence of thinking and Saying that houses Being. It grants the path of thinking "the traversable opening." "We must think *aletheia*, unconcealment, as the beginning which first grants Being and thinking and their presencing to and for each other."[72] 7) The ultimate freedom is Dasein thrown open to ex-sistence and transcends itself to the possibilities of being, "for it is man,

open toward Being who alone lets arrive as presence. Such becoming present needs the openness of a clearing."[73]

In the openness of interality, Heidegger and Lao-Zhuang have traversed time and space to meet each other. Dao and Being become one: the open, interality, clearing, throughing, *aletheia*, and illuminating all belong together in the same opening.

Being-Dao as *Ereignis*: Event of Interality and Inter-appropriation

Ereignis is another name for Being along with those discussed above. It is perhaps one of the essential terms signaling the crucial turn of his thinking from Dasein-analysis to Sein-thinking. *Ereignis* originally means "event," or a happening of something "coming into view" of one's eyes (*auge*). In Heidegger's application, *Ereignis* becomes an Ur-word, which cannot be translated as Greek "*logos*" or Laozi's Dao.[74] Current English translations include "event," "appropriation," "event of appropriation," "en-owning," and so on. Nonetheless, its meaning remains cryptic if we simply read the above words without further clarification.

In the context of what Heidegger has said about it, none of the above translations are sufficient insofar as they lack the meaning of *relation* or relationality (to concern) that impacts the ek-sistence of all beings: "For that appropriation (*Ereignis*), holding, self-retaining is the relation of all relations."[75] From the mirror play of the fourfold to the way to language (saying), "relation is thought of here always in terms of *Ereignis*, and no longer conceived in the form of reference."[76] Two points are made here: 1) *Ereignis* can be understood as the relation itself, or relation of all relations. 2) The movement of *Ereignis* amounts to the movement of relation itself. Relation relates and joins different elements to allow beings to become themselves.

In an usual sense of "event," meaning the happening or occurring of *something* (crucial, big), which has little to do with the context of Heidegger's use, the sense of event that never slips away from the meaning of *Ereignis* is the event which can be understood as the ongoing waying that opens itself to allow the encounter, interact (mirror playing), and round-dance of the Fourfold. *En-owning* and appropriation, if only with regards to self-owning, can become an atomic concept that fails to show the interactive and inter-owning entanglement of the event that actually makes the *en-owning* possible. At this point, the event of inter-owning or inter-appropriating, I suggest, can be a more suitable appropriation of Heidegger's *Ereignis*.

If read carefully, we find Heidegger's *Ereignis* shifts significantly from the onto-theological paradigm to a disparate one with a focus on relation itself. Traditional metaphysics emphasizes *what* relates and are related, but Heidegger tried to switch it to relation itself which is independent from any other related ones. It is the openness of relation that brings beings into the realm of relation and lets them encounter, conjoin, inter-act (intimate), and receive each other. This relation is the in-between of what is related.

The same can be said of the Dao. Dao represents the web of all webs and relation of all relations, without which nothing would be seen or presenced. For Lao-Zhuang, everything exists in relations that are there before things fall into them. Relation is the precondition of existence and presence. In Aristotle, relation is only a subsidiary property of substance: *beings produce relations*. Lao-Zhuang and Heidegger, however, think of relation as *a prior* to beings: *relation creates beings* in the event of *Ereignis*: letting beings be.

In Lao-Zhuang's teaching we find a familiar word (*xiang* 相) which has a similar flavor to *Ereignis*, especially in the sense of mutuality, relationality, and inter-ality. The character *xiang* combines two radicals: tree (*mu* 木) and eyes (*mu* 目) to mean: 1) "looking" or "observing"; 2) gathering together; 3) encounter and interaction; and 4) reciprocity or exchange.[77] According to Lao-Zhuang, everything comes into being by interacting with others (opposites and differences) in forms of *xiang*. Such an interaction does not subject itself to any side of what acts; on the contrary, it takes place in and as interality that makes interactions possible. For instance, chapter 2 of the *Daodejing* says: "Thing and no-thing give birth to each other, difficult and easy complete each other, long and short take shape from each other, high and low lean toward each other, music and noise make harmony out of each other, and front and back keep company with each other." Zhuangzi, in chapter 2 of his text, writes: "This genre and other genre inter-appropriate one another into their own category."[78] *Xiang* associated with giving/receiving expresses senses such as mutual-encountering, inter-giving-receiving, affection, and belonging together, all of which reverberate the core meanings of *Ereignis*. As Albert Hofstadter observes about Heidegger:

> *Ereignen* comes to mean, in his writing, the joint process by which the four of the fourfold are able, firs, to come out into the light and clearing of truth, and thus each to exist in its own truthful way, and secondly, to exist in appropriation of and to each other, belonging together in the round dance of their being (expropriation). And what is more, this mutual appropriation becomes the very process by which the emergence into light and clearing occurs, for it happens through the sublimely simple play of their mutual mirroring.[79]

The keywords extracted such as "joining process," "belonging together," "mutual appropriation and expropriation," "mutual mirroring," are all attributes of the nature of relation and interaction or *xiang*, in which Being and human, the fourfold, thinking and language, being and nothingness, and Yin-Yang, belong together, encountering and challenging one another in the circular dance that is the onefold of Dao.

Xiang or *Ereignis* thus speaks of relation itself attributed to interality. Heidegger might not have recognized words such as "*jian*," "*xiang*," and "interality," but he did pay heed to the same type of phenomenon by using synonyms like "between" and "middle." In *Identity and Difference*, Heidegger used *Ereignis* to mean concern or "to concern" in the sense of "to relate" or conjoin what happens "in the between" or "in the midst" of beings. Understood as the event of identity (gathering and *belonging* together) and difference, *Ereignis* must primarily be embedded in the realm of interality, the "between" or "middle." Heidegger has *nearly* thematized the "between" or "middle." He claims the relation of things to world should not be construed as the two that are merely coupled together. Instead, "they penetrate each other" and thus "traverse a middle," or "the between," in which "they are at one."[80] In other words, the middle or between is where things and worlds, beings and Being, identity and dif-ference inter-appropriate each other *intimately.*

> The middle of the two is intimacy—in Latin, *inter*. The intimacy of world and thing ... The intimacy of world and thing is not a fusion. Intimacy obtains only where the intimate—world and thing—divides itself cleanly and remains separated. In the midst of the two, in the between of world and thing, in the *inter*, division prevails: a *dif-ference*.[81]

Where does the middle or between come from? "It is presented in the dif-ference," the single and unique dif-ference itself that "holds apart the middle in and through." Here, the notion of middle or between contains the following connotations: 1) the *inter* or intimacy that initiates the event of inter-appropriation[82]; 2) a *rift* as dif-ference itself that separates and unifies, and thus carries out the worlding of worlds, carries out the thinging of things[83]; 3) a place (empty or open space-time) or interval in the midst of entities, or a ringing ring that circulates and envelopes all into a simple one; 4) the relation (*xiang*) itself that lets thing and world bind together and penetrate each other in the event of inter-appropriation; 5) the threshold that sustains the middle and bares the between.[84]

The middle or between as such designates immediately toward the open region and the "mystery" of interality which has been either unthought or forgotten in metaphysics while explored and developed by Daoism. Evidently enough, by emphasizing the middle and between so frequently, Heidegger is turning his task of thinking into the realm of interality.

Place of Being, Topology of Being, Location and Temporality

There are at least two additional hints in the corpus of Heidegger's work that are worth mentioning and would help us detect whether his thinking of Being is converging with Lao-Zhuang's utterance of Dao in light of interality.

The first hint lies in his reinvention of Plato's conception of *chōra* or *khôra* (χώρα), recorded in *Timaeus*. The word was used by Plato via the mouth of Timaeus to mean a receptacle, a space, a substratum, or an interval, as a "third type" [*triton genos*].[85] In the *Republic*, Plato articulated his philosophy of form/*idee* by setting up a "divided line" between two types: the intelligible and the sensible. In the middle of *Timaeus* (48d), he abruptly called a "fresh start" for the exposition of *chōra*, which is the third type on top of the other two types with regards to the origin of the cosmos.

Even though Plato, in the middle of *Timaeus* (48–52), addresses *chōra* as the *triton genos* of reality and reasons how it functions in the *middle* between intelligible and sensible, his notion of *chora* has never actually been taken seriously, let alone developed as something of magnitude in Western history until quite recently by Heidegger and a few other thinkers after him.[86] It has been lost either in translation (receptacle) or in the *orthodox* interpretation of Form/*idee*.

Heidegger, in his *Introduction to Metaphysics*, reiterated Plato's classification of the three types (*genos*) of reality (*Timaeus* 50e): 1) that which is intelligible (i.e., form or idea), which Heidegger interprets as "that which becomes" (i.e., being); 2) *chōra* or space, or in Heidegger's words, "that *within which* it becomes, the medium in which something builds itself up while it is becoming and from which it then stands forth once it has become"; 3) the sensible as the copy of form/idea, or "the source from which what becomes takes the standard of resemblance, namely sensible beings as a whole."[87]

Chōra means locus, site, place, or space in general, which is said of "the nurse of becoming" by Plato between the being and becoming. This *draft* of reality is somewhat different from the dualism in his *Republics*. Did Plato attempt to make a turn or start/begin again in the middle of *Timaeus*, one of his last dialogues, by thinking of this third type, named *chōra*? We have also wondered why such an important word could be so neglected in Western history, when Plato has been worshiped as the father of philosophy? Is it because we have put too much emphasis on beings and entities, or think of Being as one of the beings, or merely beingness of beings ontically, thereby letting *chōra* slip away and be concealed in mainstream Platonism? More importantly, why was *chōra* brought to light by Heidegger's reading of *Timaeus*? Is it something that had been in Heidegger's heart and that deeply calls for the unconcealment of *chōra*? I believe so.[88]

In *What Is Called Thinking*, Heidegger mentions *chōra* as he talks about the duality or relation *between* beings and Being:

> An interpretation decisive for Western thought is given by Plato. Plato says that between beings and Being there prevails *chōra* (χώρα) which is the locus, the place. Plato means to say: beings and Being are in different places. Particular beings and Being are differently located. Thus when Plato gives thought to the different location of beings and Being, he is asking for the totally different place of Being, as against the place of beings.[89]

Although the articulation of *chōra* and how it operates in the world of becoming in the above passages is not lucid and comprehensive, we have enough reason to account for the significant impact of the term associated with Daoism to Heidegger's thinking of Being. The signification of *chōra* resembles Lao-Zhuang's interalogical vision of Dao. Plato used examples or images illustrating the meaning of *chōra*: receptacle or container, gold as mold that gives shape/form but not itself that shape/form, sieve that sifts/locates things in order (place), the nurse of becoming, and so on. These images are also used by Laozi to indicate what Dao is supposed to mean.[90] Did not Plato, by virtue of his thinking of *chōra*, open up in Western philosophy a new beginning or other way/path, which I call the "interalogical" one?

The second hint is in the *Four Seminars* Heidegger delivered during 1966, 1968, 1969, and 1973. Heidegger makes critical remarks on his *Being and Time*, albeit his thinking of being proceeds from it. In these late lectures, Heidegger critically re-examines his own journey in the thinking of Being. He recollected three stages of this journey: 1) in *Being and Time*, the question is the meaning of Being; 2) the question then turns to the truth of Being—truth in terms of unconcealment; 3) the question becomes the place of Being or topology of Being, which started but was not really developed in the lectures. He puts the three in a simple formula: Meaning—Truth—Place (*topos*).[91] These are three terms that succeed one another while also indicating three steps along the way of thinking. The "meaning" in *Being and Time* signifies a "project region, and projection is the accomplishment of Dasein," or "ex-static instancy" (ek-sistence) in "the openness of being." From its ek-sisting, "Dasein includes meaning."[92]

When Heidegger's thinking advances, he gives up the word "meaning of being" in favor of "truth of Being," henceforth stressing "the openness of Being itself, rather than the openness of Dasein in regard to this openness of Being."[93] This is a "turn" in which the emphasis switched to Being itself. Another turn which occurs is to move from the question concerning the "truth of Being" in terms of unconcealment to that of the "place or location of Being," hence the "topology of Being."[94]

During these lectures he switched topics to something else after the above statements and did not, quite uncharacteristically, clarify what he meant by "place" or "topology." We may find some favorable sources to interpret the last turn, such as the accounts on dwelling, building, measuring, staying, stilling etc., and what Jeff Malpas has done in his *Heidegger's Topology*.[95] Yet the explicit meaning of "place" or "topology" of Being still remains covert and incomplete. Does he mean the place of Being a place or location of Being? Is Being a place or location where humans dwell? We find a note in "Language in the Poem":

> Originally the word 'site' suggests a place in which everything comes together, is concentrated. The site gathers unto itself, supremely and in the extreme. The site, the gathering power, gathers in and preserves all it has gathered, not like an encapsulating shell but rather by gathering with its light all it has gathered, and only thus releasing it into its own nature.[96]

The place is a term that ensembles all the essential meaning and truth of Being as the "gathering power," open region, clearing and unconcealment, Nothing, space-time, and all the names he uses to characterize Being. From the perspective of such gathering power, instead of what is gathered, has Heidegger found his new beginning by meditating "that place or site" in a broadest sense: interality?

Accordingly, my assumption is that the place of Being may refer to: first, the open region that clears and frees the *between* through which Being discloses itself; second, the place of belonging together of what are different as "the simple onefold"; third, the conjoining place in which all things, including humans, conjoin, relate, and inter-appropriate one another and thus take place of their dwelling and become themselves. Topology of Being thereby becomes a new study of the place of Being which leaps away from traditional metaphysics and steps back to the place of Being as Being itself. The place of Being must not be understood as a mere place or location of beings but the spatiality and temporality of ek-sistence, in the broadest sense. Are we up to now allowed to announce: Dao: Being: Interality: the Same?

Conclusion

Dao and Being, *wu* and Nothing, nature and *aletheia*, throughing and opening, interaction and *Ereignis*, middle and between, all of these elementary words used by Lao-Zhuang and Heidegger are interchangeable and intertextual. What remained *unthought* (unheeded, oblivion, neglected), in the history of Western metaphysics, could be the problem of interality, which indicates the *invisible* and other-than-being aspect of reality. Heidegger's meditation of Being "without being" from the "other beginning" well resonates to Lao-Zhuang's interalogical play of Dao.

It might be too arbitrary to claim that Heidegger was a follower of Daoism, or attribute to him a philosophy of interality. Nevertheless, we can assert that Heidegger's "other beginning," be it "fundamental ontology," "tautology," "topology of Being," or "phenomenology of inconspicuous," seems similar or in tone with Daoism's interalogy, rather than traditional ontology. The originality and significance of both Lao-Zhuang and Heidegger lie in their ingenious intuition for interality. They are "on the way" together, from the similar "new beginning," to venture a possible "transmutation" of philosophizing.

Notes

1. I coined the word "interality" to translate *jian* as opposed to "between" or "betweenness" discussed by Heidegger and other recent philosophers simply because it covers a wider range of meanings than the later. See Geling Shang, "Interality Shows Through: An Introduction to Interalogy," *China Media Research*, 11.1 (2015): 68–79.
2. Laozi (ch. 5) was probably the first person in ancient China to utter *tiandi zhi jian* 天地之間. It actually became a phrase to express the fundamental field of philosophy and the ultimate attainment of human cultivation and enlightenment. Unfortunately, most readers fail to put enough emphasis on *jian*, sometimes even omitting it.
3. "Interalogy" is another word I coined after "interality" to signify "the study or thinking of interality." I then named it in Chinese as *jianlun* 間論 or *jianxinglun* 間性論, in contrast to "ontology," to exposit the disparate problematic in early Chinese thought. For instance, *yi* 易 or change (process) belongs to the category of interality instead of being/thing which is only a product of change. Dao, according to the *Yijing*, indicates whence and whither changes come and go. For more, see Geling Shang, "Why Is It Change Instead of Being? Meditation on the Interalogical Meaning of Change/*Yi* in the *Book of Change*," *Canadian Journal of Communication*, 41.3 (2016): 383–402.
4. Martin Heidegger, *Being and Time*, trans. Joan Stambaugh (Albany: State University of New York Press, 1996), 20.
5. Martin Heidegger, *Introduction to Metaphysics*, trans. Gregory Fried and Richard Polt (New Haven: Yale University Press, 2014), 41.
6. Martin Heidegger, *On Time and Being*, trans. Joan Stambaugh (New York: Harper and Row, 1972), 24.
7. Burton Watson, trans. *The Complete Works of Chuang Tzu* (New York: Columbia University Press, 1968). References to Zhuangzi's original text are to chapters in Qingfan Guo, ed. *A Collection of Commentaries on the Zhuangzi* 莊子集釋 (Beijing: Zhonghua Shuju, 1982).
8. For further details, see Lin Ma, "Deciphering Heidegger's Connection with the *Daodejing*," *Asian Philosophy*, 16.3 (2006): 149–71.

9   Translation is my own. References to Laozi's original text are to chapters in Yulie Lou, ed., *Collected Commentaries and Annotations of Wang Bi* 王弼集校釋 (Beijing: Zhonghua Shuju, 1987); Cf. Roger Ames and David Hall, trans. *A Philosophical Translation of Dao De Jing* (New York: Ballantine Books, 2003),
10 Laozi, *Daodejing*, ch. 2.
11 Ibid., ch. 21; see also chs. 2 and 4 of the *Zhuangzi* for similar expressions.
12 Laozi, *Daodejing*, ch. 25.
13 Ibid., ch. 4.
14 Ibid.
15 Ibid., ch. 42. The second chapter of the *Zhuangzi* uses the same numeration to eliminate the possibility of representing undifferentiated one by calculative or discursive reasoning.
16 See *Zhuangzi* ch. 2. Most translations have taken the word "*tong*" lightly or rendered it insufficiently as identification, penetration, etc. which failed to show its essential meaning of "throughness" (*Das Durch*) in *Zhuangzi*. Cf. Watson, *Chuang Tzu*, 41.
17 *Zhuangzi*, ch. 4. Cf. Watson, *Chuang Tzu*, 59.
18 Ibid., ch. 3. Cf. Ibid., 51.
19 Ibid., chs. 4 and 6. Cf. Ibid., 57 and 90.
20 Martin Heidegger, *On the Way to Language*, trans. Peter D. Hertz (New York: Harper and Row, 1971), 92.
21 Ibid.
22 Laozi, *Daodejing*, ch. 5.
23 Heidegger, *On the Way*, 107.
24 Martin Heidegger, *Country Path Conversations*, trans. Bret W. Davis (Bloomington: Indiana University Press, 2010), 74–5.
25 Laozi, *Daodejing*, ch. 6. The term *gushen* 谷神, often translated as "the spirit of valley," is better understood as "the godlike valley" which emphasizes the invisible power of "valley" (interality) as something holy or godlike, rather than the spirit of the valley which emphasizes "spirit."
26 Laozi, *Daodejing*, ch. 42.
27 Ibid., ch. 40.
28 Ibid., ch. 2.
29 Ibid., ch. 1.
30 Ibid., ch. 56.
31 I discuss this in greater detail in Shang Geling, "Embracing Differences and Many: The Significance of One in Zhuangzi's Utterance of Dao." *Dao: A Journal of Comparative Philosophy*, 1.2 (2002): 229–50. See also, David Chai, *Zhuangzi and the Becoming of Nothingness* (Albany: State University of New York Press, 2019).
32 It is interesting to note what is said at the beginning of chapter 18 of the *Zhuangzi*: "In the grand opening there is (*you*) no-no-thing (*wuwu*); there is nameless (*wuming*)" (according to Guo Xiang's commentary). Another translation, based on different punctuation of the sentence, can be: "In the grand beginning there is (*you*) nothing (*wu*), which has no-there-is and no-name (*wuyou wuming*)." What is interesting about this is the use of "there-is" which indicates that no-thing is not simply a negation or annihilation of present things, but another type of existence that is no-thing. No-thing is a part of the phenomenal or apparent reality yet hides amongst or is concealed in things (physical entity or conceptual representation). Inasmuch as our thinking focuses upon things as they appear, as in traditional metaphysics, no-thing withdraws and is absent from the scene. But the presence of

no-thing, that is presencing itself, does not eliminate itself as such. It gives (*es gibt*) a way for things to take their place and come into being: all things are generated out of there-is, being is originated out of there-is-not (see chapter 40 of the *Daodejing*). Both is and is-not are "there" as "it" or "es" if translated into Western languages. The "there" or "es" as Da of Dasein or there of there-is could be more primal than "is." Dao as no-thing or no-no-thing belongs to the realm of interality.

33 *Wuwuzhe fei wu* 物物者非物. See *Zhuangzi* chs. 11 and 22.
34 Laozi, *Daodejing*, ch. 11. Cf. Ames and Hall, *Philosophical Translation*, 91. According to Lin Ma, in an article entitled "The Uniqueness of the Poet" (*Die Einzigkeit des Dichters*) written in 1943, Heidegger cites the whole of chapter 11 from the *Daodejing*. Ma, "Deciphering Heidegger," 159.
35 Laozi, *Daodejing*, ch. 2 and ch. 1.
36 We should be mindful that Zhuangzi was not as serious about the question of the origin as was Laozi. He instead left the question open with a mindset of *wuwu* which would twist free from any kind of mind fixation. See *Zhuangzi* chs. 1, 2, and 6.
37 Heidegger, *Introduction to Metaphysics*, 1.
38 Martin Heidegger, "What Is Metaphysics," in David F. Krell (ed.), *Basic Writings*, 91–112 (New York: Harper and Row, 1976).
39 Ibid., 100.
40 Ibid., 104.
41 Martin Heidegger, *Four Seminars*, trans. Andrew Mitchell and Francois Raffoul (Bloomington: Indiana University Press, 2003), 58.
42 Heidegger, "What Is Metaphysics," 110.
43 Heidegger, *Introduction to Metaphysics*, 69.
44 Heidegger, "What Is Metaphysics," 111.
45 Ibid., 105.
46 Ibid., 109.
47 Ibid., 110.
48 Ibid., 106.
49 Heidegger, *Four Seminars*, 58.
50 Heidegger, "What Is Metaphysics," 107.
51 Heidegger, *Four Seminars*, 58–9.
52 Laozi, *Daodejing*, ch. 25.
53 *Zhuangzi* ch. 17. Cf. Watson, *Chuang Tzu*, 183.
54 Laozi, *Daodejing*, chs. 32, 37, and 57.
55 *Zhuangzi* ch. 2.
56 Laozi, *Daodejing*, ch. 73.
57 Ibid., ch. 57.
58 Ibid., ch. 28.
59 Ibid., ch. 23.
60 Ibid., ch. 64.
61 Heidegger, *Introduction to Metaphysics*, 61.
62 Martin Heidegger, *Poetry, Language, Thought*, trans. Albert Hofstadter (New York: Harper and Row, 1975), 100.
63 Ibid.
64 Laozi, *Daodejing*, ch. 37.
65 Martin Heidegger, *Zollikon Seminars: Protocols, Conversations, Letters*, trans F.K. Mayr and R. Askay (Evanston: Northwestern University Press, 2001), 5.
66 Heidegger, *On Time and Being*, 64–5.

67 Ibid.
68 Heidegger, *Poetry, Language, Thought*, 106.
69 Ibid.
70 Laozi, *Daodejing*, ch. 5.
71 Heidegger, *On the Way to Language*, 150.
72 Heidegger, *On Time and Being*, 68.
73 Martin Heidegger, *Identity and Difference*, trans. Joan Stambaugh (New York: Harper and Row, 1969), 31.
74 Ibid., 36.
75 Heidegger, *On the Way to Language*, 135.
76 Ibid.
77 These meanings are according to the Kangxi dictionary.
78 *Zhuangzi* ch. 2, Cf. Watson, *Chuang Tzu*, 42–3.
79 Heidegger, *Poetry, Language, Thought*, xxi.
80 Ibid., 202.
81 Ibid.
82 Ibid., 202.
83 Ibid., 207.
84 Ibid., 204.
85 Plato *Timaeus*, 48c-e. Cf. Francis Cornford (trans.), *Plato's Cosmology: The Timaeus of Plato* (Indianapolis: Hackett Publishing Company, 1935), 177.
86 For example, Whitehead, Derrida, and Deleuze.
87 Heidegger, *Introduction to Metaphysics*, 71–2.
88 In the middle of the dialogue, Plato abruptly announced: "So now once again at the outset of our discourse let us call upon a protecting deity to grant us safe passage through a strange and unfamiliar exposition to the conclusion that probability E. dictates; and so let us begin once more." Cornford, *Plato's Cosmology*, 167. Cornford points out, "in this prefatory passage the word ἀρχή (beginning, principle, starting-point) is reiterated many times, with a certain fluctuation of sense." Did Plato tend to start over once more to experiment an "other beginning"?
89 Martin Heidegger, *What Is Called Thinking?* trans. J. Glenn Gray (New York: Harper Perennial, 1976), 227.
90 See Laozi, *Daodejing*, chs. 1, 4, 5, 6, 11, 14, etc.
91 Heidegger, *Four Seminars*, 47.
92 Ibid.
93 Ibid.
94 Ibid.
95 Jeff Malpas, *Heidegger's Topology: Being, Place, World* (Cambridge: MIT Press, 2016).
96 Heidegger, *On the Way to Language*, 159–60.

References

Ames, Roger and David Hall, trans. *Daodejing, Making This Life Significant*. New York: Ballantine Books, 2003.

Chai, David. *Zhuangzi and the Becoming of Nothingness*. Albany: State University of New York Press, 2019.

Cornford, Francis, trans. *Plato's Cosmology: The Timaeus of Plato*. Indianapolis: Hackett Publishing Company, 1935.
Guo, Qingfan, ed. *A Collection of Commentaries on the Zhuangzi* 莊子集釋. Beijing: Zhonghua Shuju, 1982.
Heidegger, Martin. *Identity and Difference*. Translated by Joan Stambaugh. New York: Harper and Row, 1969.
Heidegger, Martin. *On the Way to Language*. Translated by Peter D. Hertz. New York: Harper and Row, 1971.
Heidegger, Martin. *On Time and Being*. Translated by Joan Stambaugh. New York: Harper and Row, 1972.
Heidegger, Martin. *Poetry, Language, Thought*. Translated by Albert Hofstadter. New York: Harper and Row, 1975.
Heidegger, Martin. *Basic Writings*. Edited by David F. Krell. New York: Harper and Row, 1976.
Heidegger, Martin. *What Is Called Thinking?* Translated by J. Glenn Gray. New York: Harper Perennial, 1976.
Heidegger, Martin. *Being and Time*. Translated by Joan Stambaugh. Albany: State University of New York Press, 1996.
Heidegger, Martin. *Zollikon Seminars: Protocols, Conversations, Letters*. Translated by F.K. Mayr and R. Askay. Evanston: Northwestern University Press, 2001.
Heidegger, Martin. *Four Seminars*. Translated by Andrew Mitchell and Francois Raffoul. Bloomington: Indiana University Press, 2003.
Heidegger, Martin. *Country Path Conversations*. Translated by Bret W. Davis. Bloomington: Indiana University Press, 2010.
Heidegger, Martin. *Introduction to Metaphysics*. Translated by Gregory Fried and Richard Polt. New Haven: Yale University Press, 2014.
Lou, Yulie, ed. *Collected Commentaries and Annotations of Wang Bi* 王弼集校釋. Beijing: Zhonghua Shuju, 1987.
Ma, Lin. "Deciphering Heidegger's Connection with the *Daodejing*." *Asian Philosophy*, 16.3 (2006): 149–71.
Malpas, Jeff. *Heidegger's Topology: Being, Place, World*. Cambridge: MIT Press, 2016.
Shang, Geling. "Embracing Differences and Many: The Significance of One in Zhuangzi's Utterance of Dao." *Dao: A Journal of Comparative Philosophy*, 1.2 (2002): 229–50.
Shang, Geling. "Interality Shows Through: An Introduction to Interalogy." *China Media Research*, 11.2 (2015): 68–79.
Shang, Geling. "Why Is It Change Instead of Being? Meditation on the Interalogical Meaning of Change/*Yi* in the *Book of Change*." *Canadian Journal of Communication*, 41.3 (2016): 383–402.
Watson, Burton, trans. *The Complete Work of Chuang Tzu*. New York: Columbia University Press, 1968.

Part Two

Existence and the Arts

4

Dao of Death

Jason M. Wirth

> *If I do not decide*
> *The dwelling place*
> *Of my future,*
> *How is it possible*
> *That I should lose my way?*
>
> Ikkyū Sōjun

Introduction

One of the most striking features of the *Zhuangzi*[1] is its attachment neither to death nor life. It does not celebrate either clinging to life at any cost or carelessly and arbitrarily dispensing with it. Moreover, its acceptance of death as belonging as much to the Dao 道 (the Way) as living itself speaks as if such realizations come easily. But this is the ease of Cook Ding who, in chapter 3 of the *Zhuangzi*, effortlessly carves the ox for Lord Wenhui, needing only to sharpen his knife once a year, while mediocre cooks, even with strenuous efforts and copious experience, need to sharpen their blades every month. Free and easy equanimity before life and death are the mark of a consummate realization of Dao enacted in effortless acting without acting (*wuwei* 無為). Indeed, the consummate equanimity of both living and dying belongs to the Way of the true person (*zhenren* 真人) or sage (*shengren* 聖人).

Many of the characters throughout the *Zhuangzi* are amazed at, and sometimes befuddled by, the effortless ease in which death is embraced. The *Zhuangzi* explores and enacts the root that gives rise to a *dramatic de-dramatization* of death. In contrast, one can consider, from a vast expanse of possible examples, the Franco-Czech novelist and essayist Milan Kundera's admiring recollection of a passage from Louis-Ferdinand Céline's neglected novel, *From Castle to Castle*, which contradistinguishes the sagacious equanimity exhibited by his dog as it died of cancer—"by far nothing so beautiful, discreet"—with the inevitable bluster of human death: "the trouble with men's death throes is all the fuss … somehow man is always on stage … even the plainest men." Human death is always a huge deal and even the cessation of an otherwise wholly unremarkable life meets with great fanfare. What is more, the sages who aspire to this canine discretion will not elude this public dramatization of death. "Because it's not always the man himself who climbs on stage. If he doesn't do it, someone will put him there. That is his fate as a man."[2] Someone's life may have been so undervalued that it was cherished by no one and inspired little or no care. Perhaps this person had become permanently unhoused, eating from garbage cans and sleeping in the streets. No government entities or individuals felt obligated to help this person transition into a more dignified mode of life, yet when they die, it will be accounted a grave loss.

The latter is at least an implicit symptom of an unrelenting attachment to life as an unconditional good. Perhaps we admire those who make the "supreme sacrifice" by dying so that others may live, but we are generally reluctant to venerate those who take their own lives when they are no longer worth living. Given that this rare equanimity before death is a mark of a true person or sage, and that the ordinary mind may tolerate it in animals but not in human beings, what is it that the former has overcome in order to achieve this disposition? What are the obstacles that, left in their default mode, warp our attitudes about death?

Given that these obstacles are radically distorting, the issue at hand cannot simply be the promulgation of a philosophy of dying as if philosophy itself were somehow immune to these distortions. If these obstacles tacitly operate in their default mode, they influence or perhaps even determine the sensibility that governs what we come to value as preeminently philosophical. The *Zhuangzi* consequently requires more than the intellectual athleticism that we extoll in professional philosophy. It also requires a "fasting of the mind,"[3] that is, a winnowing away of the mind's obstructions. However, prevailing practices of professional philosophy would not generally accept that a prerequisite for study is the cultivation of practices that help render the ordinary mind more sagacious. The *Zhuangzi* is not primarily a discursive apology for the *zhenren* and *shengren*, but rather a hopefully encouraging performance of them at work and play. It enacts the symptoms or fruits of a practice of personal transformation rather than arguing for them. In chapter 2 of the text, we learn that "If the Way is made clear, it is not the Way. If discriminations are put into words, they do not suffice."[4]

If the practice of the realization of the Dao enables equanimity before both life *and death*, it also reveals that the default mode finds us much more comfortable with striving to make peace exclusively with our lives—think of the ubiquity of mindfulness practices and anti-anxiety medications—rather than making peace with the intertwining of that life with death. The pacification of life's anxieties is related to our desires for wealth, eminence or fame, longevity, and reputation, and whatever else we may believe completes life. The way we typically think of our supreme happiness belongs to our belief that life is what in all cases is most important, and it should preferably acquire what fulfills it. From this perspective, death obliterates both our hopes for fulfillment and the life that would benefit from them. This makes death decisive. For the ordinary person, it is a decisive termination of anything that they would deem positive. For the *zhenren* and *shengren*, however, life is already complete and supreme happiness (*zhile* 至樂) includes the inevitability of death.

Although the *zhenren* and *shengren* do not seek death, they do not dread it or regard it as a scandal that decimates the value of living. That death is nothing special makes it in a way special, at least inasmuch as it becomes a touchstone of sagacity, that is, a strikingly illuminating quality of the *zhenren* and *shengren*. Tell me what you think of death, and I will tell you who you are. "The Perfect Person uses her mind like a mirror, going after nothing, welcoming nothing."[5]

How does the realization of the equanimity before life and death make not only human living, but also the practice of philosophy more sagacious? Given that death is a touchstone on this issue, I initially review this issue in the *Zhuangzi* before considering it in relationship to Martin Heidegger's celebrated analysis of "being toward death" in *Sein und Zeit*.[6] His fascination, however marginal, with Dao is well known, including his quixotic attempt to translate the *Daodejing*[7] as well as his occasional but appreciative passing comments about its importance as a *Grundwort* or grounding word.

As fascinating as this relationship may be, I will not review or evaluate Heidegger's overall understanding of Dao. This chapter is rather a meditation on the Dao of death, and it is my hope to push the Heideggerian discourse on this issue beyond the vice grip of his phenomenological analysis of Dasein's being toward death. From the perspective of Dasein, Heidegger's analysis is seminal, but its strength is also its weakness, namely, death is grasped from the perspective of Dasein's ownmost. Dasein cannot give its death away or outsource it because "each Dasein must take up death for itself."[8] In disclosing the future as an unsurpassable and nonrelational possibility,[9] Dasein is exposed to its ecstatic temporality. This undoes the entanglement and tranquilization of the everyday (*Alltäglichkeit*), which enables our "constant flight" from death,[10] but it does not undo Dasein as the reference point from which death is confronted. Death is always in relationship to its owner: *my* death, *your* death, *their* death, *our* death. This is Zhuangzi's challenge: to confront death not from our mortality, our being toward death, but from Dao. Finally, I supplement my consideration of the Dao of death as it both confirms the prescience of Heidegger's analysis while simultaneously undermining its foothold in Dasein and consider another of this tradition's most challenging confrontations with death, namely Jean Améry (the *nom de plume* of Hanns Chaim Mayer). What is the Dao of death and how does it cast transformative light on philosophical practice?

The Vast Room

In chapter 18 of his text, Zhuangzi analyzes the widespread belief that people who get what they want (wealth, eminence or fame, longevity, reputation) maximize their happiness, unlike those who strived for these things in vain, only to suffer poverty, ignominy, short lives, and bad names. Zhuangzi rejected these strivings as pernicious fixations. Those who attain the presumed desiderata of supreme happiness fret about losing them and anxiously scheme about enhancing them. More is never enough, and the final satisfaction of such desires is a fantasy. Moreover, no matter what one does, there is no antidote against death as it cancels any and all human attainments. There is no formula for happiness, no schema that, once achieved, brings one to supreme happiness and a consummate enjoyment of life. Zhuangzi counsels acting without acting, as in "heaven and earth do nothing, and there is nothing that is not done."[11] Heaven and earth are the effortless enactment of *wuwei*, not the laborious and progressive fulfillment of an original lack. There is nothing to do, no tasks to accomplish, yet nothing remains undone. Heaven and earth act without acting, but who among humans can act likewise?

This implies that humans are complicit in their misery because of the manner of their efforts to be happy. They endlessly and vainly strive to fulfill a particular conception of happiness. They seek a particular form of happiness as if human living had a preordained form without which it would be inadequate and unhappy. This struggle, whether or not it is temporarily successful, is part of our distress. This contrasts with the proclamation in chapter 12 of the *Zhuangzi*: "no joy in long life, no grief in early death, no honor in affluence, no shame in poverty."[12] In what would astound our own hyper-extractive era (the Anthropocene), the *zhenren* and *shengren* would be happy to leave the gold in the mountains and the pearls in the sea. Does our mad and ecologically catastrophic acquisitive mania indicate a lack of equanimity with our mortality?

Equanimity with the Dao is equanimity with both *life and death*. One does not grasp at either, seeking neither to shorten nor to prolong life beyond its allotment. It was such a realization that enabled Zhuangzi to come to terms with his grief at the loss of his spouse:

> Zhuangzi's wife died. When Huizi went to convey his condolences, he found Zhuangzi sitting with his legs sprawled out, pounding on a tub and singing. "You lived with her, she brought up your children and grew old," said Huizi. "It should be enough simply not to weep at her death. But pounding on a tub and singing—this is going too far, isn't it?"
>
> Zhuangzi said, "You're wrong. When she first died, do you think I didn't grieve like anyone else? But I looked back to her beginning and the time before she was born. Not only the time before she was born, but the time before she had a body. Not only the time before she had a body, but the time before she had a spirit. In the midst of the jumble of wonder and mystery a change took place and she had a spirit. Another change and she had a body. Another change and she was born. Now there's been another change and she's dead. It's just like the progression of the four seasons, spring, summer, fall, winter."[13]

Zhuangzi is not opposing mourning as if it were an inappropriate and mistaken response to the death of another. He admits to grieving. It is not a question of the affirmation or negation of grief. The issue rather is the mistaken assumption that there is an adequate or appropriate form of responding to death. The ritual funeral practices of his time (or our time for that matter) can tempt one erroneously to infer that there is a proper relationship to death. There is no proper or exclusively appropriate form of being with the dead any more than there is an appropriate form for living. This extends not only to our cultural forms, but also to our bodies. The *Zhuangzi* is rife with deformed and misshapen characters, but it does not share its culture's aversion to them. Instead, it mocks culture's fixation with ideal or normal body types. Each bodily form is a momentary perspective on Dao, one of its myriad fleeting things, no more so nor more less so Dao than anything else.[14] The judgment that something is deformed relies on the assumption that it lacks something that it was supposed to have, just as the impoverished person lacks wealth and the ignominious person lacks cultural esteem. This is not only true spatially, as in, no one form is more a form of Dao than any other form. It is also true temporally, as in, there is not one momentary form of Dao that is more Dao than other momentary manifestation. I am not, for example, more my form when I am baby than when I am a child, or adult, or quite old.

Death, like deformity, allows us to see that even being alive is no more so nor less so Dao than dying. Zhuangzi mourns his wife's death, but this does not mean that mourning is proprietary. It is a single perspective on the form of a single aspect of a single moment. Just as Case 23 of the Chan and Zen classic *Wumenguan* 無門關 (Japanese: *Mumonkan*) memorably recounts the story of the Sixth Ancestor Huineng's call for his jealous rival to remember his true face before his parents were born, Zhuangzi recalls his wife's beginning, the time before she was born. She was not a "she" at all. There was nothing, no form, until the emergence of her *qi* 氣 (breath), but such spirit or energy was not yet a body in any particular form. The *qi* manifests as each and every momentary form of her life, but, after playing itself through the myriad forms of her life, it reconfigures as something (or someone) else. In a sense, we enter through the mouth of spring and exit out the ass of winter, but such a circulation is yet not to remember our face before our parents were born.

What is this time before the beginning from which we emerge and back into which we dissolve, and throughout which we are the play of fate (*ming* 命)? Zhuangzi poetically imagines it as a vast, gigantic, or tremendous room (*ju shi* 巨室): "Now she's going to lie down peacefully in a vast room. If I were to follow after her bawling and sobbing, it would show that I don't understand anything about fate. So I stopped."[15] *Ming* is the fate, lot, order, or ordination of the myriad things, but it is also their life, the face before one was born and its emergence into *qi* and its consequent progression through the four seasons, culminating in its departure through the tail-end of winter. Just as there was no moment of *ming* that was any more so or less so the life of *ming*, there is no ritual or behavior that is appropriate once and for all. Just as construing atypical or unusual bodies as misshapen and deformed reveals our attachment to an ideal form, our attachment to the belief that Dao is more the living body than it is either the face before it was born or its *qi* reveals our attachment to particular forms of Dao rather than our embrace of Dao itself. As Romain Graziani articulates it, "death, illness, and meditation are all occasions to free oneself from the perspectives of individual identity and experience the flow of the unknown forces that are the alpha and the omega of our conscious existence."[16]

A few lines later in chapter 18, Zhuangzi is traveling to the state of Chu when he discovers a desiccated human skull. In his own *Hamlet* moment, Zhuangzi interrogates the skull, wondering if it has brought this fate upon itself. Was this the result of a greedy life? Was the skull the unfortunate decapitated subject of a fallen kingdom? Was it so disgraced that it took its own life or did it starve or freeze to death or succumb to old age, its "springs and autumns piled up until they brought you to this"?[17] Of course, the skull is taciturn, and so Zhuangzi used it as a pillow. During the night, the skull spoke to Zhuangzi in his dreams: "You chatter like a rhetorician, and all your words betray the entanglements of a living man. The dead know nothing of these! … Among the dead, there are no rulers above, no subjects below, and no chores of the four seasons. With nothing to do, our springs and autumns are as endless as heaven and earth. A king facing south on his throne could have no more happiness than this!"[18] When Zhuangzi inquired if the skull would like to return to its body, the skull scoffed, retorting, "Why would I throw away more happiness than that of a king on a throne and take on the troubles of a human being again?"[19] The skull, too, is an effortless expression of Dao. As David Chai observes, "even an old, parched piece of bone has a purpose to fulfill. Such is *wuwei*, the art of useful uselessness."[20]

The skull's detachment from living, its enactment of the full circulation of *wuwei* (spring, summer, fall, and *winter*), that is, its refusal to attach supreme happiness to the first three seasons, let alone to any particular configuration within them (e.g., wealth, fame, longevity, and reputation), resonates with other passages in the Inner Chapters. In chapter 2, Zhuangzi (as Zhang Wuzi) inquires: "How do I know that loving life is not a delusion? How do I know that in hating death I am not like a man who, having left home in his youth, has forgotten the way back?"[21] In chapter 5, Lao Dan (the great sage Laozi) counsels: "Why don't you just make him see that life and death are the same story, that acceptable and unacceptable are on a single string."[22] Life and death all belong to the four seasons, the effortless and always complete dance of *ming*. And in chapter 6 we learn that detachment from living at any cost is a mark of the *zhenren*:

> The true person of ancient times knew nothing of loving life, knew nothing of hating death. They emerged without delight; they went back in without a fuss. They came briskly, they went briskly, and that was all. They didn't forget where they began; they didn't try to find out where they would end.[23]

Later in the same chapter, we learn that the *shengren* also "delights in early death; he delights in old age; he delights in the beginning; he delights in the end."[24] This is just a sampling of such proclamations in the *Zhuangzi*; just as the chapters abound with all manner of life, conventionally and unconventionally formed, human and nonhuman, they are rife with the moment of death.

When Zhuangzi banged his tub, he did not forget where his wife began—the time before she had emerged as *qi*, let alone body—and does not imagine that she merely transported to a new place. She dissolved into the vast room of her face before she was born. Death not only belongs to the Way of things, but it also helps detach the mind from its fixation with the pursuit of an appropriate form. As Roger Ames reflected:

> Zhuangzi, in reflecting on the 'loss' of his wife, discovers that he has not really lost her at all. Her continuing participation in the process of change is guaranteed, and his mourning for her death becomes the celebration of her life. Even more important than this realization, however, is the notion that life and death are both contributory aspects of the process. What has made this wife a unique and cherished companion is dependent upon the mutuality of both change and persistence in the human experience. Every moment must at once be a living and a dying in order for the process to be vibrant and productive.[25]

Each moment of *ming* is the death of the prior form and the birth of a new form. There is no continuous identity over time whose eventual termination we mourn or otherwise regret. Death and birth are the *discontinuous* fate of the ten thousand things. Death is not the cessation of one's identity, but rather itself another discontinuous moment along a single string of *ming*. This is what is continuous, not any particular person or thing.

In this respect, it misses the issue to think of *ming* in terms of the fate of an object, as if the object were an identity over time, subject to certain external determinations. Time itself is the discontinuity of *ming* as the myriad things are always coming and going, always transforming. Death may appear as the death of a person or the cessation of a thing, but that is only because we misconstrue them by thinking them abstractly as *identities in time*. To live well demands loosening our fixation with ourselves as enduring entities. To live well, this fixation must die. As Mary I. Bockover articulates it: "Since living entails dying, living well entails dying well, which the *Zhuangzi* tells us involves a mindset of contentment and ease; a willingness to freely go with the change regardless of what it may bring."[26]

Finally, there is the famous account Zhuangzi preparing for his own death, contained in chapter 32. Given that Zhuangzi is still read today, we can imagine that his contemporaries sensed his importance and likely impact on future generations. Is he not extraordinary and would it not be appropriate to acknowledge this by giving him a most memorable funeral and burial? He should not be some random skull to be discovered on the way to Chu! He is Zhuangzi! Don't we still seek out the graves and tombstones of our most important forebears? However, Zhuangzi rejected the demand for a proper burial, let alone an extravagant one:

> When Zhuangzi was about to die, his disciples expressed a desire to give him a sumptuous burial. Zhuangzi said, "I will have heaven and earth for my coffin and coffin shell, the sun and moon for my pair of jade disks, the stars and constellations for my pearls and beads, and the ten thousand things for my parting gifts. The furnishings for my funeral are already prepared—what is there to add?"
>
> "But we're afraid the crows and kites will eat you, Master!" said his disciples.
>
> Zhuangzi said, "Above ground, I'll be eaten by crows and kites; below ground, I'll be eaten by mole crickets and ants. Wouldn't it be rather bigoted to deprive one group in order to supply the other?"[27]

Why do we hate birds? Is it because we are so attached to our identities that we think that they can somehow be preserved after death as identities? Yet we cannot preserve what we never had in the first place. In his brilliant confrontation with Heidegger, Hans Ruin takes up the question of our being with the dead, with the ways that they are still here precisely as gone. We are the left behind, struggling to know how best, how most appropriately, to honor the departed who have shaped our cultural and personal horizons. But how to care for the dead whose present absence makes us who we are? How to bury and memorialize the dead?

As members of the human species we never stopped burying. Perhaps we are only just started. Perhaps we are still looking for the right and proper way to bury.

Perhaps we are only now slowly beginning to learn to live more authentically with the dead, not just with our own but with all of the dead of the earth, through our historical culture and memory.[28]

Do we burn the dead? Or do we prefer crows and kites or mole crickets and ants? Do we mark them with stone? Or art? Or scholarly commemorations? Such questions reveal that we are in part our *care* (in the Heideggerian sense) for the dead, but this does not vitiate Zhuangzi's refusal of our fixation with a single appropriate response. There is not a single appropriate body any more so than there is a single moment of my life that was its most appropriate moment. Zhuangzi does not offer arbitrary answers. He rather loosens the grip on our pernicious fixation with the uniformly appropriate.

Beyond the Logic of Life

Part of what is so shocking or causes nervous titillation for some readers about Zhuangzi's equanimity before death is his resolute refusal to confirm what many people so thoroughly take for granted: that life is an unconditional good and that its loss is a scandal of incalculable proportions. To think otherwise than the latter is considered pathological, criminal, or both. This prejudice cannot simply be explained away by invoking Heidegger's nonetheless impressive description in *Sein und Zeit* of our absorption in and tranquilization (*Beruhigung*) by the quotidian flight from death.[29] To give Heidegger his due, we are indeed entangled in mass thought and default ideologies that assimilate us into the status quo. Our flight from death reveals our attachment to the prevailing consensus about life and how it is best lived. Heidegger skillfully exposes Dasein's ecstatic relationship to the temporality of being by loosening the grip of its quotidian tranquility. He does this in part by bringing it to bear on an experience of angst,[30] a sense of the uncanny (*das Unheimliche*)[31] in which we cannot assign an object or clear point of reference to a future that emerges ineluctably and inscrutably before us as the prospect of our looming mortality. We are no longer at ease nor at home, and familiarity falls away. Death shatters the intelligibility of the world. As liberating and penetrating as such an analysis may be, it is not attuned to the *shengren*'s levity or equanimity about death. Part of Heidegger's power derives precisely from his *dramatization* of the question of being, and what could be more dramatic than an authentic encounter with my own death as it liberates me from my ontic relationship to being?

Moreover, Heidegger's analysis, rooted in Dasein's care for itself and world, would likely be bewildered by the skull's indifference to returning to the world of the living. "You chatter like a rhetorician, and all your words betray the entanglements of a living man. The dead know nothing of these!"[32] The dead know nothing of Dasein's care (*Sorge*) for being, in either the mode of its tranquilized absorption in the quotidian flight from death or the resolute ecstasy and readiness for angst in our being toward death. This is not to say that the *Zhuangzi* is indifferent to whether we live or die or that it is unappreciative of the gift of human living. The *shengren* "delights in early death;

she delights in old age; she delights in the beginning; she delights in the end." There are no angst and *Unheimlichkeit* (uncanniness), no valorous resolute openness, because the *shengren* thinks death neither from the little mind of the ordinary person nor with ecstatic resoluteness. The *shengren* is not a human point of reference for death. The ego or fixed placeholder of the *shengren* falls away and death is thought effortlessly (*wuwei*) from Dao.[33]

Of course, Heidegger came to realize the limitations of *Sein und Zeit*. His famous *Kehre* or turn is in part a turn away from Dasein and a turn toward being itself. He recognized the limitations of making Dasein the point of departure for the question of being and sought to rethink it from being itself. As important as this is, the turn did not include a sustained effort to rethink death from the perspective of death itself rather than from the earlier perspective of Dasein's ownmost (*Eigentlichkeit*). If we start from death itself, that is, from Zhuangzi's recollection of the alpha of his wife's face before she was born and the omega of her dissolution back into the "vast room," our point of departure is not Dasein's ecstatic relationship to the question of being. The latter is anchored in Dasein's care for its being. However tentative and experimental such efforts are bound to be, the deeper challenge is to think ourselves, and the myriad momentary forms of life itself, from death itself (the face before we were born and the vast room in which we dissolve) as the point of departure. Death is a clue to our inability to capture Dao with names or phrases. Yet death belongs to the Way of things. Dao is no more so but also no less so life than it is death. Dao is the way of the ten thousand things. Humans have no privilege in this respect.

One way to open up the space *between* "being toward death" and Zhuangzi's equanimity is to consider a case that *Sein und Zeit* would seem unable to grasp, namely, the motivation of those who elect to take their own lives. Death cannot be ecstatically disclosive in this case because when one takes one's own life, one severs one's relationship to anything. This is not sacrificing one's life so that others may live[34] any more so than it is shattering on the prospect of one's mortality. It is *absolute negation*, a refusal of being and life altogether. Taking one's own life does not exchange it for something better. It does not expose it to an ontological stance. It is an action whose result ends the one who would benefit from it in any way whatsoever. To be clear, this is not to advocate for taking one's own life and it is certainly not to suggest that the *Zhuangzi* made such recommendations. It is simply an effort to "fast the mind" as the *Zhuangzi* counsels in order to unblock our attachment to care for life at any cost, an attachment that diminishes both living and dying.

Jean Améry's *On Suicide: A Discourse on Voluntary Death*,[35] written between his own failed attempt to take his life and successfully doing so in 1978, ventured the difficult experiment of trying to understand what motivates the taking of one's life. It is a strange motivation, because it does not produce any benefits, but rather extinguishes the one who could reap any kind of reward. Améry's book was also not written to promote or even defend taking one's own life, but rather to come to some kind of understanding of it, however tentative and halting. The effort to do so revealed an obstacle in which we are so thoroughly embedded that not even Heidegger fully escapes its snare.

Améry's analysis requires retreating from pathologizing labels like suicide, or *Selbstmord*, murdering oneself, as if it were a criminal act or some kind of depravity. Taking one's own life and acting aggressively toward others are "radically different ways of acting."[36] We think of taking one's own life, just like dying young, as somehow less natural, but death, elective or involuntary, young or old, ineluctably belongs to nature. One could also say that it belongs to *ming*. Convention has it, however, that death is to be avoided at all costs, but this is precisely what the person who takes their own life contests. "But not to have to live: this becomes a commandment wherever dignity and liberty forbid abominable conditions to the anti-nature of a living toward death, of a life of *échec*."[37] Like being checked in chess, life has hit its limits and begun to fail. Life confronts its *échec*, its failure. This too is Zhuangzian *ming*, a natural, "resounding no to the crushing, shattering *échec* of existence."[38] This is what taking one's own life exposes: the tyranny of the demand that we *have* to live, or the tacitly operating deontological tyranny that, no matter what, we *should* live.

The refusal of living at any cost has a single power. It is an absolute *no*, "a pure and most extreme negation that no longer conceals anything positive in itself."[39] It cannot be grasped by what Améry dubs the "logic of life," a logic that governs psychology, suicidology, social science, even philosophy itself, all which are dedicated, however tacitly, to preserving life, to maintaining being, at all costs. In this logic "life is the only good."[40] Whatever would radically negate life is criminally depraved or mentally ill. Aggression against the self, given that the self gains *nothing* in taking its own life, only makes sense in the "anti-logic of death."[41] Having hit the limit of being, it realizes that it has exhausted its viable forms.

> "You are nothing, now finally be *not*;" or because they have recognized the ultimate *échec* of human existence and want to lay hands on themselves before hands—the hands of cancer, the hands of a heart attack, the hands of diabetes, etc.—are laid on them.[42]

Death as a good, which is not good for me because it is the annihilation of me, is an important clue that delimits our fixation with being, even in its ontological difference. This is not to negate Heidegger's analysis of "being toward death" in which death exposes Dasein's temporal ecstasy. Within the conditions Heidegger himself sets for such an analysis, it is exceptionally effective, and it stirs us from our ontic somnolence. It is, however, the logic of death seen from the point of view of the logic of life. Dasein shatters upon death but does not yet die.

Aging for Améry offers another important clue, one that exposes our fixation on the memories and valences that make possible our sense of identity. Let's say that you come to know yourself as a valiant mountain climber and a dexterous and physically attractive socialite. As aging sets in, the very things with which you identify (the beckoning mountains, the social successes) begin to recede, putting one's sense of self into an antagonistic relationship with them. The mountains that you once surmounted now seem to inform you that you will never climb them again. The parties in which you enjoyed your social triumphs have all faded and the youthful gatherings that replaced them regard you as an old and ugly has-been. Your presence at them now feels transgressive and unwelcome. The self that was unselfconsciously operating in its world is now estranged from it. "I am becoming a stranger to myself the more I approach them and, while doing so, becoming nonetheless myself."[43] I think that I am not my body whose creeping decrepitude contradicts the memories and valances that constitute my sense of identity. Yet this unfamiliar and disappointing body is now you. Your resistance is your mental fixation with an appropriate form of yourself. Yet you are much yourself at the moment of your birth as you are at the moment of your death. Aging, while discontinuous with the memories of youthful triumph, is not a diminishment. It is as much you now as it was you then. Despite no longer being at home in the world, one is not falling away from the fullness of life into the depletion of senescence.

Heidegger, of course, excels in his descriptions of being no longer at home in the world. What a description of senescence allows us to appreciate, however, is the crisis in which my abiding sense of self, on either an ontic or ontological register, not only becomes a source of Augustine's toil and sweat,[44] but brings us to the limit of the self as a point of departure. Aging is the agony of discontinuity, not an accident to which one's identity is subject. Taking one's life (an extreme form of negating that point of departure) or aging (the pain and disappointment of one's body contradicting a fixed sense of self) brings the self into a crisis of the self, even in its ecstatic dimension. Dasein does not yet know of the "fasting of the mind"[45] that the *Zhuangzi* counsels. The ontological difference, for all its power, is not much help with what the Buddha legendarily identified as the three great realities: sickness, old age, and death.

It was Heidegger's onetime student, Nishitani Keiji, who dislodged (from a Zen perspective) death from Dasein's tremulous preoccupation with its mortality. If the thought that I am nothing—that I am no longer *fundamentally* in any predicatively meaningful sense myself—it is not death that I fear. Rather "I" fear that I am not myself, indeed, that ultimately and radically, I am not at all. If I am nothing, then nothing is not a problem that I have, but rather the dawning revelation that there is ultimately *no one* to have or not have it as a problem. If the ground of myself disintegrates, then I substantively disintegrate along with it. I do not survive such that I can absurdly say that, of all my problems, my biggest one is that I have no ground, indeed, that I ultimately am not at all. Drawing on the Zen record, Nishitani calls the annihilation and falling away of this substantive self the "Great Death." It is the conclusion of the absolute evacuation of the ground in the "Great Doubt." The latter is not an end in itself, but rather the occasion of realizing what my mortality had obscured. It appeared hollow—I am nothing!—precisely because it was measured by my sense of self as the point of departure. The "Great Doubt" dissolves the tyrannical deontology of the logic of life, which begins and ends with command that life is the primary good and that it should be preserved at all costs.

> The Great Doubt represents not only the apex of the doubting self but also the point of its "passing away" and ceasing to be "self." It is like the bean whose seed and shell break apart as it ripens: the shell is tiny ego, and the seed the infinity of the Great Doubt that encompasses the whole world. It is the moment at which the self is at the same time the nothingness of self.[46]

In a sense, the small self, anxious for its own being above all, gives way to the Great Self, or we might say, the True Person. At this moment one can now appreciate that the Dao of life is inseparable from the Dao of death. They are on a single string.

Conclusion

I undertook these modest experiments in thought during the global pandemic and in a country whose yearlong denial of the gravity of the problem made it one of the world's most gratuitously catastrophic outbreaks. Rather than help the seemingly countless people in need, we fought each other over mask mandates. This period culminated in the invasion of the US Capitol Building and the denial by one of the two major political parties that this amounted to anything that merited further thought. Police violence and gun violence abound, and all of these events transpire against the background of a looming ecological crisis and persistently expanding economic and political inequity.

We are always in need of help with our dying and our mourning. An ontological analysis of the New World Disorder is critical and indispensable, but it does not help us with sickness, old age, and death. Even a utopian economic and political order must confront them. Zhuangzi does so effortlessly, not because of the acquisition of some virtue or through resolute readiness for anxiety, but rather because of "fasting of the self" that awakens the general economy (to use Georges Bataille's felicitous phrase) of Dao. In the falling away of the putatively proper or appropriate form of the self, the inevitable dashing of our dreams does not only produce tears and the gnashing of teeth. Zhuangzi was not indifferent to the demise of his wife any more than he was indifferent to the earth. He knew the grief of both, but he also knew that this did not render the earth unworthy of our engagement and nimble care.

Notes

1 Burton Watson, trans. *The Complete Works of Zhuangzi* (New York: Columbia University Press, 2013). Note that I alter his translation only to use less gender specific language.
2 Milan Kundera, *Encounter* [*Une rencontre*], trans. Linda Asher (New York: Harper Collins, 2010), 23.
3 Watson, *Zhuangzi*, 25.
4 Ibid., 14.
5 From chapter 7 of the *Zhuangzi*. Ibid., 59.
6 For a thorough review of the English language secondary literature on Zhuangzi on death, both in itself and in relationship to Heidegger, see David Chai, "On Pillowing One's Skull: Zhuangzi and Heidegger on Death," *Frontiers of Philosophy in China*, 11.3 (2016), 483–500.
7 See Paul Shih-Yi Hsiao, "Heidegger and Our Translation of the *Tao Te Ching*," in Graham Parkes (ed.), *Heidegger and Asian Thought*, 93–101 (Honolulu: University of Hawaii Press, 1987). This volume as a whole remains an indispensable and pioneering work on comparative engagements with Asian thought, including Daoism.

8   Martin Heidegger, *Sein und Zeit* (Tübingen: Max Niemeyer Verlag, 1986), 240. Translations are my own.
9   Ibid., 250.
10 Ibid., 254.
11 Ibid., 140.
12 Ibid., 85.
13 Ibid., 140–1.
14 For a definitive discussion of perspectivism in both the *Zhuangzi* and Heidegger, see Bret W. Davis, "Knowing Limits: Toward a Versatile Perspectivism with Nietzsche, Heidegger, Zhuangzi and Zen," *Research in Phenomenology*, 49 (2019): 301–34.
15 Watson, *Zhuangzi*, 141.
16 Romain Graziani, *Fiction and Philosophy in the Zhuangzi: An Introduction to Early Chinese Taoist Thought* (London and New York: Bloomsbury, 2021), 92.
17 Watson, *Zhuangzi*, 141.
18 Ibid., 142.
19 Ibid.
20 Chai, "Pillowing One's Skull," 494.
21 Watson, *Zhuangzi*, 16.
22 Ibid., 37.
23 Ibid., 43.
24 Ibid., 45.
25 Roger T. Ames, "Death as Transformation in Classical Daoism," in Jeff Malpas and Robert C. Solomon (eds.), *Death and Philosophy*, 51–63 (London: Routledge, 1998), at 61.
26 Mary I. Bockover, "Two Portrayals of Death in Light of the Views of Brentano and Early Daoism," in David Chai (ed.), *Daoist Encounters with Phenomenology: Thinking Interculturally about Human Existence*, 31–59 (London: Bloomsbury Academic, 2020), at 54.
27 Watson, *Zhuangzi*, 286.
28 Hans Ruin, *Being with the Dead: Burial, Ancestral Politics, and the Roots of Historical Consciousness* (Stanford: Stanford University Press, 2019), 147.
29 Heidegger, *Sein und Zeit*, 254.
30 Ibid., 266.
31 Ibid., 188.
32 Watson, *Zhuangzi*, 142.
33 As David Chai eloquently makes this point: "We can, however, forgo the need for anticipation and fear by rolling together our subjective and existential selves, and eliminating the notion that humanity is immune to the vagaries of life as witnessed in the natural world." Chai, "Pillowing One's Skull," 498. And this: "Heidegger asks us to mold our life in view of its finitude, whereas Zhuangzi asks us to forget the very notion." Ibid., 498.
34 Heidegger, *Sein und Zeit*, 240.
35 Jean Améry, *On Suicide: A Discourse on Voluntary Death*, trans. John D. Barlow (Bloomington: Indiana University Press, 1999).
36 Ibid., 101.
37 Ibid., 61.
38 Ibid., 60.
39 Ibid., 132.
40 Ibid., 97.

41 Ibid., 101.
42 Ibid., 81.
43 Jean Améry, *On Aging: Revolt and Resignation*, trans. John D. Barlow (Bloomington: Indiana University Press, 1994), 40.
44 Heidegger, *Sein und Zeit*, 43–4.
45 Watson, *Zhuangzi*, 25.
46 Nishitani Keiji, *Religion and Nothingness*, trans. Jan Van Bragt (Berkeley: University of California Press, 1982), 21.

References

Améry, Jean. *On Aging: Revolt and Resignation*. Translated by John D. Barlow. Bloomington: Indiana University Press, 1994.
Améry, Jean. *On Suicide: A Discourse on Voluntary Death*. Translated by John D. Barlow. Bloomington: Indiana University Press, 1999.
Ames, Roger T. "Death as Transformation in Classical Daoism." In Jeff Malpas and Robert C. Solomon (eds.), *Death and Philosophy*, 51–63. London: Routledge, 1998.
Bataille, Georges. *The Accursed Share*, volume 1. Translated by Robert Hurley. New York: Zone Books, 1991.
Bockover, Mary I. "Two Portrayals of Death in Light of the Views of Brentano and Early Daoism." In David Chai (ed.), *Daoist Encounters with Phenomenology: Thinking Interculturally about Human Existence*, 31–59. London: Bloomsbury Academic, 2020.
Chai, David. "On Pillowing One's Skull: Zhuangzi and Heidegger on Death." *Frontiers of Philosophy in China*, 11.3 (2016): 483–500.
Davis, Bret W. "Knowing Limits: Toward a Versatile Perspectivism with Nietzsche, Heidegger, Zhuangzi and Zen." *Research in Phenomenology*, 49 (2019): 301–34.
Graziani, Romain. *Fiction and Philosophy in the Zhuangzi: An Introduction to Early Chinese Taoist Thought*. London: Bloomsbury Academic, 2021.
Heidegger, Martin. *Sein und Zeit*. Tübingen: Max Niemeyer Verlag, 1986.
Hsiao, Shih-Yi Paul. "Heidegger and Our Translation of the *Tao Te Ching*." In Graham Parkes (ed.), *Heidegger and Asian Thought*, 93–101. Honolulu: University of Hawaii Press, 1987.
Kundera, Milan. *Encounter*. Translated by Linda Asher. New York: Harper Collins, 2010.
Nishitani, Keiji. *Religion and Nothingness*. Translated by Jan Van Bragt. Berkeley: University of California Press, 1982.
Ruin, Hans. *Being with the Dead: Burial, Ancestral Politics, and the Roots of Historical Consciousness*. Stanford: Stanford University Press, 2019.
Watson, Burton, trans. *The Complete Works of Zhuangzi*. New York: Columbia University Press, 2013.

5

Thing and World in Laozi and Heidegger

Eric S. Nelson

Introduction

The concept of the thing would seemingly designate that which is most concrete while abstracting away from the specific qualities that make particular things uniquely what they are. Edmund Husserl described phenomenology as a movement toward "the things themselves," defining the thing in the *Philosophy of Arithmetic* (1891) as that which bears characteristics with unity through time and change and in *Ideas* (1913) as the correlational object of intentional consciousness. Martin Heidegger repeatedly reposed the question "What is a thing?" in the context of phenomenologically encountering and describing the thing, confronting Occidental philosophical conceptions of the thing, and engaging with the emptiness of the thing in the *Daodejing*, attributed to Laozi, and its uselessness in the *Zhuangzi*.[1]

It is thought that Heidegger initially encountered the "Daoist" (which might be better designated as Laoist) conception of the thing and being-in-the-world in the German edition of *The Book of Tea* by Okakura Kakuzō 岡倉覚三, which he received as a gift in 1919 from Itō Kichinosuke 伊藤吉之助.[2] This popular book fuses motifs from Lao-Zhuang, Chan/Zen Buddhism, and Shinto together to draw a picture of the East Asian spirit of tea as it is enacted in concrete ritual practices.

The way and art of tea making and drinking realize the Daoist "art of being-in-the world" (*Kunst des In-der-Welt-Seins*). This art consists of a continual readjustment to the environment in which one maintains the relationship between things and makes room for others without abandoning one's own position.[3] Okakura accentuates the role of emptiness (*die Leere*) in the image of the spatial vacuum in the *Daodejing*, describing how the reality of the room is found in its emptiness, the usefulness of the water-jug (*Wasserkrug*) dwells in its emptiness rather than its material form, and how emptiness is all embracing as the space and possibility of movement.[4]

The thirty-year-old Heidegger was already thinking in 1919 of the verbal character of the world, and began a style of depersonalizing and verbalizing reified substantives of such as world in "it worlds" (*es weltet*) and value in "it values" (*es wertet*). In the 1919 lecture course *The Determination of Philosophy*, he proposed: "Living in an environing world, it signifies for me everywhere and always, it is all worldly, 'it worlds.'"[5]

Environmental meaningfulness (*das Bedeutungshafte*) loses its meaning (*ent-deutet*). The living-experiencing of the environing worlding of the world (*Umwelt erleben*) is de-vitalized or "de-lived" (*ent-lebt*). The "it worlds" undergoes processes of reification as it is distilled into and concealed in the objectness of things (*res*).

Heidegger described in the 1919–20 lecture course *Basic Problems of Phenomenology* how world is lost in the reification of lived-experiences (*Verdinglichungen der Erlebnisse*) and the devitalization of life (*Entlebung*).[6] The thing is separated from its environing worlding character and fixated. The thing is "only there as such," as correlate of the ego, and reduced to the real as existing, in the distancing theoretical attitude. Yet, Heidegger notes, the "it worlds" is still suggested in specific ways of encountering things in questions such as when one asks (perhaps in surprise) "What sort of thing is that?"[7] The "real" constructed in idealism and realism is impoverished in contrast to the abundance of the thing.

Things are primarily understood in these post-war lecture-courses as objects of a reduced notion of immediate external experience and natural scientific and theoretical inquiry.[8] Such objectivizing knowledge of things is inappropriate for grasping the self-world.[9] The reification of relations is extended to the reflexive nexus of the self-world (which is neither an ego nor a thing, neither subject nor object) that is seen as consisting of a nexus of things in which the self-world loses both its "self" and "world" character.[10] It is reified operating in an instrumental nexus as a mere object among objects.

The objectivized neutralized thing as object in his winter semester 1929–30 lecture course lacks world: "The stone is worldless, without world, has no world."[11] The stone, the stream, and the mountain are not world-disclosive, not events; they are not the worlding of the world of "it worlds" and cannot address their perceiver. The object is primarily either instrumentally ready-to-hand (*zuhanden*) in pragmatic use in a nexus of tools and equipment or objectively present-at-hand (*vorhanden*) for theoretical inquiry.[12]

Things are primarily objects of use, exchange, inquiry, yet they are still more than this. Heidegger's referential nexus determines things in their instrumental usefulness, only interrupted in their uselessness in breakdowns, such that Levinas noted how this presupposes without adequately articulating the elemental as their inappropriable atmosphere and milieu of air, earth, rain, sunlight, and wind that "suffice for themselves."[13] In freely wandering, we enjoy the fresh breeze and the sunlight not for a purpose but for themselves, and the stone and the thing appear in the elemental's play of light and shadow. Heidegger forgets that the elemental nourishes myself and things as they are encountered in non-purposive enjoyment (*jouissance*).[14] Nonetheless, despite the pragmatic instrumental tendencies rightly criticized by Levinas, Heidegger's discourse of the thing in the late 1920s is not merely pragmatist when he interprets things as dominated by a referential nexus of usage and usefulness given the facticity of interruptive breakdown, disorienting questionability and uncanniness, and other possibilities of relational attunement in encountering the thing.

In the 1935–7 "The Origin of the Work of Art," the apparently natural thing, instrumental equipmental objectness (*Zeug, Gebrauchsding*), and the work (*Werk*) are differentiated as the artwork discloses the thing that bears and opens the "there" and liberates it from the nexus of instrumentality. The work can reveal the constitutive role of things in the thereness of human existence.[15] Even prior to the ostensive turn (a notion Heidegger himself introduced in his auto-critiques of the mid-1930s) to the often poetic thinking and saying of being, there are indications of the more intimate relations with things and their life in his account of the atmosphere of attunement and mood—such as the thing as encountered in the situation of radical boredom[16] or in anxiety, indifference, or wonder—that increasingly draws Heidegger toward poetic language and Daoist discourses of the thing that indicate possibilities of the releasement and a more responsively attuned encountering of things.

This conception of releasement is no doubt informed by Meister Eckhart (1260–1328), for whom the *Gelassenheit* of the self has priority over the *Gelassenheit* of things, while also being at play in his understanding of Daoist *wuwei* 無爲 (non-coercive responsive attunement) as a releasement of and responsiveness to self-happening (*ziwei* 自為) and self-transforming of the myriad things.[17] Heidegger detects his own problematic of instrumental and self-so things in texts ascribed to Lao-Zhuang in his Daoist inspired reflections of the 1940s and '50s discussed below.[18]

Wu 物 as Sacrificial, Ritual, and Natural Event

What is the "Daoist" sense of the thing that addressed Heidegger in the early Weimar Republic—and to which he returned in the closing years of the Second World War—through Okakura Kakuzō's reflections on Daoism and tea (in which the thing is natural as well as artistically sensed and cultivated) and the translations of Richard Wilhelm (Laozi and Zhuangzi) and Martin Buber (Zhuangzi)?[19] More significantly, what is the "question of the thing" in the early Chinese context?

The earliest identified uses of *wu* 物 in Shang divination inscriptions signified a speckled cow killed in sacrifice.[20] The character *wu* 物 combines the radicals for cow (*niu* 牛) and to cut/blood on the knife (*wu* 勿) associated with sacrificial ritual practice and etymologically its early meaning was any moveable entity used in ritual sacrifices.[21] Sacrifice meant the death and destruction of the thing as well as the continued reproduction of things.

This sacrificial and ritual context is significant for the development of early Chinese conceptions of the thing and its forms of world-disclosure. A sacrificial entity has its allotted time characterized by the event of its sacrifice. The expression *wu* became interlinked with the arising, persisting, and disappearing of the thing in its own allotted time, and with that which is changing and perishable. *Wu* indicates accordingly a temporalizing duration as the thing is depicted in subsequent sources as formed in flow (*liu* 流) and transformation (*hua* 化).

The excavated pre-Qin manuscript *All Things Flow in Form* (*Fan Wu Liu Xing* 凡物流形) provides an example of the flowing and temporalizing character of the thing.[22] The text begins by posing the questions: How do things flow into taking form and shape? How does the thing dissipate after having taken on a form? Given the flux and conflict of contrary vital powers, the author of the text inquires, how do constant forces operate that are capable of generating form and the thing and then disperse? That is, how is the thing individuated and fixed for a time? *Wu* indicates a temporalizing formation of a finite form between birth and death. The momentarily persisting thing expresses a cosmological order that transpires through the flow of elemental primordial forces (*qi* 氣) and is regulated through "heavenly" or "natural" criteria (*tiandu* 天度). "The hundred things do not perish" (*baiwu busi* 百物不死) as they depart and return, dissipate and remerge.[23]

The thing was carved away from the whole of things as a particularized form, which might be construed as an early form of abstraction and fixation. Yet the microcosmic thing was aligned with a macrocosmic harmony and ritual order as is evident in the early classics and Ruist (*rujia* 儒家) sources. The semantic range of *wu* unfolded to include concrete forms such as color, person, natural phenomena, the living and the non-living thing. By the late Spring and Autumn (*chunqiu* 春秋) era, as Yuri Pine notes, *wu* indicated "a thing" no longer specifically bound to sacrificial practices while often retaining a sense of connection with a ritually reproduced cosmic order.[24]

Wu signified a naturally arising thing, and reality consisted of "all things" (*baiwu* 百物) in early Ruist sources and the "myriad things" (*wanwu* 萬物) in the literature that informed the development of the *Laozi*. One potential distinguishing mark between early Ruist and "Daoist" (or "Laoist" to refer to the materials related to the *Laozi*) texts is the use of *baiwu* and *wanwu* to express the entirety of things. The former is more characteristic of extant early Ruist materials, although not later ones, and the latter of extant Laoist materials in which the phrase *baiwu* does not appear.

The early Ruist "all things" expressed both the temporal and the ritual character of the thing. In chapter 17, section 19, of the *Analects*, Confucius famously asks: "How does heaven speak at all as the four seasons follow their courses and all things arise?" Seasons and things take their generational turns. The ritual and cosmic character of the thing is expressed in early sources such as the *Liji* 禮記 (Book of Rites). In its nineteenth chapter, the *Yue Ji* 樂記 (Record of Music) sections 12 and 14 (2.3 and 2.5), "all things" are portrayed as constituting a fluctuating harmonizing whole maintained through a ritual and sacrificial order that is enacted through music and rites.[25] In music as in natural harmony, things transform, discord, and are reconciled. In ritual as in natural order, each thing finds its appropriate place and role. Music and ritual are consequently exemplary models of governance that reproduce cosmic harmony and maintain its order.[26]

The texts attributed to the enigmatic figures of Lao-Zhuang reveal a different configuration between the thing, temporality, and the cosmos. There are chapters in the received rendition of the *Daodejing* that retain connections between the thing and sacrifice, temporal duration, and cosmic ritual order. In *Daodejing* chapter 5, heaven and earth are described as "lacking benevolence and regard the myriad things like straw-dogs." This passage is commonly interpreted as conveying the sage's indifference or even a cruel inhumaneness toward things and the people. It was explicated in the *Xiang'er* 想爾 commentary (c. 190–220 CE) in moralistic language as regarding "the good with humaneness and the bad without humaneness." This commentary made sense of the passage by correlating the nurturing aspects of *dao* with being in accordance with it and its indifferent aspects with lack of accordance. The sacrificial straw-dog served accordingly as a warning established by the Yellow Emperor (Huangdi 黃帝)

of people's futile and useless expenditure of vital forces and life, as they increase and destroy themselves, and heaven does not hear them as they fail to integrate their natural vital substance in accord with the heavenly.[27]

The image of the straw-dog indicates the appropriate and inappropriate timing of the life of the thing. It is exemplary of the temporal event of the thing in its gathering and dispersing. A different sense of its import is found in the *Zhuangzi*. As expressly noted in one of the Confucius related stories, "straw-dog" (*chugou* 芻狗) is a sacrificial object that is elegantly clothed and taken care of during a ritual ceremony and afterward left aside and trampled back into the earth or used for kindling.[28] The straw-dog in the *Laozi* and the *Zhuangzi* serves as an image of the generational life and death of the thing.[29] The *Tianyun* chapter clarifies this sense as it then compares the teachings of Confucius to a flawed endeavor to preserve the scattered remnants of the straw-dog after their allotted time has passed. The pursuit to hold on to the dead and the past can only result in the living being haunted by nightmares.

Notwithstanding the temporality expressed in the "all things" passage considered previously above, Confucius in the *Tianyun* could not adequately recognize the generational revolving nature of things as events or moments in time that form and dissipate in transformation. Rituality, righteousness, law, and measure alter over time. The straw-dog functioning as the image of the thing discloses a world and its criteria in incessant generation, formation, and dissolution.

The Self-Naturing (*ziran*) of the Thing

The study of excavated pre-Qin silk and bamboo texts has revolutionized the study of early Chinese thought. The close connection between thing, generation, and transformation is expressed in the excavated Guodian 郭店 (*c.* 300 BCE) and Mawangdui 馬王堆 (*c.* 200 BCE) renditions of the *Laozi*. These materials indicate alternative or at least more complex conceptions of the thing operative in the early "Laoist" context, as the "thing" is related to the "self" (*zi* 自) in expressions that can be translated as the self-soing (*wanwu zhi ziran* 萬物之自然 in Guodian A6), self-transforming (*wanwu jiang zihua* 萬物將自化 in Guodian A7), self-steadying (*wanwu jiang ziding* 萬物將自定 in Guodian A7), and "self-guesting" (*wanwu jiang zibin* 萬物將自賓 in Guodian A10) of the myriad things.[30]

What is the early significance of "*zi*"? It is thought to initially indicate the nose and is used in Shang oracle inscriptions to signify "to start from." In relation to the thing, it refers to the face and point of departure of the thing. The "self" of *zi* is not that of human agency, identity, or subjectivity (*wo* 我). It encompasses cosmic, human, animal, and material entities. It signifies not only the "my ownness" (*Jemeinigkeit*) of the self-world phenomenologically described by Heidegger but the "its ownness" of each thing-world. Unlike ordinary English and German language usage, the thing (*wu*) encompasses sentient and insentient beings and each thing has its own way of being a self (*zi*). The thing's own self-relational self-world (expressed in *zi*-expressions in the Chinese context) is not considered in Heidegger's early thought, where the thing is primarily either instrumentally ready-to-hand (*zuhanden*) or objectively present-at-hand (*vorhanden*), nor is it fully articulated in his later more Daoist like thinking as responsive remembering (*das andenkende Denken*) of the thing in writings such as the 1950 essay "The Thing" discussed below in the concluding sections of this chapter.

Ziran is only later fixed and objectified into nature as object. In its earlier senses, it does not so much name an object or set of objects ("nature") as much as the way in which something verbally ("naturing") and adverbially ("naturally") occurs in its movements.³¹ The discourse of *wanwu* and *ziran* appears to have been systematically articulated initially in the *Laozi* materials, functioning as its key concepts and becoming fundamental to ensuing Chinese philosophical discourse, ethical life, and aesthetic culture.

Laozian discourses can well be called "ziranist" in recognizing the priority of *ziran*. The conclusion to *Daodejing* chapter 25 (Guodian A11) asserts that *ziran* is the key to understanding the way: *dao* follows or models itself according to *ziran* (*dao fa ziran* 道法自然). The late-Han era *Heshang Gong* (河上公, Riverside Elder) commentary describes how this means that *dao* follows its own naturing (*dao xing ziran* 道性自然). The myriad things are self-sufficient in their self-becoming and self-accomplishing (*wanwu zicheng* 萬物自成).³²

The rediscovered *Heng Xian* 恆先 text (300 BCE) regards letting the thing happen—in "neither avoiding nor partaking in it" (無舍也，無與也)—as being in accord with the thing's self-happening.³³ Does the early history of the thing's "selfing" (*zi*) imply that the sage-kings and sages step back or assist in allowing the thing to determinate itself? Both possibilities are found in the different renditions and interpretations of the *Laozi* that exist as a textual and interpretive plurality. There are noticeable differences between the Guodian and received *Laozi* texts. In Guodian A6, according to Henricks' translation, the ancient sages are "able" (the first use of *neng* 能) yet are "unable to act" (its second use in *fu neng wei* 弗能為), allowing the myriad things to be themselves in their own self-soing or self-naturing. In *Daodejing* chapter 64, and in Cook's translation of Guodian A6,³⁴ the sages do not dare to (coercively or calculatedly) act (*fu gan wei* 弗敢為) while they expressly complement or assist (*fu* 輔) the myriad things to be themselves.

Guodian A6 could be read as implicitly stating the same message as *Daodejing* chapter 64 if its first use of "able" implies able to complement and its second use unable to coercively act.³⁵ It could also be read to suggest the neutrality of following *dao* with respect to the self-generative naturing of things, a model found in Huanglao 黃老 and so-called "legalist" (*fajia* 法家) discourses. In contrast, the received *Daodejing* chapter 64 indicates a correlational co-responsive attunement without compelled or artificial action (*wei*) in following *dao* in its caring, maternal, and nurturing functions by complementing and assisting things to occur as themselves.³⁶

The opening lines of Guodian A7 and *Daodejing* chapter 37 express the temporalizing constancy of *dao*'s operating without purposive activity as things transform themselves (*zihua* 自化) and determine and settle themselves (*ziding* 自定). Lords and kings emulate *dao* in knowing the limits of what is sufficient and in quietude. The constancy of *dao* is described respectively as *daoheng* 道恆 and *daochang* 道常. *Heng* was tabooed, as part of the given name of the fifth emperor of the Han dynasty, and changed to the semantically overlapping *chang*. Neither word designates an eternity outside of time but extended potentially infinite duration. *Heng* signifies persevering, long continuance, and prosperity in the explication of the thirty-second hexagram of the *Yijing* 易經 (*Book of Changes*). The earlier *heng* signifies the temporalizing of the waxing moon and a fecund generative potentially infinite perpetuity; *chang* the temporality of continuing and extending regularity.[37] The moon goes through its phases, the earth its seasons, and the repeating pattern is extended. The temporalizing of constancy is not an indeterminate neutral arena but one in which vital forces and things wax and wane according to their own natures.

The Mawangdui *Laozi* A13 states that "*dao* generates" (*daosheng zhi* 道生之) and "virtuosity nourishes" (*dexu zhi* 德畜之) "governed things" (*wuxing zhi* 物刑之) and "useful devices" (*qicheng zhi* 器成之). The corresponding line in *Daodejing* chapter 51 reads that they generate and nourish "formed things" (*wuxing zhi* 物形之) and "potentiality" (*shicheng zhi* 勢成之). While these different characters were linguistically interchangeable in antiquity, they intimate two different forms of order expressed in the subsequent lines. Generative *dao* operates in Mawangdui A13 through "ceaseless self-offering" (*heng ziji* 恆自祭) instead of the more typical (in other renditions) "constant self-naturing" (*chang ziran* 常自然). The language of Mawangdui A13 hearkens to the older sacrificial signification of thing with its language of governing/punishing things, useful instrumental products, and self-offering/sacrifice. It also points toward the *ziran* discourse of the thing. The way of itself generates and nourishes the life of things, allowing them their own life and death, determinations and transformations. The kings and sages emulate and participate in the generative temporalizing of *dao* by complementing and nurturing things in their life and letting them depart in their death.

The *Heng Xian* further contextualizes the senses of constancy in the Guodian *Laozi*. The opening line asserts that in the originary state of constancy (*heng*), there is no being (*hengxian wuyou* 恆先無有).[38] This contested line could be understood as the nothingness of or—as it has no spatial or temporal differentiation—prior to primordial constancy. Spatiality arises from emptiness and temporality arises from beginning such that the vital generative forces are self-generating and self-arising and things self-reproducing and self-reverting (*zifu* 自復).[39] Given subsequent interpretations of the generativity of nothingness, it could indicate the generative spatializing and temporalizing of being emerging from emptiness and beginning from nothingness as the indistinct and muddled is differentiated and individuated into the temporalizing being of primal forces, things, and names that each have their own time. This resonates with the much later opening chapter of the *Liezi* 列子 (c. 300 CE, although incorporating earlier materials), in which the initial state of things is described as muddled without separation and the temporality of things as one of generative metamorphosis.

Guodian A10 and *Daodejing* chapter 32 state that: "Should lords and kings be able to uphold [the way], the myriad things will bring themselves in line."[40] The myriad things are self-ordering. More literally, *zi* 自 refers to self and *bin* 賓 to visitor or guest. The lords and kings allow the thing to be the guest of itself, allowing the thing to operate in its own course. Its own course has been interpreted as its way of being or role in the moral-political order of things. The *Heshang Gong* takes being a guest as spontaneous moral obedience and submission (*fucong yude* 服從於德).[41] Wang Bi 王弼 (226–249 CE) elucidates in his commentaries on *Daodejing* chapters 10 and 32 how the functioning of the self-relation of things is a condition of the self-sufficiency, self-tranquility, and self-contentment of things and how the sovereign who nurtures them to this condition enacts and embodies the example of *dao*.[42]

The early Laozi materials do not radically distinguish between interacting with things and persons, as persons appear as a special case of rather than an exception to things. The Laozian ethos of the sage's letting and the thing's naturing or selfing is articulated in Guodian 16 (*Daodejing* ch. 57): "I engage in no affairs and the people are self-enriching. I do not (coercively) act and the people are self-transforming. I practice quietude and the people are self-rectifying. I desire without desiring and the people self-simplify."[43] Letting, quieting, and simplifying, correlated with the self-becoming of things on their own, are in the context of the *Laozi* practices of the self and political rule that have complex relations with Daoist biospiritual meditative practices as well as Huanglao, legalist (in the work attributed to Hanfei 韓非), and more anarchic (in Zhuangzi, Liezi, and Bao Jingyan 鮑敬言) biopolitical models.[44]

Freedom and Allotment: Self-Naturing and the *Zhuangzi*

Although the relationship between the *Laozi* and *Zhuangzi* materials remains unclear, they are related in expressing variations on the prioritization of the self-naturing (*ziran*) of things disclosed through non-coercive responsive attunement (*wuwei*).[45] *Ziran* only occurs ten times in the *Zhuangzi*, and the ethos of the self-letting/other-selfing correlation is often conveyed in other *zi-* expressions and in the enactment of responsive resonance (*ying* 應) with the thing. While *ying* is only used twice in the ordinary sense of reply or response in the *Daodejing*, it has a more significant role in the *Zhuangzi* and in the Heshang Gong and Wang Bi *Laozi* commentaries. The sages respond when affected (*gan er hou ying* 感而後應) in *Zhuangzi* chapter 15 that concerns undoing engraved meanings and constructed fixations.[46] As will be considered below, responsive resonance suggests an alternative to Heidegger's conception of *Befindlichkeit* (attunement, disposedness) manifested through *Stimmung* (mood) through which things and world are disclosed in his examples of the disorienting limit encounters of radical anxiety and profound boredom but also in joy, love, wonder, and—in a complex mediated way—the poetic word and saying of his later thought.[47]

The self-determination of the thing appears in the *Zhuangzi* in its self-transforming (*zihua*) and self-acting (*ziwei*). The adaptive and receptive disposition of *wuwei* is correlated with the thing's self-transformation by itself on its own in chapters 11 and 17 of the *Zhuangzi*, while the recognition of the self-acting of the thing occurs when one does not self-act, as seen in chapter 13. Things occur and act of their own by "not self-acting" such that "they did not do anything themselves … Heaven does no producing of things, yet the ten thousand things transform. Earth does no growing of things, yet the ten thousand things are nourished. Emperors and kings do nothing, engage only in non-doing, yet the deeds of the world get accomplished."[48]

The *Zhuangzi* tends not to subordinate the thing's way of being itself to an external obedient role but rather emphasizes its self-becoming that was construed later as an allotted and singularly determined self-nature (*zixing* 自性). Guo Xiang 郭象 (252–312 CE) in his commentary on the *Zhuangzi* linked "lone" (*du* 獨) with "transformation" (*hua* 化). In "lone-transformation" (*duhua* 獨化), the lone singular (*du*) and self (*zi*) retain identity while transforming: the self retains itself and its own self-nature in becoming other than itself in transformation.[49] In Guo Xiang, the relation of the thing to itself (as guest of itself), individuated and potentially isolated as uniquely lone and sole (*shenqi duhua* 神器獨化), risks being bifurcated into identity and difference, host and guest, as the thing is in danger of being monadically separated from the dynamic relational responsive resonance of the myriad things in which its own self-determination occurs.

The early fourth-century Buddhist thinker and monastic Zhi Dun 支遁 (Zhi Daolin 支道林), who fused the discourses of mysterious learning and Buddhism, accordingly criticized Guo Xiang's interpretation of Zhuangzi in his "Discourse of Free and Easy Wandering" (*xiaoyao lun* 逍遙論) for the complacency, determinism, and fatalism of its notion of complying (*yue* 約) with one's endowed particular allotment (*fen* 分) in the myriad transformations (*wanhua* 萬化), subverting the freedom of free and easy wandering. Zhi Dun identified this freedom with Buddhist *prajñā*, which recognizes things as things without being fettered by things, and in which the emptiness of both somethingness and nothingness is disclosed.[50] If Zhi Dun's criticisms of Guo Xiang are valid, then *ziran*, which promised to liberate things in their self-determination from being mere sacrificial and instrumental objects in the *Zhuangzi*, has become the self-determination of the thing's inborn self-nature (*zixing*) in its allotted share.

This problematic raises two issues: first, the *Zhuangzi* itself articulates in chapter 6 the priority of the self-occurring of *dao* rather than fixed nature in discussions of the thing. *Dao* is without forced activity and fixed form (*wuwei wuxing* 無為無形) and self-originating and self-rooting (*ziben zigen* 自本自根). The life of things transforms without its direction being known and the exemplary sages participate and wander amidst transforming things without separation or escape and without calculation and anxiety regarding their purpose and outcome. Second, the *Zhuangzi* indicates not only the sole singular self-determining transformations of things but also mutual co-determination in the synchronization and integration of the myriad things.[51]

The equalizing (*qi* 齊) of the *Zhuangzi* is described in chapter 17 as the "coherence and equality of the myriad things" (*wanwu yiqi* 萬物一齊). This equalizing is more a transforming flowing musical harmonizing than subordination to a fixed determinate uniformity.[52] Equalization transpires in transformative relationality and its recognition, in which "heaven, earth, and I live side by side together, and the myriad things and I are one," as well as in singular and sole self-nature.

The diversity of various forms of expression deploying the self-relational "*zi*" in the early sources such as the Guodian *Laozi* and the *Heng Xian* is flattened out into the concept of *ziran* that increasingly becomes fixated as an objective order and object, in which the thing appears determined by a fixed nature. This development weakens the dynamic verbal and transformative character of early *ziran* discourses conveyed in Lao-Zhuang.

Ziran and Phusis

The letting releasement and responsive attunement attributable to early Laozi related materials presuppose a cosmological natural-political order of the self-generativity of things and seasonal temporality in which they operate. What can they signify in relation to a philosopher such as Heidegger or a contemporary audience such as ourselves? In Heidegger's corpus, the question of the modern construction and technological enframing of world as an arena of universally fungible and exchangeable things is intimately interrelated with the history of Occidental metaphysics and its early Greek origins.[53]

The experiential and discursive functions of *ziran* overlap at points while entailing a distinctive form of world-event and disclosure in contrast with the early Greek experience and conception of *phusis* (φύσις), as Heidegger repeatedly reimagines it in works such as the 1935 lecture course *Introduction to Metaphysics*, revised and published as a book in 1953, as determinate of the history of Occidental metaphysics:

> What does the word *phusis* say? It says what emerges from itself (for example, the emergence, the blossoming of a rose), the unfolding that opens itself up, the coming-into-appearance in such unfolding, and holding itself and persisting in appearance—in short, the emerging-abiding sway.[54]

The early Greek *phúō* (φύω) is related to archaic Indo-European words for birth, earth, dwelling, and being. It signifies that which is brought forth, generated, and produced. The meaning of *phusis* is (akin to *ziran* to this extent) that which arises and disperses. *Phusis* was only later distinguished from what is artfully produced (*tékhnē*, τέχνη) and from the normatively lawful (*nomos*, νόμος) as distinct from *phusis* as that which physically exists. It encompasses in the early Greek context not only the natural and the physical (in the subsequent reduced senses of these words) but heaven, earth, stone, plant, humans, gods, and their works.[55] *Phusis* further signifies in Heidegger's provocative reading that which is as an emerging upsurge from being's hiddenness and concealment, an abiding holding-sway (*Walten*, which more typically means reign, preside, prevail), and essence (*Wesen*) as essencing (*Wesung*) rather than nature as the fixed determinate principle of the thing.[56] In a later note, Heidegger described *phusis* as "the self-unfolding emergence in and through which a being first is what it is."[57]

Phusis operates as a name for being itself as that by which beings appear,[58] referring to being's emerging event, emerging beings and things, and their unconcealed truth. The emerged and the submerged, the unconcealed and the concealed are interconnected, and truth (*aletheia*, ἀλήθεια) is thought negatively as "not hidden" (*a-letheia*) and as that which emerges into the openness from hiddenness. According to Heraclitus's fragment 123, "nature tends toward hiddenness" ("φύσις κρύπτεσθαι φιλεῖ"), which Heidegger translates as "emerging gives favor to self-concealing."[59]

It might be thought that *phusis* names the self-emergence of beings from being and intersects with *ziran* as the self-emergence of things from *dao*. They might both operate as originary world-orienting words, yet their relation is much more complicated as *phusis* signifies being as emergence and *ziran* the way *dao* operates of itself. It is from the self-generative watery yet fecund depth of nothingness that things emerge in early *Laozi* related sources.

Phusis and the Thing

Early Greek *phusis* is depicted as the "first beginning"[60] from which Occidental metaphysics emerges. There is also the "other beginning" that confronts this first beginning. It is described in the 1935 *Contributions to Philosophy* as the referral and offering/sacrifice of beings to being ("Im anderen Anfang wird alles Seiende dem Seyn geopfert") that essences as event and in the clearing of self-hiddenness.[61] In the mid-1930s, the establishment and institution of beings are conceived through "work and deed and sacrifice" ("Werk und Tat und Opfer")[62] and linked with creativity and violence. The thing in creative work is not only a product or representation as it discloses a world. The thing is no longer determined by use and breakdown, as it emerges from and is potentially sacrificed to being or a given historical configuration of the event of being and what Heidegger portrays as, in the politically highly problematic context of National Socialist totalitarianism, the creativity of originary "poets, thinkers and state creators, who actually ground and establish the historical existence of a nation."[63]

What then is the relation between *phusis* and things? Heidegger already in the 1930s calls for liberating the thing from being a particular carrier of properties and the paradigm of representational thinking and truth as correctness and correspondence. The thing is no longer worldless as it was in 1929, but does Heidegger ever arrive at an appropriate interpretation of the thing as it is in itself (in its *ziran*) and in its own world openness?

There are already a number of indications that point toward the prioritization of the thing conveyed in his later thought. *Phusis* is called the first beginning and *da-sein*, as the "openness of the there," the other beginning in his notes for the 1935 Frankfurt lectures version of the "The Origin of the Work of Art" that was eventually reworked for publication in 1949.[64] In this work, earth is the emerging, upsurge, and showing forth of that which is hidden and the clearing is an "open middle" or center that is not enclosed or encircled by beings, but "circles around all beings like the nothingness that we hardly know."[65]

The thing can only be encountered in the midst of the clearing and, later beginning in the 1949 *Bremen Lectures*, in the fourfold gathering (*das Geviert*) into place between earth and sky, mortals and immortals. Perhaps informed by his intensive engagement with Lao-Zhuang in the mid-1940s, things disclose worlds in poetic saying.[66] Things now partake in an elemental being of their own, albeit threatened and circumscribed by their positioning and ordering in metaphysical and technological enframing (*Gestell*), which was lacking in the primarily instrumental analysis of the thing in *Being and Time* and the creative violence of being interpretation of *Introduction to Metaphysics* and the early versions of "The Origin of the Work of Art." Revealingly, in the latter, the thing in its thingliness, as carrying and opening the there,[67] plays an increasingly noteworthy role from the lecture's initial 1935 version to its 1949 publication.

The Thing as Moment and as Gathering

As noted earlier, Heidegger introduced the expression "it worlds" in his 1919 lecture course to indicate the verbal character of world as worlding. He proposed that "the nothing nothings" in his 1929 lecture "What Is Metaphysics?" Only later did he arrive at the theme of the first 1949 Bremen lecture, revised as the 1949 essay "The Thing," namely that "the thing things" in statements such as "the thinging gathers" ("*das Dingen versammelt*") and—in contrast to the 1929 worldlessness of the thing—"the thing things world" ("*das Ding dingt Welt*").[68] It is not the projection of temporalizing human existence or the swaying of being but the thing's lingering time spent and earthly dwelling place (i.e., both senses of "*verweilen*") that gathers and brings near earth and sky, mortals and immortals into the fourfold.[69] "Thing" in its modern usage can signify an indeterminate object, somethingness, or in its plural form reality. The more archaic meanings of the Germanic word ding/thing (*þenga-) include a moment or duration in time and gathering as in the assembling of the people or a court to make a judgment and decision. It is this sense of the thing's temporalizing and gathering that Heidegger emphasizes in "The Thing."

In Heidegger's turn toward the thing in its priority as more than an intentional correlate, time and space are not given as merely objectively present as a neutral arena for that which phenomenally appears as bearing qualities, as in the paradigm of representational thinking. In contrast to the "each time my own" (*Jeweiligkeit*) temporalizing of human existence in *Being and Time*, Heidegger articulates in 1949 the prominence of things in the duration of an "awhile" (*Weile*) and the nearness and proximity of place. The lingering of things gathers time as an encountered duration and their dwelling gathers space as an encountered locality. The verbal sense of the thinging of the thing is the nearing in which "world as world" is held near.[70] The thing discloses world and, more than this, it gathers, carries, and opens the worlding of the world in the specificity of a durational "for a while" and locality of place.

What then is the relation of thing, earth, and world first thought of in terms of strife and contest in the mid-1930s? According to their archaic roots, hints that Heidegger plays off of, earth means ground, the earth as the dwelling place of mortal things was called the middle enclosure (Midgard), and world (*Welt* from old German *weralt*) the generational age or life of man or world-age (*Weltalter*).

A world-age and its world-picture consist not only in a human generation; it is a configuration of things. The thing opens and discloses world and world conceals the event of the thing as it becomes one object with or without value in what Heidegger earlier described as a pragmatically determined referential nexus. Whereas Heidegger was primarily concerned with the reification of human existence in the 1920s, as we have seen, he is concerned in 1949 with the fixation of thingly existence in which natural and human life have become objectified and instrumentalized. Heidegger speaks now of the picturing and enframing of world in which things are fixed and frozen in their positionality. Confronting the alienation and reification of human existence calls for confronting what has become of things in order to encounter them anew, although Heidegger inadequately addresses their basis in material relations of production, exchange, and consumption.[71]

The enframing of things contrasts with their releasement in thoughtful encounter: "We think of the thing as thing when we release the thing in its thinging from the worlding of the world. In this way we thoughtfully let ourselves be approached by the encompassing essencing of the thing."[72] Heidegger's expression "thoughtfully allow" (*andenkend lassen*) means to let the thing (as it is of itself) near and approach in responsive reminiscence of it in its lingering duration and dwelling place. Phenomenologically speaking, time and space are accordingly not absolute, nor forms of intuition through which things are constituted in experience. Time and space occur and are encountered vis-à-vis the temporalizing and spatializing of things that is world-formative and full of the world in which it is concealed: hiding the thing in the world.

The Emptiness and Uselessness of the Thing

Heidegger's turn toward the thing during the period from 1943 to 1950 coincided with his intensive engagement with the *Daodejing* and the *Zhuangzi*, as I and others have considered elsewhere.[73] This turn toward the thing is intertwined with his multiple engagements with the Daoist thing. His interpretive encounter with these two early Daoist sources center on his concern with the thing and the word in relation to his own context of technological modernity that has neutralized words and devastated non-living and living things.

Heidegger repeatedly returns to the emptiness of the thing, expressed in the image of the empty vessel in chapter 11 of the *Daodejing*, from "The Uniqueness of the Poet"[74] and the first of the *Country Path Conversations*[75] to the first Bremen lecture[76] and "The Thing."[77] Instead of the work-in-the-thing that was emphasized in "The Origin of the Work of Art," it is its emptiness that allows the formed vessel to function and flourish as what it is. The vessel, serving as an image of the thing, is filled and emptied, gathering and releasing world through its emptiness. This emptying and filling of the thing is possible because of emptiness. It is in Wang Bi's interpretation an example of *wuwei* as an acting (*wei* 為) of and from nothingness (*wu* 無), as being is the functioning (*yong* 用) of the body or essencing (*ti* 體) of nothingness.[78]

Heidegger addresses the uselessness of things and words through the "usefulness of uselessness" (*wuyong zhi yong* 無用之用) in the *Zhuangzi* in the third of the *Country Path Conversations* and in his 1962 lecture "Transmitted and Technological Language" in which he ponders the "languaging" (the "it speaks") of language. The Zhuangzian "useful uselessness," exhibited in a series of narratives in which the useless thing (tree, person, and so on) flourishes while the useful thing is destroyed in being used, becomes the condition of use in contrast with the thing being principally characterized by its ready-to-hand pragmatic availability and usability. Pure usefulness and instrumentality suppress and forget while presupposing the thing in the functioning (*zhiyong*) of its non-use (*wuyong*) and self-so-ing of itself (*ziran*).

A number of passages help contextualize the notion of the thing and use in the *Zhuangzi*. In chapter 22 of the *Zhuangzi*, it is noted that "what things the thing is not itself the thing" and in chapter 20 that the genuine person lets "things thing without being thinged by things."[79] This need not entail a rejection of thing as thing. It is its own emptiness or nothingness and self-naturing (the thinglessness of things) that things the thing. The exemplary attunement with things is one of uselessness that lets things thing, as they are of themselves, while remaining in an attunement that is free, at ease, and undetermined (unthinged) by their thinging.[80]

Heidegger's later discourse of uselessness diverges from its deployment in the texts of the mid-1930s. It is an expression to which Heidegger repeatedly returns in his later works, typically without either directly or indirectly referring to the *Zhuangzi*, where it is coordinated with the letting go of *Gelassenheit* that steps back from coercive creating and willing as well as instrumental calculation and use. "Letting releasement" does not signify in Heidegger's works a mystical unification of the soul with God. It appears quasi-Daoistic, functioning in ways like *wuwei*, as an intra-worldly art of being-in-the-world that quiets and simplifies the self, desire, and will while releasing things to themselves in an attunement of free receptivity and responsiveness to things.[81]

Conclusion

Heidegger's philosophy of the thing shifts through a number of variations and intermediary positions from which three moments have been highlighted in the present chapter: (1) the thing as instrumental, objectively present, and worldless in relation to human existence as ecstatic world-opening Dasein; (2) the thing as ensnared in the creativity and violence of the work and offered to being; (3) the event of the "it things" as the duration and gathering of the world that conditions (*Be-Dingten*) a duration in a place.

The first strategy, unfolded particularly in the late 1920s, remains overly anthropocentric and subjectivistic, as Heidegger noted in his own auto-critiques of the project of *Being and Time*, as the thing remains an object of use and theorizing separated from animal and human life. The second strategy of the mid-1930s overly emphasizes the event of being and the being-historical deeds, works, and mission of creative and violent artists, poets, thinkers, and law-givers to sacrifice things in giving shape to new worlds. His third strategy of the late 1940s promises to unveil the world-generative event of the thing, as it things of itself, and the necessity of the thing's releasement, in its own way of being itself, in relation to human existence and being.

The thing shifts from isolation and worldlessness to gathering and worlding in Heidegger's thought. It moves from the periphery of his early phenomenology to the center of his confrontation with the environmental and existential destructiveness of technological modernity. Heidegger's philosophical pathway is characterized less by the question of being, the constitution of meaning, or truth as unconcealment, and more by the question of and the changing locus of the happening of the event: human existence as Dasein, nothingness, being, thing, and word.

The last moment, informed to some degree by his interaction with *ziran*-oriented Daoist texts in translation, brings Heidegger into his closest proximity to the responsive attunement (*wuwei*) with ongoing transforming (*hua*) and self-soing (*ziran*) of the thing in Lao-Zhuang discourses and into his most appropriate way of addressing the life of the thing. It is here that Heidegger intimates a *dao* and an ethos of responsive releasement of and attunement with things and the environments that they shape.

Notes

1 On the thing in Heidegger, Daoism, and Chinese philosophy, see Mark Kevin S. Cabural, "Daoism and the German Mission in Martin Heidegger's 'The Thing,'" *Frontiers of Philosophy in China*, 14.4 (2020): 570–92; David Chai, "Meontological Generativity: A Daoist Reading of the Thing," *Philosophy East and West*, 64.2 (2014): 303–18; Sai-Hang Kwok, "Zhuangzi's Philosophy of Thing," *Asian Philosophy*, 26.4 (2016): 294–310; Ann Pang-White, "Nature, Interthing Intersubjectivity, and the Environment: A Comparative Analysis of Kant and Daoism," *Dao: A Journal of Comparative Philosophy*, 8.1 (2009): 61–78; and Franklin Perkins, "What Is a Thing (*wu* 物)? The Problem of Individuation in Early Chinese Metaphysics," in Franklin Perkins and Chenyang Li (eds.), *Chinese Metaphysics and Its Problems* (Cambridge: Cambridge University Press, 2015), 54–68. On Heidegger and Lao-Zhuang Daoism, see Fabian Heubel, *Gewundene Wege nach China: Heidegger-Daoismus-Adorno* (Frankfurt: Klostermann, 2020); Reinhard May, *Heidegger's Hidden Sources: East-Asian Influences on his Work* (London: Routledge, 1996); Eric S. Nelson, *Chinese and Buddhist Philosophy in Early Twentieth-Century German Thought* (London: Bloomsbury Academic, 2017), 109–57; and Eric S. Nelson, "Heidegger's Daoist Turn," *Research in Phenomenology*, 49.3 (2019): 362–84.
2 Kakuzō Okakura, *Das Buch vom Tee* (Leipzig: Insel, 1919), 29. On the story of the gift and its possible influence on Heidegger, see Tomonobu Imamichi, *In Search of Wisdom: One Philosopher's Journey* (Tokyo: International House of Japan, 2004), 123; May, *Heidegger's Hidden Sources*, 118.
3 Okakura, *Das Buch vom Tee*, 29.
4 Ibid., 30.
5 "In einer Umwelt lebend, bedeutet es mir überall und immer, es ist alles welthaft, 'es weltet,'" in Martin Heidegger, *Zur Bestimmung der Philosophie* [GA 56/57], ed. Bernd Heimbüchel (Frankfurt: Vittorio Klostermann, 1987), 73.
6 Martin Heidegger, *Grundprobleme der Phanomenologie* [GA 58], ed. Hans-Helmuth Gander (Frankfurt: Vittorio Klostermann, 1993), 183.
7 Heidegger, *Zur Bestimmung der Philosophie*, 89.
8 Heidegger, *Grundprobleme der Phanomenologie*, 51.
9 Ibid., 223.
10 Ibid., 232.
11 Martin Heidegger, *Die Grundbegriffe der Metaphysik: Welt, Endlichkeit, Einsamkeit* [GA 29/30], ed. Friedrich-Wilhelm von Herrmann (Frankfurt: Vittorio Klostermann, 1983), 289.
12 Martin Heidegger, *Geschichte der Philosophie von Thomas von Aquin bis Kant* [GA 23], ed. Helmuth Vetter (Frankfurt: Vittorio Klostermann, 2006), 24.

13   Emmanuel Levinas, *Totality and Infinity: An Essay on Exteriority*, trans. Alphonso Lingis (Pittsburgh: Duquesne University Press, 1969), 132.
14   Ibid., 134.
15   Martin Heidegger, *Zu Eigenen Veroffentlichungen* [GA 82], ed. Friedrich-Wilhelm von Herrmann (Frankfurt: Vittorio Klostermann, 2018), 484–7.
16   Heidegger, *Die Grundbegriffe der Metaphysik*, 132.
17   Things are secondary to self and God in Eckhart. He identified *Gelassenheit* with Christian relinquishment (*relinquere*) of the world, detachment (*Abgeschiedenheit*), and the emptiness and freedom of self and things: "Swenne ich predige, sô pflige ich ze sprechenne von abegescheidenheit und daz der mensche ledic werde sîn selbes und aller dinge." Meister Eckhart, *Die Deutschen Werke*, volume 2, Josef Quint (ed.) (Stuttgart: Kohlhammer, 1971), 528. The letting be or releasement of self and things signified an unchanging and unmoving constancy of the self: "Der mensche, der gelâzen hât und gelâzen ist und der niemermê gesihet einen ougenblik ûf daz, daz er gelâzen hât, und blîbet stæte, unbeweget in im selber und unwandellîche, der mensche ist aleine gelâzen." Ibid., 61. Heidegger's this-worldly thingly oriented releasement often functions more along the lines of responsive releasement (*wuwei*) to the self-so event (*ziran*) of the thing. On the problems with employing the Western category of mysticism in the early ziranist context, see Eric S Nelson, "Questioning Dao: Skepticism, Mysticism, and Ethics in the *Zhuangzi*," *International Journal of the Asian Philosophical Association*, 1 (2008): 5–19.
18   The problematic of natural and technologically-framed things is found in the understanding of Daoism in Martin Buber as well as Heidegger. See Nelson, *Chinese and Buddhist Philosophy*, 109–29.
19   See Heubel, *Gewundene Wege nach China*; May, *Heidegger's Hidden Sources*; Nelson, *Chinese and Buddhist* Philosophy, 109–57; Nelson, "Heidegger's Daoist Turn," 362–84.
20   For an overview of the early use of *wu*, see Yuri Pines, "Lexical Changes in Zhanguo Texts," *Journal of the American Oriental Society*, 122.4 (2002): 691–705.
21   Perkins, "What is a Thing," 57; Pines, "Lexical Changes," 697–8.
22   For English language translations and discussions of the *Fan Wu Liu Xing*, see Shirley Chan, "Oneness: Reading the 'All things are flowing in form' (*Fan Wu Liu Xing*) 凡物流形 (with a translation)," *International Communication of Chinese Culture*, 2.3 (2015): 285–99; Feng Cao, *Daoism in Early China: Huang-Lao Thought in Light of Excavated Texts* (New York: Palgrave Macmillan, 2017), 87–123; Franklin Perkins, "*Fanwu Liuxing* ('All Things Flow into Form') and the 'One' in the *Laozi*," *Early China*, 38 (2015): 195–232; and Zhongjiang Wang, *Order in Early Chinese Excavated Texts: Natural, Supernatural, and Legal Approaches* (New York: Palgrave Macmillan, 2016), 49–81 and 169–74.
23   Chan, "Oneness," 289–90.
24   Pines, "Lexical Changes," 697–8.
25   Scott Cook, "*Yue Ji* 樂記: Record of Music: Introduction, Translation, Notes, and Commentary," *Asian Music*, 26.2 (1995): 1–96, at 45 and 47.
26   In addition to Cook's discussion on the social-cultural significance of the *Yue Ji*, see Barry D. Steben, "The Culture of Music and Ritual in Pre-Han Confucian Thought: Exalting the Power of Music in Human Life," アジア文化研究, 38 (2012): 105–24.
27   Stephen R. Bokenkamp, *Early Daoist Scriptures* (Berkeley: University of California Press, 1997), 82.
28   Brook Ziporyn (trans.), *Zhuangzi: The Complete Writings* (Indianapolis: Hackett Publishing, 2020), 121.

29 On the ethical and environmental implications of these straw-dog passages, also note Eric S. Nelson, *Daoism and Environmental Philosophy: Nourishing Life* (London: Routledge, 2020), 58–9.
30 Note that thing is *wu* 勿 in the Guodian materials. For the Guodian *Laozi* texts and English translations, see Scott Cook, *The Bamboo Texts of Guodian: A Study and Complete Translation* (Ithaca: Cornell University Press, 2012), 244; and Robert G. Henricks, *Lao Tzu's Tao Te Ching: A Translation of the Startling New Documents Found at Guodian* (New York: Columbia University Press, 2000), 44, 47, and 54.
31 Compare with Xiaogan Liu, "Laozi's Philosophy: Textual and Conceptual Analyses," in Xiaogan Liu (ed.), *Dao Companion to Daoist Philosophy*, 71–100 (Dordrecht: Springer, 2015), at 75.
32 Erkes translates *wanwu zicheng* 萬物自成 as "All things are spontaneously perfected." Eduard Erkes, "Ho-Shang-Kung's Commentary on Lao-Tse II (Continued)," *Artibus Asiae*, 9.1/3 (1946): 197–220, at 170.
33 "Regarding the actions of the world: by neither avoiding nor partaking in them, they can happen of themselves." Erica Brindley, Paul R. Goldin, and Esther S. Klein, "A Philosophical Translation of the *Heng Xian*," *Dao: A Journal of Comparative Philosophy*, 12.2 (2013): 145–51, at 150.
34 Cook, *Bamboo Texts*, 245.
35 Ibid.
36 On care (*ci* 慈), see Ann Pang-White, "Daoist Ci 慈, Feminist Ethics of Care, and the Dilemma of Nature," *Journal of Chinese Philosophy*, 43.3–4 (2016): 275–94; on Daoist care and nourishing life, see Nelson, *Daoism and Environmental Philosophy*, 60–1. The feminine disposition of care, in which the sage is disposed toward affairs and things with motherly concern, is also interestingly discussed in the *Laozi* commentary in chapter 20 of the *Hanfeizi* 韓非子.
37 Qingjie Wang takes the difference to be between "living longer" and "constant extension." See Qingjie Wang, "*Heng* and Temporality of Dao: Laozi and Heidegger," *Dao: A Journal of Comparative Philosophy*, 1.1 (2001): 55–71.
38 Compare Brindley et al., "Philosophical Translation of the *Heng Xian*," 146.
39 Ibid., 147.
40 Cook, *Bamboo Texts*, 253.
41 Compare Eduard Erkes, "Ho-Shang-Kung's Commentary on *Lao-Tse*," *Artibus Asiae*, 8.2/4 (1945): 119–96, at 181.
42 Compare Richard J. Lynn (trans.), *The Classic of the Way and Virtue; A New Translation of the Tao-te Ching of Laozi as Interpreted by Wang Bi* (New York: Columbia University, 1999), 65–7 and 109.
43 Compare Cook, *Bamboo Texts*, 273–5: "I serve no end and the people prosper on their own. I act to no purpose and the people transform of themselves. I am fond of tranquility and the people of themselves are rectified. I desire the lack of desire and the people of themselves become innocent."
44 Bao Jingyan is a completely unknown figure outside of the *Baopuzi* 抱朴子 of Ge Hong 葛洪 (see ch. 48 of the outer chapters). Ge perhaps invented Bao for polemical or hidden political reasons. Given Ge's authoritarian Confucian-legalist political thought, and his criticisms of the disorderly moral-political consequences of Lao-Zhuang, pure conversation (*qingtan* 清談), and mysterious learning (*xuanxue* 玄學) philosophizing, it seems unlikely that he was secretly advocating Bao's deconstruction of ruler and ruled. In addition to this issue, varieties of biospiritual and biopolitical models are discussed at length in Nelson, *Daoism and Environmental Philosophy*.

45 On reasons for a *ziran*-oriented reading of the *Zhuangzi*, in contrast to mystical, skeptical, and overly impersonal fatalistic interpretations, see Nelson, "Questioning Dao," 5-19.
46 Compare Nelson, *Daoism and Environmental Philosophy*, 37-8.
47 Heidegger mentions the moods of "joy, contentment, bliss, sadness, melancholy, anger" in GA 29-30: 96.
48 Ziporyn, *Zhuangzi: The Complete Writings*, 111.
49 Brook Ziporyn, *The Penumbra Unbound: The Neo-Taoist Philosophy of Guo Xiang* (Albany: State University of New York Press, 2003), 100. Guo Xiang reportedly borrowed heavily from the now lost commentary of Xiang Xiu 向秀. See Yiqing Liu, *Shih-Shuo Hsin-Yü: A New Account of Tales of the World*, trans. Richard B. Mather (Ann Arbor: Center for Chinese Studies, University of Michigan, 2002), 105-7.
50 The *Shishuo Xinyu* 世說新語 contains many anecdotes concerning Zhi Dun, including his new anti-deterministic interpretation of Zhuangzi's free and easy wandering. Liu, *Shih-Shuo Hsin-Yü*, 115-18. The *Xiaoyao lun* survives only in quotations and descriptions; it concerns wisdom (*prajñā*), equalizing things in emptiness, and the emptiness of somethingness and nothingness that cannot be self-occurring. As it is empty of any self-nature, the nothing does not self-nothing, but rather—restating the mutual correlation between form (*rūpa*) and emptiness (*śūnyatā*)—nothingness occurs through material existence (form) just as material existence occurs through nothingness. See his "Preface to a Synoptic Extract of the Larger and Smaller Versions [of the *Perfection of Wisdom*]" (*Daxiaopin duibi yaochao xu* 大小品对比要抄序) in Taisho, volume 55, number 2145.
51 For instance, "integrate the myriad things and make them into one," "the myriad things are one," and so on. See the discussion of such expressions in Chiayu Hsu, "The Authenticity of Myriad Things in the *Zhuangzi*," *Religions*, 10.3 (2019): 218-39 at 219.
52 "變化齊一，不主故常" in ch. 14.
53 Concerning Heidegger's discourse of the archaic Greek origins of philosophy, the first and other beginning, and the pluralistic alternative of Georg Misch, see Nelson, *Chinese and Buddhist Philosophy*, 131-57.
54 Martin Heidegger, *Einführung in die Metaphysik* [GA 40], ed. Petra Jaeger (Frankfurt: Vittorio Klostermann, 1983), 16; Martin Heidegger, *Introduction to Metaphysics*, trans. Gregory Polt and Richard Polt (New Haven: Yale University Press, 2014), 15-16. For an excellent overview of *phusis* in this work, see Susan Schoenbohm, "Heidegger's Interpretation of *Phusis* in *Introduction to Metaphysics*," in Richard Polt and Gregory Fried (eds.), *A Companion to Heidegger's Introduction to Metaphysics* (New Haven: Yale University Press, 2001), 143-60.
55 Heidegger, *Einführung in die Metaphysik*, 17; Heidegger, *Introduction to Metaphysics*, 16.
56 Ibid., 17; Ibid. Also compare with Martin Heidegger, *Der Anfang der abendländischen Philosophie; Auslegung des Anaximander und Parmenides* [GA 35], ed. Peter Trawny (Frankfurt: Vittorio Klostermann, 2012), 19.
57 Martin Heidegger, *Zum Ereignis-Denken* [GA 73], ed. Peter Trawny (Frankfurt: Vittorio Klostermann, 2013), 85.
58 Heidegger, *Einführung in die Metaphysik*, 17.
59 Martin Heidegger, *Heraklit* [GA 55], ed. Manfred S. Frings (Frankfurt: Vittorio Klostermann, 1979), 110 and 121.
60 Martin Heidegger, *Die Geschichte des Seyns* [GA 69], ed. Peter Trawny (Frankfurt: Vittorio Klostermann, 1998), 142.

61 Martin Heidegger, *Beiträge zur Philosophie (zum Ereignis)* [GA 65], ed. Friedrich-Wilhelm von Herrmann (Frankfurt: Vittorio Klostermann, 1989), 230.
62 Heidegger, *Beiträge zur Philosophie*, 298.
63 Martin Heidegge, *Hölderlins Hymnen "Germanien" und "Der Rhein"* [GA 39], ed. Susanne Ziegler (Frankfurt: Vittorio Klostermann, 1980), 144; also compare Heidegger, *Einführung in der Metaphysik*, 66. On Heidegger, the Daoist thing, and the politics of the thing, see Cabural, "Daoism and the German Mission," 570–92.
64 Heidegger, *Zu Eigenen Veroffentlichungen*, 494.
65 Martin Heidegger, *Holzwege* [GA 5], ed. Friedrich-Wilhelm von Herrmann (Frankfurt: Vittorio Klostermann, 1977), 40.
66 The arguments for the role of Daoist sources in Heidegger's thinking are explored in Nelson, "Heidegger's Daoist Turn," 362–84.
67 Heidegger, *Zu Eigenen Veroffentlichungen*, 494.
68 Martin Heidegger, *Vorträge und Aufsätze* [GA 7], ed. Friedrich-Wilhelm von Herrmann (Frankfurt: Vittorio Klostermann, 2000), 175 and 182; Martin Heidegger, *Bremer und Freiburger Vorträge* [GA 79], ed. Petra Jaeger (Frankfurt: Vittorio Klostermann, 1994), 13 and 24.
69 Ibid., 170; Heidegger; Ibid., 17.
70 Ibid., 179; Ibid., 24.
71 Theodor W. Adorno, for instance, underscored what he designated the "priority of the object" and criticized Heidegger in *The Jargon of Authenticity* and *Negative Dialectics* for an empty formalism that reduced things and beings, as entangled in capitalist material relations, to being.
72 Heidegger, *Vorträge und Aufsätze*, 182; Heidegger, *Bremer und Freiburger Vorträge*, 20.
73 This is discussed in greater detail in Heubel, *Gewundene Wege nach China*; May, *Heidegger's Hidden Sources*; Nelson, *Chinese and Buddhist Philosophy*, 109–57; and Nelson, "Heidegger's Daoist Turn," 362–84.
74 Martin Heidegger, *Zu Hölderlin: Griechenlandreisen* [GA 75], ed. Curd Ochwadt (Frankfurt: Vittorio Klostermann, 2000), 43.
75 Martin Heidegger, *Feldweg-Gesprache* [GA 77], ed. Ingrid Schüssler (Frankfurt: Vittorio Klostermann, 1995), 133–8.
76 Heidegger, *Bremer und Freiburger Vorträge*, 11–13.
77 Heidegger, *Vorträge und Aufsätze*, 173.
78 See Lynn, *Classic of the Way and Virtue*, 69 and 119–21.
79 See the analysis of these two statements in Perkins, "What Is a Thing," 63 and 67.
80 On the questions of freedom and determinism that this potentially raises, recall the previous discussion above of Guo Xiang and Zhi Dun.
81 On the development and significance of Heidegger's discourse of willing, not-willing, and *Gelassenheit*, see Bret W. Davis, *Heidegger and the Will: On the Way to Gelassenheit* (Evanston: Northwestern University Press, 2007).

References

Bokenkamp, Stephen R. *Early Daoist Scriptures*. Berkeley: University of California Press, 1997.
Brindley, Erica, Paul R. Goldin and Esther S. Klein. "A Philosophical Translation of the *Heng Xian*." *Dao: A Journal of Comparative Philosophy*, 12.2 (2013): 145–51.

Cabural, Mark Kevin S. "Daoism and the German Mission in Martin Heidegger's 'The Thing.'" *Frontiers of Philosophy in China*, 14.4 (2020): 570-92.

Cao, Feng. *Daoism in Early China: Huang-Lao Thought in Light of Excavated Texts.* New York: Palgrave Macmillan, 2017.

Chai, David. "Meontological Generativity: A Daoist Reading of the Thing." *Philosophy East and West*, 64.2 (2014): 303-18.

Chan, Shirley. "Oneness: Reading the 'All Things Are Flowing in Form' (*Fan Wu Liu Xing*) 凡物流形 (with a translation)." *International Communication of Chinese Culture*, 2.3 (2015): 285-99.

Cook, Scott. "*Yue Ji* 樂記: Record of Music: Introduction, Translation, Notes, and Commentary." *Asian Music*, 26.2 (1995): 1-96.

Cook, Scott. *The Bamboo Texts of Guodian: A Study and Complete Translation.* Ithaca: Cornell University Press, 2012.

Davis, Bret W. *Heidegger and the Will: On the Way to Gelassenheit.* Evanston: Northwestern University Press, 2007.

Eckhart, Meister. *Die Deutschen Werke.* Edited by Josef Quint. Stuttgart: Kohlhammer, 1971.

Erkes, Eduard. "Ho-Shang-Kung's Commentary on *Lao-Tse*." *Artibus Asiae*, 8.2/4 (1945): 119-96.

Erkes, Eduard. "Ho-Shang-Kung's Commentary on *Lao-Tse* II (Continued)." *Artibus Asiae*, 9.1/3 (1946): 197-220.

Heidegger, Martin. *Holzwege* [GA 5]. Edited by Friedrich-Wilhelm von Herrmann. Frankfurt: Vittorio Klostermann, 1977.

Heidegger, Martin. *Heraklit.* [GA 55]. Edited by Manfred S. Frings. Frankfurt: Vittorio Klostermann, 1979.

Heidegger, Martin. *Hölderlins Hymnen "Germanien" und "Der Rhein"* [GA 39]. Edited by Susanne Ziegler. Frankfurt: Vittorio Klostermann, 1980.

Heidegger, Martin. *Die Grundbegriffe der Metaphysik: Welt, Endlichkeit, Einsamkeit* [GA 29/30]. Edited by Friedrich-Wilhelm von Herrmann. Frankfurt: Vittorio Klostermann, 1983.

Heidegger, Martin. *Einführung in der Metaphysik* [GA 40]. Edited by Petra Jaeger. Frankfurt: Vittorio Klostermann, 1983.

Heidegger, Martin. *Zur Bestimmung der Philosophie* [GA 56/57]. Edited by Bernd Heimbüchel. Frankfurt: Vittorio Klostermann, 1987.

Heidegger, Martin. *Beiträge zur Philosophie (zum Ereignis)* [GA 65]. Edited by Friedrich-Wilhelm von Herrmann. Frankfurt: Vittorio Klostermann, 1989.

Heidegger, Martin. *Grundprobleme der Phanomenologie* [GA 58]. Edited by Hans-Helmuth Gander. Frankfurt: Vittorio Klostermann, 1993.

Heidegger, Martin. *Bremer und Freiburger Vorträge* [GA 79]. Edited by Petra Jaeger. Frankfurt: Vittorio Klostermann, 1994.

Heidegger, Martin. *Feldweg-Gespräche* [GA 77]. Edited by Ingrid Schüssler. Frankfurt: Vittorio Klostermann, 1995.

Heidegger, Martin. *Die Geschichte des Seyns (1939)* [GA 69]. Edited by Peter Trawny. Frankfurt: Vittorio Klostermann, 1998.

Heidegger, Martin. *Zu Hölderlin: Griechenlandreisen* [GA 75]. Edited by Curd Ochwadt. Frankfurt: Vittorio Klostermann, 2000.

Heidegger, Martin. *Vorträge und Aufsätze* [GA 7]. Edited by Friedrich-Wilhelm von Herrmann. Frankfurt: Vittorio Klostermann, 2000.

Heidegger, Martin. *Geschichte der Philosophie von Thomas von Aquin bis Kant* [GA 23]. Edited by Helmuth Vetter. Frankfurt: Vittorio Klostermann, 2006.
Heidegger, Martin. *Der Anfang der abendländischen Philosophie; Auslegung des Anaximander und Parmenides* [GA 35]. Edited by Peter Trawny. Frankfurt: Vittorio Klostermann, 2012.
Heidegger, Martin. *Zum Ereignis-Denken* [GA 73]. Edited by Peter Trawny. Frankfurt: Vittorio Klostermann, 2013.
Heidegger, Martin. *Introduction to Metaphysics*. Translated by Gregory Polt and Richard Polt. New Haven: Yale University Press, 2014.
Heidegger, Martin. *Zu Eigenen Veroffentlichungen* [GA 82]. Edited by Friedrich-Wilhelm von Herrmann. Frankfurt: Vittorio Klostermann, 2018.
Henricks, Robert G. *Lao Tzu's Tao Te Ching: A Translation of the Startling New Documents Found at Guodian*. New York: Columbia University Press, 2000.
Heubel, Fabian. *Gewundene Wege nach China: Heidegger-Daoismus-Adorno*. Frankfurt: Klostermann, 2020.
Hsu, Chiayu. "The Authenticity of Myriad Things in the *Zhuangzi*." *Religions*, 10.3 (2019): 218–39.
Imamichi, Tomonobu. *In Search of Wisdom: One Philosopher's Journey*. Tokyo: International House of Japan, 2004.
Kwok, Sai Hang. "Zhuangzi's Philosophy of Thing." *Asian Philosophy*, 26.4 (2016): 294–310.
Levinas, Emmanuel. *Totality and Infinity: An Essay on Exteriority*. Translated by Alphonso Lingis. Pittsburgh: Duquesne University Press, 1969.
Liu, Xiaogan. "Laozi's Philosophy: Textual and Conceptual Analyses." In Xiaogan Liu (ed.), *Dao Companion to Daoist Philosophy*, 71–100. Dordrecht: Springer, 2015.
Liu, Yiqing. *Shih-Shuo Hsin-Yü: A New Account of Tales of the World*. Translated by Richard B. Mather. Ann Arbor: Center for Chinese Studies, University of Michigan, 2002.
Lynn, Richard J., trans. *The Classic of the Way and Virtue: A New Translation of the Tao-te Ching of Laozi as Interpreted by Wang Bi*. New York: Columbia University, 1999.
May, Reinhard. *Heidegger's Hidden Sources: East-Asian Influences on His Work*. London: Routledge, 1996.
Nelson, Eric S. "Questioning Dao: Skepticism, Mysticism, and Ethics in the *Zhuangzi*." *International Journal of the Asian Philosophical Association*, 1 (2008): 5–19.
Nelson, Eric S. *Chinese and Buddhist Philosophy in Early Twentieth-Century German Thought*. London: Bloomsbury Academic, 2017.
Nelson, Eric S. "Heidegger's Daoist Turn." *Research in Phenomenology*, 49.3 (2019): 362–84.
Nelson, Eric S. *Daoism and Environmental Philosophy: Nourishing Life*. New York: Routledge, 2020.
Okakura, Kakuzō. *Das Buch vom Tee*. Leipzig: Insel, 1919.
Pang-White, Ann. "Nature, Interthing Intersubjectivity, and the Environment: A Comparative Analysis of Kant and Daoism." *Dao: A Journal of Comparative Philosophy*, 8.1 (2009): 61–78.
Pang-White, Ann. "Daoist *Ci* 慈, Feminist Ethics of Care, and the Dilemma of Nature." *Journal of Chinese Philosophy*, 43.3-4 (2016): 275–94.
Perkins, Franklin. "*Fanwu Liuxing* ('All Things Flow into Form') and the 'One' in the *Laozi*." *Early China*, 38 (2015): 195–232.

Perkins, Franklin. "What Is a Thing (*wu* 物)? The Problem of Individuation in Early Chinese Metaphysics." In Franklin Perkins and Chenyang Li (eds.), *Chinese Metaphysics and Its Problems*, 54–68. Cambridge: Cambridge University Press, 2015.

Pines, Yuri. "Lexical Changes in Zhanguo Texts." *Journal of the American Oriental Society*, 122.4 (2002): 691–705.

Schoenbohm, Susan. "Heidegger's Interpretation of *Phusis* in *Introduction to Metaphysics*." In Richard Polt and Gregory Fried (eds.), *A Companion to Heidegger's Introduction to Metaphysics*, 143–60. New Haven: Yale University Press, 2001.

Steben, Barry D. "The Culture of Music and Ritual in Pre-Han Confucian Thought: Exalting the Power of Music in Human Life." アジア文化研究, 38 (2012): 105–24.

Wang, Qingjie James. "*Heng* and Temporality of Dao: Laozi and Heidegger." *Dao: A Journal of Comparative Philosophy*, 1.1 (2001): 55–71.

Wang, Zhongjiang. *Order in Early Chinese Excavated Texts: Natural, Supernatural, and Legal Approaches*. New York: Palgrave Macmillan, 2016.

Ziporyn, Brook. *The Penumbra Unbound: The Neo-Taoist Philosophy of Guo Xiang*. Albany: State University of New York Press, 2003.

Ziporyn, Brook, trans. *Zhuangzi: The Complete Writings*. Indianapolis: Hackett Publishing, 2020.

6

Zhuangzi, Heidegger, and the Self-Revealing Being of Sculpture

David Chai

Introduction

Wherein lies the importance of sculpture? Is it its aesthetic beauty or its ability to stand-in for human being? Is it its multi-dimensionality or the rawness of its material? Unlike architecture, whose self-enclosing space hinders a complete and continuous encounter with it, sculpture releases its being into the openness of the world without interruption. The openness of being that is symbolized by sculpture is not dissociated from the hidden nothingness permeating the world; rather, it is its extension. What is more, the spatial voids that sculpt sculpture not only bequeath it its being, but embody the ineffable spirit of the world such that one cannot but stop and ponder the nature of being.

For Martin Heidegger, the question of being supersedes all others. What is more, thinking the question of being as it relates to art, or in the case of this chapter, sculpture, is to think of its unconcealment. The purpose of this chapter is to have Heidegger stand before the mirror of Daoism and see what is reflected back. We will ask Heidegger to relinquish his position as "the philosopher" in order that he may learn something from the ancient masters of Daoism, for "teaching is more difficult than learning because what teaching calls for is this: to let learn. The real teacher, in fact, lets nothing else be learned than learning."[1] While Heidegger was no stranger to the traditions of East Asia, Daoism touched him the most profoundly.

Evidence for this resonance can be found as early as 1930, the same year Heidegger started to write about art. When it comes to sculpture, however, we have to wait until the 1949 lecture "The Thing"[2] to see proof (i.e., the image of the clay vessel from *Daodejing* ch. 11). Heidegger himself admitted holding to Laozi despite the fact he could only do so through translators such as Richard Wilhelm.[3] Indeed, Heidegger famously hung on his study wall two lines of text from the *Daodejing*.[4] Be this as it may, this chapter will focus on Heidegger's relationship with the *Zhuangzi*. In the lecture course "What Is Called Thinking?" which was held at the University of Freiburg in 1951–2, Heidegger spoke of the cabinetmaker who brings forth "shapes slumbering within wood." This expression is a direct reference to the story of woodcarver Qing in chapter 19 of the *Zhuangzi*, and is one Heidegger discussed on two other occasions: the first was during the discussion period after his 1930 lecture "On the Essence of Truth,"[5] while the second was in his 1960 seminar course in Bremen entitled "Word and Image."[6]

In addition to the aforementioned, Heidegger employs other terms common to Daoism in his writings on sculpture: emptiness, hiddenness, mystery, clearing, and so forth. Not counting his essay "Building Dwelling Thinking" from 1951, which is predominantly concerned with space and place, Heidegger's ideas on sculpture are found in the following: a speech entitled "Remarks on Art, Sculpture, Space" from 1964, a lecture in 1967 entitled "The Origin of Art and the Definition of Thinking," and the essay "Art and Space" written in 1969. It is in "Art and Space" that Heidegger argues sculpture is "the embodiment of the truth of being in its work of instituting places." By probing the nature of sculpture and how it engages the emptiness of space to create a place of self-revealing,[7] we will discover how Heidegger and Zhuangzi use sculpture as a beacon to locate authentic being in a world threatened by artificial untruths. Our examination will end with a reading of the *Zhuangzi*'s story of the useless tree to illustrate how the sculptural naturalism of the world can be taken as model for life.

Art and Sculpture

Heidegger's 1964 speech "Remarks on Art—Sculpture—Space" (Bemerkungen zu Kunst—Plastik—Raum) took place at the opening of Bernhard Heiliger's exhibition at the Erker-Galerie in St. Gallen, Switzerland. In this talk, Heidegger presents sculpture as a confrontation whereby the invisible comes to appearance.[8] By rendering the invisible visible, the sculptor is said to engage in an act of *poiesis* which, Heidegger notes, is the "bringing-here-forth, forth into unconcealment, and here from out of concealment, so that the concealed and the concealing are not pushed aside, but instead are precisely preserved."[9] If the function of sculpture is to reveal the truth of being as the unconcealed, it cannot do so by forcibly displacing what is concealed as this will simply replace one kind of truth for another. What sculpture is qualified to do, according to Andrew Mitchell, is "provide the impetus for thinking space and body together."[10]

Heinrich-Wiegand Petzet has recorded Heidegger's desire to preserve the concealed and the concealing aspect of sculpture in order to invert their spatial relation "so that what is outside becomes the inner space and one is tempted to say that what the observer does not perceive with the physical eye becomes important."[11] The question is why? What is gained through such internalization and how is space, as a result, affected by this reprioritization? Before examining these questions, we need to first read what Heidegger says about space:

> What therefore is space as space? Answer: Space spaces. Spacing means clearing out, making free, setting free into a free area, an open. Insofar as space spaces, freely gives a free area, then it first affords with this free area the possibility of

regions, of near and far, of directions and bounds, the possibilities of distances and magnitudes.[12]

This passage repeats much of what he said in "Building Dwelling Thinking" where he argued space was not of the mathematical sort but an interval and "in this interval in turn there is space as pure extension."[13] By spacing things apart, space creates a clearing into which things are released and thereby stand free in the world. The freedom that comes with this open standing in the world is not the result of space making it so; rather, space becomes a region from which the world knows the thingliness of things. "Only things that are locations in this manner allow spaces," Heidegger writes, because "space is something that has been made room for, something that is cleared and free, namely within a boundary ... [and] the boundary is that from which something begins its presenting."[14] This is sculpture qua *poiesis*.

As we shall soon see, Daoism will reframe the human-sculpture relationship from an act of knowing creation to self-unfolding via oneness with the Dao. The premise is that things are already self-sculpted, and in a myriad of possibilities; the problem is that most people are not aware of this due to their narrow understanding of sculpture. For Daoism, sculpture can be likened to a burning candle: it stands alight in space yet its presence neither disrupts the coherency of said space nor enhances it; on the contrary, the candle shines forth in the emptiness of space allowing things to reveal their own sculpting. This self-revealing is not the result of human hands but the silent carving of the Dao. In his speech from 1964, Heidegger spoke of sculpture and space as existing in a relationship whose defining region is dynamic. As sculpture encroaches into space, space yields itself to sculpture; however, this adjustment is not one of overcoming but merely the shifting of a shared boundary. Such is why, Heidegger says, "the artist brings the essentially invisible into figure and, when he corresponds to the essence of art, each time allows something to be caught sight of which hitherto had never been seen."[15]

What our analysis has so far revealed is an appreciation of the hidden potential of sculpture to lay bare an aspect of being that is unbeknownst to many. Sculpture may have a presencing stance in the world, one it creates by way of its own being, but were it not for the nothingness lying within, the space that is its external self would be impossible. Given this, Daoism would agree with Heidegger's claim that "*poiesis* is to bring forth into unconcealment from out of concealment" but with one important distinction: Daoism holds that what is being shaped is not corporeal matter but the veins of nothingness inside.

Indeed, shortly after his speech in 1964, Heidegger would proclaim in his 1967 lecture in Athens entitled "The Provenance of Art and the Determination of Thinking" (Die Herkunft der Kunst und die Bestimmung des Denkens) that the artist brings forth not a product per se, but something situated in the invisible. Why? His answer is as follows:

> Because art as *techne* resides in a knowing, because such knowing resides in that which indicates the form, gives the measure, but remains yet invisible, and which first must be brought into the visibility and perceptibility of the work, for this

reason such a glance forward into what has not yet been sighted requires vision and light in an exceptional way.[16]

Heidegger's use of *poiesis* and *techne* to describe sculpture would be short-lived however. His essay "Art and Space" would replace these terms with place and space, to which we shall now turn.

Space and Sculpture

"Art and Space" (Die Kunst und der Raum) was written in 1969 for inclusion in a book about the Spanish sculptor Eduardo Chillida (1924–2002). Heinrich-Wiegand Petzet first met Chillida in 1962 and shared the latter's views on sculpture and space with Heidegger until, in 1968, Chillida and Heidegger were able to meet in person for the first time.[17] Anyone reading "Art and Space" will be struck by its opening line of inquiry: "The sculptured body embodies something. Does it embody space? Is sculpture an occupying of space, a domination of space?"[18] All physical bodies embody something, this is for certain. In the case of sculpture, one would presume they also embody the space they occupy, as Heidegger noted in his lectures from 1964 and 1967, however, the position taken in "Art and Space" is different insofar as space itself embodies the invisible properties of sculpture through its capacity to create place and thus it has its own form of being. Jeff Malpas is one of the few scholars to have noticed this subtle but important shift in Heidegger's framing of the localization of space in the form of place. He writes: "In 'Art and Space,' the emphasis is on the settled locality—die Ortschaft—rather than the solitary place [as was the case in 'Building Dwelling Thinking'], and on the belonging together of things, rather than on the gathering that occurs in the single thing."[19]

Drawing upon an idea first raised in "The Origin of the Work of Art"—that "art is the fixing in place of a self-establishing truth in the figure. This happens in creation as the bringing forth of the unconcealedness of what is"[20]—Heidegger in "Art and Space" explores space in relation to sculpture by probing the root meaning of the word space: "In speaking the word space, clearing-away is uttered therein. This means to clear out, to free from wilderness. Clearing-away brings forth the free, the openness for man's settling and dwelling."[21] Sculpture, he goes on to say, does not occupy space, does not even deal with space; rather, "sculpture is the embodiment of places. Places, in preserving and opening a region, hold something free gathered around them which grants the tarrying of things under consideration and a dwelling for man in the midst of things."[22] In the words of Paul Crowther: "The sculptural work will always be caught in the act of seeming to become something else. Sculpture is where that event of finding or bringing together different things, which is also constitutive of place, is itself fixed in place through the work's distinctive character as thingly, three-dimensional image."[23] On the ability of art, including sculpture, to embody the truth of being, Alejandro Vallega notes two aspects of Heidegger's thought at play: one, sheltering the truth of being is not an abandonment or forgetting of beings in their finitude; two, the concreteness of beings must be thought in terms of the task of sheltering the truth of being, their finitude and ephemeral passages, as well as their alterity and exilic character.[24]

There are a number of stories in Daoism illustrating the "seeming to become something else" that Crowther spoke of, but that of woodcarver Qing from chapter 19 of the *Zhuangzi* is the only one specifically about sculpture. It reads:

> Woodworker Qing carved a piece of wood and made a bell stand, and when it was finished, everyone who saw it marveled, for it seemed to be the work of gods or spirits. When the marquis of Lu saw it, he asked, "What art is it you have?" Qing replied, "I am only a craftsman—how would I have any art? There is one thing, however. When I am going to make a bell stand, I never let it wear out my energy. I always fast in order to still my mind. When I have fasted for three days, I no longer have any thought of congratulations or rewards, of titles or stipends. When I have fasted for five days, I no longer have any thought of praise or blame, of skill or clumsiness. And when I have fasted for seven days, I am so still that I forget I have four limbs and a form and body. By that time, the ruler and his court no longer exist for me. My skill is concentrated, and all outside distractions fade away. After that, I go into the mountain forest and examine the heavenly nature of the trees. If I find one of superlative form and I can see a bell stand there, I put my hand to the job of carving; if not, I let it go. This way I am simply matching up "heaven" with "heaven." That's probably the reason that people wonder if the results were not made by spirits."[25]

When woodcarver Qing sets off into the forest to match his heavenly nature with that of the trees, he is not assessing the trees by the quality of their wood but is letting the Dao guide his connectedness to them in such a way that whichever one he chooses, it will accord with his ability to release its inner object, in this case a bell stand. In other words, woodcarver Qing uses his tools to facilitate the tree's own self-carving; he does not wield them to alter its being. Daoist sculpture, therefore, is not about transforming one thing into something else, a destructive process that brings no benefit to the material being shaped, nor is it exclusively driven by the pronouncement of space in which it is to be situated; rather, sculpture in the Daoist sense is a matter of letting things transform by way of their own inborn nature. The woodcarver's tools are thus an extension of his connectedness to the world and are not the means by which he superimposes his being onto it. If anything, the opposite happens: woodcarver Qing abandons his being in order to become one with the nothingness of the Dao.

Just now we spoke of woodcarver Qing's tools becoming an extension of his connectedness to the Dao, and he does so in typical Daoist fashion—self-forgetting. How interesting, then, that Heidegger should also speak of tools and forgetting:

> When one is "really" busy with something and totally immersed in it, one is neither only together with the work, nor with the tools, nor with both "together." Being in relevance, which is grounded in temporality, has already founded the unity of the relations in which taking care of things "moves" circumspectly. A specific kind of *forgetting* is essential for the temporality that constitutes being in relevance. In

order to be able to "really" get to work "lost" in the world of tools and to handle them, the self must forget itself.[26]

What is more, Heidegger sees tools as making a continuous yet invisible contribution to an object's creation:

> Handiness is not grasped theoretically at all, nor is it itself initially a theme for circumspection. What is peculiar to what is initially at hand is that it withdraws, so to speak, in its character of handiness in order to be really handy. What everyday association is initially busy with is not tools themselves, but the work. What is to be produced in each case is what is primarily taken care of and is thus also what is at hand. The work bears the totality of references in which useful things are encountered.[27]

We can interpret this as indicating "among the most basic drives of the sculptor is the need to bring forth our withness with things as thingly. And as depth is an essential attribute of things, the sculptor presumably must impart to the surface the quality of the substance within, much as the skin shows forth the muscle."[28] To restrict the tools of sculpture to their function of carving and nothing more is to overlook the role of space in said carving. Indeed, "sculptural space does not withdraw or cut itself off from real space, as with the space of the painted portrait; rather, sculptural space is a metamorphosis of real space, making it more dynamic perceptible."[29] This is especially true for Daoism in that as hard as one might try to pare-away unwanted aspects of life, the one thing that cannot be decreased is the space of the Dao in which we dwell.

The Dao, however, generates both being and nothingness. When Heidegger argues that the truth of art is the unconcealment of being, what is cleared-away is the invisibility of nothingness in order to create a place within and around which being can gather. Indeed, at the end of "Art and Space" he makes this exact point, asking: "What would become of the emptiness of space?" He answers: "Emptiness is closely allied to the special character of place, and therefore no failure, but a bringing-forth."[30] Gunter Figal was critical of Heidegger's response insofar as "grasping emptiness via gathering places, Heidegger misses the fact that the gathering that belongs to the essence of places is impossible without emptiness. Emptying is not gathering; instead, gathering presupposes emptiness."[31] From the point of view of Daoism, Figal's statement is problematic because it presupposes gathering only occurs in human society and not in the natural world.

While some species deliberately create a clearing for the purpose of gathering, in more cases than not, places that are cleared of their inherent fullness tend to be avoided whenever possible. It would be far easier for woodcarver Qing to chop down a large number of trees and haul them back to his workshop for inspection than to wander amongst them in the forest, hoping to discover a seemingly perfect specimen. And yet, this is precisely what he does, for in the spirit of Daoism: "When the tailorbird builds her nest in the deep wood, she uses no more than one branch. When the mole drinks at the river, he takes no more than a bellyful."[32] In other words, the Daoist artist only uses the minimally required amount of material to complete the task, nothing more. They certainly do not manipulate the world to create a specific space to construct their work but do so *in situ*. Nature speaks through the myriad things inhabiting it, each one sculpting their way through life in harmonious unity. Humanity, however, divides and molds things to suit our likes while striving to eliminate our dislikes. We fail to realize that in carving up the world, we are carving up ourselves. By erroneously believing that paring away material from the source creates something new, we yet again fail to comprehend the inclusiveness and co-dependency of things.

The plastic arts such as sculpture try their utmost to convey a sense of fluidity, airiness, and unsayability; such being the case, why do we not approach them in an equally fluid, airy, and unsayable manner? Is it because we don't see the world in such terms, or is it because we are unable to think about the world in this way? True sculpture, which has a spiritual presence about it, lets the world speak through it. The skill required to produce it goes unnoticed and this is because the artist has transcended ordinary skill and reached a level only heaven can match. Matching the heavenly with the heavenly cannot be achieved through the exertion of being, however, but is only possible when being fades into obscurity and we are free to dwell in nothingness. Thus, sculpture as the place of truth's revealing is more about the unfolding of nothingness than the enrapturing of being; it is more about discovering how nothingness uplifts being, setting it free, than the concreteness of being itself. Without the invisible participation of nothingness, sculpture would not be possible, and without the gift of space qua nothingness, we could not take up residence in the clearing of being.[33]

This leads to a question: Who teaches the sculptor this most profound of truths? The answer might surprise you: the sculptor learns to sculpt through sculpting. The teacher, therefore, does not lead by his teaching but follows the learning of the learner. Chapter 11 of the *Zhuangzi* describes this teacher as follows:

> The great man in his teaching is like the shadow that follows a form, the echo that follows a sound. Only when questioned does he answer, and then he pours out all his thoughts, making himself the companion of the world. He dwells in the echoless, moves in the directionless, takes by the hand you who are rushing and bustling back and forth and proceeds to wander in the beginningless. He passes in and out of the boundless and is ageless as the sun. His face and form blend with the great unity, the great unity that is selfless.[34]

When Heidegger gave his lecture course "What Is Called Thinking?" at the University of Freiburg in 1951–2, he also spoke of the teacher:

> Teaching is more difficult than learning because what teaching calls for is this: to let learn. The real teacher, in fact, lets nothing else be learned than—learning. His conduct, therefore, often produces the impression that we properly learn nothing from him, if by "learning" we now suddenly understand merely the procurement of useful information. The teacher is ahead of his apprentices in this alone, that he has still far more to learn than they—he has to learn to let them learn.[35]

These examples are certainly instructive but what of the teacher of sculpture? Chapter 13 of the *Zhuangzi* contains the well-known story of wheelwright Pian, who offers this insight into his craft:

> When I chisel a wheel, if the blows of the mallet are too gentle, the chisel will slide and won't take hold. But if they're too hard, it will bite and won't budge. Not too gentle, not too hard—you can get it in your hand and feel it in your mind. You can't put it into words, and yet there's a knack to it somehow. I can't teach it to my son, and he can't learn it from me.[36]

The story of woodcarver Qing was one Heidegger spoke of on several occasions throughout his life, but nowhere is its influence more obvious than in his account of the cabinetmaker:

> A cabinetmaker's apprentice, someone who is learning to build cabinets and the like, will serve as an example. His learning is not mere practice, to gain facility in the use of tools. Nor does he merely gather knowledge about the customary forms of the things he is to build. If he is to become a true cabinetmaker, he makes himself answer and respond above all to the different kinds of wood and to the shapes slumbering within wood—to wood as it enters into man's dwelling with all the hidden riches of its nature. In fact, this relatedness to wood is what maintains the whole craft.[37]

Recall how woodcarver Qing stated that upon finding a tree of superlative form and seeing a bell stand therein, he would set about carving it. For Heidegger, the cabinetmaker *par excellence* responds to the wood and the shapes slumbering within, releasing their hidden riches into the world. He is able to do this, Heidegger says, because he has learned how to think with his hands: "Only a being who can speak, that is, think, can have hands and can be handy in achieving works of handicraft."[38] The extraordinary vision of woodcarver Qing, however, does not emanate from his hands but his spirit. Indeed, the program of mental fasting that woodcarver Qing embarks on before entering the forest should not be taken as intellectual abstinence but mental composure. After seven days of preparation, one of the outcomes woodcarver Qing lists is a concentration of skill such that the external world no longer disturbs his inner clarity. Forgetting his form and body, woodcarver Qing is able to partake in the heavenly or naturally endowed nature of things. Such being the case, the boundary between inner and outer space vanishes, allowing nothingness to roam free. The paradigmatic sculptor thus roams in harmony with the nothingness of space, creating pockets of being that signify sculpture's standing in the world.

Heidegger, too, recognized the importance of nothingness to sculpture and space, writing: "Emptiness is not nothing. It is also no deficiency. In sculptural embodiment, emptiness plays in the manner of a seeking-projecting instituting of places."[39] We can understand this seeking-projecting as Alejandro Vallega does—as a letting the events of beings "broach their possibilities by enacting their passage as a passing [such that] the emptiness of space offers possibilities neither objectively nor ideally present, possibilities intimated in the futurity of events of beings and thought"[40]—or we can frame the issue in this way: if sculpture is unable to serve as a clearing for being, then the space in which it stands will not be conducive to thinking the question of being. Heidegger adds to this the fact that "sculpture would be the embodiment of places. Places, in preserving and opening a region, hold something free gathered around them which grants the tarrying of things under consideration and a dwelling for man in the midst of things."[41] For Paul Crowther, "the concept of space, which is decisive ultimately, is that which can be linked to the unconcealment of Being. This 'genuine space' is the primordial basis of all spaces, and thence the artistic space of sculpture must involve some distinctive articulation of it."[42]

By saying emptiness is neither an absolute nothingness nor a deficiency, Heidegger adopts the definition of nothingness used by Daoism to grant it the role of seeking-projecting instituting of places. Since places receive the gift of space that allows humanity to dwell therein, the tarrying of things in any given place is not because they have created said place but is due to the open region of space in which said place exists. The space that serves as the open region of sculpture is an emptiness that seeks the being of things while simultaneously projecting its own nothingness as the mystery of being's horizon. Because the horizon of being does not exist in Daoism, it would be incorrect of us to say sculpture signifies a futural self; the transformation of things is a process that precedes the birth of things and extends beyond their death. The *Zhuangzi* uses the examples of woodcarver Qing and wheelwright Pian as a pedagogical tool, one that should be forgotten upon mastering the art of sculpting.

What woodcarver Qing produces is not a work of art but a mere shadow of the candlelight of the Dao. This shadow of the Dao is what woodcarver Qing means when he says his sculpture is held by others to be a creation of the spirits. Rather than portraying art as the unconcealment of the truth of being, as Heidegger does, Daoism casts superlative artworks as the epitome of humanity's ability to harmonize with the Dao. Given this, what sculpture impresses on us is not only as Andrew Mitchell says— if the artist is no longer separated from the world by a divide, if there is no longer the confrontation with a recalcitrant material, but instead some manner of mutual interpenetration, then the idea of the tool as literally a stopgap measure for bridging such divides must be abandoned[43]—but that sculpture stands in the world, and during the course of this enduring, its surrounding space lays bare the transience of being. Heidegger himself appears to have ruminated on this last point when he says: "Even a cautious insight into the special character of this art causes one to suspect that truth, as unconcealment of Being, is not necessarily dependent on embodiment."[44]

We dance from one sculptural being to the next, losing sight of the nothingness interconnecting them. And yet, sculpture's fixity can be overcome by viewing it within the fluidity of space, an emptiness that allows for sculpture's inner light to radiate forth while the space of said light effects the closeness of being things have with one another. Said differently, the Dao's light is a reflection of the shadow produced by the "shapes slumbering within" and can be thought of as akin to the Daoist notions of Yin 陰 and Yang 陽. When a thing's outer form is manifested, its inner potential becomes hidden; when a thing's potency reaches its maximum level of concentration, it thereupon descends into a state of weakness and dormancy. Applying this principle to human beings, one can say we each have a shape slumbering within us which is none other than the potential of self-realization in the Dao. The openness of sculpture is hence a reminder for us not to be closed-off like a painting or live a one-dimensional life; rather, as Andrew Mitchell writes:

> Sculpture changes the space around it. Its entrances and invitations change the density and thickness of things. Sculpture changes the texture of the space around it as each work eddies forth turbulences into the smoothness of the world. Sculptures push at the space that runs through us. Sculptures touch us for this reason, they pull us out of ourselves as well. The sculpture in place disrupts the homogeneity of space and the encapsulation of the subject. It tugs both of these at once and testifies to our belonging to world.[45]

Whether woodcarver Qing or Heidegger's cabinetmaker, sculpture has the unique ability to transcend its own craftliness and become something magical, not in the sense of being beyond belief, but in reinforcing our belief in being and that the darkness of nothingness forms an indubitable part of such existence. Creation is never a solitary act insofar as it feeds off of its own creativity. We create things out of images yet the forms of images are themselves a carving of ideas. To what do ideas owe their existence? The answer is nothingness. Incorporeal space is nothingness in waiting, an awaiting and abiding in accordance with its own empty quietude. Sculpture does not disrupt the harmony of nothingness; on the contrary, it refines and makes it more pronounced by bringing its formerly obscure presence to light. Sculpture is thus sculpted by its own nothingness. Every natural thing in the world is a sculpture yet humanity does not see the world in such a manner. Why? Perhaps it is because we see things as tools but tools violate the space of things instead of conjoining them. What is more, tools have a purpose whereas sculpture does not; tools are a means to an end while sculpture teaches us to think. Thinking is also a tool but Daoism and Heidegger warn us against misconstruing thought of the technical kind for that which probes the question of being. The latter writes:

> We think of creation as a bringing forth. But the making of equipment, too, is a bringing forth. Handicraft—a remarkable play of language—does not, to be sure, create works, not even when we contrast, as we must, the handmade with the factory product. But what is it that distinguishes bringing forth as creation from bringing forth in the mode of making? It is as difficult to track down the essential features of the creation of works and the making of equipment, as it is easy to distinguish verbally between the two modes of bringing forth. Going along with first appearances we find the same activity of potter and sculptor, of joiner and painter. The creation of a work requires craftsmanship. Great artists prize craftsmanship most highly. They above all others constantly strive to educate themselves ever anew in thorough craftsmanship.[46]

In order to illustrate the possibility of thinking sculpturally, we will turn to the *Zhuangzi*'s well-known example of the crooked tree, an artifact of sculptural naturalism and a symbol of Daoist life praxis.

Sculpture of Nature

Having examined what Heidegger and Zhuangzi say about manmade sculpture, it is time for us to set those ideas aside and turn our attention to sculpture of an altogether different sort. At the outset of this chapter, I mentioned the *Zhuangzi* offers several examples of natural sculpture, the predominant one being the withered tree. Before we see how this tree serves as a place of self-revealing thanks to the sheltering of nothingness, here is one of the stories in which the archetypical tree occurs:

> Carpenter Shi went to Qi and, when he got to Crooked Shaft, he saw a serrate oak standing by the village shrine. It was broad enough to shelter several thousand oxen and measured a hundred spans around, towering above the hills. The lowest branches were eighty feet from the ground, and a dozen or so of them could have been made into boats. There were so many sightseers that the place looked like a fair, but the carpenter didn't even glance around and went on his way without stopping. His apprentice stood staring for a long time and then ran after carpenter Shi and said, "Since I first took up my ax and followed you, Master, I have never seen timber as beautiful as this. But you don't even bother to look, and go right on without stopping. Why is that?" "Forget it—say no more!" said the carpenter. "It's a worthless tree! Make boats out of it and they'd sink; make coffins and they'd rot in no time; make vessels and they'd break at once. Use it for doors and it would sweat sap like pine; use it for posts and the worms would eat them up. It's not a timber tree—there's nothing it can be used for. That's how it got to be that old!"[47]

This story is interesting for several reasons: it provides insight into the mindset of the Daoist sculptor while simultaneously describing the ways Nature can sculpt something as innocuous as a tree. It should be said that Zhuangzi's purpose in writing this story is to explicate the praxis of useful uselessness; however, we will not discuss that topic here.[48] We will instead focus on how the tree symbolizes the epitome of natural sculpture. We know from carpenter Shi's words that the common person takes trees to be nothing more than a disposable means to an end. They fashion boats from them but boats merely carry people from one place to another. In becoming a boat, the tree is forgotten; should the boat take on water and sink, it too will be relegated to the ghostly terrain of memory. Whereas boats are used to transport things from one region of life to another, coffins can only reunite the dead. We box up the deceased and offer them to the earth; embraced by the ground as such, what is cherished is not the coffin but the clearing of soil into which the departed are laid to rest. Furniture eases our labored bodies while doors enable or arrest our movement; neither contributes to our understanding of being nor enhances our spiritual connectivity with the world. Finally, we assign trees the role of life-protector by turning them into the beams and pillars of our homes, never realizing that in uprooting them, we are sacrificing their home for the benefit of our own. Ironically, the pillar of the house is seen by the ancient Chinese as a metaphor for the stability of one's family and the entire country; should the pillar of one fall down, calamity will befall all others.

Daoism does not perceive trees in this manner (i.e., as carpenter Shi does). For someone of woodcarver Qing's repute, the entire natural world is a forest of interconnected trees vacillating in perfect synchronicity to the breath of the Dao. People are attracted to the great oak in the carpenter Shi story due to its girth and not its beauty, to its towering height and not the fragrance or strength of its wood. The oak tree is far from graceful in stature yet it still manages to attract people from far and wide. What beckons them, draws them into its encircling space, is the void beneath its canopy. The nothingness demarcating the region of the tree is also responsible for bringing beings to life. Recall Heidegger's words at the end of "Art and Space" when he said "in sculptural embodiment, emptiness plays in the manner of a seeking-projecting instituting of places." Our relationship with the tree is such a seeking-projecting in that we seek the projection of its space and in doing so, establish the place of its being. However, the region we take to be its ontological boundary is, in fact, not the full extent of its self-projecting. What is missing is its own emptiness—not the direct emptiness cast downwards from its canopy, but that which emanates up and outward. Moreover, the great oak tree is not a two-dimensional entity but a three-dimensional canvas sculpted by the Dao. For the throngs of beings taking shelter under its shielding mass, and within its labyrinth of limbs and branches, the oak tree is a world of light and shadow, clarity and indiscernibility, openness and constriction. Within the living statue that is this towering tree, beings thrive and receive shelter from it; such is the gathering power of the Dao, a gathering that is free of partiality and covetousness.

By growing as tall as it did, the old tree was able to avoid the occupation of its lowest region of space, creating a zone of emptiness in its place. This open region protects the being of the tree from strife and injury, a fate smaller and more useful trees cannot avoid. With its lower branches too high for many to reach, the oak tree's canopy becomes its defining feature; however, what is defining is not the physicality of its canopy but the shadow it casts on the ground beneath. We thus have horizontal and vertical zones of being and nothingness when it comes to deconstructing the oak tree, and the same holds true for sculpture in general. On the usefulness, or lack thereof, of the empty space within and around a sculpture, it does not affect the self-standing of said object. It is we, as outsiders, that lay claim to a sculpture's onto-spatial power. It is we, as being-centric thinkers, that deny a sculpture its sense of belonging with nothingness.

Using the innocuous example of the tree, the *Zhuangzi* reveals a key principle of Daoism:

> As a symbolic representation of Dao, the tree roots itself in the endless darkness of the earth's soil, soaring toward heaven as if trying to embrace it. With its great height, said tree offers refuge to the beings on the ground below, just as the harmonizing oneness of Dao shelters the myriad things of the world from succumbing to the petty desires of their ethical selves.[49]

Art, and in particular the plastic arts, carries with it the task of releasing us from our own ethical pettiness. Sculpture, as presented in the thought of Heidegger and Zhuangzi, strives to capture the movement of being while grounding it in the space of nothingness. What is more, sculpture invokes a feeling of togetherness in that it uplifts and injects humanity with a fuller sense of belonging to the world and the great expanse of Nature. As a result, sculpture's presence becomes otherworldly, for it guides us away from calculative human carving toward the authentic encirclement of space and non-space. This, we can say, is the ultimate expression of artistic creativity, a discovering of the root of our own ontological potential.

In order to authentically realize our ontological potential, we should carve our place in the world with our heart-mind and not tools, and having learnt to carve with our heart-mind, we should set it aside and learn to carve with our spirit. The mysterious ground of the soul that is said to be epitomized by superlative sculpture is mysterious not because it belongs to heaven and is hence inaccessible to us; rather, its profundity stems from its inner nothingness that is concealed by its surface appearance. Indeed, humanity is overly reliant on our minor senses and we do not pay enough attention to our most primal sense in the form of touch. Entering the space of a sculpture, we are touched by the emptiness of the air in which it stands. Before we lay hands on a sculpture, the displacement of space caused by the shape of the object invites us to connect with it on a bodily level. We feel the sculpture, sensing its volume, more than we are able to see it. Our interaction with it constantly changes, as is the case with Zhuangzi's oak tree, because the sculpture invites us to do so. It is here, in the realm of mutual co-operation, that things are able to be true to themselves; it is here, in the oneness of the Dao, that being gives way to nothingness. To think of one's encounter with sculpture in this way is to no longer see it as standing outside of oneness, but as an essential component of one's inner flourishing.

Indeed, Heidegger employed the Greek temple in his essay "The Origin of the Work of Art" as a way of challenging our conservative reasoning of the artwork's reality and how it captures the openness of the world. He writes:

> By contrast the temple-work, in setting up a world, does not cause the material to disappear, but rather causes it to come forth for the very first time and to come into the Open of the work's world. The rock comes to bear and rest and so first becomes rock; metals come to glitter and shimmer, colors to glow, tones to sing, the word to speak. All this comes forth as the work sets itself back into the massiveness and heaviness of stone, into the firmness and pliancy of wood, into the hardness and luster of metal, into the lighting and darkening of color, in to the clang of tone, and into the naming power of the word.[50]

Thus, art teaches us that such reasoning replaces what is with constructions of the human spirit [and that] to be open to the reality of things is to be open to the dimension of things that will always resist human mastery.[51] Daoism, however, would argue the natural world is a temple, one that requires no work to establish or maintain. Nature is the freely sculpted work of the Dao, a world whose material stands in its midst without calling attention to its standing. Instead of having the material of sculpture emerge into the openness of the work's world, Daoism's stance is the opposite: the openness of the world and the work of natural sculpture are one and the same. It is we, human beings, that create the spatial distinction between the nothingness molding things, the clearing that stands between things, and the emptiness sweeping across the earth. To connect with things in their own nothingness is to connect with their heavenly spirit, and when one is able to use what is of heaven to recognize the heavenly in others, this is to attain the skill of woodcarver Qing and is why carpenter Shi declared the tree at Crooked Shaft to be useless.

Conclusion

Heidegger's "Art and Space" serves as a reminder that even short pieces of genuine thinking can be just as provoking as long ones. Being one of the few places where Heidegger discusses the art of sculpture, "Art and Space" not only shows the stamp of Eduardo Chillida's artistic vision, but also cleverly incorporates allusions to the conceptual motifs of Daoism. Using Daoism in such a covert manner not only allowed Heidegger to prod and set aside ideas traceable to ancient Greece, the former resonated with him in a way that other Eastern traditions could not. In Daoism, Heidegger found a style of writing and a method of philosophizing that felt wholly familiar to him, despite the language barrier. What sculpture teaches us, no matter for Heidegger or Daoism, is that thinking the question of being is an activity that transcends time and place. Our urge to touch sculpture arises from our being touched by it and the spiritual presence of sculpture touches us as if it were an extension of heaven itself such that we become one with it. Sculpture, therefore, provides a place for the things of the world to encounter what is heavenly, laying bare the nature of being in the process. It is here, in the clearing of being, that sculpture reflects the self of humanity for all to see.

Notes

1 Martin Heidegger, *What Is Called Thinking?* trans. Fred Wieck and J. Glenn Gray (New York: Harper and Row, 1968), 15.
2 For more, see David Chai, "Meontological Generativity: A Daoist Reading of the Thing," *Philosophy East and West*, 64.2 (2014a): 303–18.
3 Heinrich-Wiegand Petzet, *Encounters and Dialogues with Heidegger, 1929–1976*, trans. Parvis Emad and Kenneth Maly (Chicago: University of Chicago Press, 1993), 174.
4 Petzet, *Encounters and Dialogues*, 168. The lines in question are from chapter 15 and read: "Who can take his turbidity and, by stilling it, gradually become clear? Who can take his quietude and, by stirring it long, gradually come alive?" See Richard J. Lynn, trans. *The Classic of the Way and Virtue: A New Translation of the Tao-te Ching of Laozi as Interpreted by Wang Bi* (New York: Columbia University Press, 1999). To read more about Heidegger's interest in the *Daodejing*, see Lin Ma, "Deciphering Heidegger's Connection with the *Daodejing*," *Asian Philosophy*, 16.3 (2006): 149–71.
5 Petzet, *Encounters and Dialogues*, 18.
6 Ibid., 169.
7 For an excellent overview of the concept of "place" in Heidegger's thought, see Jeff Malpas, *Heidegger's Topology: Being, Place, World* (Cambridge: MIT Press, 2006), 17–37.

8   Andrew Mitchell, *Heidegger among the Sculptors: Body, Space, and the Art of Dwelling* (Stanford: Stanford University Press, 2010), 36.
9   Ibid., 39. For the original German, see Martin Heidegger, *Bemerkungen zu Kunst-Plastik-Raum* (St. Gallen: Erker-Verlag, 1996), 15–16.
10 Ibid., 43.
11 Petzet, *Encounters and Dialogues*, 157.
12 Mitchell, *Heidegger among the Sculptors*, 43; Heidegger, *Bemerkungen zu Kunst-Plastik-Raum*, 13.
13 Martin Heidegger, *Poetry, Language, Thought*, trans. Albert Hofstadter (New York: Harper Collins, 2001), 153.
14 Ibid., 152.
15 Mitchell, *Heidegger among the Sculptors*, 48; Heidegger, *Bemerkungen zu Kunst-Plastik-Raum*, 14.
16 Ibid., 60.
17 See Petzet, *Encounters and Dialogues*, 156–8.
18 Martin Heidegger, "Art and Space," trans. C.H. Seibert, *Man and World*, 6 (1969), 3. For the original German, see Martin Heidegger, *Die Kunst und der Raum—L'Art et L'Espace* (Frankfurt: Vittorio Klostermann, 2007), 506.
19 Malpas, *Heidegger's Topology*, 263.
20 Heidegger, *Poetry, Language, Thought*, 69.
21 Heidegger, "Art and Space," 5; Heidegger, *Die Kunst und der Raum*, 8–9.
22 Ibid., 7; Ibid., 9.
23 Paul Crowther, "Space, Place, and Sculpture: Working with Heidegger," *Continental Philosophy Review*, 40 (2007): 167.
24 See Alejandro Vallega, *Heidegger and the Issue of Space: Thinking on Exilic Grounds* (University Park: Pennsylvania State University Press, 2003), 179–80.
25 Burton Watson, trans. *The Complete Works of Zhuangzi* (New York: Columbia University Press, 2013).
26 Martin Heidegger, *Being and Time*, trans. Joan Stambaugh (Albany: State University of New York Press, 2010), 337. Italics in original.
27 Heidegger, *Being and Time*, 65.
28 F. David Martin, "Sculpture and Truth to Things," *Journal of Aesthetic Education*, 13.2 (1979): 22.
29 Ibid., 16–17.
30 Heidegger, "Art and Space," 7; Heidegger, *Die Kunst und der Raum*, 12.
31 Gunter Figal, *Aesthetics as Phenomenology: The Appearance of Things* (Bloomington: Indiana University Press, 2015), 203.
32 Watson, *Zhuangzi*, 3–4.
33 See David Chai, "Nothingness and the Clearing: Heidegger, Daoism and the Quest for Primal Clarity," *The Review of Metaphysics*, 67.3 (2014b): 583–601.
34 Watson, *Zhuangzi*, 82.
35 Heidegger, *What Is Called Thinking*, 15.
36 Watson, *Zhuangzi*, 107.
37 Heidegger, *What Is Called Thinking*, 14.
38 Ibid., 16.
39 Heidegger, "Art and Space," 7; Heidegger, *Die Kunst und der Raum*, 12.
40 Vallega, *Heidegger and the Issue of Space*, 181.
41 Heidegger, "Art and Space," 7; Heidegger, *Die Kunst und der Raum*, 11.
42 Crowther, "Space, Place, and Sculpture," 156.

43   Mitchell, *Heidegger among the Sculptors*, 76.
44   Heidegger, "Art and Space," 8; Heidegger, *Die Kunst und der Raum*, 13.
45   Mitchell, *Heidegger among the Sculptors*, 56.
46   Heidegger, *Poetry, Language, Thought*, 56–7.
47   Watson, *Zhuangzi*, 30.
48   For more, see David Chai, *Zhuangzi and the Becoming of Nothingness* (Albany: State University of New York Press, 2019), 99–100.
49   Ibid., 99–101.
50   Heidegger, *Poetry, Language, Thought*, 45–6.
51   Karsten Harries, *Art Matters: A Critical Commentary on Heidegger's "The Origin of the Work of Art"* (Dordrecht: Springer, 2009), 117.

References

Chai, David. "Meontological Generativity: A Daoist Reading of the Thing." *Philosophy East and West*, 64.2 (2014a): 303–18.

Chai, David. "Nothingness and the Clearing: Heidegger, Daoism and the Quest for Primal Clarity." *The Review of Metaphysics*, 67.3 (2014b): 583–601.

Chai, David. *Zhuangzi and the Becoming of Nothingness*. Albany: State University of New York Press, 2019.

Crowther, Paul. "Space, Place, and Sculpture: Working with Heidegger." *Continental Philosophy Review*, 40 (2007): 151–70.

Figal, Gunter. *Aesthetics as Phenomenology: The Appearance of Things*. Bloomington: Indiana University Press, 2015.

Harries, Karsten. *Art Matters: A Critical Commentary on Heidegger's "The Origin of the Work of Art."* Dordrecht: Springer, 2009.

Heidegger, Martin. *What Is Called Thinking?* Translated by Fred Wieck and J. Glenn Gray. New York: Harper and Row, 1968.

Heidegger, Martin. "Art and Space." Translated by C.H. Seibert. *Man and World*, 6 (1969): 3–8.

Heidegger, Martin. *Bemerkungen zu Kunst-Plastik-Raum*. St. Gallen: Erker-Verlag, 1996.

Heidegger, Martin. *Poetry, Language, Thought*. Translated by Albert Hofstadter. New York: Harper Collins, 2001.

Heidegger, Martin. *Die Kunst und der Raum—L'Art et L'Espace*. Frankfurt: Vittorio Klostermann, 2007.

Heidegger, Martin. *Being and Time*. Translated by Joan Stambaugh. Albany: State University of New York Press, 2010.

Lynn, Richard J., trans. *The Classic of the Way and Virtue: A New Translation of the Tao-te Ching of Laozi as Interpreted by Wang Bi*. New York: Columbia University Press, 1999.

Ma, Lin. "Deciphering Heidegger's Connection with the *Daodejing*." *Asian Philosophy*, 16.3 (2006): 149–71.

Malpas, Jeff. *Heidegger's Topology: Being, Place, World*. Cambridge: MIT Press, 2006.

Martin, David F. "Sculpture and Truth to Things." *Journal of Aesthetic Education*, 13.2 (1979): 11–32.

Mitchell, Andrew. *Heidegger among the Sculptors: Body, Space, and the Art of Dwelling*. Stanford: Stanford University Press, 2010.

Petzet, Heinrich-Wiegand. *Encounters and Dialogues with Heidegger, 1929–1976.* Translated by Parvis Emad and Kenneth Maly. Chicago: University of Chicago Press, 1993.

Vallega, Alejandro. *Heidegger and the Issue of Space: Thinking on Exilic Grounds.* University Park: Pennsylvania State University Press, 2003.

Watson, Burton. *The Complete Works of Zhuangzi.* New York: Columbia University Press, 2013.

Part Three

Language and Identity

7

Rivers to the East: Heidegger's Lectures on Hölderlin as Prolegomena for Daoist Engagements

Daniel Fried

Introduction: Being-toward an "Orient"

Although Heidegger had read the Martin Buber translation of the *Zhuangzi* no later than 1930,[1] his engagements with Daoism are more visible in his later work, a time when he was also turning toward poetic language, especially what he saw as the utterly German *poiesis* of Hölderlin. There is nothing contradictory about simultaneous interest in one's own national traditions and those of another civilization, but one might also assume that such disparate interests are separable and coincidental. In Heidegger's case they are not, as can be seen from three sets of lectures on Hölderlin: a lecture course on both "Germania" and "The Rhine," delivered in 1934–5, and then two more lecture courses, on "Remembrance" and "The Ister," both of which were given during 1941–2. All of these lectures focus on the necessity of constructing a German identity through the experience of the Other, and hold that intellectual motions toward the Other are inseparable from the return toward self-understanding.

In those lectures, there is no engagement with Daoist texts or ideas. Nonetheless, a close examination of Heidegger's lectures can be useful for understanding his late turn toward engagement with Daoism, because they clearly establish a set of principles for how and why one should read texts alien to one's own national tradition. In these writings, his orientalism is not just on display, it is given a lengthy intellectual grounding in deliberate solipsism. Heidegger argues at length that one seeks out the other not to understand something alien in its own terms, with a responsibility to correct assessment of historical context, but rather in order to find oneself and one's own interests defined in relief against the other. Heidegger's fascinating misreadings of Daoism may have been largely the result of insufficient background and lack of proficiency in Chinese. Nevertheless, contextual knowledge was also irrelevant to his goals: despite his stated values, his lectures on Hölderlin make clear that his readings in Daoism were never intended to center the actual kind of attentive listening to the Other, through patient research, which we might think of as normal scholarly practice. Instead, projection for the sake of self-understanding was an affirmative goal of his engagement.

Few who have read the speculations on *kotoba* in "A Dialogue on Language between a Japanese and an Inquirer"[2] will later be surprised to read Tezuka Tomio's assessment that "There was perhaps an element here of forcing the word into a preconceived idea, but I was not in a position to contradict this interpretation."[3] Early work on Heidegger's engagements with East Asian traditions had to build up a case for the importance of those connections, and hence there was little space for a focus on his mistakes. As the reality of Heidegger's connections to Asian thought has been better established, however, there has been more room to note and explore his distance from it. Steven Burik, arguing for the positive value of difference to comparative philosophy, has compared Heidegger's own caution about losing the Self in the Other to a disdain for cultural adventurism or the desire to "go native."[4] The present chapter will be more critical of that difference, arguing that it is born out of a solipsism that leaves Heidegger's reading of civilizational Others both politically and philosophically suspect.

The following account of Heidegger's reading of Hölderlin will be directed only toward highlighting those aspects of his argument that provide a methodological framework for the Orientalism that shapes his Daoist engagements. In the hundreds of pages of the three separate lecture series, there is much that bears on Heidegger's detailed understanding of Hölderlin, his philo-Hellenism, and his ongoing questioning of thinking per se, which must be rushed past. There are, in fact, many streams of Heidegger's postwar thought that can be better understood in light of the Hölderlin lectures;[5] but the tracing of his lectures that follows will bypass most of those to maintain a focus on those aspects of Heidegger's development that are of most interest to comparative philosophy. Following the explication of how his Hölderlin lectures provide a method for finding Germany's national self in the phantasm of its Others, this chapter will then offer a brief review of how this approach affects his understanding of Daoism in several postwar texts: the *Country Path Conversations*, "The Thing," and "The Nature of Language."

Preliminary Journeys: "Germania" and "The Rhine"

Heidegger's first lecture course dedicated to Hölderlin's poetry focused on the two hymns, "Germania" and "The Rhine," and was delivered during the winter of the 1934-5 academic year in Freiburg. This was the year following his holding of the rectorate, in which he worked to make the university into an exemplar of Nazi higher education. Because that was a disastrous tenure, the lectures have been read with some confidence "as the answer to and justification for an abortive political commitment."[6] That is true in the sense that the lectures do refer obliquely to, and move away from, certain forms of direct political engagement. However, as Tom Rockmore has written, "Heidegger may have desired to portray his initial Hölderlin lectures as in fact coming to grips with Nazism. But the text, which does not support that interpretation, in fact reveals that he has not changed his mind about National Socialism or even about the shared concern to bring about German authenticity."[7] Despite ongoing conflicts with those in the educational and cultural hierarchies, Heidegger was still understood as a prominent philosopher of National Socialism, and was being considered as the first director of a proposed elite "Academy of Professors of the Reich."[8] Although the present analysis is not primarily concerned with the details of Heidegger's political involvement, it is impossible to avoid the politics that lies at the heart of his understanding of Hölderlin. These lectures still endorse a peculiarly Heideggerian form of nationalism that must be understood in order to think through his vision of who civilizational Others were, and to what uses they could be put.

In its philosophical content, this lecture series is closer to his early work than to the later writings in which he shows more substantial interest in and engagement with Daoist texts and traditions. There is a deep focus on *Sein* and *Dasein* that grows out of *Being and Time*. In fact, the lectures on these two poems are chronologically halfway between that book's 1927 publication and the later lectures on Hölderlin, delivered in the winter and summer sessions of 1941–2. Therefore, it is worthwhile examining in brief this earlier lecture series, to establish points of reference for Heidegger's early engagements with Hölderlin, before observing how his patterns of reading changed during the war years in ways that would shape his later orientalist desire for national affirmation within cultural Others.

From the first sections of the series, Heidegger speaks of "we" readers, and "our" readings in ways that cannot be reduced to the magisterial voice of the authoritative lecturer: the cultural *Dasein* of a corporate Germany is named as the reader who struggles into being under the pressure of Hölderlin's lyrics. "This originary, historical time of the peoples is therefore the time of the poets, thinkers, and creators of the state—that is, of those who properly ground and found the historical Dasein of a people."[9] When he turns from methodological preliminaries to a direct engagement with the content of the poem, what he finds as the content is a series of philosophical lessons on the proper sphere for national consciousness. He asserts that the poem begins by calling for "attunement" (*Stimmung*), which engages people at the roots of their being. Heidegger denounces the notion of "culture," but only in a reductionist mode of light cultural attainment: "Culture and the furthering of culture, culture clubs, and even cultural programs exist and make sense only where historical Dasein stands under the domination of what is today called 'liberalism.'"[10] It is clear that the attunement that he seeks for "historical Dasein" is what we might call "cultural" in a more totalizing sense, which engages the whole being of a historically determined people. This attunement happens on Earth, yet Earth is to be understood as a homeland rather than an abstract principle of nature. It happens within time, but time is properly understood as history, rather than an abstracted system of date-measurement. There is an oddly ahistorical quality to Heidegger's fondness for history: as Annemarie Gethmann-Siefert observed, "Heidegger believes he can disregard the concretion of the poetic world-projection," never accounting for the post-Napoleonic context of Hölderlin's actual politics.[11] The confluence of Earth and time within a Fatherland is "sealed in a mystery,"[12] an actual felt connection to generations lived in a space, rather than "Fatherland" as a mere patriotic abstraction. "*The 'fatherland' is beyng itself*"[13] he writes.

Heidegger begins his discussion of "The Rhine" by noting Hölderlin's interest in demigods, and claiming that he begins to think them in relation to the nation. "Standing at the threshold of the homeland has the dual meaning that from there the poet's longing can range into the foreign and remote, and that there, at the threshold, the gods that belong to the homeland must also be received for it."[14] He later goes on to identify "beyng" for Hölderlin as that which springs forth from an enigmatic origin, and argues that it is well represented by the image of the river—while at the same time the river is not merely an abstracted trope, but is itself central to the founding essence of a people. Somehow, the springing-forth of essence in the form of rivers is asserted always also to include a return to the source. This return is associated with the motion of demigods described in the later strophes of the poem, and whose presence among the people is interpreted as finally revealing the nature of corporate being in relation to its Others:

> A historical people, as a people, is community only when the community knows—and that means, wills—the fact that community can be as historical only if those Others as Others venture and sustain their being Other. This necessity for the Others to be Other is certainly not a license for all those stubborn and vain, those irksome and unproductive types who think their mere standing on the periphery is itself an accomplishment. The necessity of being the Other is such only out of the need and for the need of those who actually create—that is, on the grounds of the work that is effected.[15]

The offhand note about "stubborn and vain … irksome and unproductive types" who remain aloof on the periphery of German society is chilling in historical context. Nevertheless, the "Others" whom Heidegger speaks of as proper Others are praiseworthy, the demigods who are not fully encased in the nation, because they bring prophecies from outside. In the closing of the analysis, the poet is identified as such an Other.

This location of the nation's needed Otherness in divinity and poetizing is the most obvious limitation that the later lecture courses in 1941–2 would exceed. Much that he establishes in the course of these initial lectures is foundational: the notion that a poem is engaged with by a corporate, national readership; the idea that a poem becomes a space within which a nation finds its being; the notion that that being has to be founded from within a consciousness of history. Most important of all is his idea of the necessity of a double motion out from the national space toward an Other, and then back again, in order to capture some essential wisdom from outside. That is figured as a quasi-theological journey here; but it is one that would later be turned to Orientalist use in Heidegger's readings of "Remembrance" and "The Rhine."

"Remembrance" and the Wandering to the East

Although some scholars, building off of Heidegger's postwar statements, have argued for a turning-away from Nazism, there is no strong reason to think that, by 1941, Heidegger had abandoned his particular brand of phenomenological nationalism in favor of liberal internationalism. John W. Hoffmeyer has persuasively argued that the pattern of Heidegger's misreadings of Hölderlin, even into the postwar period, reflects an ongoing influence of Nazi ideals.[16] It is therefore not surprising that the geographical motions of "Remembrance" lead immediately to extended meditations on ideas of German national identity. What has changed from the lectures on "Germania" and "The Rhine" is a new emphasis on determining that identity in relation to geographical others, rather than to the demigods alone.

Heidegger begins with an exegesis of the opening line, "The northeasterly blows,"[17] as a declaration of spatiality and temporality without abstraction. This sending-off of the wind to the southwest sends it back along the track which Hölderlin had followed to Bordeaux during 1802, when he had worked there as a tutor. The "remembrance" is of course the poet's own, and his sending-off of the wind is a way to imaginatively follow it back into his own past, in a foreign land which was—in Heidegger's reading—a place of *ecstasis* and self-foreignizing learning. Bordeaux is noted as a place of quasi-racialized foreignness. Its "brown women"[18] who are the first humans to appear in the poem are tanned white women, but nonetheless of a literally elemental difference from German women: "This specifically recalls the southern land, where the sun's light is of intense transparency and its glow is overwhelming ... The encountering of gods and humans is different in the southern land."[19] Citing a letter of Hölderlin's upon his original return from Bordeaux that had associated southern France with classical Greece, Heidegger declares that the brownness of these sunny women is in fact a Greek brownness. Over the remainder of the poem, he continues to discuss the place of distance and ecstatic discovery as Greece rather than France; later, this pattern of geographic-semiotic slippage will enable a further motion, from Greece to India.

The motion to the foreign, slipping as it does from place to place, is also a journey to a certain ecstatic time: the holiday during which the brown women go walking. Holiday, festival, and celebration are identified as the markers of time out of time, a way to pause and escape from routine during which one can consider the nature of one's essential connection to life and to the world. It is, in Julian Young's phrase, an "antidote to *Gestell*,"[20] or life-sapping technological framing, which the Hellenic world possessed, but which has been lost to modernity. Through a series of turns in the exposition, this ecstatic festival encounter is associated with a motion toward the source of a river that confuses the foreign and the local:

> "The source"—that is the origin of the waters of the homeland, whose course speaks of the homeland as the soil that is to be consecrated for the festival. The source, however, names that which is originally indigenous to the homeland, that which is authentically one's own. To find one's way there and to take up free residence in the free realm of the homeland is what is most difficult ... And yet, one's ownmost and the origin retain difficulty within them; only it now appears transformed, insofar as now, for one who *has* once gone to the source, it is abandoning the homely locale that is, by converse, difficult, if it does not indeed become impossible.[21]

Heidegger has been associating Hölderlin's motions toward the foreign with motions back toward the German homeland, and his reading of the fluvial "source" does the same. Shy motion toward the headwaters of the river is turned around: the wealth one finds there only can become wealth insofar as it moves back down the river, to its mouth, and to the ocean, and the lands that lie beyond that ocean. It is here that the core of Heidegger's argument, the finding of one's own origin in that which is foreign, really comes to a head:

> The initial task, therefore, is to go away from the source, downstream, in the direction of the river's flowing out, to set out upon the ocean. Away from the source, that is, away from the homeland into the foreign ... The stay in the foreign and alienation in the foreign must be, in order for one's own to begin to light up in relation to the foreign. This distant lighting up awakens a remote inclining toward one's own.[22]

Following "Remembrance" in its narration of men going out from the river onto the open ocean, and ultimately to the "Indians," Heidegger traces this self-foreignization to the furthest point which the poem allows. It is unfortunately a place where Heidegger is simultaneously near his darkest and most compromised, and a place that holds the most clues toward the philosophical value in his Orientalism:

> To "Indians"? To the Indus? Thus still further away from what, for the poet, is the land of his home. Still further away, if we measure the remoteness numerically in terms of distance. Nonetheless nearer, if we ponder the essential, the passage to the source, the arrival in Germania ... To the Indians by the Indus? As if the distant provenance of Germania were at the Indus and the parents of our native homeland had come from there ... "Indus," in the realm of the hymnal poetry, is the poetic name for the primordial homeland, which, however, nonetheless remains remote. It is only for those who are homely and for those who seek what is their own, in such a way that they have gone there, yet at the same time returned from the Indus. Those who have returned home are who they are as those arrived from afar.[23]

The "Indus" as a river-image is entirely an interpolation by Heidegger; Hölderlin only mentions "Indians." The constant motion between the foreign and the domestic that has suffused his reading of the previous stanzas may have accustomed us to read past the shifting geographies; and the ongoing mystification of experience in the place of the foreign might lull us into thinking this rhetoric too quickly into spiritual forms.

Nevertheless, in the Germany of 1941, a line such as "if the distant provenance of Germania were at the Indus and the parents of our native homeland had come from there" echoed with the language of Aryan origins, despite the fact that Heidegger opposed the idea that race-"science" should be central to Nazi philosophy. Using his reading to trace the poet's imaginary journey into the heart of an essentialized foreign other allows Heidegger space for reflection on what it means to be an essentialized and authentically German self. Precisely because he opposed Nazi pseudo-biologism, it is likely that he intended this discussion of the "Indus" as primordial homeland as a way to redirect discussions of Aryan superiority from genetics to a certain power of historical vision.

One must read this book with a cold eye. Never does the text offer an argument for German racial superiority, much less for genocide. It consistently directs its exegetical energies at phenomenological questions, asking questions about the character of life as a process which occurs through motion in space and time, tied to active memory and reflection. At the same time, Heidegger is not shy about identifying the motion toward the Other as a way of self-understanding as somehow entirely consonant with the most nationally rooted version of German identity. The analysis constantly returns to Hölderlin's Germanness; he repeatedly cites Hölderlin's "Germania" for corroborating evidence, and once calls "Remembrance," "this most German of all German poetry."[24] Moreover, at the climax of his analysis, he asserts that the meaning of life as a German is to be found in the nation's Aryan roots—even though those roots are likely being defined away from standard Nazi biological reference terms.

Throughout the lecture series, Heidegger argues that cultural self-knowledge must be pursued through the cultural Other. This is not about an individual quest within interpersonal engagement; it is very far indeed from the Levinasian claim of the face of the other upon one's ethical being. Heidegger's vision of the questioning and remembering poetic self is as one who launches an imaginative quest on behalf of the homeland: self-definition is always national self-definition, and the poet seems to be undifferentiated from any other individual for whom he might speak.

The national self-knowledge that is to be sought happens in distant and exotic others, not ethnic minorities close at hand. And there is a semiotic slippage in who those exotic others might be, so that Bordeaux can easily be switched out as really meaning classical Greece; Greece again can be swapped out for India, so that we are given the possibility of measuring a national European identity against an assumed oriental Other. What is odd is that the content of this self-knowledge is never defined. He does not speculate on the characteristics of German character that Hölderlin makes clear, despite strong belief that Hölderlin is deeply German in some essentialist fashion. Nor does he even essentialize the cultural identity of Bordeaux, Greece, or India with any list of characteristics that could allow us to deduce what Germany must be, if we were to read those exotic locales as complex foils for the cultural self.

What we are thus given in the lecture series is a content-free argument for comparative methodology. Cultural analysis of the other is the proper and only way to know the national self; it is also only performed for the sake of knowing the national self. In the final lecture series the following year, on "The Ister," Heidegger continues to elaborate comparative cultural framing as a methodological principle. He still does not provide any content for what cultural self-knowledge Hölderlin actually reveals. Nevertheless, he does add detail on the nature of historicization and its central role in the process of cultural self-discovery, as well as on how the embodied character of symbolic language promotes a form of self-knowledge that cannot be extracted as a list of principles from the texts used to promote it.

The Ister and the German "Polis"

Heidegger's analysis of "The Ister," delivered in a 1942 lecture series, continues on many of the same themes that occupied his analysis of "Remembrance." Musings on the nature of rivers play an even larger role, and this carries on into his similar speculations on what is "homely" and what is foreign. He begins by unpacking the etymology of the name "Ister" as a Greek way of identifying the lower Danube; in his reading, Hölderlin's use of the name for the upper Danube again introduces into this poem as well the salutary confusion of directionality, from the source to the mouth of the river, and back again. He then begins an extended meditation on the nature of rivers in human life. Although he notes with interest the "dwelling" by the river as a key feature that Hölderlin's text proposes, the main line of his discussion connects the river to the form of the hymn, as he understands the poem to be.

He discovers the character of the river as the instantiation of that which it represents. That is a certain kind of double motion across different categories, geographical, temporal, and philosophical: "The river is simultaneously vanishing and full of intimation in a double sense. What is proper to the river is thus the essential fullness of a journey. The river is a journey in a singular and consummate way."[25] Yet because the river was previously identified as a place of dwelling, it is also a journey that incorporates stillness: "Our claim is this: the river is the locality of the dwelling of human beings as historical upon this earth. The river is the journeying of a historical coming to be at home at the locale of this locality. The river is locality and journeying."[26] As with the previous lectures, motion out toward the foreign (geographically, temporally, ideationally) is key toward understanding life at the home's center. The Ister can be key to this motion precisely because, in the words of Rafael Winkler, "[it] is not a thing in the world. It is a mode of disclosure of world and earth, of where there is."[27] By way of an excursus on the mechanistic character of modern ideas of location within a spatio-temporal grid, Heidegger seems to rescue Hölderlin for philosophical understanding of place, while actually planting him more than ever within the framework of nationalist consciousness:

> What is one's own in this case is whatever belongs to the fatherland of the Germans. Whatever is of the fatherland is itself at home with [*bei*] mother earth. This *coming to be* at home in one's own in itself entails that human beings are initially, and for a long time, and sometimes forever, not at home ... What is one's own, which the poetic meditation and telling is concerned with finding and appropriating, itself contains the relations to that foreign through which coming to be at home takes its path.[28]

The encounter with the foreign is immediately an encounter with the Greeks, an apparent diversion that occupies the whole of a lengthy second section on the *Antigone*. The argument of that second section focuses on the relation of the "uncanny" (*das Unheimliche*, in Hölderlin's translation of *ta deina*) to the "unhomely" (*das Unheimische*, unmentioned by either Hölderlin or Sophocles). Homeliness (in the sense of becoming native to a place) is identified as a historical process; unhomeliness, or a motion toward deliberate self-alienation, puts one into an experience of the uncanny. The uncanny is that which is anxiety inducing, something not at home in the ordinary and daily space of the homely. Moreover, as the famous line of the *Antigone* makes clear, human beings are the most uncanny (*deinoteron*, more literally "fearsome" or "wondrous") thing of all, and hence the self-alienation of the homely becoming unhomely is an encounter with a human, presumably one not from the home of the "homely," identified as the political unit of the *polis*.

Heidegger identifies Antigone as the obvious figure of the uncanny who stands in an ambiguous and disturbing relation to the political order of Thebes. Julian Young has offered a clever reading of that section as a covert anti-Nazi polemic, with Cleon standing in for Hitler,[29] but Antigone is figured as structurally parallel to the poet as a mediator of the uncanny/unhomely, rather than as a dissident. Given the need for the foreign poet which he had previously outlined, as well as the similar directions of his prior reading of "Remembrance," this valorization of the human uncanny certainly seems to imply a potential for geographical Others as the bringers of self-knowledge. Antigone might be Hölderlin, the figure of the German poet who cannot be contained within the polity; she might also literally be herself, a Greek character who can be used as the uncanny foil for the national self.

In any case, it is necessary to the logic of the lectures that Antigone, insofar as she is a representative of Greece, be recognizable to Germany without being wholly assimilable:

> One therefore does no service either to contemporary political thought or to the Greeks if one mixes together, in the overenthusiasm of the "scientific approach," everything that stands by itself in its own essence and in its specific historical uniqueness. One does no service whatsoever to our knowledge and evaluation of the historical singularity of National Socialism if one now interprets the Greek world in such a way as to say that the Greeks were all already "National Socialists."[30]

Praise of the "historical singularity" of National Socialism is in no way mitigated by Heidegger's rejection of absurd claims that it was consonant with the Hellenic world, and Hugo Ott is right to cite this passage as evidence that "there had been no movement in Heidegger's thinking between 1935 and 1942."[31] Nonetheless, for the purposes of tracking his overall argument, it is noteworthy how this series of political statements frames identity and difference. Greece is only valuable as a counterpoint for understanding German homeliness within the Nazi state because it exhibits cultural difference, through which one could pass on a circular journey back to the banks of the Ister.

The final part of the book, in effecting its own return from Greek literature to Hölderlin, prioritizes a certain vision of Hölderlin as a presence within his own poem, as an equivalent to the Ister itself. In the first part, as well as in his exegesis of "Remembrance," he had already established rivers as a sort of being that mediates between opposing directions: they go up to the headwaters in the national home, and out toward the mouth beyond which the foreign and exotic lie. But now in this final part of his reading, Heidegger associates this double motion with the act of poetizing, as well as the person of the poet, as the agent who brings the uncanny/unhomely from ecstatic realms back into the heart of the nation: "The poet is the river. And the river is the poet. The two are the same on the grounds of their singular essence, which is to be demigods, to be in the between, between gods and humans."[32] This hearkens back to the themes of the 1934–5 lectures, but here the nature of the poet as a demigod is more clearly geographical, someone who travels on imaginative journeys to real places. Figuratively, he points at soul, or mind, or even "the stars of the heavens."[33] Nevertheless, in reality he is still pointing only at those wholly locatable places to which both the Ister and the Rhine stretch, "determined from the direction of the East and from Asia."[34]

Asia as such is only lightly touched on in this final part of the exegetical narrative, to the degree that Andreas Grossmann argues that the exclusion of Asia is necessary for Heidegger's positing of Hölderlin as a heroic champion of "poetic dwelling."[35] There is less geographical specificity in this poem than in "Remembrance," with no particular river or region mentioned corresponding to that poem's foregrounding of the Indus. However, though not a specified place, the most significant geographical space in the section is an unnamed and generalized "Colony," cited from an unrelated poetic fragment of Hölderlin's:

> namely at home is spirit
> not at the commencement, not at the source. The home consumes it.
> Colony, and bold forgetting spirit loves.
> Our flowers and the shades or our woods gladden
> the one who languishes. The besouler would almost be scorched.[36]

Heidegger's gloss runs as follows:

> "Colony"—this does not mean whatever is merely foreign in the sense of the alien and exotic, that which the adventurer sets out in search of in order to settle his conscience. Spirit is not befallen by some arbitrary desire for the foreign. Spirit "loves" colony. Love is the essential will for what is of the essence. "Colony" is always the land of the daughter that is related and drawn back to the motherland. Spirit "loves" colony; in the foreign it essentially wills the mother who, according to the hymn "The Journey" (IV. 170) is indeed "difficult to attain: the closed one." Yet in spirit's "love" of "colony," it is, in an essential sense, "not at home": it has taken up being un-homely into the will pertaining to its love.[37]

The voyage into the Other, the unhomely, by which one comes to know the self and define the homely national space, is explicitly declared not to be about an arbitrary experience of the exotic. It is about love of the colonizer for the colonized, Heidegger insists; and just as importantly, about the positive will of the colonized to remain in that relationship. It is about that relation as both natural and constitutive, and as justified power-over.

This colonialist mindset tells us a great deal about how Heidegger views the actual intellectual process of the visionary journey he describes, from the domestic space to the foreign and back again. In no way does his enlarged emphasis on the value of history translate into a truly historicist approach to foreign texts or engagement with them. The lengthy excursus into the *Antigone*, despite insistent engagement with the idea of the *polis*, has nothing to say about the actual political state of the fifth-century *polis*, much less the details of family law which could have been expected to inform spectators' understanding of the central conflict of the tragedy. Katrin Froese is correct to write (about similar sentiments voiced in the 1946 *Letter on Humanism*), "Heidegger claims that Hölderlin's concept of nationalism exemplifies a greater respect for the particularity of other nations than what he considers to be a more vacuous cosmopolitanism or internationalism."[38] That is indeed his claim. Nevertheless, there is no indication that Heidegger has any idea of what particularity looks like in practice, without resorting to ill-informed speculation on cultural essentialisms.

Ignoring historiography, Heidegger posits history as a category of poetic vision. Like rivers, history is discussed as something which does not simply flow in one direction, but which involves the future in the past, calling out for new beginnings to start from within a legacy. "At root, Heidegger's Hölderlin becomes *the* poet who poetizes that the beginning of our history is still to come, that is, still coming as a kind of homecoming to our concealed origin, an origin whose potencies have hardly been able to unfold their poetic power."[39] This power of history to gather the past into new beginnings is what allows it the potential for a holistic rootedness against technological reductionism. In other words, it is justified mythmaking—small wonder he can so easily ignore the actuality of colonial relations in favor of mother-daughter archetypes.

Although it might seem paradoxical, this willingness to use the other as a quasi-colonial playground for Dasein's self-seeking could partially explain why there were so few explicit references to Asian thought in the works published during Heidegger's lifetime. Gadamer's remark to Graham Parkes, that Heidegger would have been reluctant to comment formally on texts he was unable to read in the original, is unsatisfying.[40] Little in Heidegger's corpus suggests intellectual modesty, and in these lecture series, he has been explicit about not needing to worry about fidelity to original contexts. However, if the journey into the unhomely has always been about the self of Dasein, rather than about the Other, there really should not be any need to cite the Other's text explicitly.

Heidegger's Postwar Daoist Appropriations

This overview of Heidegger's lectures on Hölderlin has aimed to explicate the philosophical underpinnings of his methodological Orientalism. His developing belief, over the course of those lectures, that the journey out toward civilizational Others is necessary for the self-definition of a nation, something integral to its very being, leads us to expect that Heidegger's postwar encounters with Daoism should be both solipsistic and appropriative. A few brief sketches of some of his postwar engagements with Daoism should make clear that the vision of an appropriative journey to the unhomely indeed does drive his method in his late period.

A first example comes from the brief invocation of the *Zhuangzi* in the closing pages of the *Country Path Conversations*. The third conversation, a dialogue between an old and a young German soldier, is set in a Russian prisoner of war camp, and dated May 8, 1945—the date of German surrender. In many ways, it recapitulates the themes of his lectures on "Remembrance" and "The Ister," but modulated to a minor key. It can be understood as an attempt to save his model of knowing the self through the other from the failures of German nationalist warmaking, and his paraphrase of the *Zhuangzi* shows how he can continue to practice intellectual neocolonialism without an overtly nationalist project.

As Bret W. Davis notes, the dialogue was written while Heidegger's own sons were still missing on the eastern front.[41] Nonetheless, the locale also has ironic resonance with the theory propounded in his lectures on Hölderlin: in Heidegger's ethereal phenomenological vocabulary, their conversation circles around the primary problem of how to understand German national identity in the face of calamitous loss and unending devastation. Like Hölderlin, they are discovering the true nature of German being from a geographical journey to someplace very much Other, but with no freedom to make the return journey associated with the return to rivers' sources. This model is not merely left as an implication of the setting, but explicitly invoked: "it was as if my essence were walled up and wholly expelled from the open expanse of thinking," says the Younger Man. "At the same time, however, I was allowed to presage and learned to presage this thinking like a distant land."[42] Nevertheless, Heidegger's argument is new in divorcing the self-foreignizing journey of thinking from the actual geographical motions of military conquest that Germany had chosen. Jingoism is identified as a "rash pseudo-essence"[43] which is in fact the true danger. To put it crassly: Germany, having been defeated militarily, can look for a true identity in philosophy.

In closing, the Older Man quotes Zhuangzi on the "unnecessary," partly as authority and partly as ornamental flourish:

> The one said: "You are talking about the unnecessary."
> The other said: "A person must first have recognized the unnecessary before one can talk with him about the necessary. The earth is wide and large, and yet, in order to stand, the human needs only enough space to be able to put his foot down. But if directly next to his foot a crevice were to open up that dropped down into the underworld, then would the space where he stands still be of use to him?"
> The one said: "It would be of no more use to him."
> The other said: "From this the necessity of the unnecessary is clearly apparent."[44]

This story is not given any commentary; after it is cited, the dialogue ends. Apparently, it is assumed to speak for itself, offering a grace note of "eastern wisdom" which just happens to endorse their conversation about the necessity of the unnecessary. In fact, the anecdote is a dialogue between Zhuang Zhou and Hui Shi, excerpted from chapter 26 of the *Zhuangzi*. This chapter, classified by Xiaogan Liu as belonging to a "Transmitter" school relatively close in time and approach to the historical Zhuang Zhou, does replicate an interest in uselessness that can indeed be found in the inner chapters.[45] Most early readers, understanding Zhuangzi's disputes with the Logicians (*mingjia* 名家) would presumably have understood the polemics of uselessness here: Huizi's accusation is that it is Zhuangzi's words that are useless, because they are wild, incautious, overly literary. In other words, Zhuangzi's actual argument is against the reduction of philosophical argument to precise and measurable words—an argument Heidegger could have made great use of on its own terms. This fact only emphasizes the arbitrariness of Heidegger's actual choice, to tear "uselessness" out of context and put it to use in ways thoroughly alien to its own meaning. This is not to say that Heidegger was deliberately misreading the source text in the form it was available to him; Eric S. Nelson has recently demonstrated that Heidegger's understanding is dependent on Richard Wilhelm's 1912 translation. Nonetheless, he certainly should have known that praise for the "unnecessary" in ancient China was not a renunciation of fascism, and that the earth around Zhuangzi's feet was not a nationalist territorial claim.

Why cite the passage at all? Even given Heidegger's misreading, it merely provides a putative echo for what Heidegger had explicated on his own, with no further comment. Its citation fits the model of geographic semiotic slippage established in the lectures on "Remembrance": the real Germany is found in an Other that is first Russia, and then the more distant Orient. He has seemingly made a thought-journey over into the realm of the Unhomely, in order to find a postwar self for Germany; but in actuality has performed an act of simple dominance.

In Heidegger's more substantial postwar engagements with Daoism, there also remains a clear habit of appropriative overwriting. "The Thing," originally delivered as a 1950 lecture, is on the surface an attempt to reframe the post-Kantian problem of the epistemological status of objects. The thing is that which cannot be reduced to the status of an epistemological object, and attempts to treat it as an object through either classical epistemology or modern scientific analysis will inevitably miss the point. The thing is defined not by what it is, but by what it does, gathering the "fourfold" unity of heaven and earth, gods and humans. "The thing stays—gathers and unites—the fourfold. The thing things world."[46]

It is well-recognized that the essay is indebted to Daoism. The paradigmatic object that Heidegger uses as an example of the thing is the jug: "The emptiness, the void, is what does the vessel's holding. The empty space, this nothing of the jug, is what the jug is as the holding vessel."[47] Related discussion of the jug as a thing can be found in "The Origin of the Work of Art,"[48] but this version of the description in "The Thing" is more clearly borrowing from *Daodejing* chapter 11: "Knead clay in order to make a vessel. Adapt the nothing therein to the purpose in hand, and you will have the use of the vessel."[49] Reinhard May, noting the closeness of Heidegger's description to the *Daodejing* translations of both Wilhelm and Von Strauss, has identified this as a direct paraphrase, and he is likely correct.[50] One should not read "The Thing" as an exposition of Daoism: Heidegger never acknowledges any appropriation, and moves quickly from the paraphrase of Laozi into etymological questions from High German, Greek, and Latin. The basic concerns of the essay can be traced back to central issues of *Being and Time*, but David Chai is quite correct to note that "this notion of a self-originating thingness is quite Daoist in tone insofar as it is an attempt to explain how the space between the Thing and human reality can be bridged rather than driven farther apart."[51]

Paradoxically, the essay's distance from Daoism, and its Orientalizing disruptions of Daoism, can best be understood through other, seldom-noticed borrowings. It seems likely that the notion of the "fourfold," a union of heaven, earth, demigods, and humans that is used to explain the gathering function of the thing, might owe something to *Daodejing* chapter 25: "Hence the way is great; heaven is great; earth is great; and the king is also great. Within the realm there are four things that are great, and the king counts as one."⁵² However, the clearest appropriation is in this description of the jug:

> But the jug does consist of sides and bottom. By that of which the jug consists, it stands. What would a jug be that did not stand? At least a jug *manqué*, hence a jug still—namely, one that would indeed hold but that, constantly falling over, would empty itself of what it holds. Only a vessel, however, can empty itself.⁵³

The notion of a self-emptying jug is mystifying, until one recognizes the concept from the classic Guo Xiang 郭象 (252–312 CE) gloss on chapter 27 of the *Zhuangzi*: "This *zhi* is [a thing which] tips when full, and rights [itself] when empty, and does not stay fast."⁵⁴ This gloss is also clearly related to the idea of *Daodejing* chapter 9: "Rather than fill it to the brim by keeping it upright/Better to have stopped in time."⁵⁵ The origin of this language in description of self-tipping vessels first of agricultural, and then ceremonial use, has been described at length;⁵⁶ although that is a sinological question beyond what Heidegger could have accessed directly, it is broached in classical commentaries. Whether he learned about it in reference to the *Daodejing* or the *Zhuangzi*, his usage here is clearly taking the self-tipping jug out of its context. In the *Daodejing*, the image is used to suggest the value in a life of quiet contentment away from avarice, praising the half-full rather than the empty. In the *Zhuangzi*, it is used as a metaphor for the value of allusive philosophical language, precisely because of its inherent instability. Both of these would have been plainly evident through available translations.

That Heidegger understood his own decontextualizing appropriations as a version of Hölderlin's journey to the unhomely can be seen from the seldom-remarked framing of the essay. Geography is not a particularly covert subtext. On the contrary, it is trumpeted in the opening sentences: "*All distances in time and space are shrinking. Man now reaches overnight,* by plane, places which formerly took weeks and months of travel … Distant sites of the most ancient cultures are shown on film as if they stood this very moment amidst today's street traffic."⁵⁷ This technological triumph is characterized as a failure, an annihilation of space and time which somehow utterly fails at actually bringing one into true nearness and actual presence. It is as an alternative to the technologically mediated version of physical globalization that Heidegger offers a phenomenological route to nearness, and it is in that context that he first introduces the Daoist jug:

> What about nearness? How can we come to know its nature? Nearness, it seems, cannot be encountered directly. We succeed in reaching it rather by attending to what is near. Near to us are what we usually call things. But what is a thing? Man has so far given no more thought to the thing as a thing than he has to nearness. The jug is a thing. What is the jug? We say: a vessel, something of the kind that holds something else within it.⁵⁸

This would be a strange and sudden shift without the knowledge of the jug as a symbol of Asian wisdom; but as it stands, it makes perfect sense to find the solution to geographic annihilation in the allusion-thing laying perfectly at hand. Moreover, this is where a strange anxiety over the jug's possible independence from the German philosopher-subject begins to reveal itself. In the pages that follow, Heidegger repeatedly stresses the fact that the jug's base makes it "something self-sustained, something that stands on its own."[59] Although it has a handle and supposedly lies to hand, although it is fashioned by the potter, Heidegger keeps returning to its "self-support" and "over-againstness" as a threat to the kind of nearness which he claims to crave. Self-support becomes a metaphor for the objecthood of the jug in traditional epistemological assessment: "But from the objectness of the object, and from the product's self-support, there is no way that leads to the thingness of the thing."[60] It is that independence of the jug that must be eliminated, if one is to overcome both epistemology and technology: in order to be a thing and not an object, Heidegger needs it to stop being independent and self-supporting. He needs a relation to it that eliminates its separation. And this is precisely the conclusion that draws him on to focus on the jug's emptiness as a solution: it exists to be filled. (The self-tipping function of the jug, undercutting the notion that it ever really was wholly distant object, is a simple grace note.)

The image of the jug is, on one level, "about" a point of epistemology. Yet everything explicit in Heidegger's philosophical system militates against reductionist approaches that would narrow postulates to a set of equations. In his analysis of Hölderlin he repeatedly argued against reductionist readings of symbolic imagery, and practiced an associative mode of poetic exegesis. As readers who know the origin of his jug-image in Daoist texts, we also know that he had his own appropriation clear in his mind during the composition of the essay. Therefore, it is not a stretch to say that, while about epistemology, the essay is also about cross-cultural philosophical appropriation. Deliberately introducing his essay in geographical terms, he has openly confessed his continuing interest in the same journeys across time and space that fueled his reading of Hölderlin. His assertions about the jug parallel his exegetical action on the Daoist image of the jug. Apparently, something from a tradition that stood independent from himself, over and against himself, he has asserted that that independence is illusory. The Daoist image is defined at its core by emptiness: it has been waiting millennia for a German to fill it with the substance of his own phenomenology.

Despite the rhetorical connections to *Daodejing* chapter 11, Heidegger's use of the jug remains an appropriation that tears the image entirely loose from its specific local contexts in the Lao-Zhuang texts. He pours out its original meanings, and fills it instead with content that does have some affinities with Asian philosophy, but much greater ones with Heidegger's own earlier writings. This action also re-enacts the same mental journey, and the same colonial-style appropriations, which Heidegger had identified for praise in Hölderlin's hymns. He travels off toward the civilizational Other in order to find himself.

Again, in "The Nature of Language" from the winter of 1957–8, Heidegger enacts this same appropriative journey. This despite the fact that it is one of the few essays in which Heidegger directly acknowledges a substantive borrowing from Daoist traditions: "Perhaps the mystery of mysteries of thoughtful Saying conceals itself in the word 'way,' *Tao*, if only we will let these names return to what they leave unspoken ... All is way."[61] Unsurprisingly, Heidegger reaches this borrowing by means of a speculative journey to the East that by now should feel familiar. Over the course of this three-lecture series, he frames his discussion around the Stefan George poem "The Word," which describes a motion nearly identical to those in the Hölderlin hymns: motion toward an exotic land, followed by a return motion carrying a cultural treasure intended to enrich the homeland. Throughout, he stresses that the relationality of language and Being must happen in a quasi-geographical space of an ideational "country," "region," or "neighborhood," and Daoism is introduced in terms which stress that geography in the terms of George's treasure-seeking: "the reflective use of language cannot be guided by the common, usual understanding of meanings; rather, it must be guided by the hidden riches that language holds in store for us, so that these riches may summon us for the saying of language. The country offers ways only because it is country. It gives way, moves us."[62] Heidegger imagines the "country" as that which yields a bounty, by yielding to appropriative inquiry.

In addition, that which he immediately goes on to take from Laozi is simply wrong: "*Tao* is then translated as reason, mind, *raison*, meaning, *logos*."[63] It does seem that in the closing lines of the essay, Heidegger comes closer to Daoist language (without citing Daoism), proposing that "the sounding word returns into soundlessness."[64] However, this does not overwhelm the entire focus of the piece, which argues throughout the necessity of conceiving of Being as something that happens inside language, and through an experience of language. One could hardly find a sentiment more directly alien to the Daoist conception of language, which repeats in many ways across many texts the famous opening words of *Daodejing* chapter 1: "The way that can be spoken of/Is not the constant way."[65] Heidegger frames Laozi as an exotic source of wisdom from whom he claims a treasure and brings it back into European philosophy, acting out both Hölderlin and George. Nevertheless, that which he forces the text to yield is a rhetoric and a style made to hold the diametric opposite of its actual propositional content.

Conclusion

In the three-lecture series on Hölderlin, Heidegger develops a clear model of how national self-knowledge is acquired. One starts from the national space, making a journey outward, often along a river. Distant locales (which tend to blend into each other via a chain of substitution) are an uncanny/unhomely space in which one encounters an Other. That Other might be a demigod, or simply a foreigner. However, one does not really listen to the Other for the Other; one brings one's own national concerns to the exotic space, in order to understand oneself better there. The resulting wisdom is brought home to refound the nation.

In his postwar engagements with Daoism, Heidegger hews closely to this model. He repeatedly frames his discussion in explicitly geographical terms, introducing rhetorical structures that highlight globalization and discussing philosophical encounters as spatialized events. Whether acknowledged or not, Daoist intertexts are the foreign, uncanny foils against which he articulates his ideas. Moreover, they are his own: even when he gets some general Daoist atmospherics correct, the details of contexts are erased under the pressure of his desire to express his own phenomenological position. What is brought back is ultimately that which he himself had carried into his readings of Lao-Zhuang.

Ultimately, this fault is less important as a political critique than as a philosophical one. Heidegger's orientalist habits are real, and richly deserving of condemnation. However, those habits are not more scandalous than the Nazism for which he has long since been universally condemned, and there is no need to emphasize how unacceptable his politics are.

The problem is that the model that Heidegger both proposes in his reading of Hölderlin, and enacts through his reading of Lao-Zhuang, is a bad and unhelpful model for comparative philosophy, unless one recognizes its limits. Daoist texts do seem to have given Heidegger inspiration, in ways that proved fruitful for the maturation of his later thought. Nevertheless, he read those texts in relatively shallow and mistake-prone ways, while using the rhetoric of depth and true connection. He engages with a distant tradition with the explicit goal of finding a true cultural self, and downplays the importance of actual historical legwork in favor of History as a power of vision. Without recognizing that history can only ever be granular, this approach would create a constant danger of mistaking one's own guesses for the object of analysis.

Notes

1 Otto Pöggeler, "West-East Dialogue: Heidegger and Lao-Tzu," in Graham Parkes (ed.), *Heidegger and Asian Thought*, 47–78 (Honolulu: University of Hawaii Press, 1987), at 52.
2 Martin Heidegger, *On the Way to Language*, trans. Peter D. Hertz (New York: Harper Collins, 1971), 45–8.
3 Reinhard May, *Heidegger's Hidden Sources*, trans. Graham Parkes (London: Routledge, 1996), 62.
4 Steven Burik, *The End of Comparative Philosophy and the Task of Comparative Thinking: Heidegger, Derrida, and Daoism* (Albany: State University of New York Press, 2009), 38.
5 "Heidegger's reading of Hölderlin therefore opens up a number of the paths in his later thought. The project of overcoming metaphysics, the questioning concerning technology, and poetic dwelling all become clearer and more developed if we follow the confrontation between thinker and poet." Stuart Elden, "Heidegger's Hölderlin and the Importance of Place," *Journal of the British Society for Phenomenology*, 30.3 (1999): 258–74, at 270.
6 Annemarie Gethmann-Siefert, "Heidegger and Hölderlin: The Over-Usage of 'Poets in an Impoverished Time,'" trans. Richard Taft, in Christopher Macann (ed.), *Martin Heidegger: Critical Assessments*, volume 3 (London: Routledge, 1992), 247.
7 Tom Rockmore, *On Heidegger's Nazism and Philosophy* (Berkeley: University of California Press, 1992), 132.
8 For a summary of Heidegger's political entanglements during that year, see Victor Farias, *Heidegger and Nazism* (Philadelphia: Temple University Press, 1989), 191–212.
9 Martin Heidegger, *Hölderlin's Hymns "Germania" and "The Rhine,"* trans. William McNeill and Julia Ireland (Bloomington: University of Indiana Press, 2014), 49–50.

10   Heidegger, "*Germania*" and "*The Rhine*," 89.
11   Gethmann-Siefert, "Heidegger and Hölderlin," 250.
12   Heidegger, "*Germania*" and "*The Rhine*," 108.
13   Ibid., 109. Italics in original.
14   Ibid., 155.
15   Ibid., 257-8.
16   John W. Hoffmeyer, "Poetics of History, Logics of Collapse: On Heidegger's Hölderlin," *The German Quarterly*, 93.3 (2020): 374-89.
17   Martin Heidegger, *Hölderlin's Hymn "Remembrance*," trans. William McNeill and Julia Ireland (Bloomington: University of Indiana Press, 2018), 16.
18   Heidegger, "*Remembrance*," 17.
19   Ibid., 71.
20   Julian Young, *Heidegger's Later Philosophy* (Cambridge: Cambridge University Press, 2002), 58.
21   Heidegger, "*Remembrance*," 147.
22   Ibid., 149.
23   Ibid., 156-7.
24   Ibid., 102.
25   Heidegger, "*The Ister*," 30.
26   Ibid., 33.
27   Rafael Winkler, "Dwelling and Hospitality: Heidegger and Hölderlin," *Research in Phenomenology*, 47.3 (2017): 366-87, at 371.
28   Heidegger, "*The Ister*," 49.
29   Julian Young, "Poets and Rivers: Heidegger on Hölderlin's 'Der Ister,'" in Hubert Dreyfus and Mark Wrathall (eds.), *Heidegger Reexamined*, volume 3 (New York: Routledge, 2002), 96.
30   Heidegger, "*The Ister*," 86.
31   Hugo Ott, *Martin Heidegger: A Political Life* (New York: Harper Collins, 1993), 295.
32   Heidegger, "*The Ister*," 165-6.
33   Ibid., 151.
34   Ibid., 145.
35   Andreas Grossmann, "The Myth of Poetry: On Heidegger's 'Hölderlin,'" *The Comparatist*, 28 (2004): 29-38, at 34.
36   Heidegger, "*The Ister*," 126.
37   Ibid., 131.
38   Katrin Froese, *Nietzsche, Heidegger, and Daoist Thought: Crossing Paths In-Between* (Albany: State University of New York Press, 2006), 86.
39   Charles Bambach, "Who Is Heidegger's Hölderlin?" *Research in Phenomenology*, 57.1 (2017): 39-59, at 52.
40   Graham Parkes, "Heidegger and Japanese Thought: How Much Did He Know and When Did He Know It?" in Christopher Macann (ed.), *Martin Heidegger: Critical Assessments*, volume 4 (London: Routledge, 1992), 399.
41   Martin Heidegger, *Country Path Conversations*, trans. Bret W. Davis (Bloomington: University of Indiana Press, 2010), xix.
42   Heidegger, *Conversations*, 142.
43   Ibid., 152.
44   Ibid., 156.
45   Xiaogan Liu, *Classifying the Zhuangzi Chapters*, trans. William Savage (Ann Arbor: University of Michigan Press, 1995), 114-16.

46 Martin Heidegger, *Poetry, Language, Thought*, trans. Albert Hofstadter (New York: Harper Collins, 2001), 178.
47 Ibid., 167.
48 That essay had been evolving since an original 1935 lecture until published in *Holzwege* in 1950, the same year as "The Thing" was originally delivered.
49 Lao Tzu, *Tao Te Ching*, trans. D.C. Lau (New York: Penguin, 1963), 15.
50 May, *Hidden Sources*, 31.
51 David Chai, "Meontological Generativity: A Daoist Reading of the Thing," *Philosophy East and West*, 64.2 (2014): 303–18, at 307.
52 Lao Tzu, *Tao Te Ching*, 30.
53 Heidegger, *Poetry, Language, Thought*, 167.
54 Qingfan Guo, ed., *Collected Explanations to the Zhuangzi* (Taipei: Dingyuan, 2001), 947. My translation.
55 Lao Tzu, *Tao Te Ching*, 13.
56 Daniel Fried, "A Never-Stable Word: Zhuangzi's Zhiyan and 'Tipping-Vessel' Irrigation," *Early China*, 31 (2007): 145–70.
57 Heidegger, *Poetry, Language, Thought*, 163. Italics in original.
58 Ibid., 164.
59 Ibid.
60 Ibid., 165.
61 Heidegger, *On the Way to Language*, 92.
62 Ibid., 91–2.
63 Ibid., 92.
64 Ibid., 108.
65 Lao Tzu, *Tao Te Ching*, 5.

References

Bambach, Charles. "Who Is Heidegger's Hölderlin?" *Research in Phenomenology*, 57.1 (2017): 39–59.
Burik, Steven. *The End of Comparative Philosophy and the Task of Comparative Thinking: Heidegger, Derrida, and Daoism*. Albany: State University of New York Press, 2009.
Chai, David. "Meontological Generativity: A Daoist Reading of the Thing." *Philosophy East and West*, 64.2 (2014): 303–18.
Elden, Stuart. "Heidegger's Hölderlin and the Importance of Place." *Journal of the British Society for Phenomenology*, 30.3 (1999): 258–74.
Farías, Victor. *Heidegger and Nazism*. Philadelphia: Temple University Press, 1989.
Fried, Daniel. "A Never-Stable Word: Zhuangzi's *Zhiyan* and 'Tipping-Vessel' Irrigation." *Early China*, 31 (2007): 145–70.
Froese, Katrin. *Nietzsche, Heidegger, and Daoist Thought: Crossing Paths In-Between*. Albany: State University of New York Press, 2006.
Gethmann-Siefert, Annemarie. "Heidegger and Hölderlin: The Over-Usage of 'Poets in an Impoverished Time.'" Translated by Richard Taft. In Christopher Macann (ed.), *Martin Heidegger: Critical Assessments*, volume 3, 247–76. London: Routledge, 1992.
Grossmann, Andreas. "The Myth of Poetry: On Heidegger's 'Hölderlin.'" *The Comparatist*, 28 (2004): 29–38.
Guo, Qingfan, ed. *Collected Explanations to the Zhuangzi* 莊子集釋. Taipei: Dingyuan, 2001.

Heidegger, Martin. *Hölderlin's Hymn "The Ister."* Translated by William McNeill and Julia Ireland. Bloomington: University of Indiana Press, 1996.
Heidegger, Martin. *On the Way to Language.* Translated by Peter D. Hertz. New York: Harper Collins, 1971.
Heidegger, Martin. *Poetry, Language, Thought.* Translated by Albert Hofstadter. New York: Harper Collins, 2001.
Heidegger, Martin. *Country Path Conversations.* Translated by Bret W. Davis. Bloomington: University of Indiana Press, 2010.
Heidegger, Martin. *Hölderlin's Hymns "Germania" and "The Rhine."* Translated by William McNeill and Julia Ireland. Bloomington: University of Indiana Press, 2014.
Heidegger, Martin. *Hölderlin's Hymn "Remembrance."* Translated by William McNeill and Julia Ireland. Bloomington: University of Indiana Press, 2018.
Hoffmeyer, John W. "Poetics of History, Logics of Collapse: On Heidegger's Hölderlin." *The German Quarterly,* 93.3 (2020): 374–89.
Lao Tzu. *Tao Te Ching.* Translated by D.C. Lau. New York: Penguin, 1963.
Liu, Xiaogan. *Classifying the Zhuangzi Chapters.* Translated by William Savage. Ann Arbor: University of Michigan Press, 1995.
May, Reinhard. *Heidegger's Hidden Sources.* Translated by Graham Parkes. London: Routledge, 1996.
Nelson, Eric S. "Heidegger's Daoist Turn." *Research in Phenomenology,* 49.3 (2019): 362–84.
Ott, Hugo. *Martin Heidegger: A Political Life.* New York: Harper Collins, 1993.
Parkes, Graham. "Heidegger and Japanese Thought: How Much Did He Know and When Did He Know It?" In Christopher Macann (ed.), *Martin Heidegger: Critical Assessments,* volume 4, 377–406. London: Routledge, 1992.
Pöggeler, Otto. "West-East Dialogue: Heidegger and Lao-Tzu." In Graham Parkes (ed.), *Heidegger and Asian Thought,* 47–78. Honolulu: University of Hawaii Press, 1987.
Rockmore, Tom. *On Heidegger's Nazism and Philosophy.* Berkeley: University of California Press, 1992.
Watson, Burton, trans. *The Complete Works of Chuang Tzu.* New York: Columbia University Press, 1968.
Winkler, Rafael. "Dwelling and Hospitality: Heidegger and Hölderlin." *Research in Phenomenology,* 47.3 (2017): 366–87.
Young, Julian. *Heidegger's Later Philosophy.* Cambridge: Cambridge University Press, 2002.
Young, Julian. "Poets and Rivers: Heidegger on Hölderlin's 'Der Ister.'" In Hubert Dreyfus and Mark Wrathall (eds.), *Heidegger Reexamined.* Volume Three—*Art, Poetry, and Technology,* 79–104. New York: Routledge, 2002.

8

Thinking through Silence: (Non-) Language in Heidegger and Classical Daoism

Steven Burik

Introduction

For Heidegger, "[w]hoever discourses about keeping silent is in danger of proving in the most immediate way that he neither knows nor understands keeping silent."[1] Also, "I renounced and sadly see: Where word breaks off no thing may be."[2] I have nothing to say. Although this may not be the usual way one starts a chapter contribution to a book, I mean it quite literally. How can one not say anything, but more importantly, how to speak of, how to say "nothing"? The question of how to speak of or understand nothing has been posed in many different ways.[3] In this chapter, I examine the relation between understanding nothingness and silence in Martin Heidegger and classical Daoism. Through this examination I seek to understand how these protagonists aspire to another interpretation and/or use of language via silence.

At first glance, Heidegger and Lao-Zhuang seem to be advocating silence as a way of being, superior to that of speech, writing, or any use of language, and symbolizing a return to understanding nothingness as a way of being more originary than possible through a focus on beings. It therefore seems that those who understand are silent, and those who do not understand have to resort to language. We shall find evidence in Heidegger and Daoism that they think this is the case. But I will further claim that this focus on silence is only a preliminary step, and that the warning Heidegger gives us (in the first quote above) about not discoursing on silence is, although important and necessary, also premature. This chapter thus challenges an overly facile understanding of both Heidegger and Daoism, and argues that although some form of silence constitutes an important and necessary stage of understanding, it is in the end not sufficient. In other words, although language needs to be overcome by silence, it is silence itself which in turn needs to be overcome by another kind of language to arrive at a full(-er) understanding of the world and our being in it.

I will, therefore, challenge the idea that silence would be the endpoint of understanding and seek to prove that "real" understanding consists in an awareness of the necessity of using language, as well as the awareness that our "normal" ways of using language are insufficiently suited to such deeper understanding. Not only will we need language to come to understand and explain that silence should follow or supersede "normal" language, in other words we need language to overcome language but, more importantly, we also need another kind of language to understand and seek to convey what this silence actually aims to achieve for us. And it is understanding through that other language that Heidegger and Daoism seek to convey via silence. Silence in my exposition may be understood in a variety of ways, as non-spoken language, writing for example, but also other non-spoken or non-written forms of signification, and as a form of non-signification or a challenge to signifying structures.

Heidegger on Silence

As many know, to say that Heidegger is fond of language would be an understatement, and this fondness and focus on language is evidenced throughout his work. For example, in the "Letter on Humanism" where he emphasizes that language is the way that Dasein is in Being, Heidegger goes so far as to famously call language "the house of Being"[4] and the "clearing-concealing advent of Being itself."[5] But the fact that language is this so-called house of Being does not mean we automatically dwell in this house in the right way. We all know that one can live in a house that is not a home. As Heidegger says: "Only because language is the home and the essence of man can historical mankind and human beings not be at home in their language."[6]

Throughout his work, Heidegger suggests that at least *a certain type* of language, closely associated with both the metaphysical use and our normal language use, informed as they are by the subject-object distinction, is inadequate to convey Being, and on numerous occasions he suggests that silence is to be preferred over our normal and metaphysical/philosophical language use. This is because Heidegger believes that "the metaphysical-animal explanation of language covers up the essence of language in the history of Being."[7] In other words, our normal language use as understood in the Western history of philosophy precludes an entrance into thinking Being.

But this in itself does not call for silence. Yet the kind of thinking Heidegger envisions is intimately related to silence. Heidegger says that for "the truth of Being to come to language … language requires much less precipitate expression than proper silence. But who of us today would want to imagine that his attempts to think are at home on the path of silence?"[8] To find that appropriate way of existing and saying that would be attuned to Being, one needs to go through silence, the silence that results from the realization that conventional and traditional forms of (metaphysical) language are inadequate to the "*Sage*," the Saying of Being. Heidegger says: "But if man is to find his way once again into the nearness of Being he must first learn to exist in the nameless … Before he speaks man must first let himself be claimed again by Being, taking the risk that under this claim he will seldom have much to say."[9]

There are many occasions where Heidegger attests to this preference of silence over language. In the earlier work, *Sein und Zeit* §34 argues that discourse (*Rede*) is grounded in silence. First of all, Heidegger establishes in this paragraph that silence and hearing belong as much to language, speech, discourse (*Rede*), as does speaking itself.

"*Hearing* and *keeping silent* are possibilities belonging to discoursing speech."[10] And he argues that discourse is "equiprimordial with attunement and understanding."[11] Then he proceeds to argue that as an essential possibility of discourse:

> Authentic silence is possible only in genuine discourse. In order to be silent, Da-sein must have something to say, that is, must be in command of an authentic and rich disclosedness of itself. Then reticence (*Verschwiegenheit*) makes manifest and puts down 'idle talk.' As a mode of discourse, reticence articulates the intelligibility of Da-sein so primordially that it gives rise to a genuine potentiality for hearing and to a being-with-one-another that is transparent.[12]

Verschwiegenheit is the German word for reticence and comes from the root *schweigen*, to be or to keep silent. Further on in *Sein und Zeit*, Heidegger talks about the call of conscience, which calls Da-sein to itself, in the same terms:

> *Conscience speaks solely and constantly in the mode of silence.* Thus it not only loses none of its perceptibility, but forces Da-sein thus summoned and called upon to the reticence of itself. The fact that what is called in the call is lacking a formulation in words does not shunt this phenomenon into the indefiniteness of a mysterious voice, but only indicates that the understanding of 'what is called' may not cling to the expectation of a communication or any such thing.[13]

The call to Dasein's authentic self thus happens silently, or to put it in other words: according to Heidegger we are not called by some external speech or language, some "mysterious voice," but this call is what we are, as Dasein that is, and not as everyday existence:

> In the summons, Da-sein gives itself to understand its ownmost potentiality-of-being. Thus this calling is a keeping silent. The discourse of conscience never comes to utterance. Conscience only calls silently, that is, the call comes from the soundlessness of uncanniness and calls Da-sein thus summoned back to the stillness of itself, and calls it to become still. Wanting to have a conscience thus understands this silent discourse appropriately only in reticence. It takes the words away from the commonsense idle chatter of the they.[14]

Dasein is called, calls itself to itself, and again, what is important is that all of this is done in silence. The call is a silent call, and not because it comes from some transcendental source, but because only in silence can our authentic selves be heard: "*In keeping silent*, authentic *being*-one's-self does not keep on saying 'I,' but rather '*is*' in reticence the thrown being that it can authentically be."[15] Silence, or rather reticence, is thus for Heidegger the way to step back from the subject-object distinction of metaphysics, from the clatter of idle talk and the "they," and toward true or authentic "being." The more we speak, the less we "are." We may then find that we really do not have much to say, or rather that we do not have to say much. The realization of the limitations and inadequacy of language cannot be experienced in language, but must be "heard" in silence. Authentic being of Dasein is really ineffable, but not because authentic being is somehow in touch with some transcendent higher being such as a god, but because the experience of our existence, our being, can neither be reduced to nor experienced via language. *Verschwiegenheit* or reticence is how we display this. Reticence lets us be.

This term "reticence" (*Verschwiegenheit*) returns in the two most important works following *Sein und Zeit*, the *Beiträge zur Philosophie* (*Contributions to Philosophy*), and *Besinnung* (*Mindfulness*). In the *Contributions*, Heidegger says that "we can never say be-ing itself in any immediate way, precisely when it arises in the leap. For every saying comes from be-ing and speaks out of its truth."[16] Because of this inability to say Being, what we need then, Heidegger calls "reticence in silence."[17] Since it is not us who speak of Being, but Being which *may* speak to us, silence is the proper attitude: "What is ownmost to language is also grasped first of all in *sigetic*."[18] Heidegger coins the word "*sigetic*" from the Greek *sigan*, meaning silent, and with this term "*sigetic*" as the "teaching of silence" he seeks to indicate a counterforce to logic: "the teaching of words." Yet it seems that Heidegger was not content with this idea of a "teaching of silence" and he abandons the term *sigetic* accordingly. Even the idea of *sigetic* is to him "only a title for those who still think in 'disciplines' and believe to have knowledge only when what is said is classified."[19] Heidegger realizes that there cannot really be any "teaching" of silence, for if taught, it would have to be in words and thus suffer from their inevitable categorizations, and that would bring it back to where he wants to depart from. "Reticence in silence has a higher law than any logic."[20]

Back to reticence then. It indicates, as the meaning of the word conveys, an unwillingness to speak. Reticent, from Latin, meaning "remaining silent." The Oxford English Dictionary has the following entry for reticent: "Reserved; disinclined to speak freely; given to silence or concealment." The Latin root of reticent is *tacere*, "to be silent." Some normal connotations, as can be seen from the entry, involve some form of deliberately concealing something, but in Heidegger's case we of course directly think of something else when we hear the word concealment. The German *Verschwiegenheit* has similar connotations to hiding and concealing. There are two things worth mentioning here: First, like unconcealment and concealment in Heidegger, this chapter will seek to argue that both language *and* reticence in silence belong together intimately. Second, concealment in Heidegger of course has no negative connotations, it is part and parcel of reality and closely related to the German *bergen*, securing or preserving or salvaging, which is the root of both *entbergen* (disclosing, unconcealing) and *verbergen* (concealing).

In this context we may also think for example of Heidegger's excursion into the cryptic Heraclitus fragment 123: "nature loves to hide itself" (Φύσις κρύπτεσθαι φιλεῖ).[21] Heidegger translates it differently: "emerging bestows favor on self-concealing."[22] While not wanting to go into the details of Heidegger's discussion of this fragment, it should be clear from these two different translations alone what he is trying to achieve. First of all, a "normal" translation such as "nature loves to hide itself (or its essence)" clearly displays the metaphysical imports of subject and object, something Heidegger claims was not yet present in Heraclitus' times. It also introduces physis as nature, which is a later interpretation. And it creates a paradoxical tension between disclosing (what physis is said to be about) and concealing, which cannot be solved within our normal logical ways of thinking, given the law of noncontradiction. We then try to solve such tensions by either saying that Heraclitus is contradicting himself (that is why he is referred to as the "obscure") or to solve the tension in a dialectical reading where we understand the emerging and concealing either in sequential and hierarchical fashion, or seek some kind of transcendental deeper essence to nature. Either way, such readings distort the original and give a fake sense of security because they make Heraclitus sound "familiar" to us: Nature loves to hide its essential secrets, but science will bring those out in the open. Therefore, according to Heidegger, the metaphysical language of subject and object will not do. Secondly, and following from this, Heidegger conceives of a necessary retreat from such metaphysical interpretations, and this is where reticence surfaces. Reticence involves an unwillingness to draw things out, an unwillingness to draw things to the fore with our interpretations, because such drawing out or into the open is characteristic of the metaphysical approach and the consequent scientific or technological understanding of the world. Heidegger does not want to *make* things show themselves, he wants to *let* them show themselves. With normal language we try to grasp things, represent them within the sphere of subject and object (*vorstellen*), and assert things about them through propositions. Heidegger's turn to silence is a retreat from that dominant and dominating way of thought. Reticence is retreat, and retreat is reservedness, and Heidegger thinks that such reservedness preserves, secures.

With reticence, Heidegger then proclaims his novel way of thinking: "For here the new style of thinking must announce itself—the reservedness (*Verhaltenheit*) in the truth of be-ing; the saying of silence in reticence (*Das Sagen des Erschweigens*)."[23] But how exactly does Heidegger understand this reticence? More than just an unwillingness to speak, reticence indicates an attitude that is both reserved and resolute. "Foundational reticence is the firmness of a gentleness ... Those sayers must come, who habitually ponder beforehand every word so that all stress remains suspended in the word and the word resists consumption."[24] "Consumption" here would mean that words and language are focused on classifying beings, that we merely use them to indicate beings, things, and the trick is to let that focus go: "What happens then, when beings and the beingness (*a priori*) that is always appended to them lose their preeminence? *Then there is be-ing* [*Dann is das Seyn*]. Then, the 'is' and all language undergo a fundamental transformation."[25] When we let go of the dominant metaphysical subject-object attitude present in our normal language and thinking, only then we will be able to reach a language where in lovely Heideggerian "the be-ing-historical saying says the pure swaying of be-ing; it says the granting of what is charged with decision as well as the taking back of be-ing unto the stillness of the ab-ground."[26] And in the *Nietzsche* volume Heidegger puts this in the following way:

> The thinker inquires into being as a whole and as such; into the world as such ... He thinks in the direction of the *sphere* within which a world becomes world. Wherever that sphere is not incessantly called by name, called aloud, wherever it is held silently in the most interior questioning, it is thought most purely and profoundly. For what is held in silence (*das Verschwiegene*) is genuinely preserved ... Supremely thoughtful utterance does not consist simply in growing taciturn (*zu verschweigen*) when it is a matter of saying what is properly to be said;

it consists in saying the matter in such a way that it is named in nonsaying. The utterance of thinking is a telling silence (*Erschweigen*).[27]

In this passage two terms are used which may need further elaboration, that is *Erschweigen* and *zu verschweigen*. Earlier both translated as "reticence," *zu verschweigen* seems to have connotations with a keeping silence, as well as having the more standard meanings of hiddenness and concealment, which again, in Heidegger's lexicon, have different meanings. *Erschweigen* may suggest a deeper holding or remaining in silence, but also seems as a verb an active approach or disposition. The former may be associated with concealment and the latter with unconcealment,[28] and we shall this these links come back in other passages.

A superficial translation of both *erschweigen* and *verschweigen* as "reticence," "taciturn," or "silence" might then confuse us into thinking that Heidegger is only about silence. Understood as linked to concealment and unconcealment, we can more fittingly see this passage as not advocating a jump into silence per se, but rather as pointing to a transformation of our attitude that would somehow allow Being to come to the fore in Saying, while preserving Being in silence at the same time. But as we have just seen, we cannot just *make* that happen (in fact that is exactly the wrong disposition to have in the first place), we can only prepare for the advent of this, as it is really not something of our making, but comes from out of the granting of Being itself, which we can only try to secure or preserve in silence. In that preparation for the Saying of/from Being, we see that again silence remains fundamental. In the *Contributions* Heidegger puts it in the following way:

> Every saying of be-ing is kept in words and namings which are understandable in the direction of everyday references to beings and are thought exclusively in this direction, but which are mis-construable as the utterance of be-ing. Therefore it is not as if what is needed first is the failure of the question ... but the word itself already discloses something (familiar) and thus hides that which has to be brought into the open through thinking-saying. This difficulty cannot be eliminated at all; even the attempt to do so already means misunderstanding all saying of be-ing. This difficulty must be taken over and grasped in its essential belongingness (to the thinking of be-ing).[29]

One cannot just think to take some kind of vow of silence and be done, or provide any other way to circumvent or escape from the problem of language. Heidegger clearly indicates that the problem of language *and* silence must be taken up again and again, and that there really is no "solution" to or escape from this problem: "The truth of be-ing cannot be said with the ordinary language that today is ever more widely misused and destroyed by incessant talking. Can this truth ever be said directly, if all language is still the language of beings? Or can a new language for be-ing be invented? No."[30] In this extraordinary passage we hear Heidegger, the one who said that language is the house of Being, flatly deny the possibility to convey Being in language, yet that is basically what he tried to do his whole life and what the idea of "Saying," *Sage*, or other ideas such as *Ereignis* (appropriation) are all about. The paradox that seems to ensue can be understood as a recognition of the failure of *any* kind of language, including Heidegger's own attempts at "authentic words," and of the importance to prepare for a transformation and a different attitude that would, out of the recognition of this failure, be attuned differently to language, and not only to language. And that requires a leap away from the familiar and comfortable, into the abyss (*Ab-Grund*) of paradox and silence. Or in more Heideggerian terms, into the abyss of Being as Nothing, or of *entbergen* and *verbergen*, unconcealing and concealing.

"What is Metaphysics" is one of the many works where Heidegger discusses this "Nothing," and again, there are close connections to silence. He says that in everyday existence, we lose ourselves in beings, without regard for Being. Only in such rare moments of, for example, anxiety (*Angst*), when beings fall away, can we experience this nothingness. And again, this fundamental experience is understood to be essentially nonlinguistic: "Anxiety robs us of speech. Because beings as a whole slip away, so that just the nothing crowds round, in the face of anxiety all utterance of the 'is' falls silent."[31]

We can now conclude that in Heidegger's earlier work, reticence and silence are meant to convey the idea that we should be extremely careful with words, and should refuse to speak (only) the language of metaphysics (or later the language of science and technology) which has resulted in what Heidegger arguably finds a one-sided way of existing. Reticence mirrors the play of *entbergen* and *verbergen*, or dis-closing, unconcealment, and concealment understood as belonging together, which is how Being is. In reticence we withhold the word, and we do so because we realize that there is no word that would accurately say Being. And so to convey this reticence, Heidegger naturally often resorts to (the metaphor of) silence.

In his later work, this trend is continued in a number of ways. Even as language itself (think of *das dichtende Denken*, poetic thinking, or the work *On the Way to Language*) seems to become increasingly prominent in Heidegger's thinking, the notion of silence progresses in tandem, and remains the go-to on many occasions. For example, in "The Way to Language" it is implied in *Ent-sprechen*, un-saying, nonsaying as grounding or corresponding. Here Heidegger says that "silence corresponds to the noiseless ringing of stillness, the stillness of the saying that propriates and shows."[32] In the "Dialogue on Language," it is said that a proper dialogue "would have a character all its own, with more silence than talk. Above all, silence about silence, because to talk and write about silence is what produces the most obnoxious chatter. Who could simply be silent of silence? That would be authentic saying."[33] To be silent about silence would be the ultimate, but of course as a philosopher, Heidegger cannot help himself, he needs to talk, and write about silence. And of course we shall see a similar problematic back in Daoism, for example, in the *Daodejing* chapter 1. And with the very chapter you are reading!

Heidegger in his later work is always on a quest for authentic words, words or language which could somehow bring us closer to that experience of Being, which he also calls an experience of/with language. And he does find such words, for example, in *Ereignis, Aletheia, Weg, Logos*. But when discussing *dao* in "On the Way to Language," Heidegger also says the following: "Perhaps the mystery of mysteries of thoughtful Saying conceals itself in the word 'way,' *Tao*, if only we will let these names return to what they leave unspoken."[34] So it seems Heidegger was well aware of the provisionality of such so-called authentic words as "way," *dao*, or *logos*, and points to what is left in silence by thinking through these words carefully, that is, in what they of necessity leave unsaid, essentially what they cannot say. In this context one could also point to his crossing out the word "being" in various works to indicate this inadequacy of language. All these strategies point in a different way to reticence again.

Heidegger does not simply deny language in favor of silence, but seeks to establish a transformed relation to language, another language, which he refers to as "*Sage*," or Saying. Prerequisite for this transformation of thinking depicted by the word *Sage* is that "saying will not allow itself to be captured in any assertion. It demands of us a telling silence as regards the propriative, way-making movement in the essence of language, without any talk *about* silence."[35]

The question then becomes what this other-than-philosophical/metaphysical or transformed thinking would consist of, and what its relation to silence should be. Heidegger has expressed this in many ways, we may think of terms like *Andenken*, *Erdenken*, *das dichtende Denken*, *Besinnliches Denken*, or just *Denken*, or even *Gelassenheit*, a way of thinking instead of philosophizing. In the "Letter on Humanism" he states it in the following way: For thought to be fitting to Being, it needs "rigor of meditation, carefulness in saying, frugality with words."[36] The point of this kind of thinking is to reengage with Being, instead of the metaphysical focus on beings and the highest being. Since this new kind of thinking is not concerned with beings, it is also the case that "Such thinking has no result. It has no effect … for it lets Being-be."[37] In other words, "In all this it is as if nothing at all happens through thoughtful saying."[38] Instead of "reengaging with Being," perhaps it would be better to say that we should reengage with the fact that we are always already in Being.

The connection of this transformed kind of thinking to silence lies (again) in the fact that Heidegger continues to refer to silence in his depictions of this other thinking. "For thinking in its saying merely brings the unspoken word of Being to language."[39] By using language differently, Heidegger believes he may at least point to the departure of thinking from the philosophy of metaphysics:

> Saying, as the way-making movement of the world's fourfold gathers all things up into the nearness of face-to-face encounter and does so soundlessly, as quietly as time times, space spaces, as quietly as the play of time-space is enacted. The soundless gathering call, by which Saying moves the world-relation on its way, we call the ringing of stillness … This breaking up of the word is the true step back on the way of thinking.[40]

To truly think Being, our relation to the word, to language, must be broken up, language itself must be broken up, and silence is again instrumental in that process. It may be argued that Heidegger seeks to undo the primacy of the spoken word in favor of the silent, written word, preempting Derrida's later moves. But Heidegger is well aware that such a move does not solve any of his problems:

> Then everything would hinge on reaching a corresponding saying of language. Only a dialogue could be such a saying correspondence … And it would remain

of minor importance whether the dialogue is before us in writing, or whether it was spoken at some time and has now faded ... because the one thing that matters is whether this dialogue, be it written or spoken or neither, remains constantly coming.[41]

The dialogue with Heidegger's Japanese interlocutor is of course to a large extent about translation issues. But in this dialogue Heidegger perceives an encounter with language again, and this encounter is silent as well, for as he says elsewhere: "The truly fateful encounter with historic language is a silent event. But in it the destiny of Being speaks."[42] So although Heidegger is well known as a definite proponent of the voice and the spoken word, this does not mean he necessarily subscribes to the orthodoxy just by this preference. Both written language and spoken language are equally originary:

> The word of language sounds and resounds in the spoken word, shines and clears itself in the written image. Sound and writing are certainly something sensible (*Sinnliches*), but the sensible in which a sense or meaning (*Sinn*) sounds and appears.[43]

These passages show that Heidegger thinks that it does not matter whether a dialogue is "written or spoken or neither."[44] Although much emphasis is often put on Heidegger's notions of hearing (*hören*) and belonging (*gehören*) and other related notions, indeed such as "saying" (*Sage*), we should not forget Heidegger's equal insistence on language as showing (*zeigen*), and his writings on paintings, art, that betray the "visual" aspect of his thought. Each of these examples shows that Heidegger is really seeking for a different understanding of language, and of our inhibiting and use of language to understand our being in the world. We should understand Heidegger's jargon as attempts to both circumnavigate traditional, metaphysical language, as well as an attempt to create an experience of Being with language after the silence.

To wrap up this section on Heidegger I now want to turn to a long and complicated passage from his *Heraklit*:

> The saving/securing (*bergende*) gathering of Being as such is more originarily already that relation (*Bezug*) in which humans first remain silent (*schweigend*) and then still remaining silent (*schweigend*) hear (*ver-nimmt*) the Being of beings, beings in their Being, beings as such. This silencing/not talking (*Be-schweigen*) of Being is the originary Saying and naming of beings, it is the originary word that, encountering the region of Being, is the first answer, in which any word swings that unfolds itself in Saying and announces itself in the words of language. Silencing/not talking (*Be-schweigen*) sways (*west*) as originary self-gathering of humans onto Being and vice-versa. The λέγειν as saving/securing does not just occur silently, but it and only it is the collected gathering of the keeping silence/reticence. The λέγειν is originarily the keeping silence. All comportment of humans to beings and all relationship with humans and gods rests in the reservedness of silence. What goes for λέγειν, that it, as originary gathering, is the saving/securing silencing (*Beschweigen*) of Being, holds even more originarily for Λόγος. Λόγος is

the originary saving/securing keeping silent or concealment (*Verschweigung*) and as such the (be-)fore-word (*Vor-wort*) to every Saying of the word in the answer. To the essence of the word, the (be-)fore-word is the prior and preceding silence (*Erschweigen*) of stillness, which only must be broken when the word should be. The Λόγος is not the word. More originary than this, it is the foreword to each language. Its call to humans is the silent one of the before-word that silences (*zu-schweigt*) Being to humans. Only unbecomingly and already from the human context of the speaking Saying do we call this 'silencing' (*Zu-schweigen*) the response (*Zuspruch*) or call (*Anspruch*). More becomingly we say: the Λόγος is the region silencing (*zu-schweigende*) towards humans, that is the all opening hints and indications securing and in itself resting expanse. When the region silences (*zu-schweigt*) towards the human, it returns into its own stillness.[45]

In this dense and very Heideggerian passage there are numerous wordplays on *Schweigen*, with *Beschweigen* and *Zu-schweigen*, as well as the aforementioned *Erschweigen* and *Verschweigen*. With the exception of *Verschweigen* and possibly *Erschweigen*, these word(-plays) are either rarely used or not even actual German words, but neo-logisms used by Heidegger for his own purposes. Aside from this there is the *Vor-wort*, in common language understood as foreword or preface, but its literal meaning is here alluded to by Heidegger through the hyphen, and that is pre-word, that is, what is before the word. The same seems to apply to the word *Zu-spruch*, which means encouragement or response, but also seems to Heidegger to have connotations with something that is prior to speech, *Zu-spruch* literally meaning to-speech. And I have translated *Zu-schweigen* as "silencing," which may need some explanation. In this translation, I do not mean "silencing" in a negative way, as not allowing someone to speak, as stopping someone from expressing herself. Silencing, *Zu-schweigen*, seems rather to suggest a giving silence that opens up the possibility of Being showing itself. We must first of all "silence" ourselves and only thus can we prepare for the silent advent of Being. But that is only the unbecoming and preliminary understanding of this "silencing." Rather, and more appropriately understood, it is Being itself which "silences" toward us, in other words, shows (and conceals) itself in silence. In my understanding, this passage tells us that prior to the word, the gathering, being, is really only "given" to humans in silence, and as soon as the word arrives, this magic is broken and the "delivery" is upset and derailed. No effort should be spared to keep the silence. I now turn to Daoism to see if a similar understanding is to be found.

Daoism and Silence

In classical Daoism we find an equal emphasis on the provisionality of language, and although the background is very different in that the Daoists were not fighting against a dominant metaphysical history of philosophy, we find similarities with Heidegger's ideas of reticence, silence, and a transformation of language and thinking.

The idea that language is inadequate and provisional is a steady feature of both the *Daodejing* and *Zhuangzi*. In both works there is a healthy mistrust of the possibility of language to convey what really matters. And in both works some way of dealing with this is sought. And it is there again that silence plays a crucial role. The fact that language tends to categorize, substantialize, reify, leads Roger Ames and David Hall to say: "We can easily and at real expense overdetermine the continuity within the life process as some underlying and unchanging foundation. Such linguistic habits can institutionalize and enforce an overly static vision of the world, and in so doing, deprive both language and life of their creative possibilities."[46] And in a longer passage they claim that:

> A misunderstanding of the nature of language has the potential to promote the worst misconceptions about the flux and flow of experience in which we live our lives. There is an obvious tension between the unrelenting processual nature of experience and the function of language to separate out, isolate, and arrest elements within it. To the extent that it is the nature of language to arrest the process of change and discipline it into a coherent, predictable order, there is the likelihood that an uncritical application of language might persuade us that our world is of a more stable and necessary character than it really is. The assumption, for example, that there is a literal language behind the metaphorical can introduce notions of permanence, necessity, and objectivity into our worldview that can have deleterious consequences.[47]

In short, language of necessity and by its very nature seems to be about halting the processual nature of the world, language artificially names things as things, objects, instead of doing justice to processuality. This is exactly what Daoism seeks to avoid. So we expect and do find numerous passages seeking to address this. How then, do the *Daodejing* and *Zhuangzi* deal with language? What is role of silence in their efforts at overcoming the obstacles presented by language? We will see that in similar ways as Heidegger, the Daoists, in the words of David Chai, also believe that "saying nothing is to approach Dao while saying something is to be driven from it. The more one speaks, the less insightful are one's words; hence it is better to remain silent."[48] The most interesting connection I perceive between Heidegger and the Daoists lies in the fact that both try to think *through* silence toward a transformed relation to language. And that transformed relation to language informs and is informed by the idea of silence pointing to an experience of Being in the world and interdependence that language cannot do justice to.

Language and Silence in the *Daodejing*

The notion of *dao* 道 itself, as chapter 1 of the *Daodejing* famously proclaims, cannot be pinned down in language. It is indeterminate, or un-determinable. In chapter 14 it is said of *dao*: "Ever so tangled, it defies discrimination and reverts again to indeterminacy. This is what is called the form of the formless and the image of indeterminacy. This is what is called the vague and the indefinite."[49] Commenting on this passage, Ames and Hall state that *dao* "will not yield itself up to our most basic categories of location and determination: bright and dark, inside and outside, subject and object, one and many."[50] So language as a means of categorizing is inadequate, because *dao* defies categorization. And that is why chapter 15 says that the profundity of "those of old who were good at forging their way (*dao*) in the world … [were] beyond comprehension."[51] In Ames and Hall language this means: "The processive and synergistic forces at work in way-making render the language of discreteness and closure inappropriate."[52] And that may also be why chapter 15 talks about being *forced* to describe something, in the same way as chapter 25 does.

The same ideas with regards to the inadequacy of language are expressed in chapter 21: "As for the process of way-making, it is ever so indefinite and vague."[53] And again in chapter 14 where it is said that while we may look for it we do not see it, listen for it but not hear it. This means the senses, through which language of necessity works, cannot convey *dao*. In chapter 35 this hesitance with regards to language is reiterated again.

If language is inadequate, then how does the *Daodejing* seek to get us in touch with *dao*? Inadequacy itself, like in Heidegger, need not mean a turn to silence. But in both chapter 2 and chapter 43 there is mention of "teachings that go beyond what can be said"[54] and in both chapters this is connected to *wuwei* 無為. *Wuwei* has been translated as "non-assertive action." Taking some liberties here, assertion can be understood here both as an action and in a linguistic way. We should not assert ourselves, that is, remain in reticence, and make no assertions, knowing full well that any such assertions are in some important way wrong. Instead, we act so that we are in unison with the myriad processes, and this is seen in the *Daodejing* as something which requires at least a phase of silence. A prime example to corroborate my reading here is chapter 56: "Those who really understand it do not talk about it, and those who really talk about it do not understand it."[55] This seems very much to suggest that *dao*, which is what this chapter is about, cannot be understood in any form of language, and is thus something that needs silence in order to truly understand it. The rest of the chapter indeed suggests some form of silent meditative state that is of the "Profoundest consonance."[56] We should not dismiss this idea of meditative practice, it is in fact found throughout the *Daodejing* in various chapters, from breathing exercises to concentrating on *qi* 氣, etc. Such meditative practices go beyond language and are usually connected to a return to silence.

There are other chapters conveying the same idea. In chapter 73, *tiandao* 天道 is said to lie in: "answering effectively without saying a word."[57] In chapter 81 we are told that the wise do not debate, or are not erudite. The discriminating/debating that comes naturally to language use is here seen as unwise. Such an attitude is also constantly debunked in the *Zhuangzi*. Again, the kind of language that halts the process should be avoided if possible. And both the *Daodejing* and *Zhuangzi* realize that language of necessity always halts the process.

In the appendix of Ames and Hall's translation, "The Great One Gives Birth to the Waters," there is a sentence which talks about both the original name and the style name, and says that "in trying to venture beyond these categories, we do not think that such names are fitting."[58] Neither normal naming nor "style-naming" are adequate, and that is because *dao* is considered in chapter 25, which also talks about naming and a style name, to be "silent and empty."[59]

And then of course there is the term *wuming* 無名, the nameless. *Wuming* in chapter 1 of the *Daodejing* is understood to be the "fetal beginnings of everything that is happening."[60] The nameless is the source from which the named springs, or in other words, language is based on silence. But chapter 1 continues to say that the nameless and the named together both come from the same darkness. This means that we cannot just assume that the *Daodejing* urges us to stop using language and jump into the silence.

In chapter 32 it is said that *dao* is nameless, again language is inadequate to describe it. This is also the reading of the chapter 37 first line in the Mawangdui version, which also refers to a "nameless scrap of unworked wood"[61] and that *dao* is nameless is reiterated again in chapter 41.[62] All of these instances tell us that any form of language will distort *dao* and hinder our efforts to understand it. So it must be understood in silence, or if you will in nonlanguage.

Throughout the *Daodejing* we can read a philosophy that seeks to realign us with the unnamed nature of things, with the process of the world as it is before humans start artificially making distinctions through language, which can only be done by going beyond language. Naturally metaphors of silence crop up here in trying to convey this artificiality or categorizing of language, as they do in Heidegger. But like Heidegger, the *Daodejing* does not stop there. We have to go *through* silence, but cannot stay there, and instead have to move toward a language that is provisional and more conducive to understanding process. Chapter 23 of the *Daodejing* has it that "it is natural to speak only rarely"[63] and not that it is natural not to speak at all. Remember, chapter 1 already told us it does not stop with silence, with the nameless. This can be related to Heidegger's reticence. Neither Heidegger nor the *Daodejing* is against language, but they are against its uncritical and normal use. In chapter 32 it is said: "When we start to regulate the world we introduce names. But once names have been assigned, we must also know when to stop. Knowing when to stop is how to avoid danger."[64] Again, reticence as understood in Heidegger's terms seems to be the way to avoid falling into the trap that language seemingly inadvertently sets for us. Yet it is not only reticence or being reluctant or frugal with words. It is also about changing *how* we speak. After all, chapter 78 tells us that "appropriate language seems contradictory."[65] And this brings me to the *Zhuangzi*.

Language and Silence in the *Zhuangzi*

We now know that basically all language already amounts to misunderstanding in Daoism, since language is the artificial construct that halts the spontaneity of *ziran* 自然. The best understanding would then be "speechless" or silent, in awareness of this artificiality. The idea that knowing and saying do not go together, as found in the *Daodejing*, is clearly reiterated in the *Zhuangzi*. For example, in chapter 22 it is said in repeating chapters 2 and 56 of the *Daodejing*: "He who knows does not speak, and he who speaks does not know. Hence the sage practices the teaching of no words."[66] The sage's realization that all is process, and that there have never begun to be individuated things, flows over into the argument against the setting up of artificial boundaries by language, by naming, which suggests that language is useless, since language is there to identify and create boundaries, and thus things. But realistically, knowing that human life in complete silence is virtually impossible, the *Daodejing* then tells us that knowing when to stop relying on language is the next best, a move we see happening in Heidegger as well in the arguments for a transformed relation to language. Where does the *Zhuangzi* take it from there?

At first, we find in the *Zhuangzi* a similar appeal to stop using language and revert to silence. Zhuangzi first identifies language as having this property of "discriminating," "dividing," of "deeming" something to be either "this" or "that," or what Heidegger would call the categorizing function of language. Zhuangzi says in chapter 2 that "the Way has never known boundaries, speech has no constancy ... Those who discriminate fail to see."[67] Those who have more than a cursory knowledge of the *Zhuangzi* know that this kind of discriminating and categorizing is exactly the kind of thinking that Zhuangzi does not appreciate. Because of his perspectivism, he fairly easily dismisses this kind of thinking that divides the world into "this-es" and "that-s," and with it the correspondent use of language:

> For wherever a division is made, something is left undivided. Wherever debate shows one of two alternatives to be right, something remains undistinguished and unshown. What is it? The sage hides it in his embrace, while the masses of people debate it, trying to demonstrate it to one another. Thus I say that demonstration by debate always leaves something unshown. The greatest Course (*dao*) is thus always unproclaimed. Greatest argument is that which uses no words.[68]

All important things are considered silent or nameless, unspoken, such as *dao* or even the sage.[69] When the realization of this namelessness is complete, we could according to Zhuangzi hopefully return to being like the people of old:

> The understanding of those ancient people really got somewhere! Where had it arrived? To the point where there had never existed any definite thing at all. This is really getting there, as far as you can go. When no definite thing exists, nothing more can be added! Next there were those for whom specific things existed, but no sealed boundaries between them. Next there were those for whom there were sealed boundaries, but never any rights and wrongs. When rights and wrongs wax bright, the Course begins to wane.[70]

A way of living is sought that attests to the processual nature of the world and of ourselves in it, and this processual nature again cannot be understood through language. As a number of passages from both the inner chapters and outer testify, it is better to "just sit and forget"[71] or to be "a nameless man."[72] Or in another passage: "Debate about it is no match for silence. The Course (*dao*) cannot be learned, so hearing about it is no match for plugging up your ears. This is called the Great Attainment."[73] To this kind of mistrust of looking and hearing and language we may add that this is also why the sage is said to be "Canny! Seems he likes to keep his mouth shut."[74] We may only speculate as to how much Heidegger was influenced by these thoughts in his thinking about the possibilities of an experience of Being, but the similarities are striking.

In this context of thinking beyond language, we can equally reflect on all the stories in the *Zhuangzi* of craftsmen and skilled people who act in a certain way, but seem unable to convey this skill in words, such as the carpenter Pian who says that language (the books of the sages) are really just dregs and that his knack, his skill cannot be conveyed in words.[75] Cook Ding's cutting of the ox,[76] the swimmer's skill in staying afloat[77] all indicate the inadequacy of language, the impossibility to reach *dao* with language. They indicate an experience not conveyable in language. At the same time, all these stories (in language!) attempt exactly to make us aware of this. That is the paradox of language, and again, it suggests that silence is a necessary stage, but not the necessary endpoint. As Angus Graham puts it:

> Taoists are trying to convey a knack, an aptitude, a way of living, and when the carpenter tells Duke Huan that he cannot put into words how much pressure to exert in chiseling wood we both understand and agree. [Taoists] have the good sense to remind us of the limitations of the language which they use to guide us towards that altered perspective on the world and that knack of living.[78]

In all the *Zhuangzi* says, it really attempts to convey what cannot be said. Summed up by Zhuangzi: "When nothing is said, everything is equal. But the saying and this original equality are then not equal to one another. Thus it is that I speak only nonspeech. When you speak nonspeech, you can talk all your life without ever having said a word, or never utter a word without ever failing to say something."[79]

The point is of course that the craftsmen do communicate something somehow. They are the ones that are making finer distinctions than can be put into words. Maybe this is what Heidegger has in mind, when in "What Calls for Thinking?" speaking of the hand and of thinking as craft (*Hand-werk*), he says: "But the hand's gestures run everywhere through language, in their most perfect purity precisely when man speaks by being silent."[80]

Be that as it may, in the *Zhuangzi* being silent is still preferred above using language. As one of the outer chapters has it:

> If someone answers when asked about the Course (*dao*), he does not know the Course. Though one may ask about the Course, this does not mean one has heard of the Course. The Course is not susceptible to questions, and any questions about it have no answers. To ask after it by asking no questions is to be through with all questions. To answer by giving no answer is to be free from harboring anything within.[81]

Even saying that all is process, or in other words that all is one, cannot do. Zhuangzi sees right through that move:

> But if we are all one, can there be anything to say, anything to refer to? But since I have already declared that we are 'one,' can there be nothing to say, nothing to refer to? The one and the saying are already two, the two and the original unsaid one are three. Going on like this even a skilled chronicler could not keep up with it, not to

mention a lesser man. So even moving from nonexistence to existence we already arrive at three—how much more when we move from existence to existence! Rather than moving from anywhere to anywhere, then, let us just go along with 'thisness,' relying on the rightness of whatever is before us as the present 'this.'[82]

The *Zhuangzi* then, in many ways, urges a return to a way of life that is nonlanguage based, or silent: "In the great beginning, what there was was nothing—devoid of definite being, unnameable by any name."[83] Avoiding using language is best, but this is impossible. Yet if we allow ourselves to get into any argument, there is no possible end to it. This Zhuangzi realized and actively applied to his own sayings, and like Heidegger, he will offer a use of language that would first of all be aware of its provisionality, and second would be more attuned to the process nature of the world.

After Silence, After-Word?

In ways similar to Heidegger, we see that Zhuangzi finds himself in a paradox. Not to use language, to be silent, yet to use language after that move is exhausted. But he is not one who is bothered by paradoxes. What is his solution? Does he advocate a retreat into silence, or becoming a hermit? It is often argued that Daoists in general and Zhuangzi in particular propose to totally do away with language because of its impermanence, but I think this is a misreading. One of the passages often invoked in this argument is based on the following passage:

> A fish trap is there for the fish. When you get the fish, you forget the trap. A rabbit snare is there for the rabbits. When you get the rabbit, you forget the snare. Words are there for the intent. When you get the intent, you forget the words. Where can I find a man who has forgotten words, so I can have a word with him?[84]

It is important to understand this passage not as saying that we can do without language once we have reached the meaning of things, but as saying we must always return to language after forgetting it, even when we think we no longer need it. You can only forget the fish trap for a short moment, while you have fish. Once the fish runs out, is consumed, you need the fish trap again, and you might have to do some repairs as well. The same goes for the rabbit snare. On the level of language this means that the metaphysical idea that there is some ultimate and unchanging reality conveyed by words but essentially in a different realm, is undone by pointing to the provisionality of words, not with respect to this ultimate truth, but with respect to the description of the world. You need first to forget about words as having a fixed reference, and this occurs in the move to silence, but you do not continue to leave words behind permanently. Silence in this sense is, as it is in Heidegger, a stage.

Zhuangzi, like Heidegger, complicates the necessary but easy flight into silence itself as ultimately inadequate. After forgetting words, the realization that you will still need them sets in, and then you need to reinvent or reintroduce, or reinscribe them. Zhuangzi's answer of course lies in two things: the "spillover-goblet" words of chapter 27, and the "reckless" use of language advocated in chapter 2. Trying to do justice to fluidity and process in language means language should be seen as provisional, much like a spillover-goblet, in that the goblet does not get rid of itself, but of what it has too much of, as it rights itself after spilling over and emptying itself. Such language, at least according to Zhuangzi, would, although still not perfectly, be more attuned to the changes that reality consists of. Like Heidegger, who keeps reinventing words from either German or ancient Greek, who uses existing words in different meanings, or creates neo-logisms when current language is found inadequate, spillover-goblet words supposedly do not fixate, instead they "give forth [new meaning] constantly"[85] and are considered the kind of language that would somehow do justice to the process nature of the world. Another way of putting this for Zhuangzi is to talk about "reckless"[86] or "abandoned" words.[87] Reckless or abandoned words risk losing meaning (or actually seek not to fix meaning), because they are not spoken with considerations of ulterior motives, or with the aim of categorizing or classifying, but their result is supposed to reinforce the idea that for the sage "each thing is just so, and through the rightness of each, the thisness of each, he lets each enfold each."[88]

In the end Zhuangzi does not suggest overcoming language in some mystical state of silent being, he is quite adamantly not in favor of such "retreating into silence" as the mystics fleeing to the mountains seem to embrace. So, I understand Daoist "forgetting" as only a preliminary stage of the process. Instead, he argues for the equality and provisionality of *all* language and thus of all views, including his own, which means that any mystical state of silence is not better or worse than another state, but also suffers from the same provisionality. The state of being in language is just another state of being. As Graham puts it: "It is all right to make fluid distinctions varying with circumstances, it is when we make rigid distinctions misleading us into judging that something is permanently what it is temporarily convenient to name it that thinking goes wrong."[89] Even the distinction between *tian* and man is questioned in this way in the *Zhuangzi*.

Zhuangzi is acutely aware that he needs language. And his words reflect that. In the words of Graham: "Although Chuang-tzu rejects *bian*, 'disputation,' the posing and arguing out of alternatives, he always speaks favorably of *lun*, 'sorting, grading,' thought and discourse which orders things in their proper relations."[90] It is important to understand this sorting and grading as according to situation and circumstance, and not as according to fixed categorizations or conceptual schemes with little flexibility. Zhuangzi does not always flat-out deny that language has meaning, but instead articulates that "human speech is not just a blowing of air. Speech has something of which it speaks, something it refers to. Yes, but what it refers to is peculiarly unfixed."[91] And that is why Zhuangzi in the end wants to be "Walking Two Roads."[92] Because we need to be sometimes of *tian*'s party, and sometimes of man's party, ultimately what Zhuangzi believes is that:

> If words were completely adequate, one could speak all day and all of it would be the Course (*dao*). If words were completely inadequate, one could speak all day and all of it would concern only particular beings. The ultimate reaches both of the

Course and of beings cannot be conveyed by either speech or silence. Only where there is neither speech nor silence does discussion really come to its ultimate end.[93]

That would be the kind of speaking that would respond spontaneously to what is, in mirror-like fashion. Is this still similar to what Heidegger is trying to achieve? If I am correct, then the similarity lies in the fact that both Heidegger and the Daoists realize that we cannot rest in an inversion move from language to silence. I believe that the Daoists, for all their talk about "sitting and forgetting," do not actually believe we can reach some permanent transcendent state styled *dao*. Neither does Heidegger, probably under the influence of Daoism to a certain extent, believe we can just be. But our attitudes and ways of being, including the use of language, could better approximate what in essence is not. But the greatest similarity lies to me in the fact that both the Daoists and Heidegger realize that this is an ever-continuing process.

Conclusion

In talking a lot about silence and about not using language, I have already betrayed my authentic self, if such a thing exists, and missed my shot at finding *dao*. But is that really so? It is this paradox that I believe both Heidegger and the Daoists understood. They employed the concept of silence understood only as a necessary stage to abandon a certain kind of language and thinking, before one can truly appreciate another kind of language and thinking. All our protagonists move from the Word through the *Vor-Wort* to the After-Word. In the end, both Heidegger and the Daoists realize that even a renewed and provisional language is inadequate, but that we have nothing else and are actually always already tied to this provisionality. But this leads to a realization that thinking in terms of inadequacy might just be a remainder of the attitudes Heidegger and the Daoists were trying to redress. The problem then becomes how to deal with that provisionality, how to live in a world of change and with the realization of our finitude. Ames and Hall claim that for the Daoist: "The precise referential language of denotation and description is to be replaced by a language of 'deference' in which meanings both allude to and defer to one another in a shifting field of significances."[94] This language of "deference" that Ames and Hall mention is a language which refuses the reification and substance thinking characteristic of classical Western philosophy. In Heidegger's language this would be a language of attunement, of Saying Being, of letting things be. And in both Heidegger and the Daoists such a way of saying is found in the language of silence.

Notes

1 Martin Heidegger, *Being and Truth*, trans. Gregory Fried and Richard Polt (Bloomington: Indiana University Press, 2010), 85.
2 "So lernt ich traurig den Versicht, kein Ding sei wo das Wort gebricht." Stefan George, *Das Wort*, in Martin Heidegger, *Unterwegs zur Sprache* [GA 12], ed. Friedrich-Wilhelm von Herrmann (Frankfurt: Vittorio Klostermann, 1985), 153.

3 See for example Jacques Derrida's *Denials: How to Avoid Speaking*. Or think of schools of negative theology.
4 Martin Heidegger, *Basic Writings*, ed. David F. Krell (New York: Harper Collins, 1993), 217.
5 Ibid., 230.
6 Ibid., 262.
7 Ibid., 236.
8 Ibid., 246.
9 Ibid., 223.
10 Martin Heidegger, *Being and Time*, trans. Joan Stambaugh (Albany: State University of New York Press, 1996), 151. Italics in original.
11 Ibid., 150.
12 Ibid., 154. German added.
13 Ibid., 252–3. Italics in original.
14 Ibid., 273.
15 Ibid., 297.
16 Martin Heidegger, *Contributions to Philosophy (from Enowning)*, trans. Parvis Emad and Kenneth Maly (Bloomington: Indiana University Press, 1999), 55.
17 Ibid.
18 Ibid.
19 Ibid.
20 Ibid., 55.
21 See Martin Heidegger, *Heraklit* [GA 55], ed. Manfred S. Frings (Frankfurt: Vittorio Klostermann, 1994), 109–41.
22 Ibid., 110: "Das Aufgehen dem Sichverbergen schenkt's die Gunst."
23 Martin Heidegger, *Mindfulness*, trans. Parvis Emad and Thomas Kalary (London: Continuum, 2006), 377. German added.
24 Ibid., 50.
25 Ibid., 300–1. Italics in original, German added.
26 Ibid., 306.
27 Martin Heidegger, *Nietzsche*, trans. David F. Krell (New York: Harper and Row, 1984), 207–8. German added.
28 I am grateful to Eric Nelson for suggesting the links to concealment and unconcealment.
29 Heidegger, *Contributions to Philosophy*, 58.
30 Ibid., 54.
31 Heidegger, *Basic Writings*, 101.
32 Ibid., 420.
33 Martin Heidegger, *On the Way to Language*, trans. Peter D. Hertz (New York: Harper and Row, 1971), 52–3. Translation modified.
34 Ibid., 92.
35 Heidegger, *Basic Writings*, 424.
36 Ibid., 265.
37 Ibid., 259.
38 Ibid., 263.
39 Ibid., 262.
40 Heidegger, *On the Way to Language*, 108.
41 Ibid., 52.
42 Martin Heidegger, *Early Greek Thinking*, trans. David F. Krell and Frank A. Capuzzi (New York: Harper and Row, 1984b), 57.

43 Martin Heidegger, *Aus der Erfahrung des Denkens* [GA 13], ed. Hermann Heidegger (Frankfurt: Vittorio Klostermann), 150 and 209. Translation including German in Graham Parkes ed., *Heidegger and Asian Thought* (Honolulu: University of Hawaii Press, 1987), 70.
44 Heidegger, *On the Way to Language*, 52.
45 Heidegger, *Heraklit*, 382–3. My translation.
46 Roger T. Ames and David L. Hall, trans., *Daodejing, Making This Life Significant* (New York: Ballantine Books, 2003), 45.
47 Ames and Hall, *Daodejing*, 113.
48 David Chai "Thinking through Words: The Existential Hermeneutics of Zhuangzi and Heidegger," in Paul Fairfield and Saulius Geniusas (eds.), *Relational Hermeneutics: Essays in Comparative Philosophy*, 205–19 (London: Bloomsbury Academic, 2018), 207.
49 Ames and Hall, *Daodejing*, 96.
50 Ibid., 97.
51 Ibid.
52 Ibid., 99.
53 Ibid., 107.
54 Ibid., 80 and 145.
55 Ibid., 164.
56 Ibid., 164.
57 Ibid., 192.
58 Ibid., 230.
59 Ibid., 115.
60 Ibid., 77.
61 Ibid., 134.
62 Ibid., 141.
63 Ibid., 111.
64 Ibid., 127.
65 Ibid., 198.
66 Brook Ziporyn, trans., *Zhuangzi: The Complete Writings* (Indianapolis: Hackett Publishing, 2020), 174.
67 Burton Watson, trans., *Zhuangzi: Basic Writings* (New York: Columbia University Press, 2003), 39.
68 Ziporyn, *Zhuangzi*, 17. Pinyin added.
69 A.C. Graham, *Chuang-Tzu: The Inner Chapters* (Indianapolis: Hackett Publishing, 2001), 45.
70 Ziporyn, *Zhuangzi*, 16.
71 Ibid., 62.
72 Ibid., 69.
73 Ibid., 178.
74 Graham, *Chuang-Tzu*, 85.
75 Ziporyn, *Zhuangzi*, 116.
76 Ibid., 29.
77 Ibid., 154.
78 Graham, *Chuang-Tzu*, 199.
79 Ziporyn, *Zhuangzi*, 225–26.
80 Heidegger, *Basic Writings*, 381.
81 Ziporyn, *Zhuangzi*, 180.

82 Ibid., 17.
83 Ibid., 102.
84 Ibid., 224.
85 Ibid., 225.
86 Ibid., 19.
87 Graham, *Chuang-Tzu*, 59.
88 Ziporyn, *Zhuangzi*, 20.
89 A.C. Graham, *Disputers of the Tao: Philosophical Argument in Ancient China* (La Salle: Open Court, 1989), 190.
90 Graham, *Chuang-Tzu*, 12.
91 Ziporyn, *Zhuangzi*, 13.
92 Ibid., 16.
93 Ziporyn, *Zhuangzi*, 216.
94 Roger T. Ames and David L. Hall, trans., *Focusing the Familiar: A Translation and Philosophical Interpretation of the Zhongyong* (Honolulu: University of Hawaii Press, 2001), 10.

References

Ames, Roger T. and David L. Hall, trans. *Focusing the Familiar: A Translation and Philosophical Interpretation of the Zhongyong*. Honolulu: University of Hawaii Press, 2001.

Ames, Roger T. and David L. Hall, trans. *Daodejing, Making This Life Significant*. New York: Ballantine Books, 2003.

Chai, David. "Thinking through Words: The Existential Hermeneutics of Zhuangzi and Heidegger." In Paul Fairfield and Saulius Geniusas (eds.), *Relational Hermeneutics: Essays in Comparative Philosophy*, 205–19. London: Bloomsbury Academic, 2018.

Graham, Angus C. *Disputers of the Tao: Philosophical Argument in Ancient China*. La Salle: Open Court, 1989.

Graham, Angus C. *Chuang-Tzu: The Inner Chapters*. Indianapolis: Hackett Publishing, 2001.

Heidegger, Martin. *On the Way to Language*. Translated by Peter D. Hertz. New York: Harper and Row, 1971.

Heidegger, Martin. *Heraklit*. [GA 55]. Edited by Manfred S. Frings. Frankfurt: Vittorio Klostermann, 1979.

Heidegger, Martin. *Aus der Erfahrung des Denkens* [GA 13]. Edited by Hermann Heidegger. Frankfurt: Vittorio Klostermann, 1983.

Heidegger, Martin. *Early Greek Thinking*. Translated by David F. Krell and Frank A. Capuzzi. New York: Harper and Row, 1984.

Heidegger, Martin. *Nietzsche*. Translated by David F. Krell. New York: Harper and Row, 1984.

Heidegger, Martin. *Unterwegs zur Sprache* [GA 12]. Edited by Friedrich-Wilhelm von Herrmann. Frankfurt: Vittorio Klostermann, 1985.

Heidegger, Martin. *Basic Writings*. Edited by David F. Krell. New York: Harper Collins Publishers, 1993.

Heidegger, Martin. *Being and Time*. Translated by Joan Stambaugh. Albany: State University of New York Press, 1996.

Heidegger, Martin. *Contributions to Philosophy (from Enowning)*. Translated by Parvis Emad and Kenneth Maly. Bloomington: Indiana University Press, 1999.

Heidegger, Martin. *Mindfulness*. Translated by Parvis Emad and Thomas Kalary. London: Continuum, 2006.

Heidegger, Martin. *Being and Truth*. Translated by Gregory Fried and Richard Polt. Bloomington: Indiana University Press, 2010.

Parkes, Graham, ed. *Heidegger and Asian Thought*. Honolulu: University of Hawaii Press, 1987.

Watson, Burton, trans. *Zhuangzi: Basic Writings*. New York: Columbia University Press, 2003.

Ziporyn, Brook, trans. *Zhuangzi: The Complete Writings*. Indianapolis: Hackett Publishing, 2020.

9

The Politics of Uselessness: On Heidegger's Reading of the *Zhuangzi*

Fabian Heubel

> *Your foot itself has effaced the way behind you,*
> *and over it stands written: Impossibility.*
>
> Nietzsche

Heidegger's Transcultural Turn?

"On the day the world celebrated its victory, without yet recognizing that already for centuries it has been defeated by its own rebellious uprising." This is the final note in a text by Martin Heidegger bearing the lengthy title "Evening Conversation: In a Prisoner of War Camp in Russia, between a Younger and an Older Man" and dated to May 8, 1945.[1] The posthumously published "Evening Conversation" belongs to the hitherto less discussed texts from Heidegger's extensive collected writings. The relation to Chinese philosophy that permeates the text has been largely ignored, also by those who have dealt with the "Evening Conversation" in greater detail.[2] Even the editor of the text himself did not take the trouble to find out where the quoted passages came from and who the two Chinese thinkers mentioned in it were. The quote from chapter 26 of the *Zhuangzi* was in fact from Richard Wilhelm's German translation first published in 1912 under the title *Dschuang Dsi: Das Wahre Buch vom Südlichen Blütenland* [*Dschuang Dsi: The True Book of the Southern Flower Land*] to which Wilhelm had added the subtitle "The Necessity of the Unnecessary" ("Die Notwendigkeit des Unnötigen").[3] Were it not for the symbolic date and the irritating afterword cited above, this text would probably have been condemned to even greater oblivion.

What I am suggesting here, however, is that the transcultural potential of Heidegger's thought is expressed in the "Evening Conversation" in a profound and astonishingly radical way. I say this although, or precisely because, after the publication of his *Black Notebooks* from the 1930s and 1940s, the deep entanglement of Heidegger's thought with National Socialism has become even more obvious. The evidence is so overwhelming this time that attempts to again whitewash Heidegger seem hopeless. These are challenging, but also suitable conditions for some rather awkward reflections on the difficulties of philosophical interaction between East and West, not only in the German-speaking world.

Since Kejun Xia, a Chinese friend and specialist on Heidegger, repeatedly indicated to me the importance of the "Evening Conversation," I have been impressed by the eerie, even almost shocking actuality of the text and have experienced simultaneous repulsion and attraction toward it. It was exactly this rather paradoxical attitude that motivated me to write about it. Any contemporary significance of the text seems eerie, because the vision of a new historical task for the German people which Heidegger addresses in the "Evening Conversation" opens up a bleak perspective on the continuing importance of nationalist, if not populist (*völkisch*) conservatism in Germany and beyond. At the same time, Heidegger discusses a short passage from a classical text of Chinese philosophy in a manner that not only reflects the cultural and political situation in 1945 Germany, but also that of a contemporary China.

The "Evening Conversation" inspired me to philosophically pursue the presumption that there may be a historical correspondence between Germany of the early twentieth century and China of the early twenty-first. The philosophical debate concerning the rise and fall of German National Socialism may also be significant, at least indirectly, for critical reflections on the rise of the People's Republic of China to a world power. I will try to approach this correspondence in a way which may appear to be a strange detour, namely, by way of discussing Heidegger's dream of a paradoxical German turn (*Kehre*) from a "vanquished German people" into a "useless people" fit to fulfill a new world-historical mission. In Heidegger's dream, Zhuangzi's "necessity of the unnecessary" (or "use of the useless" in Watson's translation) plays an outstanding role.

I will, therefore, assume in the following that Heidegger's momentary, but nevertheless extraordinary, interest in the *Zhuangzi* as expressed in the "Evening Conversation" is interwoven with problems of identity-formation and a quest for self-awareness that characterize both contemporary Germany and contemporary China. This historical constellation may not be gratifying for both sides, but it may partly explain why Chinese philosophy hardly receives any attention in contemporary German philosophy, and may, furthermore, open up possibilities of at least partly removing a barrier of communication, which obstructs a genuinely philosophical (and not only Sinological or historical) interaction with Chinese sources. In light of this possibility, the transcultural dynamics between Chinese and German philosophy is understood as a back-and-forth movement that does not try to circumvent painful problems, but recognizes them as spaces of transit or temporal residence on a philosophical way which necessarily involves working through individual and collective urgency and danger (*Not*).

"The Necessity of the Unnecessary" ("Die Notwendigkeit des Unnötigen") is Wilhelm's subtitle to his translation of the short dialogue between the two Chinese thinkers in chapter 26 of the *Zhuangzi* to which Heidegger refers. Here I will not enter into a detailed discussion of Wilhelm's translation and other possibilities of translation and interpretation. What I need to mention, however, is that I prefer the translation of *wuyong zhi yong* 無用之用 as "use of the useless," although I do recognize that it was probably due to Wilhelm's problematic translation that Heidegger became strongly attracted to this passage. In the "Evening Conversation" a possibility appears which, at first sight, seems to be not only paradoxical but also absurd or even crazy: that the "vanquished German people" may, with the help of Chinese philosophy, enter its "still-withheld essence" (*immer noch vorenthaltenes Wesen*).[4] For a moment at least, Heidegger does not seem to situate, as usual, the source of philosophical learning, self-awareness, and of an "other beginning" in ancient Greece, but in ancient China.

This shift, however, does not interest me in terms of whether a certain cultural identity (Occidental, Western, or German) is replaced by another cultural identity or identification (with the East or China) and so in terms of whether ancient China replaced ancient Greece as a spiritual source. Therefore, I am neither interested in whether there is an orientalist or occidentalist attitude behind his impulse to learn not only from Greek but also from Chinese thinkers. What I am concerned with is whether the possibility of a double or perhaps even multiple cultural identity emerges at this crucial moment in German history. Such a perspective comes to the fore because the language used by Heidegger in the "Evening Conversation" contains peculiarities which can be traced back to the influence of the *Zhuangzi*—the "necessity of the unnecessary" or the idea of a "useless people"—but also because his interpretation abounds with traces of the influence of the pre-Socratics, Friedrich Hölderlin, and the writings of Meister Eckhart. Is Zhuangzi thereby, at least as a possibility of thought, placed next to Heraclitus and Anaximander, ranked as an equally valuable source which the modern world urgently needs in order to achieve self-awareness? And does it perhaps need this source, because the paradoxical figure of the "necessity of the unnecessary" and the "use of the useless" provides an unknown, more or less unthinkable key to an alternative way of thinking and doing?

World-Historical Awareness and Sense of Urgency

What does it mean to explore the transcultural potential of Heidegger's thought? We might first want to explore whether the transcultural character of the way in which Heidegger relates Old and New, South and North, Greek-speaking and German-speaking thought can be extended to the relation between East and West. From a geopolitical perspective, this extension is confronted with the fact that the "pivot to the West" undertaken by the Federal Republic of Germany after 1949 has been accompanied by the creation of strong structural obstacles for any philosophical interest in Eastern or Asian philosophy. Therefore, extending the relation between the East and the West should encompass or even highly controversial aspects of Heidegger's relationship to ancient Greek philosophy. For instance, in the context of his interpretation of Heraclitus in the 1943 lectures on *The Inception of Occidental Thinking* (*Der Anfang des abendländischen Denkens*) Heidegger writes: "The planet is in flames. The essence of the human being is out of joint. An awareness [*Besinnung*] that is sufficiently world-historical can only come from the Germans, provided that they find and safeguard 'the German.' This is not arrogance, but rather the knowledge of the necessity [*Notwendigkeit*] of bearing out an inceptual urgency need [*Not*]."[5] In the "Evening Conversation" he reformulates the idea of a "world-historical awareness," again linked to necessity (*Notwendigkeit*) and need, urgency, or "poverty" (*Not*) that may come from the Germans, if they were only able "to begin to turn and enter [*einzukehren*] the still-withheld essence of our vanquished people."[6]

Heidegger seems concerned with "the Germans" and "German essence" even after 1945. In his speculations, the expression of despair about the terrible "fate of the Germans," their "ignorance,"[7] and "treason against their own being"—for him, "more blinded and destructive than the obvious widespread devastation"[8]—is mixed with weird ideas about the salvation of the world which is to start with the Germans and indeed with Heidegger's native state in the southwest.[9] I would not have given a second thought to such aberrations from a thinker so strongly attached to his homeland, a thinker who even burdens himself with the historical task of giving birth to the spirit of the Occident, if he had not drawn Zhuangzi and Chinese philosophy into the realm of that world-historical awareness. What kind of link is there between Heidegger's idea that the Germans should turn into a waiting and useless people and his use of the *Zhuangzi*? Does it make sense to speak of a "second turn" (*zweite Kehre*): a transcultural turn (*Kehre*) of Heidegger's thought, this time not through the Greek South, but through the Chinese East?[10]

In his *Remarks V* (*Anmerkungen V*), one of the *Black Notebooks* from 1948, Heidegger writes: "The German people is ruined in its political, military, economic, and best national power, both by the criminal madness of Hitler and by the will to extermination finally exercised by foreign countries. Do not be fooled ... The task is still to eradicate the Germans spiritually and historically."[11] This is one of the testimonies of the nationalist thought which Heidegger did not abandon even after the war. In the course of my encounters with contemporary Chinese philosophy, I repeatedly came across expressions strongly resembling Heidegger's nationalist language and corresponding to the idea of "self-affirmation" (*Selbstbehauptung*) he put forth in 1933. An example would be the whole discourse of "self-strengthening" (*ziqiang* 自強), very influential well up to the twenty-first century. Moreover, in the context of the Chinese cultural and political modernization since the nineteenth century, a consciousness of despair and urgency about the possibility of China being "spiritually and historically" wiped out as a nation and as a people spread widely and across different political positions. One of the most well-known philosophical expressions of this attitude was the Confucian Manifesto of 1958. Recently, the success of the long struggle for self-strengthening is expressed in the formula of the "great renaissance of the Chinese nation," encapsulating a popular yearning for and belief in the rise of China to an economic, political, and cultural power, even though the normative potential of such a power remains largely unclear. Throughout the twentieth century, China's self-understanding was shaped by the unconditional will to survive and to strengthen herself. But now the question is to what extent the Chinese way of modernization could become normatively meaningful by turning against the self-destructive tendency inherent in different European and North American ways of modernization so far, or whether it will only lead to prolonging and intensifying their tendency to devastation and destruction. The German way of modernization, culminating in National Socialism, is of particular importance because it can serve as a thought-provoking example of the extent to which the dialectic of progress can lead an entire people into the abyss of catastrophic failure.

This historical situation at least partly explains why Heidegger's idea of an "other beginning," his evocation of a German essence accumulated in poetry and thought, seems so appealing to Chinese thinkers. It at least also allows us to understand Kejun Xia's deep concern about Heidegger's critical response to the National Socialist cult of the will, inspired, as we saw, by a passage from the *Zhuangzi*, but also, if only indirectly, the cultural and political situation of Communist China which, for Xia, is in danger of repeating the self-destructive development of Nazi Germany.

With the possible correspondence between the "socialism with Chinese characteristics" and German National Socialism, the question which arises from a philosophical point of view is whether understanding the failure of modern metaphysics of the will in Germany and the critique Heidegger elaborated against it might help to develop a discourse that analyzes the dangers of any blind faith in willpower. Heidegger's vision of turning the "vanquished German people" into a "useless people" capable of "releasement" (*Gelassenheit*) appears, against this background, as the normative potential of the Chinese people rather than the German, all the more because Heidegger's understanding of releasement received decisive inspiration from paradoxical thought developed in Chinese antiquity. While the Germans, according to Heidegger's conviction, ignored this visionary possibility succumbing to Americanization, Chinese intellectuals may look for a way to make this possibility fruitful for the critical self-reflection of Chinese modernization. From this perspective it seems that the historical condition for this possibility lies in the fact that the spiritual and cultural foundations necessary for the realization of Heidegger's vision have been rather neglected in German philosophy in particular and in Western philosophy in general, and that, therefore, Heidegger had to turn against Western metaphysics in order to express this possibility in a rather tentative way. By contrast, those foundations have been strongly developed in Chinese philosophy since antiquity, and may undergo a modern transformation in order to unfold their normative potential in a new way.

This roughly sketched perspective already makes clear in which sense the relation between Heidegger and Zhuangzi touches upon delicate and difficult issues in both contemporary Chinese and German philosophy. It also reveals what kind of insight may be gained from the discussion of the "Evening Conversation" within an intercultural discourse between contemporary Chinese and German philosophy which would be both comparative and transcultural; "comparative" in the sense of working with cultural and linguistic identities that are problematic and at the same time indispensable; "transcultural" insofar as both sides engage in dynamic and creative interaction in which the awareness of the nonidentical dimension within these identities is strengthened and both sides are drawn into a process of mutual learning and transformation. In this sense, intercultural philosophy in Heidegger's "Evening Conversation" seems to relate to a certain "consciousness of urgency" (*Bewußtsein von Nöten*), to a way of philosophizing that does not shrink from painful questions when entering into the twisted communication between different linguistic and cultural sources and positions.

Was Zhuangzi a Nazi?

Zhuangzi was fond of bizarre stories and strange questions. So, he might forgive me for oddly asking: Was he a Nazi? The view that his writings cannot be pressed into political service is already found in ancient historical sources. For more than two thousand years his teachings had been understood as useless for the purposes of political ideology. In twentieth-century Germany, however, Heidegger found a way to undermine this uselessness. Well known in China and controversial almost everywhere else because of his support for National Socialism, in his "Evening Conversation" Heidegger quotes from the *Zhuangzi*:

> Older Man: But as a good night parting, and perhaps also as a thanks, I would still like to relate to you now a short conversation between two thinkers.
> In my student days I copied it down from a historical account of Chinese philosophy because it struck me, though I did not quite understand it earlier. This evening it first became bright around me, and probably because of that, this conversation also occurred to me. The names of the two thinkers escape me. The conversation goes like this: The one said: "You are talking about the unnecessary." The other said: "A person must first have recognized the unnecessary before one can talk with him about the necessary. The earth is wide and large, and yet, in order to stand, the human needs only enough space to be able to put his foot down. But if directly next to his foot a crevice were to open up that dropped down into the underworld, then would the space where he stands still be of use to him?" The one said: "It would be of no more use to him." The other said: "From this the necessity of the unnecessary is clearly apparent."
> Younger Man: I thank you for this conversation.
> Older Man: And I you for your poem [*Gedicht*], in which perhaps after all something densely composed [*Gedichtetes*] is concealed.
> Younger Man: Let us think of what poetically condenses [*das Dichtende*].
> Older Man: A good night to us both and to all in the camp.
> Younger Man: And to the homeland the blessing of its destined assignment.[12]

This is how the text ends. Below Heidegger added the following remark, already partly quoted above: "Schloß Hausen im Donautal, on May 8, 1945. On the day the world celebrated its victory, without yet recognizing that already for centuries it has been defeated by its own rebellious uprising."[13]

In the afterword to the *Country Path Conversations* the editor notes: "Now, fifty years after the German surrender in May 1945, these thoughts of Heidegger's during that time appear in print for the first time ... Yet those who, on account of the dates of these conversations, expect a word from the philosopher concerning the end of the Nazi regime, will find themselves disappointed."[14] Anyone who expects a certain direct, explicit word—of repentance or confession—will undoubtedly be disappointed. If instead one assumes that Heidegger might have expressed himself indirectly and allusively about the end of the Nazi regime will perhaps consider the major idea of the text—the necessity of the unnecessary (*die Notwendigkeit des Unnötigen*)—insufficient and provocative or even repulsive, but will hardly be able to deny that it is a philosophically profound answer. Apparently, on this symbolic day, Heidegger attempts to turn the victory of the Allies over Nazi Germany into a historical defeat in order to then derive the vision of a new world-historical mission of the German people out of this defeat; "Older Man: 'Thus, we must learn to know the necessity of the unnecessary and, as learners, teach it to the peoples [*den Völkern*].' Younger Man: 'And for a long time this may perhaps be the sole content of our teaching—the need and the necessity of the unnecessary.'"[15]

Does Heidegger instrumentalize the *Zhuangzi* in the service of the nationalist vision of paradoxically turning Germany's devastating defeat into victory? But what kind of victory would that be? Perhaps a victory without victory? Any attempt to realize the "necessity of the unnecessary" requires renouncing the "arrogant will to have an effect" (*Anmaßung des Wirkenwollens*),[16] as well as breaking away from the claim to power of all ideological "worldviews" (*Weltanschauungen*). According to this vision, the German people should become "entirely useless," "squander its essence purely on the unnecessary" in order to finally "begin to turn and enter [*einzukehren*] the still-withheld essence of our vanquished people."[17] Does Heidegger not push the exercise in "counter-turning" (*Gegenwendigkeit*) paradoxical thinking to the point where this imagined victory will at the same time appear as a non-victory, because the German people who may achieve it will have left the will to victory behind? And does the new historical mission which Heidegger bestows to the "people of poets and thinkers"[18] not consist in learning, along with the "necessity of the unnecessary," what he calls "pure waiting," that is to learn and exercise the ability to wait and let come (*Kommenlassen*), obviously in stark contrast to the failed ideology of will and action (*Tat*)?

At this point, it is obvious that the assumption that Heidegger has put Zhuangzi at the service of volkish thought leads to a strangely reversed vision of the Germans as a people that have renounced the metaphysics of will to embrace "a strange doing, which is a letting"[19]—a doing no one can make use of. It is in this attempt to think of the Germans as turning from a people of will to a useless and unusable people that Heidegger's transcultural turn comes into play. Nevertheless, Heidegger's philosophical use of the "necessity of the unnecessary" is, to say the least, ambivalent and confusing, making it difficult to simply dismiss a seemingly absurd suspicion: that Zhuangzi could have been a precursor of volkish, perhaps even National Socialist thought. More than two thousand years after Zhuangzi's death, Heidegger seems to have succeeded in assigning a political use to his writings, making selected passages from this ancient text useful in a new, hitherto unknown way. This use, however, entails rejecting any instrumentalizing intention—a paradoxical precondition of any successful instrumentalization. The only way to instrumentalize the *Zhuangzi* is to lack deliberation to do so.

Even if the idea that Zhuangzi could have been a historical predecessor of National Socialism belongs to the realm of distasteful absurdities, the question still remains whether he will ever again be able to free himself from the malicious suspicion of having unwillingly collaborated with a Nazi philosopher who reached out to him through the millennia. Or is the Heidegger who embraces the Zhuangzian "necessity of the unnecessary" (use of the useless) no longer a Nazi philosopher, but a thinker who has turned away from national-socialist ideology? Is the paradoxical idea of using the useless by definition incompatible with the philosophical foundations of National Socialism?

Strictly speaking, Zhuangzi steps out of the remoteness of Chinese antiquity and moves into the proximity of contemporary German philosophy only at the moment in which Heidegger's "Evening Conversation" draws him into the horizon of a thoughtful but also highly problematic response to the end of the Nazi regime. Germany's history in the twentieth century has forced this one main topic onto the mind of German philosophers, urging them to directly or indirectly investigate the reasons for and the aftermath of Adolf Hitler and National Socialism. Paraphrasing a well-known statement by Theodor W. Adorno, one might even say that any philosophizing after Auschwitz which does not immerse itself into painful and patient "meditations" on Hitler, National Socialism, and the destruction of the European Jews is ultimately "garbage." Taking this perspective, we might wonder about the possibility of a discussion of Heidegger's response to the end of the Nazi regime on the basis of Adorno's *Negative Dialectics* and its "meditations on metaphysics" as an important reference and normative yardstick. Aren't these meditations in themselves somehow pathological? Was Adorno not very well aware of this problem when he pointed out that all urgent criticism of Hitler and National Socialism remains entangled in their regime? As he declares, "Hitler has imposed a new categorical imperative upon humanity in the state of their unfreedom: to arrange their thinking and conduct, so that Auschwitz never repeats itself, so that nothing similar ever happens again."[20] Now a particular individual in German history becomes the starting point for a categorical imperative which is perceived as having universal content. And if "Auschwitz" was an event whose moral significance is supposed to surpass other mass murders and massacres of the twentieth century, where does the criterion for judging what is "similar" and what "should not happen again" come from?

Even if the (negative) Germanocentrism that determines Adorno's perspective is by no means easy to understand, especially outside of Europe and North America, it can hardly be denied that Hitler and National Socialism pose philosophical problems that have significance beyond Germany. If this is the case and if the "Evening Conversation" and the paradoxical figure of the "necessity of the unnecessary" can be read as Heidegger's answer to the end of the Nazi regime—also difficult to grasp and in need of further explanation—he has then dragged the *Zhuangzi* into the dark side not only of German, but also of global contemporary philosophy.

Lovers of Chinese wisdom may see this as an act of unfriendly appropriation or even arbitrary violation. It does, however, contain the important hint that Chinese philosophy may be perceived as globally significant, if it is able not only to contribute to China and her self-understanding, but also to provide valuable sources for dealing with dark and painful experiences of the present age in the West. For Heidegger, the German defeat has undoubtedly been such an experience and one might, again, wonder how Heidegger's response to the end of the Nazi regime is *not* disappointing.

Asia!

The "Evening Conversation" is marked by references to the already quoted short passage from chapter 26 of the *Zhuangzi*. Heidegger does not explicitly state his source, introducing it as a "brief conversation between two thinkers." The names of the two thinkers remain unknown, Heidegger calls them "the one" and "the other," although he was familiar with Richard Wilhelm's translation of the passage, since he attached it to a letter to his brother Fritz Heidegger dated March 5, 1945.[21] The "Older Man," one of the two interlocutors in the "Evening Conversation," says that the dialogue between the two unnamed thinkers comes from a "historical account of Chinese philosophy" which he came across during his student days. He had copied it down, because "it struck" him, even though he "did not quite understand it earlier."[22] It is likely that, very early on, Heidegger was familiar not only with Martin Buber's partial translation of the *Zhuangzi* published in 1910 (and not including *Zhuangzi* chapter 26, section 7), but also with Richard Wilhelm's more extensive translation, published in 1912, and that he was probably greatly impressed by it without knowing why. But now, in the unprecedented situation of urgency and upheaval at the end of the Second World War, he remembered this passage again and "it became bright around him"; the phrase "necessity of the unnecessary" suddenly struck him in a much deeper and unexpected way.

Was it the specific historical situation that prompted or even forced Heidegger to recall the conversation between the two Chinese thinkers? Or was not even the experience of "devastation" and "annihilation" necessary to allow him, for a fleeting but decisive moment, to let go of all the otherwise very strong reservations with which academically educated people in Europe often fend off Chinese philosophy? As the cliché goes, nothing is more foreign and distant than China, not only geographically, but also historically, culturally, and linguistically. So, is not the experience of approaching these distant things inevitably illusory, doomed to fall into the trap of exoticism or orientalism? Such and related reasons may have persuaded Heidegger not to further pursue that intuitive experience of proximity with the distant that runs through the "Evening Conversation"; an urgent problem in the present can suddenly and unexpectedly open up correspondences and suggest historical leaps through which the distant suddenly comes closer in a way that is hardly explicable by any causal and linear justification.

Given Heidegger's high philological standards in his work with Greek texts, it is hardly surprising that his postwar attempts to translate the Daoist classic *Daodejing* with a Chinese student did not lead very far. A closer look at the *Zhuangzi* passage quoted in the "Evening Conversation" reveals that the textual basis for Heidegger's speculations is rather flimsy (and Richard Wilhelm's translation raises many questions itself). It seems that, in this case, Heidegger simply trusted Wilhelm's translation, following the possibilities of thought which it opened up. The contrast with his meticulous reading of ancient Greek texts is immediately apparent. We might assume, therefore, that his inability to work on a translation from the original was for him a serious and embarrassing impediment not only for the "Evening Conversation," but for a study of Chinese philosophy in general. If he had been able to establish a relationship between the original text and its translation, as he had been in the case of Greek texts, the "Evening Conversation" would certainly have developed very differently. Even under these academically and philologically unsolid conditions, however, Heidegger manages to engage with the text in a way which seems to me philosophically more profound and far-reaching than many discussions of the *Zhuangzi* not only in Western Sinology.

The "Evening Conversation" does not approach section 7 of chapter 26 of the *Zhuangzi* from the outside, does not regard it as a foreign or unfamiliar object to be examined, but leaves no doubt that it proceeds from the point of being struck by it. I would even say that the "Evening Conversation" traces the experience of a self-transformation triggered by this passage from the *Zhuangzi*. It seems as if Heidegger wanted to continue the Chinese tradition of commentaries on the book, mimetically adapting to the way of reading texts cultivated by Chinese thinkers: they are meant to be read repeatedly, perhaps even memorized, but their understanding, their "taste," is not immediately revealed. It is to be savored again and again. The content of particular sentences, even individual characters, may be constantly investigated until the text, under certain circumstances and against the background of a very individual experience, unexpectedly emerges from the darkness of diffuse memory and imposes itself upon conscious awareness. It then begins to unfold a meaning that is bound to the singularity of one individual experience and, so to speak, one aesthetic event, but nevertheless, or perhaps for this very reason, accumulates a general meaning which can be perceived and (re)recognized by others. This gives a broader meaning to the brief, completely incidental reference to the circumstances under which a conversation between two Chinese thinkers attracted Heidegger's attention. Here, at this very moment, Heidegger's thinking shows, even if only fleetingly, a relationship between text and experience, between classical culture and a way of life, which can be regarded as crucial for any deeper understanding of Chinese philosophy.

In a letter to his brother dated March 5, 1945, Heidegger writes: "The little conversation between two Chinese thinkers (Asia!) will certainly bring you joy."[23] Zhuangzi would probably not have objected to the role of the nameless "other," since the *Zhuangzi* explicitly plays with namelessness and presents "the nameless" as an idealized figure. Nevertheless, Heidegger's short comment already indicates the many difficulties raised by his use of the Chinese passage. Huizi and Zhuangzi become two nameless Chinese thinkers whose thinking is immediately placed in the general horizon of "Asia," so that it may not be exaggerated to see in them, partly revealed, the nature of Heidegger's interest in Chinese philosophy in general and in this passage in particular. What seems to play a decisive role here is the philosophical, cultural, but also geopolitical relationship between Europe (the West) and Asia. The exclamation mark ("Asia!") points to the importance Asia is granted in the difficult circumstances toward the end of the Second World War. To speak, in this context, of a turn to Asia, perhaps even of a "second turn" associated with it, a turn to the East in Heidegger's thinking, may not therefore be entirely absurd; it is exactly this turn that makes the transition from a people that celebrated the triumph of the will to a useless people thinkable in the first place. It would admittedly be a very experimental and unsatisfactory turn, but one which deserves to be taken seriously as an abandoned and unrealized possibility.

I am, therefore, not interested in finding philological proof for the turn to the East in Heidegger's writings or even in establishing a causal link between the development of his thought and Daoism, but rather in "discovering and developing from a transcultural perspective" something still largely unthought of in his thinking.[24]

It is obvious that Heidegger views the Asians, in this case the Chinese, and the Germans or Europeans as philosophically unequal, as the cursory and passing manner in which the former are mentioned reveals. Even if the "Evening Conversation" suggests that Heidegger's search for an "other beginning" temporarily and experimentally shifted in the direction of Chinese philosophy, "Asia!" remains vaguely general and nameless. There is undoubtedly an East Asian influence in Heidegger's thought, but it seems rather pointless to me to put much effort into attempts to prove it in greater detail.[25]

It would perhaps be more meaningful to operate on the assumption that Heidegger has not only himself opened up and also closed down the possibilities associated with non-Western philosophy, but that his writings contain correspondences with important aspects of Eastern philosophy which he himself, as well as most Western researchers, overlooked; unfamiliar with the richness and complexity of the three great traditions of Confucian, Daoist, and Buddhist thought in China, Western thinkers simply failed to develop a sense for those internal and hidden references that have, reversely, and for decades, inspired Japanese and Chinese readings of Heidegger. In Europe and, ironically, especially in Germany, the philosophical potential of Heidegger's transcultural turn is still largely unexplored. The linguistic and cultural conditions of the possibility of a more open and unblocked communication between Europe and Asia have in fact even worsened, compared with the situation in the early twentieth century. One reason for this is that Eastern philosophy never became more familiar through Heidegger's attempt at rapprochement. On the contrary, his attitude to Chinese philosophy has cast a shadow of deep suspicion on it as a whole, investing it with a dubious aura of esotericism or even mystical totalitarianism and so condemning it to unapproachable distance and sinister foreignness.

German Non-identity

The significance of Heidegger's use of the *Zhuangzi* in the "Evening Conversation" lies, in my view, in the fact that this classical work is pulled into the horizon of problems of contemporary German philosophy which are still highly controversial and will probably remain so in the foreseeable future. I will attempt to approach this horizon by touching upon Heidegger's archaic use of the German language which Adorno polemically rejected in his *Jargon of Authenticity*. My own experience of translating classical Chinese texts into German has shown me that there is in fact a lot to learn from Heidegger's language. His work with and on the limits of his native tongue is no less than a reminder of the courage against conventions necessary for engaging in philosophical translation. But Heidegger's language is also a warning. It seems, at times, so hermetic, self-referential, and self-satisfied, to the point of absurdity, that it annuls any attempt at serious discussion. At the same time, however, it makes clear to me that translating classical Chinese into a more or less modern, digestible language may be possible for some texts, but in most cases any such effort is doomed to failure. I have often had the impression that the task of translating classical Chinese texts in a thoughtful way unavoidably involves the presumptuous claim of constantly testing, renewing, and expanding the possibilities of the target language. It is, therefore, necessary not to limit oneself to the thin layer of current language use, but, if possible, to draw on sources that originate from the historical depths of one's "own" language(s). Resorting to a language that archaizes in this sense, however, does not seem desirable to me for the purpose of shielding German from external influences in a protectionist way. On the contrary, I consider increased attention to the entire breadth and depth of the German language as indispensable in the process of opening it up to transcultural communication, in this case with the Chinese language. Such communication remains superficial if it only knows the New and disregards the Old.

Seen from this perspective, the German language is, at least today, rather unsuitable for transcultural philosophizing, because it is a language in which the communication between the Old and the New, as well as East, West, South, and North—between the temporal and spatial dimensions of transculturality—is interrupted and distorted. The reason for this rupture, for this barrier to free communication, can also be traced in Heidegger's "Evening Conversation." In his longing for and bizarre description of a new historical mission for the defeated Germans (to become an "entirely useless people"), an understanding of people and language comes forth which was also expressed in the early twentieth century in the context of revolutionary conservatism and aesthetic fundamentalism, albeit in a will-critical and antiheroic disguise.[26] Is the "Evening Conversation" a contemplation on the possibility of revolutionizing the so-called conservative revolution? The normative meaning of this revolution of revolution appears in it as its potential detachment from a fixation on the German Volksgeist and the cultural unity of the nation, in order to explore an alternative possibility: that of searching for a tradition of German spirituality concentrated in writing and language that does not need to be confirmed by the identitary exclusion of seemingly distant and foreign otherness, but that is able to open itself to classical literature in other languages in order to preserve the liveliness of classical culture expressed in German.

In this respect, Heidegger and Adorno are probably not as far apart as they seem. For both thinkers, German identity, in linguistic and cultural terms, is only possible as "German non-identity";[27] perhaps there is hardly a more accurate term to describe what contemporary German philosophy, aware of the tension between Heidegger and Adorno as it is, focuses on. "German non-identity" refers to a paradoxical communication between identity and non-identity through which individual and collective subjectivities are formed. For intercultural philosophy, as I would like to understand it, the back and forth between a comparative dimension emphasizing identity and a transcultural dimension highlighting non-identity is crucial in a similar way.

German-speaking philosophers and poets of the eighteenth and nineteenth centuries were quite familiar with this matter. At least their use of language was formed and refined by opening up to and dealing with other languages—mostly classical Greek. The historical correspondence between Greek and German testifies to a transcultural dynamics within Europe in which Old and New, South and North communicated with each other in a far-reaching manner. Heidegger's German dream of a new beginning of Occidental thinking in Germany still draws on the tenacious influence of this far-reaching cultural correspondence and can be understood as its radical, indeed almost extremist, continuation. To speak of aesthetic fundamentalism in this respect is also quite reasonable, because, since the eighteenth century, there has been a tendency in the field of German aesthetics to understand aesthetics as a comprehensive cultivation program carrying an almost religious significance and even elevated to the level of a substitute for religion, with the relationship between the Old and the New, the classical and the modern, at its core. An idea found in Baumgarten expresses the philosophical radicality inherent in modern aesthetics as a cultivation program: ἄσκησις (askesis) or *exercitatio aesthetica*, aesthetic ascesis or exercise.[28]

There is a current in the German tradition that has tried to oppose an academic-methodological style of philosophizing with an aesthetic-ascetic one (oriented toward aesthetic education and practice). Not so much Baumgarten himself, but aesthetic thinkers from Sulzer, Herder, Goethe, and Schiller to Hölderlin and Nietzsche can be understood as contributors to a German tradition of "aesthetic ascetics," for which the reference to ancient Greece and classical *Bildung* associated with it was an invaluable source of inspiration. Schiller and, more than him, Hölderlin and Nietzsche conjured up the classical culture of *Bildung* as indispensable nourishment of self-cultivation in the contemporary world. They abhorred any tendency to reduce classical culture to a museum exhibit lacking any force for creative transformation and poetic inspiration or *Begeisterung*, as Hölderlin often refers to it. Even parts of the so-called conservative revolution can be understood as a movement of aesthetic fundamentalism intent on rescuing this old program of aesthetic cultivation under the political conditions of the early twentieth century. This aesthetic program aimed at no less than a revolutionary "spiritual upheaval" (*Geistesumwälzung*)—as Hofmannsthal calls it at the end of a lecture—comparable only to the Renaissance or the Reformation.[29] It sometimes even dreamt of a new beginning for Europe, achieved, supposedly, through a radical reinterpretation of ancient Greek philosophy. Heidegger was one of those who worked on the realization of this German dream—which would soon turn into a nightmare.

The entanglement between the tendency toward aesthetic fundamentalism within revolutionary conservativism and the political movement of National Socialism is a tragic event in German cultural history. How could it happen that a transcultural and cosmopolitan culture of language and *Bildung* joined an identitarian and ethnocentric nationalism, only to be ultimately dragged into its downfall? Heidegger's reflections in the *Black Notebooks* can be taken as evidence that, at least for a time, he really equaled these events with the collapse of the West. "Everything Western is the end," he writes in a 1943 letter to his brother.[30] It was in this situation of radical change and urgency that Zhuangzi's "necessity of the unnecessary" struck him profoundly. For a brief but nevertheless philosophically highly significant moment, a new historical correspondence emerged in Heidegger's thinking: that between the German and the Chinese language, between German and Chinese philosophy.

The seemingly arbitrary correspondence between old Chinese and new German philosophy is born out of a historical catastrophe that has been weighing heavily on the latter ever since, even though it remains largely unrecognized and unrecognizable.

Heidegger's writings thus seem to be a very bad and hopeless way of gaining access to the transcultural potential of this correspondence. If he had not exerted such strong influence in East Asia, which remains strong today, if his thinking had not been much more influential in East Asia than Adorno's, and if, moreover, the reception and interpretation of classical German philosophy of the eighteenth and nineteenth centuries were not of such far-reaching importance in contemporary China, there would probably be little reason on the German side to continue exploring the correspondence between Heidegger and Daoism or Chinese philosophy in general.

In Germany, as elsewhere, there is a tendency to dismiss the influence of classical Chinese philosophy on Heidegger as marginal or to warn against overestimating its importance. If we were to measure this influence in terms of the number of references Heidegger explicitly makes to Chinese texts quoting them in translation, the findings would indeed be quite poor. The quotation from the *Zhuangzi* in the "Evening Conversation" and the one from the *Daodejing* in a text on Hölderlin[31] are among the most important of these references. More significant than the explicit references, however, are the implicit ones, in the form of the inspiration Heidegger drew from chapter 11 of the *Daodejing* for his repeated discussion of the relationship between the "jug" (*Krug*) and emptiness, nothingness, or withoutness (*wu* 無). There are also, however, those more hidden correspondences which Heidegger himself was rather unaware of, but which readings of Heidegger based on a profound knowledge of East Asian philosophy in general and Chinese philosophy in particular can help bring to light. An obvious example is the connection between "thing" (*Ding*) and "the fourfold" (*Geviert*) in Heidegger's "Das Ding," while a less obvious one is Heidegger's concern with "habit" (*Brauch*) and "use" (*Gebrauch*). Within this horizon, the meaning of his discourse on the necessity of the unnecessary or the use of the useless in the "Evening Conversation" gains considerably in theoretical depth and richness.

Heidegger's reflections on the word *Brauch* (habit, use), often with reference to a quotation from Anaximander, mark the relationship between the Greek and the German language with archaisms difficult to comprehend and with an attitude of thinking that rejects rapid utilization. What I want to suggest, however, is that, if contemporary German philosophy is prepared to open itself up to possibilities of transcultural communication with sinophone or, more precisely, sino-grammatic philosophy at all, the use of such uselessness is imperative. I would even say that the "necessity of the unnecessary" or the "use of the useless" is Heidegger's concise and necessary response to the end of the Nazi regime.

The assumption, therefore, that Heidegger's thinking turns away from National Socialism in and with these words does not seem implausible. This turning away becomes possible precisely because it takes place from within, in the mode of immanent critique. Because Heidegger knew National Socialism from within, out of his own conviction, his transcultural turn was able to gain a "meditative" force and depth without which the universalistic, even normative content of the late Heidegger cannot be explained. For this reason, his *Country Path Conversations* can be read not only as a radical critique of the national-socialist ideology of will and usefulness, but also as a critique of a technical and economic modernization whose destructive dynamics has long since become a global problem. To understand the normative potential of the late Heidegger, the idea of a second, transcultural turn to the East seems to be very helpful. It can help explain how he managed to escape, at least partially and temporarily, the Germanocentrism of the first turn, namely, his turn to the history of being. If nothing else, the idea of a second turn at least helps in shedding new light on Heidegger's past and future significance in East Asia. The fact that he only hinted at possible ways to the East, hardly embarking on them himself, probably effaces any possibility of following him on this way, but it speaks more in favor of the idea of a second turn than against it. It is in this sense that I want to highlight the need to take Heidegger's transcultural thought experiments seriously as paradigmatic experiences, even if or precisely because these experiences are inevitably also exercises in thinking against oneself.[32]

Conclusion

The global significance of Chinese philosophy never only depends on Chinese philosophy itself, but is linked to translations and transformations into different languages and historical situations which always develop an independent dynamic of their own. Paradoxically, the global significance of Chinese classics can only emerge when they prove their ability to respond to urgent local or regional problems and concerns, when they enter into a kind of transcultural turmoil similar to Heidegger's use of the *Zhuangzi* in a terrible historical moment, the moment in which he was confronted with the German defeat, and when, moreover, this response inspires new philosophical developments in the Chinese context. The "Evening Conversation" may be an extreme example for the reception and transformation of Daoism in German philosophy, but, as I have tried to show, it is highly significant for understanding the enormous difficulty of dealing with the barriers to communication which separate philosophical discourses in China and the West. Those barriers are never merely in the hearts and minds, but are deeply entrenched in historical and political experiences and sensibilities that strongly influence the ways in which we are thinking and doing. The irritation and the pain inflicted by the changing forms of those barriers to communication can never be fully overcome or removed. Paradoxical communication, therefore, is a way to live with and through barriers to communication.

Notes

1 "Abendgespräch in einem Kriegsgefangenenlager in Rußland zwischen einem Jüngeren und einem Älteren." See Martin Heidegger, *Feldweg-Gespräche* [GA 77], ed. Ingrid Schüssler (Frankfurt: Klostermann, 1995), 203–40. For an English translation, see: Martin Heidegger, "Evening Conversation: In a Prisoner of War Camp in Russia, between a Younger and an Older Man," trans. Bret W. Davis, in *Country Path Conversations* (Bloomington: Indiana University Press, 2010), 132–57.
2 See Peter Trawny, *Heidegger und Hölderlin oder Der Europäische Morgen* (Würzburg: Königshausen and Neumann, 2010), 191–201.

3   Richard Wilhelm, *Dschuang Dsi: Das Wahre Buch vom Südlichen Blütenland* (Jena: Diederichs, 1912), 203–4.
4   Heidegger, *Feldweg-Gespräche*, 234; Cf. Heidegger, "Evening Conversation," 134.
5   Heidegger, Martin. *Heraclitus, The Inception of Occidental Thinking and Logic; Heraclitus's Doctrine of the Logos*. Translated by Julia G. Assaiante and S. Montgomery Ewegen (London: Bloomsbury Academic, 2018), 92; Cf. Martin Heidegger, *Heraklit*. [GA 55], ed. Manfred S. Frings (Frankfurt: Vittorio Klostermann, 1979), 123.
6   Heidegger, *Feldweg-Gespräche*, 234; Cf. Heidegger, "Evening Conversation," 154.
7   Walter Homolka and Arnulf Heidegger, ed., *Heidegger und der Antisemitismus: Positionen im Widerstreit* (Freiburg: Herder, 2016), 131.
8   Ibid., 133.
9   Ibid., 129–30.
10 See Kejun Xia, *A Waiting and Useless People. Zhuangzi and Heidegger's Second Turn* 一個等待與無用的民族：莊子與海德格爾的第二次轉向 (Beijing: Beijing University Press, 2017).
11 Martin Heidegger, *Anmerkungen I-V* [GA 97], ed. Peter Trawny (Frankfurt: Vittorio Klostermann, 2015), 444.
12 The German translation by Richard Wilhelm reads "Hui Dsï sprach zu Dschuang Dsï: Ihr redet von Unnötigem. Dschuang Dsï sprach: Erst muß einer das Unnötige erkennen, ehe man mit ihm vom Nötigen reden kann. Die Erde ist ja weit und groß, und doch braucht der Mensch, um zu stehen, nur soviel Platz, daß er seinen Fuß darauf setzen kann. Wenn aber unmittelbar neben dem Fuß ein Riß entstünde bis hinab zu der Unterwelt, wäre ihm dann der Platz, worauf er steht, noch zu etwas nütze? Hui Dsï sprach: Er wäre ihm nichts mehr nütze. Dschuang Dsï sprach: Daraus ergibt sich klar die Notwendigkeit des Unnötigen."
13 Heidegger, *Feldweg-Gespräche*, 239–40; Cf. Heidegger, "Evening Conversation," 157.
14 Heidegger, *Feldweg-Gespräche*, 247; Cf. Heidegger, "Evening Conversation," 162.
15 Ibid., 237; Cf. Ibid., 155.
16 Ibid., 238; Cf. Ibid.
17 Ibid., 234; Cf. Ibid., 153.
18 Ibid., 233; Cf. Ibid., 152.
19 Ibid., 234; Cf. Ibid.
20 Theodor W. Adorno, *Negative Dialektik*, in *Gesammelte Schriften* (Frankfurt am Main: Suhrkamp, 1997), vol. 6, 358.
21 Homolka and Heidegger, *Heidegger und der Antisemitismus*, 123–4.
22 Heidegger, *Feldweg-Gespräche*, 239; Cf. Heidegger, "Evening Conversation," 156.
23 Homolka and Heidegger, *Heidegger und der Antisemitismus*, 123.
24 Kejun Xia, *A Waiting and Useless People*, 15.
25 See Alfred Denker et al., eds., *Heidegger und das ostasiatische Denken* (Freiburg: Alber, 2013).
26 "Conservative revolution" is a concept evoked, for instance, in Hugo von Hofmannsthal's influential discourse on "Das Schrifttum als geistiger Raum der Nation" (Writing as the spiritual space of the nation) (1927). On the concept of "aesthetic fundamentalism" see Stefan Breuer, *Ästhetischer Fundamentalismus: Stefan George und der deutschen Antimodernismus* (Darmstadt: Wissenschaftliche Buchgesellschaft, 1995). In my view, Breuer's approach of interpreting aesthetic fundamentalism as anti-modernism is misleading. I tend to understand conservative revolution and aesthetic fundamentalism as part of modernity; even its anti-modern features are profoundly modern and should not be excluded from a normatively

narrowed concept of modernity. Indeed, we are unavoidably faced with the question of how warranted it is to speak of a normative content of revolutionary conservatism. In this sense, I already see in the program of aesthetic cultivation developed in eighteenth-century Germany clear features of an aesthetic fundamentalism that ultimately considered itself a substitute for (Christian) religion.

27   For the concept of "German non-identity" see Peter Trawny, "Adornos Deutschland," in *Was ist deutsch? Adornos verratenes Vermächtnis* (Berlin: Matthes and Seitz, 2016), 27, 37, and 50. He writes: "Nach Adorno gibt es eine deutsche Nicht-Identität. Nicht-Identität—da er durchaus davon ausgeht, dass es ein deutsches, narrativ vermitteltes Selbstverhältnis gibt. *Nicht-*Identität—weil dieses deutsche Selbstverhältnis durch eine selbst-kritische Anerkennung des Leidens in und an der Shoah stets in einen Verlust umschlägt, der noch den ohnehin notwendigen Verlust einer jeden Herkunft übersteigt. Die deutsche Identität ist nach Adorno durch einen nie zu heilenden Riss gezeichnet. Schließlich gehört zu einer solchen Nicht-Identität, dass ihre Instabilität sich als Offenheit für das Menschliche schlechthin erweist." Ibid., 50.

28   Alexander Gottlieb Baumgarten, *Ästhetik* (Hamburg: Meiner, 2009), 38-9. Also see Christoph Menke, *Force: A Fundamental Concept of Aesthetic Anthropology*, trans. Gerrit Jackson (New York: Fordham University Press, 2013), especially ch. 2.

29   Hugo von Hofmannsthal, "Das Schrifttum als geistiger Raum der Nation," in *Reden und Aufsätze III (1925-1929)* (Frankfurt: Fischer, 1980), 41.

30   Homolka and Heidegger, *Heidegger und der Antisemitismus*, 89.

31   Martin Heidegger, *Zu Hölderlin: Griechenlandreisen* [GA 75], ed. Curd Ochwadt (Frankfurt: Vittorio Klostermann, 2000), 75.

32   See Fabian Heubel, "Kritik als Übung: Über negative Dialektik als Weg ästhetischer Kultivierung," *Allgemeine Zeitschrift für Philosophie*, 40.1 (2015): 63-82.

References

Adorno, Theodor W. *Negative Dialektik*. Frankfurt: Suhrkamp, 1997.
Baumgarten, Alexander Gottlieb. *Ästhetik*. Hamburg: Meiner, 2009.
Breuer, Stefan. *Ästhetischer Fundamentalismus: Stefan George und der deutschen Antimodernismus*. Darmstadt: Wissenschaftliche Buchgesellschaft, 1995.
Denker, Alfred et al., eds. *Heidegger und das ostasiatische Denken*. Freiburg: Alber, 2013.
Heidegger, Martin. *Heraklit*. [GA 55]. Edited by Manfred S. Frings. Frankfurt: Vittorio Klostermann, 1979.
Heidegger, Martin. *Feldweg-Gespräche* [GA 77]. Edited by Ingrid Schüssler. Frankfurt: Vittorio Klostermann, 1995.
Heidegger, Martin. *Zu Hölderlin. Griechenlandreisen* [GA 75]. Edited by Curd Ochwadt. Frankfurt: Vittorio Klostermann, 2000.
Heidegger, Martin. "Evening Conversation: In a Prisoner of War Camp in Russia, between a Younger and an Older Man." In Bret W. Davis (trans.), *Country Path Conversations*, 132-60. Bloomington: Indiana University Press, 2010.
Heidegger, Martin. *Anmerkungen I-V* [GA 97]. Edited by Peter Trawny. Frankfurt: Vittorio Klostermann, 2015.
Heidegger, Martin. *Heraclitus: The Inception of Occidental Thinking and Logic; Heraclitus's Doctrine of the Logos*. Translated by Julia Goesser Assaiante and S. Montgomery Ewegen. London: Bloomsbury Academic, 2018.

Heubel, Fabian. "Kritik als Übung: Über negative Dialektik als Weg ästhetischer Kultivierung." *Allgemeine Zeitschrift für Philosophie*, 40.1 (2015): 63–82.

Homolka, Walter and Arnulf Heidegger, eds. *Heidegger und der Antisemitismus: Positionen im Widerstreit*. Freiburg: Herder, 2016.

Menke, Christoph. *Force: A Fundamental Concept of Aesthetic Anthropology*. Translated by Gerrit Jackson. New York: Fordham University Press, 2013.

Trawny, Peter. *Heidegger und Hölderlin oder Der Europäische Morgen*. Würzburg: Königshausen and Neumann, 2010.

Trawny, Peter. "Adornos Deutschland." In *Was ist deutsch? Adornos verratenes Vermächtnis*. Berlin: Matthes and Seitz, 2016.

von Hofmannsthal, Hugo. "Das Schrifttum als geistiger Raum der Nation." In *Reden und Aufsätze III (1925-1929)*. Frankfurt: Fischer, 1980.

Wilhelm, Richard. *Dschuang Dsi: Das Wahre Buch vom Südlichen Blütenland*. Jena: Diederichs, 1912.

Xia, Kejun. *A Waiting and Useless People: Zhuangzi and Heidegger's Second Turn* 一個等待與無用的民族：莊子與海德格爾的第二次轉向. Beijing: Beijing University Press, 2017.

10

"We Have Been Schooled by the Cabin Haven't We?" Heidegger and Daoism in the Provinces

Mario Wenning

Small retreat consists in hiding in the mountains,
Genuine retreat occurs downtown.

Chinese proverb

Introduction

One motif that seems to connect Heidegger's philosophy and classical Daoist thought is a radical critique of urban dwelling. Undoubtedly, part of the popular appeal of the twentieth-century existential philosopher and the author(s) of the *Daodejing* and *Zhuangzi* is that they allude to the possibility of resisting the stresses associated with a civilization marked by ambition, uprootedness, acceleration, and the striving for recognition. These social pathologies have become associated not only, but especially, with life in cities. Both Daoists and Heidegger seek to critically question the desires and temptations that have come to be associated with urban modes of being-in-the-world. Rather than drawing upon experiences characteristic of city dwellers, they appeal to peasants and craftsmen as exemplars of what it means to live authentically and resist a technologically advanced, but existentially alienating urban civilization. Huts serve as the symbolic topoi that connect Heidegger and the classical Daoists in their respective attempts of getting away from the city in order to get back into place. Heidegger was fond of Bertholt Brecht's poem "Legend of the *Origin* of the Book Tao-Te-Ching on Lao-Tsu's Road into Exile." In the poem, Laozi leaves the kingdom—or city—by traveling with his ox and a boy at a slack pace. When asked by the tax collector at the border gate what he had taught, the boy reports "nothing at all" and adds "He learnt how quite soft water, by attrition, over the years will grind strong rocks away. In other words, that hardness must lose the day."[1] It may be doubted that Heidegger perceived the poem's subtle revolutionary message. Brecht emphasizes the practically important roles of the ox, the boy, and the tax collector to balance the commonly recognized role of the old master.[2] Another orientalization of Heidegger is performed by his friend Heinrich Petzet when he recounts that when Heidegger was sitting in front of his hut he was "like one of those sages painted on one of the Chinese folding screens in the Museum of Ethnology in Bremen, which had inspired Heidegger's great admiration. Each of the sages is sitting in front of his hut, meditating and writing."[3] Indeed, hermits who withdraw from the world either because they are seeking spiritual freedom from mundane concerns or refugees escaping specific political crises are a common reference point in the Daoist imagination and have continued to shape the image of modern literati who study and pursue a life dedicated to philosophy and the arts in isolated country retreats that are surrounded by beautiful landscapes.[4]

It has become customary to emphasize the hidden sources and entanglements with Daoist themes in Heidegger's work.[5] It is well known that Heidegger was endeavoring a co-translation of the *Daodejing*.[6] There are parallels between the guiding conceptual metaphor of the Way in some of Heidegger's writings (the term appears in three book titles) and the fourfold (*das Geviert*), which resonates with Daoist cosmology. Traces of Daoism can be perceived especially in Heidegger's thinking toward the end of the Second World War and during the immediate postwar period. Philologically oriented research in recent years has convincingly revealed the extent to which Heidegger was at least aware of and often influenced by East Asian and especially Daoist motifs ranging from a rejection of willing in *Country Path Conversations* (1944/45) to a philosophy of nothingness in the lecture "The Thing" (1949) and his talk on releasement or "*Gelassenheit*" (1955). Undoubtedly, the focus on remote living and thinking spaces seems like another candidate to underscore an elective affinity between Heidegger and Laozi. The Eurodaoist reception has often interpreted motifs into Daoism,[7] especially the *Daodejing* which has been a projection screen for the Western imagination due to its ambiguous and polysemous nature.

In spite of parallels on the surface, it may be a disservice to Daoism if one were to overemphasize the alleged proximity between the classical Chinese tradition and Heidegger's existential philosophy. It is at least questionable whether the image of Heidegger as a solitary hermit sitting in his mountain hut captures the essentially dialogical spirit of Daoist philosophy. In this chapter, I will turn to the surface similarity between Heidegger's provincialism and Daoist localism as another example of what may be perceived as a deeper philosophical parallel. Upon closer examination, the critique of urbanism by Heidegger and the idealization of small utopian spaces that are depicted in Daoist texts are developed in a different key. In what follows I will first address the theme of Heidegger's provincialism and then move to that of Daoist localism. By way of a conclusion, I will suggest that some proto-modern themes in Daoism are revealed to be better equipped to address the question how to dwell today than Heidegger's anti-modern provincialism.

Heidegger's Provincialism

In Heidegger's writings, despite the original intention of elucidating the ordinary everyday existence of Dasein, the reader senses a certain disdain for the average everydayness as it characterizes the majority of modern people: urban dwelling. In a letter to his wife Elfriede dated July 21, 1918, Heidegger describes his impressions when visiting Berlin as "disgusted to the marrow" by "an atmosphere of artificially cultivated, most vulgar and sophisticated sexuality."[8] Furthermore, he diagnoses that "in such a milieu there can be no true intellectual culture—a priori there cannot—and even if every perfect remedy were to hand—it lacks what is simply Great and Divine … the people here have lost their soul—their faces don't have any expression at all—at most one of vulgarity, there's no staying this decadence now." He goes on to juxtapose the fallen "'spirit' of Berlin" to the "home-grown culture at the provincial universities."[9] In short, small-town Freiburg with the Black Forest mountains in the background is the ideal soil for authentic philosophy while Berlin is not a fertile ground for true thinking and authentic existence. For Heidegger, the intellectual scene in Berlin is characterized as being "sophisticated," "clever, over-clever, but disappointing in terms of content."[10] Even though Heidegger, in contrast to his reputation, traveled extensively, foremost in Germany, but also to France, Italy, and Greece, he tends to have been skeptical of modern modes of displacement and complains about the superficial character of city life. When visiting the city of Dresden, for example, he reports: "Dresden isn't a fertile ground for my work."[11] By contrast, Heidegger idealizes to the point of fetishizing the isolated existence in the cabin designed by his wife and constructed in the early 1920s. While the construction of the hut originally may have served the purpose of preserving a second home in Southern Germany while Heidegger was teaching in Marburg in the North, it soon evolved into what Heidegger considered to be his true intellectual home. In particular, he emphasizes that the simple cabin existence is essential for his concentrated work: "I've got well into my work and live with the woods and mountains, the meadows and brooks—which give me what I need. Quite away from all contingency—in profound indifference to the non-necessary."[12] The cabin takes on an increasingly prominent place in Heidegger's imagination and reflection on space and the place of thinking and resisting the forces of modernity. It is being imbued with the status of one of the few constants and reliable reference points in his life. The cabin allows Heidegger to experience and withstand the freezing winter temperatures. It has served as a singularly important educational role against which other experiences are measured. One of the letters to Elfriede thus recalls: "It's almost like up at the Cabin … We've been schooled by the Cabin, haven't we?"[13]

Heidegger's correspondence and his published work are filled with references to the Black Forest. Especially his hut stands for the possibility of a productive retreat for a solitary thinker for whom dwelling places were essential for authentic existence. The fact that Heidegger sends greetings "from house to house" or to the "whole house"[14] expresses the importance of houses as constitutive of family life and human experience. The tropes of enclosures that are not mere shelters, but enable the constitution of a distinctive world, reveal an aspect of Heidegger's philosophy that has not been sufficiently acknowledged. Especially the hut is endowed with an almost magical quality. For Heidegger, it served as a medium that enables work and communication with Being by way of being intuitively connected to the—mostly threatening—forces of nature. He writes to Jaspers as if speaking of an experience of the sublime: "A storm sweeps over the mountains; the beams creak in the cabin; life lies before the soul: pure, simple, and great." This characterization of the harsh and productive conditions "up here" is juxtaposed to the strange life marked by the pretense of role behavior down below: "Sometimes I no longer comprehend how we can play such strange roles down below."[15]

Philosophical being-in-the-world was for Heidegger essentially being-in-the-hut. Existence worthy of its name is "hut-existence" (*Hüttendasein*).[16] The hut epitomizes the aura of cultural provincialism that permeates Heidegger's writing and has become a central target for critical reactions, especially from the perspective of Critical Theorists. Thus, Habermas credits Heidegger's student Gadamer to have achieved an "urbanization of the Heideggerian province"[17] by highlighting dialogue; Habermas's successor Honneth calls for a "reclamation" and a "civilization" of the Heideggerian wilderness;[18] and Sloterdijk bemoans that

> [I]n Heidegger there is something that did not relocate, that turned away from the world, that harbored a rage for remaining where it was. One can enumerate what his old *Da* (here/there) consists in: the silhouettes of the village and the alleys of the small town, meadows, forests, hills and chapels, classrooms, school hallways, book spines, the banners of the Kirchweih, and bells tolling in the evening.[19]

Habermas, Honneth and Sloterdijk seek to unmask an author who is at odds with the Zeitgeist of urbanism with its anonymity, drive to communication, an accelerated pace of living and its reliance on technology. The movement of goods, ideas, and persons that has become subsumed under the banner of globalization is presented as a perversion of the gravitas of human existence. When visiting France, Heidegger felt "soon struck by the increased traffic … from Paris streaming back on the main road—queues kilometers long in the 2nd and 3rd lanes all moving very slowly," but also emphasizes "how largely unpopulated and beautiful the countryside is."[20]

The short text "Creative Landscape: Why Do We Stay in the Provinces?" perhaps best reveals the particular place of Heidegger's thought. The text was written in 1933 and published in the following year by the journal "Der Alemanne" ("The German"), a journal run by the National Socialists and dedicated to the promotion of the blood and soil ideology in the Freiburg region. The text was broadcasted via Berlin Radio in 1933. In this brief address, Heidegger declines the—already second—offer to take up a prestigious position of chair professor at the University of Berlin. Instead of providing academic or personal reasons for turning down this call to transition to the capital, Heidegger juxtaposes the superficial life in Berlin to the potential for a profound immersion in the landscape he associates with the Black Forest. The reader—or the radio listener—is told that Heidegger's philosophical work "belongs right in the midst of the peasants' work."[21] The solitary thinker emphasizes that, in contrast to the person from the city, he does not contemplate the landscape and the breaks from work are usually spent in silence sitting and smoking a pipe with the peasants from the village: "A city dweller thinks he has gone 'out among the people' as soon as he condescends to have a long conversation with a peasant. But in the evening during a work break, when I sit with the peasant by the fire or at the table in the Lord's corner, we mostly say nothing at all."[22] Heidegger stages himself as standing in an equal or at least structurally parallel relationship with the peasants, a relationship that transcends the need for verbal communication that only snobby city people cherish. The intimate relationship to the place, its landscape, and its inhabitants provide a sense of spatial rootedness and historical depth: "The inner relationship of my own work to the Black Forest and its people comes from a centuries-long and irreplaceable rootedness in the Alemannian-Swabian soil."[23] The theme of rootedness in the soil of the South-West German province is a recurring one in Heidegger's work of the 1930s and 1940s. Literally, the term "*bodenständig*" means "standing on the ground." More idiomatically, one can render it as being uncomplicated, direct, and traditional. At times, Heidegger's staged "*Bodenständigkeit*" comes across as an unwillingness to deliberate or engage with everything considered urban: technology, the media, and cultural diversity. Fittingly, at the end of the short text, Heidegger's silent old peasant friend reacts to the job offer from Berlin. After reading about the "call" to Berlin in the newspaper he reacts as follows: "Slowly he fixed the sure gaze of his clear eyes on mine, and keeping his mouth tightly shut, he thoughtfully put his faithful hand on my shoulder. Ever so slightly he shook his head. That meant: absolutely no!"[24] Not only does the imagined friend not speak, but Heidegger interprets his resolute gesture as leaving no room for deliberation or even second thoughts.

From a strategic perspective, Heidegger's text follows the maxim that offence is the best form of defense. He presents himself as a resolute provincial: someone whose work is bound up with the province, its earth, landscape, weather patterns, and people—especially peasants. He thereby justifies why he refuses to expose himself to the alienating experiences of the city. City dwelling is conceived of as implying uprootedness. Idle chatter and urban pretension is at odds with serious philosophical work of the philosopher of authenticity. Philosophy resembles the arduous tasks performed by peasants rather than the communication among citizens.

Any critical reader of Heidegger will notice the contradictions of this romanticized image of the solitary hut philosopher up high who is nevertheless broadcasting his message to city folks down below. In spite of his critique of the enframing role of modern technology, Heidegger used and listened to the radio, a piece of enframing that was not absent in his hut, to follow, among other events, the unfolding dynamics of the Cuba Missile Crisis. Adam Scharr comments on the contradictions of Heidegger's academic hut existence when he writes about the philosopher's complex *Hüttendasein*:

> The hut, not least because of the ambitions of its inhabitant, was indivisible from a human world with boundaries far beyond the Black Forest. The philosopher dreamed of the lost intellectual and temporal rigor he perceived at Todtnauberg and mythologized the virtues he perceived in it. However, if Heidegger found traces of that life there for himself, they were fragments caught at full stretch: moments of daydream between teaching and other commitments, always supported by a professorial salary. Despite his leanings toward the anti-academic, when working at the hut he nevertheless remained a tactician in the expertise games of professional philosophy, a tendency fatefully epitomized by his attempts at political influence. Although Heidegger carefully sought to submit himself to the rhythms and lessons of the landscape, a parallel life full of human concerns was always somewhere in attendance.[25]

In itself, there is nothing wrong with idealizing one's weekend escape. Arguably, the yearning to take some time off, to decelerate and focus in a hut—or, alternatively, a monastery, or a boat—in order to focus on what is truly important is part of late modern subjects. Somewhat paradoxically, while Heidegger idealizes his mountain hut, the Black Forest peasants Heidegger cherishes and considers his models have often moved to the city drawn by urban thrills ranging from better educational and medical institutions, a diversity of life, and modern amenities such as public transportation. If they stayed, the former peasants profited from an increased connectivity between city and countryside and discovered the advantages of making use of modern farming and telecommunication technology. Not rarely are they generating a good income by offering the necessary infrastructure for skiing, hiking, or ecotourism paid for by city tourists. Rather than the yearning for a retreat in resonance with nature, what is problematic in Heidegger's self-representation is the assumption that a contemporary philosopher of human existence could escape the modern world with its distinctive promises and challenges by withdrawing into a hut. The price paid for is that not only of territorial but of intellectual provincialism. Before addressing the charge of Heidegger's philosophical provincialism again, let us turn to Daoism to focus on the alleged parallel with Daoist localism.

Daoist Localism

Classical Daoism is often understood as primitivism. According to this interpretation, the authors of the *Daodejing* and *Zhuangzi* embrace a life in accordance to nature (*ziran* 自然), which is a life according to the Dao 道. The depiction of village life in *Daodejing* chapter 80 is one of the most well-known passages to support the primitivist interpretation. The passage, translated by Hans-Georg Moeller, reads:

> A small state, few people. Let there be a militia and weapons, but people do not use them. Let people take death seriously, and migrating is far from their mind. There are boats and carriages which no one rides. There are shields and swords which no one takes up. Let people return to the use of knotted cords for writing. Sweet be the food. Beautiful be the clothing. Happy be the customs. Peaceful be the homes. Neighboring states are within the distance of sight, and the sounds of chickens and dogs are mutually heard. But people reach old age and die without traveling back and forth.[26]

On the surface, this passage addresses themes that are also important to Heidegger: an idealization of village life characterized by simplicity and death anxiety. The inhabitants are content with their circumscribed lives and do not travel far. In short, they recognize their existential as well as territorial limits without striving for more. While the depiction of what has been interpreted as an ideal village is unique to chapter 80, the importance of a recognition of human finitude also appears in other chapters of the *Daodejing*. Chapter 72, for example, mentions that people fear authority (*weiwei* 畏威) and chapter 74 explicitly mentions the fear of death (*weise* 畏死). The phrase "ponder on death" or "take death seriously" (*zhongsi* 重死) mentioned in chapter 80 is inverted in the phrase "*qingsi*," to take death lightly in chapter 75, where taking death lightly is considered to be a consequence of a lack of effective governance.[27]

The acknowledgment of limits and death in particular does not imply a rejection of worldly pleasures for Laozi. Thus, the villagers enjoy their food, their clothes, their peaceful homes, and their rituals (translated as "customs" above). Upon closer examination, there is a profound abyss separating Heidegger's praise of his hut existence in the provinces from the Daoist focus on a community of people who ponder death and live out their years in peace without having a need to venture into the distant. The Daoist text is free of the heroic confrontation with the forces of nature and the immanence of death that Heidegger typically associates with death anxiety.[28] Also, the villagers of the *Daodejing* do not emphasize the importance of work, a central theme in Heidegger's essay "Creative Landscape: Why We Remain in the Provinces?"

For Heidegger, the remote hut and dispersed farm houses represent an escape from the city that enabled him to think and work hard in solitude. In fact, Heidegger often exaggerated the hut's remoteness while making increasing use of the public transportation options that allowed him to enrich his urban professorial existence with his regular trips and work-retreats in the Black Forest hills. At times Heidegger also needed a retreat from the hut. *Being and Time* was written primarily in a room that Heidegger rented in a farmhouse in the vicinity of his hut, most likely to concentrate on his work while his young children were playing around the hut.

For Laozi, the focus on the village over the city represents a form of social organization that is relatively independent and yet highly developed and interconnected. Max Weber traced the absence of democratic structures in China to the reduction of cities to administrative and militaristic purposes. He argued that a city was experienced in imperial China by most of its inhabitants as an alien body that is far away from one's true home in the village of one's ancestors. Weber writes: "The alien character of the city was further sharpened by the … absence of the organized self-government found in the village … A 'city' was the seat of the mandarin and was not self-governing; a 'village' was a self-governing settlement without a mandarin."[29] Weber's interpretation is indebted to the observations of Leong and Tao who had observed in *Village and Town Life in China* (1915):

> The village in China is less governed than any other in the world. In China the central government plays but an infinitesimally small part in the village life. The village has perfect freedom of industry and trade, of religion, and of everything that concerns the government, regulation, and protection of the locality. Whatever may be required for its well-being is supplied, not by Imperial Edicts or any other kind of governmental interference, but by voluntary associations.[30]

According to the authors, one of the defining characteristics of a Chinese village is that it is being run by families that secure significant degrees of equality and chances for self-cultivation. Women, in particular, enjoy a high social status within the village family, and education is being promoted across generations. The political order fosters emancipation among the villagers: "The Chinese village folks are most capable (of self-organization and self-government.) On the other hand, they are extremely jealous of external interference. Reform, should any be needed, must come from within, and not from without."[31]

In a related manner, Angus Graham argues that the village presented in the *Daodejing* is characterized by self-rule. Daoists, on his account, favor a form of what he calls "hierarchical anarchism."[32] Daoist utopianism is rooted in the primitivist conception of Shennong 神農, the god of agriculture. It is associated with the ideal of

> a world of village communities where a man's word can be trusted by his neighbors without the need of oaths and covenants, where only idle hands make mischief and disputes are better settled by local custom than by calling in the law, under leaders who work their own fields and are obeyed because everyone can see the point of their decisions.[33]

In a village the inhabitants trust each other and are naturally suspicious of the distant emperor's tendency to impose taxes and wage wars to expand his reign rather than focusing, as they do, on what is next to him.

Furthermore, Graham remarks that "the people are best ordered when interfered with least, but only if there are no thoughts in their hearts of a better life elsewhere, no advertisements between the television programs to tempt them with the promise of 'goods difficult to obtain.'"[34] Yet, it seems to me important that in the ideal village there is no mention of an emperor or forms of rulership as there is in other chapters. Instead, there is a genuine concern for the happiness of the villagers. Rather than political rule, there is the (self-)regulation of desires. In contrast to primitivist interpretation, the chapter suggests a cultivation of a specific sense of awareness. The Daoist utopia of village life is aiming, like the Shennong utopia, at the production of "simple-hearted people who do not hanker after 'goods difficult to obtain.'"[35] Yet, they do so while having sophisticated technology and the option to leave open to them and not making use of these options out of freedom rather than necessity.

In the commentary to their "philosophical translation" of the *Daodejing*, Roger Ames and Henry Rosemont point to the parallel between chapters 80 and 47. While chapter 80 seems to idealize small communities, chapter 47 warns against leaving one's home and seeking what is distant. Ames and Rosemont represent localism as a "responsive and efficacious participation in one's environments, and through one's full contribution at home in the local and the focal relationships that, in sum, make one who one is."[36] For Lin Ma the emphasis on localism by Ames and Rosemont is problematic for the following reason:

> To state Laozi's view as localism (or contextualism) may risk taking the local to be something immutable and self-evident. Ames and Hall place such a strong emphasis on the local that, for them, leaving home seems to necessarily endanger one's defining roles and relationships. They regard concentrating on local life as a necessary condition for knowing the world. This interpretation is suggestive of deterministic ideas that do not accord with Laozi's insight that there are many ways of going about in the world.[37]

While Heidegger may have sympathized with a "localist" interpretation of Laozi along the lines of Ames and Hall, a potentially more convincing interpretation needs to account for the essential difference between the focus on what is in one's environment while keeping the myriad things and all-under-heaven in view from a self-affirmative, one-sided, and ultimately provincial embrace of the provinces one happens to find oneself in.

Today's world is the product of complex processes of exchange: the exchange of goods, people, and ideas. The internet has further exacerbated the trend toward a detachment of human existence from the geographical and cultural traditions she has been born or—in Heideggerian jargon—thrown into. We are no longer bound to the soil we happened to be born on, nor are we standing within culturally clearly demarcated histories. Transculturalization processes as well as an increase in exchange have been an empirical reality that poses new normative challenges. Even though their authors were obviously not familiar with what we discuss under the banner of globalization and transculturalization, the Daoist classics provide a reservoir of anti-provincial motifs that may be a better fit to critically come to terms with the modern world than Heidegger's one-sided appeal to holding onto one's provincial roots. The warning against travel is to be taken with a grain of salt. In fact, the Mawangdui version of the *Daodejing* says "be distant from emigration" rather than "not be distant from emigration." It is likely that the "not" was introduced at a later point. Chapter 80 can be more plausibly interpreted as a warning against aimless traveling back and forth rather than a radical prohibition of travelling.

But what allows the villagers to cherish their lives while living out their years? Ames and Hall comment:

> A life is lived most fully in the immediacy and concreteness of ordinary experience. We can only thrive by further articulating and extending ourselves within those constitutive relationships that locate us in a specific time and place. We must grow from here to there. Whatever the temptations to wealth and grandeur that lure us away from these relationships, such distractions from what we really are serve only to diminish our opportunities for consummate experience. On the other hand, a fully responsive appreciation of the local redirects us back to unmediated feeling as the real site of efficacious knowing and living.[38]

However, chapter 80 does not refer to personal growth or an intensification of experience. While such an interpretation is possible, it risks reducing the Daoist classic to a form of personal self-help and identity-seeking literature. Emphasizing intensive experiences may not capture the philosophically profound, reflective and, most importantly, self-reflective, and critical dimension of the Daoist classic.

The passage presents an unusually concrete vision of a communal life, one that is technologically advanced and connected. The village depicted in chapter 80 is a "global village" in that it perceives the "chickens and dogs" from afar. Chickens may stand for the richness of other food while dogs stand for the—military or other—strength of neighboring polities. While the villagers are focused on the present and near, they also perceive the non-present and far. Rather than depicting a primitivist settlement, the passage presents the reader with an image of a small, but technologically advanced and well-informed community. The people in this community are equipped with sophisticated technology and military equipment, but do not make use of it. Rather than being a depiction of a primitive society, I interpret it as a utopian image of a society that displays high degrees of progress in the areas of technology, but, more importantly, an advanced cultivation of a sense of self-restrained and a prioritization of reflecting on the constitutive limits of existence.[39] The inhabitants of this community—either deliberatively or by habit—leave certain options at their disposal unused. Daoists know when to stop. Mortality is being perceived without either running away or running toward it, but as a reminder to focus on what is important and in reach. The inhabitants of this community are dwellers who have accepted the human condition and know who they are and what they should cherish. Rather than radically juxtaposing inside and outside, the familiar and the foreign, as is typical of Heidegger's thought, Daoism emphasizes the art of focus and transformation. The transformation of inside and outside is exemplified by an awareness of the threshold under one's feet, the doorstep that is the transition from the inside to the outside.[40] Gates and liminal encounters are essential categories in East Asian philosophical traditions and in Daoism in particular. Architecturally, they are represented by passageways that do not seem to serve the typical Western purpose of radically dividing inside and outside (and often blocking one from the other). They do not serve the purpose of clearly separating one's own from what is foreign, but serve as connecting links that invite the traveler to pause and become aware of transitions beyond limits.

The conception of a utopian space such as the one presented in *Daodejing* chapter 80 has been accompanying the radical critique of civilizational pathologies ranging from over-ambitiousness to restlessness. From the beginning, Daoists have not only revealed the cracks in the Confucian appeals to the underlying ambitions of civilizational projects and normative orders by advocating a concern for situational existence; they have also emphasized a critical attitude toward provincialism. This is particularly visible in the *Zhuangzi*. This classic of what one could call liminal existence emphasizes the need for becoming aware of the constitutive limits of one's perspective. The stories combine an appreciation of living in an always finite natural environment with an appreciation of a "global" bird's eye perspective on reality that, however, is also limited, in part due to its overly large-scale perspective.[41]

Steven Burik captures Zhuangzi's oscillation between small and large perspective as an attempt to think "between local and global" that presents a fruitful image of the tasks of comparative philosophy. He writes:

> Zhuangzi is an advocate of "provincial" thinking, if "provincial" is ... understood as a criticism of the traditional understanding of "global" or "cosmopolitan." Although Zhuangzi obviously never spoke about cosmopolitanism, by extension we could say that in advocating for both the smaller and the larger views, he seeks to overcome the traditional global/local distinction altogether and tries to replace it with a different kind of thinking.[42]

In contrast to a Daoist ethos of encounter, for Heidegger, an engagement with what is foreign and distant would need to begin and end in a deeper appreciation of what is proximate. He writes to Jaspers at the occasion of being asked whether he would consider going to work at an institute dedicated to the study of European culture in Tokyo: "The advantages would be broadening of horizon, possibility of undisturbed work, and money to build a house upon return."[43] Heidegger was, at least during certain moments and when considering potential options for increasing his world of references, interested in the foreign, but only from the perspective of how it could be used for his own purposes, including a broadening of horizons of Western metaphysics. More mundane, he was interested in building his family a house in addition to his hut. In contrast to Burik, who sees a similarity between the double perspective of focusing on the local and the global in Daoism and Heidegger's emphasis on homecoming or returning home, I would emphasize the importance of open-ended transformations as well as "free and easy wandering" (*xiaoyaoyou* 逍遙遊) emphasized by Zhuangzi or Laozi's leaving the kingdom for the West.

Daoist utopianism has had significant influences on the Chinese imagination. Most notable is perhaps Tao Qian's (Tao Yuanming, 365–427 CE) influential poem "Peach Blossom Spring" which depicts a fisherman who stumbles upon an egalitarian community living happily hidden away from mainstream society. The community consists of refugees who have escaped an earlier authoritarian regime yet they treat their surprised visitor in a hospitable manner. Peach Blossom Spring is a "powerfully critical utopia"[44] in the Daoist tradition. It is intended to present a counter-image to the oppressive imperial bureaucratic state. The poem also presents a "subtle but powerful self-critical element"[45] in calling into question the very act of evoking utopian images, including Daoist ones, and thereby establishing desires that one chases in vain. When a recluse by the name of Liu Ziji sets out to find the way to the utopian village, he dies in the process.

Conclusion

By way of conclusion, I have argued that the utopian village depicted in *Daodejing* chapter 80 springs from the critical imagination and is intended to expose problematic forms of civilization while also pointing to potentials for a new form of freedom that knows when to stop. This stands in contrast to Heidegger's imagination of the essentially reactionary hut-existence in the German province. Against mainstream scholarship, I have emphasized the difference rather than points of contact between the classical Chinese tradition and Heidegger's existentialism. I am not primarily thinking of the obvious temporal, linguistic, and cultural differences separating the Black Forest philosopher from the ancient Daoist sages. There can be similarities between philosophical ideas across very different traditions that may not have much else in common and lack a direct history of reception.

One philosophically essential difference is that Heidegger's philosophy and Daoism are premised on different media and corresponding forms of action: Heidegger is a thinker of the soil, especially the soil of his homeland to which he retreats during times of crisis or productivity. In contrast, Lao-Zhuang are philosophers of water and air who emphasize not only stillness, but also movement and the enabling features of transformation processes.

The philosophical difference is mirrored by a different architecture. Heidegger's hut is located on a southward facing slope facing West. In traditional Daoist-inspired *feng shui* 風水 belief, huts should face South. Heidegger's hut is made to withstand the raging forces of the times, while Daoist-inspired enclosures emphasize the transition from inner to outer, the enabling conditions of empty spaces such as windows and doors as well as courtyards.[46] While Heidegger emphasizes the distance of his hut to other human dwellings, Daoist utopias consist of an assembly of huts and common spaces in which people can encounter each other.

This chapter has demonstrated that Heidegger's anti-urbanism is rooted in his self-ascribed provincialism. This is documented not only in his philosophically nuanced rejection of the potentials of engaging in intercultural dialogue, especially with Asia, but also in his conception of philosophy as an engagement with the sources of one's own philosophical tradition to which one needs to return. Heidegger seems to have been aware that the idealized word of his hut-existence was a remnant of a past. Especially in "Building Dwelling Thinking," he mourns for this world in a nostalgic tone of voice without, however, critically engaging with the dark sides of provincialism or the reasons for modernization and urbanization.[47] Rather than revealing the limitations of a world of assigned social roles and expectations, narrow-mindedness and xenophobia usually associated with life in the provinces, Heidegger simply blames the allegedly uprooting forces of modernity for the decay of authentic dwelling.

Departing from the observation that what divides Heidegger and Daoism is more significant than what unites them, I have suggested that the Daoist utopia presented in chapter 80 of the *Daodejing* can be interpreted as an attempt to present a form of dwelling in the provinces that acknowledges the need for certain technologies while also cultivating a freedom from becoming enslaved by them. Drawing on this condensed representation of achieved form of living, one could conclude by drawing consequences for the design of livable communities by highlighting five dimensions. First, livable communities would have to be sufficiently small in order to be self-governing and free from social alienation and an overly complex administrative apparatus. Secondly, such communities would have to be capable of protecting themselves without seeking confrontation with its neighbors. Third, life in this community would allow a focus on what is important. For Daoists, this includes a reflection on mortality as much as the cherishing of the proximate features that provide the life of villagers with meaning: the sweetness of their food, the beauty of their clothes, the peacefulness of their homes, as well as the delightfulness of their customs. Fourth, a well-ordered community would have to be well connected and thus capable of receiving news about what is going on outside of its limits. Fifth, they would be communities that would not force—but neither prohibit—its citizens to come and go. From a contemporary perspective marked by the current Coronavirus pandemic, one can conceive of the utopian Daoist village as an attractive home. It would be a village that would be sufficiently attractive to stay, with or without roots.

Notes

1 Bertholt Brecht, *Poems 1913–1956*, trans. John Willett (New York: Routledge, 1998), 314–15.
2 On Brecht's creative reception of the subversive potential of Chinese philosophy and Daoism in particular, see Heinrich Detering, *Bertolt Brecht und Laotse* (Göttingen: Wallstein, 2008).
3 Heinrich Wiegand Petzet, *Encounters and Dialogues with Martin Heidegger, 1929–1976*, trans. Parvis Emad and Kenneth Maly (Chicago: University of Chicago Press, 1993), 216–17.
4 An example of the philosophical hermit is Xu You while Bo Yi and Shu Qi embody political recluse. See Jürgen Weber, "Die Vier Weißhaarigen vom Shang-Berg: Die Verkörperung eines chinesischen Eremitenideals," *Oriens Extremus*, 39.2 (1996): 131–61.
5 The literature on Heidegger's relationship to East Asia is extensive. It includes, among others, Hartmut Buchner, ed., *Japan und Heidegger* [Japan and Heidegger] (Sigmaringen: Thorbecke, 1989); Bret W. Davis, "Heidegger and Asian Philosophy," in *The Bloomsbury Companion to Heidegger*, ed. Francois Raffoul and Eric S. Nelson, 459–71 (London: Bloomsbury Academic, 2013); Reinhard May, *Heidegger's Hidden Sources: East Asian Influences on His Work*, trans. Graham Parkes (London: Routledge, 1996); Graham Parkes, ed., *Heidegger and Asian Thought* (Honolulu: University of Hawaii Press, 1987); Lin Ma, *Heidegger on East-West Dialogue: Anticipating the Event* (New York: Routledge, 2008); and Fabian Heubel, *Gewundene Wege nach China: Heidegger-Daoismus-Adorno* (Frankfurt am Main: Klostermann, 2020).
6 Shih-Yi Hsiao, "Heidegger and Our Translation of the *Tao Te Ching*," in Graham Parkes (ed.), *Heidegger and Asian Thought*, 93–101 (Honolulu: University of Hawaii Press, 1987).
7 The term "Eurodaoism" designates the European reception of East Asian thought as part of a Western Oriental Renaissance. This neologism has been coined by Peter Sloterdijk in his *Infinite Mobilization: Towards a Critique of Political Kinetics*, trans. Sandra Berjan (London: Polity, 2020).
8 Martin Heidegger, *Letters to His Wife: 1915–1970*, trans. R.D.V. Glasgow (Cambridge: Polity 2008), 45.
9 Ibid.
10 Ibid., 124.
11 Ibid., 134.
12 Ibid., 138.
13 Ibid., 165.
14 Heidegger, *Letters to his Wife*, 215.
15 Martin Heidegger, *The Heidegger-Jaspers Correspondence, 1920–1963*, trans. Gary E. Aylesworth (Amherst: Humanity Books, 2003), 64–5; 65–6.
16 Martin Heidegger, "Creative Landscape: Why Do We Stay in the Provinces?" in *The Weimar Republic Sourcebook*, ed. Anton Kaes, Martin Jay, Edward Dimenberg (Berkeley: University of California Press), 426–8, at 427.
17 Jürgen Habermas, "Urbanisierung der Heideggerschen Provinz," in *Philosophisch-politische Profile*, 392–401 (Frankfurt: Suhrkamp, 1981).
18 Axel Honneth, "On the Destructive Power of the Third: Gadamer and Heidegger's Doctrine of Intersubjectivity," *Philosophy and Social Criticism*, 29.1 (2003): 5–21, at 5–6.

19 Peter Sloterdijk, *Not Saved: Essays after Heidegger* (London: Polity, 2016), 27.
20 Heidegger, *Letters to his Wife*, 307.
21 Heidegger, "Creative Landscape," 427.
22 Ibid.
23 Ibid.
24 Ibid., 428.
25 Adam Scharr, *Heidegger's Hut Existence* (Cambridge: MIT Press, 2006), 71.
26 Hans-Georg Moeller, trans., *Daodejing: A Complete Translation and Commentary* (La Salle: Open Court, 2007), 185.
27 Based on the overlap of the themes of death anxiety, and a concern for common people, Franklin Perkins argues that chs. 72, 74, 75, and 80 present a coherent group that can be interpreted separately from other sections of the *Daodejing*. See Franklin Perkins, "Divergences within the *Laozi*: A Study of Chapters 67–81," *T'oung Pao*, 100.1–3 (2014): 1–32.
28 For the analysis of the possibility of Being-a-Whole of Da-sein and Being-toward-Death, see Martin Heidegger, *Being and Time*, trans. Joan Stambaugh (Albany: State University of New York Press, 1996), paragraphs 46–53.
29 Max Weber, *The Religion of China: Confucianism and Taoism*, trans. Hans H. Gerth (Glencoe: The Free Press, 1959), 90–1.
30 Y.K. Leong and L.K. Tao, *Village and Town Life in China* (London: George Allen and Unwin, 1915), 5.
31 Ibid., 40.
32 Angus C. Graham, *Disputers of the Tao: Philosophical Arguments in Ancient China* (La Salle: Open Court, 1989), 303.
33 Ibid., 69–70.
34 Ibid., 233.
35 Ibid. 303.
36 Roger T. Ames and David L. Hall, trans., *Daodejing: A Philosophical Translation* (New York: Ballantine Books, 2003), 150.
37 Lin Ma, *Heidegger on East-West Dialogue: Anticipating the Event* (New York: Routledge, 2008), 132.
38 Ibid., 203.
39 Guying Chen develops a non-primitivist reading of chapter 80 following the Daoist directive that the sage "knows civilization and maintains simplicity." See Guying Chen, *The Annotated Critical Laozi: With Contemporary Explication and Traditional Commentary*, trans. Paul D'Ambrosio and Ouyang Xiao (Leiden: Brill, 2020), 400. For a related interpretation, see Feng Youlan, *A New History of Chinese Philosophy* 中國哲學史新編 (Beijing: People's Press, 2001).
40 Martin Buber emphasizes the role of the gateway (*Pforte*), turning-around, self-transformation and mutual encounter rather than a self-assertive return to an alleged ideal condition in his interpretation of Daoism. See also Eric S. Nelson, "Buber's Phenomenological Interpretation of Laozi," in David Chai (ed.), *Daoist Encounters with Phenomenology: Thinking Interculturally about Human Existence*, 105–20 (London: Bloomsbury, 2020).
41 I have traced the importance of bird motifs in China and the European tradition in relation to discussions of perspectivism and its relationship to wisdom in Mario Wenning, "Birds of Wisdom," *Philosophy East and West*, 71.3 (2021): 683–703.

42 Steven Burik, "Between Local and Global: The Place of Comparative Philosophy through Heidegger and Daoism," in Peter D. Hershock and Roger T. Ames (eds.), *Philosophies of Place: An Intercultural Conversation*, 34–50 (Honolulu: University of Hawaii Press, 2019), at 46.
43 Heidegger, *Heidegger-Jaspers Correspondence*, 52.
44 Nathaniel R. Walker, "Reforming the Way: The Palace and the Village in Daoist Paradise," *Utopian Studies*, 24.1 (2013): 6–22, at 12.
45 Ibid., 14.
46 Following Daoist aesthetics, Chinese houses orchestrate an interplay of solid and void spaces. The essential elements of Chinese architecture consist of enclosure, symmetry, axiality, and hierarchy. See Ronald G. Knapp, *Chinese Houses: The Architectural Heritage of a Nation* (North Clarendon: Tuttle, 2004), 159.
47 Martin Heidegger, "Building Dwelling Thinking," in *Poetry, Language and Thought*, trans. Albert Hofstadter (New York: Harper Collins, 1971), 143–62.

References

Ames, Roger T. and David L. Hall, trans. *Daodejing: A Philosophical Translation*. New York: Ballantine Books, 2003.

Brecht, Bertolt. *Poems, 1913–1956*. Translated by John Willett. New York: Routledge, 1998.

Buchner, Hartmut, ed. *Japan und Heidegger* (Japan and Heidegger). Sigmaringen: Thorbecke, 1989.

Burik, Steven. "Between Local and Global: The Place of Comparative Philosophy through Heidegger and Daoism." In Peter D. Hershock and Roger T. Ames (eds.), *Philosophies of Place: An Intercultural Conversation*, 34–50. Honolulu: University of Hawaii Press, 2019.

Chen, Guying. *The Annotated Critical Laozi: With Contemporary Explication and Traditional Commentary*. Translated by Paul D'Ambrosio and Ouyang Xiao. Leiden: Brill, 2020.

Davis, Bret W. "Heidegger and Asian Philosophy." In Francois Raffoul and Eric S. Nelson (eds.), *The Bloomsbury Companion to Heidegger*, 459–71. London: Bloomsbury Academic, 2013.

Detering, Heinrich. *Bertolt Brecht und Laotse*. Göttingen: Wallstein, 2008.

Feng, Youlan. *A New History of Chinese Philosophy* 中國哲學史新編. Beijing: People's Press, 2001.

Graham, Angus C. *Disputers of the Tao: Philosophical Arguments in Ancient China*. La Salle: Open Court, 1989.

Habermas, Jürgen. "Urbanisierung der Heideggerschen Provinz." In *Philosophisch-politische Profile*, 392–401. Frankfurt: Suhrkamp, 1981.

Heidegger, Martin. *Poetry, Language and Thought*. Translated by Albert Hofstadter. New York: Harper Collins, 1971.

Heidegger, Martin. "Creative Landscape: Why Do We Stay in the Provinces?" In Anton Kaes, Martin Jay and Edward Dimenberg (eds.), *The Weimar Republic Sourcebook*, 426–8. Berkeley: University of California Press, 1995.

Heidegger, Martin. *Being and Time*. Translated by Joan Stambaugh. Albany: State University of New York Press, 1996.

Heidegger, Martin. *The Heidegger-Jaspers Correspondence, 1920–1963*. Translated by Gary E. Aylesworth. Amherst: Humanity Books, 2003.
Heidegger, Martin. *Letters to His Wife: 1915–1970*. Translated by R.D.V. Glasgow. Cambridge: Polity, 2008.
Heubel, Fabian. *Gewundene Wege nach China: Heidegger-Daoismus-Adorno*. Frankfurt am Main: Klostermann, 2020.
Honneth, Axel. "On the Destructive Power of the Third: Gadamer and Heidegger's Doctrine of Intersubjectivity." *Philosophy and Social Criticism*, 29.1 (2003): 5–21.
Hsiao, Shih-Yi. "Heidegger and Our Translation of the *Tao Te Ching*." In Graham Parkes (ed.), *Heidegger and Asian Thought*, 93–103. Honolulu: University of Hawaii Press, 1987.
Knapp, Ronald G. *Chinese Houses: The Architectural Heritage of a Nation*. North Clarendon: Tuttle, 2004.
Leong, Y.K. and L.K. Tao, *Village and Town Life in China*. London: George Allen and Unwin, 1915.
Ma, Lin. *Heidegger on East-West Dialogue: Anticipating the Event*. New York: Routledge, 2008.
May, Reinhard. *Heidegger's Hidden Sources: East Asian Influences on His Work*. Translated by Graham Parkes. London: Routledge, 1996.
Moeller, Hans-Georg, trans. *Daodejing: A Complete Translation and Commentary*. La Salle: Open Court, 2007.
Nelson, Eric S. "Buber's Phenomenological Interpretation of Laozi." In David Chai (ed.), *Daoist Encounters with Phenomenology: Thinking Interculturally about Human Existence*, 105–20. London: Bloomsbury, 2020.
Parkes, Graham, ed. *Heidegger and Asian Thought*. Honolulu: University of Hawaii Press, 1987.
Perkins, Franklin. "Divergences within the *Laozi*: A Study of Chapters 67–81." *T'oung Pao*, 100.1–3 (2014): 1–32.
Petzet, Heinrich Wiegand. *Encounters and Dialogues with Martin Heidegger, 1929–1976*. Translated by Parvis Emad and Kenneth Maly. Chicago: University of Chicago Press, 1993.
Scharr, Adam. *Heidegger's Hut Existence*. Cambridge: MIT Press, 2006.
Sloterdijk, Peter. *Not Saved: Essays after Heidegger*. London: Polity, 2016.
Sloterdijk, Peter. *Infinite Mobilization: Towards a Critique of Political Kinetics*. Translated by Sandra Berjan. London: Polity, 2020.
Walker, Nathaniel R. "Reforming the Way: The Palace and the Village in Daoist Paradise." *Utopian Studies*, 24.1 (2013): 6–22.
Weber, Jürgen. "Die Vier Weißhaarigen vom Shang-Berg: Die Verkörperung eines chinesischen Eremitenideals." *Oriens Extremus*, 39.2 (1996): 131–61.
Weber, Max. *The Religion of China: Confucianism and Taoism*. Translated by Hans H. Gerth. Glencoe: The Free Press, 1959.
Wenning, Mario. "Birds of Wisdom." *Philosophy East and West*, 71.3 (2021): 683–703.

Index

Ab-grund (abyss) 18, 25–6, 28, 47, 209, 229, 249
Aletheia (unconcealment) 37–8, 64, 66, 74, 88n109, 93n152, 105, 112–14, 117–18, 150, 154, 164–5, 168, 171, 206, 208–9, 221n28
Ames, Roger 132, 213–14, 220, 250–1
Angst (anxiety) 25–8, 110, 128, 134–5, 138, 143, 149, 197, 209, 248–9
Anklang (echo, resonance) 65, 67–70, 73, 92n148
Antigone 190–2
Aristotle 56, 115
aufgehende Walten (arising holding-sway) 73, 77, 93
Auseinandersetzung (con-versation) 50, 59

Berlin 47–9, 51, 245–7
Black Notebooks 5, 225, 228, 237
Bremen 1, 2, 11, 55, 70–1, 73–4, 77, 80n13, 93n153, 151–3, 164, 244
brightness / clarity 70–1, 73, 80n13, 113, 170, 174, 214, 216, 230, 233
Buber, Martin 1–2, 6n5, 39n10, 74, 93n153, 93n154, 143, 156n18, 183, 233, 256n40
Buddhism 14, 36, 44n56, 71, 84n67, 141, 149

candle 165, 171
carve 42n32, 94n164, 112, 127, 144, 167, 175
Chillida, Eduardo 166, 176
Cook Ding 庖丁 42n32, 94n164, 105, 107, 127, 217

dao 道 5, 13–14, 16, 23, 40n13, 48–9, 60, 79n7, 94n164, 103–6, 112, 114, 127–30, 138, 165, 167–8, 171–2, 174–5, 213, 248
dao shu 道樞 (Dao pivot) 49, 55–6, 94n164

darkness 35, 37, 70, 80n13, 93n150, 94n164, 113, 172, 174, 215, 234
Dasein (there-being) 15–17, 20, 27, 29, 42n28, 47, 55–6, 59, 61–4, 67–9, 75–7, 87n91, 91n124, 110–11, 113–14, 118, 121n32, 129, 134–7, 151, 154, 185, 193, 204–6, 244, 256n28
death 5, 15, 25–31, 43n39, 43n44, 66, 86n83, 127–38, 143–5, 147, 171, 231, 248, 249, 256n27
Ding (thing) 2, 16–17, 24, 32, 34–5, 42n29, 43n49, 47, 56, 59, 61, 63, 69, 77, 83n52, 85n69, 85n70, 141–3, 145, 151–4, 156n17, 163, 184, 195–7, 238, 244
dunklen Öffnung (dark opening) 56, 77

earth 15–16, 18, 21, 27, 35–7, 41n18, 44n60, 49, 52, 55–6, 60, 63–6, 68, 71, 76–7, 79n7, 83n55, 86n83, 88n109, 91n136, 94n165, 104, 106, 108, 110, 112–13, 129–30, 132–4, 138, 142, 144–5, 147–52, 173–4, 176, 185, 190, 194–5, 230, 247
Eckhart, Meister 66–7, 89n112, 143, 156n17, 227
ekstasis 62
Entscheidung (de-cision) 60, 67
equiprimordial 61, 68, 73, 92n149, 205
Ereignis (event, appropriation) 47, 55–6, 70, 73, 91, 105, 114–15, 118, 208–9
Erklüftung (encleavage) 56
Erschlossenheit (disclosedness) 29, 63
Erschweigen 207–8, 212

forget (*wang* 忘) 25, 29, 31, 76, 94n164, 107, 166–7, 170, 218–20
Frankfurt 35, 151

Index

Freiburg 2–3, 12, 33, 48, 80n13, 88n110, 163, 169, 184, 245–6
Fug (jointure) 69, 71–3, 87n91, 92n139, 92n147

Gelassenheit (releasement) 22, 32, 43n49, 47, 62, 66, 89n112, 143, 154, 156n17, 159n81, 210, 229, 244
Gestell (framing) 55, 151, 187
Gestimmtheit (attunement) 76
Geviert (fourfold) 55, 60, 83n52, 151, 238, 244
God(s) 26, 38, 47, 50, 53–6, 58–60, 63, 66, 68, 71–2, 82n41, 88n109, 150, 154, 156n17, 167, 186–7, 191, 195, 206, 211
Graham, Angus C. 27, 29, 31–2, 39n5, 43n48, 217, 219, 250
Guo Xiang 郭象 59, 85n72, 94n164, 120n32, 149, 158n49, 159n80, 196
Guodian 郭店 145–9, 157n30

heaven 15–16, 18, 21–2, 29, 32, 35, 41n18, 49, 55–6, 59, 71, 76–7, 79, 81n13, 82n48, 86n83, 88n109, 91n136, 94n158, 94n165, 104, 106, 108, 110, 112–13, 129–30, 132–3, 144–5, 148–9, 150, 167, 169–70, 174–6, 195, 251
Heraclitus 11–12, 14–15, 27, 40n12, 40n13, 44n59, 47, 54, 71–7, 82n41, 92n141, 93n155, 150, 206–7, 227
Heshang Gong 河上公 146–8
Hölderlin, Friedrich 73, 183–94, 196–9, 199n5, 227, 237–8
Hsiao, Paul Shih-Yi 2–3, 12, 65, 78–9n7, 83n49, 88n109, 88n110
Huizi 惠子 2, 12, 18, 21–2, 24, 55, 130, 194, 234
Hüttendasein (hut-existence) 246–7

interality (*jian* 間) 5, 103–4, 106–9, 111–16, 118–19, 120n25, 121n32

Jaspers, Karl 65, 67, 245, 253
ji 跡 (footprint, trace) 47, 58–9, 77, 85n72

Kehre (the turn) 16, 47, 61, 77, 85n72, 135, 226, 228

Leere (void) 47–8, 56, 63–4, 71, 77, 80n13, 83n48, 91n124, 141
Leibniz, Gottfried Wilhelm 50, 60, 86n80
Leitfäden (guiding threads) 74–5
Lichtung (clearing) 3, 20, 37, 64–5, 67, 70, 76, 79n7, 86n83, 89n112, 105, 107, 109, 112–15, 118, 151, 164–5, 168–9, 171, 173, 176, 204
Liezi 列子 71, 91n136, 147–8

Ma, Lin 1, 4, 121n34, 250
maieutics 63
Mawangdui 馬王堆 39n5, 145, 147, 215, 251
Munich 80n13
mystery 3, 49, 57, 60, 63–4, 67, 77, 80n13, 89n112, 116, 130, 164, 171, 185, 197, 209

National Socialism 2, 5, 184, 191, 225–6, 228–32, 237–8
Nazi / Nazism 1, 184, 186, 188–9, 191, 199, 229–32, 238
Nichts (nothing) 24–7, 31, 33, 37, 58–9, 110–11, 151–2, 170–1, 195, 203, 209, 240n12, 244
Nietzsche, Friedrich 4, 14, 18, 26, 37, 40n12, 41n21, 42n27, 72, 225, 237

Parkes, Graham 1, 4–5, 65, 71–2, 77, 79n7, 92n141, 193
Parmenides 15, 47, 58, 66–7, 73, 84n62, 88n109, 90n118, 90n119
Petzet, Heinrich-Wiegand 1–3, 12, 78n6, 164, 166, 243
Pforte (passageway, portal) 48–50, 54, 256n40
phusis 73, 150–1, 158n54
Plato 13–14, 28, 72, 116–17, 122n88
Pöggeler, Otto 1, 43n34, 73, 76–7
poiesis 164–6, 183
polis 191–2

qi 氣 (breath) 93n154, 131–2, 144, 214

reckless / abandoned words 219
ruler / king 56, 132, 148, 157n44, 167, 195–6, 250

Sage (saying) 204, 208, 210–11
sage (*shengren* 聖人, *zhenren* 真人) 2, 23, 27, 38, 47, 75, 77, 85n72, 94n164, 112, 127–30, 132, 138, 146, 157, 215–16, 219, 256n39
Schelling, Friedrich 47–54, 56–64, 66–7, 69, 73, 75–7, 78n6, 80–1n13, 82–3n48, 85n69, 87n91, 88n109, 89n112, 90n124
Schritt züruck (step back) 47, 59
Schweigen 47, 59
sculpture 163–76
Selbstbehauptung (self-affirmation) 228
shadow 61, 71, 142, 169, 171, 174
sigetic (silence) 206
silence 75, 79, 83n55, 203–20, 246
spirit 5, 14, 25–6, 49, 52, 61, 71, 89n112, 113, 120n25, 130–1, 163, 168–70, 173, 175–6, 188, 192, 227–9, 236–7, 240n26, 244–5
Stimmung (attunement, mood) 20, 148, 185

taiji 太極 (Ultimate One) 37, 104
techne 165–6
tong 通 (throughness) 107, 120n16
tree 19, 21, 32, 42n31, 65, 74, 75, 77, 113, 115, 128, 153, 164, 167–8, 170, 172–6

Umwelt (environment) 15, 20–1, 142, 155n5
Unbedingt (unbethinged) 51, 59, 77, 85n69
uncarved block (*pu* 樸) 28, 81n13, 111
Unheimische (unhomely) 190
Unheimliche (uncanny) 134, 190
Unheimlichkeit (uncanniness) 25, 135
Unnötige (unnecessary) 240n12

Verbergen (concealing) 206, 209
Verlassenheit (abandonment) 62, 66
Vernehmen (ap-prehension) 47, 57, 61, 63, 67–8, 77, 86n89, 90n119
Verschweigen (hiddenness, concealment, silence) 207–8, 212
Verschwiegenheit (reticence) 205–6

von Gebsattel, Viktor 1
vorhanden (on-hand, present-at-hand) 16–17, 19–20, 25–6, 32, 40n17, 42n29, 142, 146
Vorhandenheit (on-handness) 17, 19
Vorstellung (representation) 61, 77

Wang Bi 王弼 76, 147–8
Weg (Way) 78n7, 105, 108–209
Wilhelm, Richard 2, 44n56, 143, 163, 195, 225, 240n12
Woodworker / Carpenter Qing 32, 76, 93n154, 164, 167–8, 170–2, 176
wu 無 (nothingness, no-thing, void) 24, 27, 34, 49, 51, 52, 56, 58–9, 64, 71, 77, 80–1n13, 86n83, 94n164, 104, 107–12, 115, 118, 120–1n32, 147, 149, 151, 153–4, 158n50, 163, 165, 167–76, 203, 209, 218, 238, 257n46
wu 物 (thing) 24, 32–3, 85n70, 94n164, 104, 106, 108–12, 115, 141, 143–9, 153–5, 157n30, 159n63, 172, 195–6, 219
Wu, Kuang-Ming 55, 74, 84n67
wuming 無名 (nameless) 120–1n32, 215–16, 234
wuwei 無為 (non-action, effortless acting) 29, 31, 67, 79, 89n112, 94n158, 127, 129–30, 132, 135, 143, 148–9, 153–5, 156n17, 214

Yijing 易經 (*Book of Changes*) 52, 76, 90n124, 104, 119n3, 147
Yin-Yang 陰陽 80n13, 88n109, 104, 107, 115

ziran 自然 (self-so, natural, spontaneity) 28–9, 41n18, 41n22, 69, 85n72, 94n164, 107, 111–12, 143, 145–51, 153, 155, 156n17, 157n32, 158n45, 164, 172, 215, 220, 248
zuhanden (to-hand) 15–27, 29–31, 33, 35–6, 40n17, 43n45, 43n46, 142, 145, 153
Zuhandenheit (to-handness) 15, 17, 19–20, 41n23

Printed in the USA
CPSIA information can be obtained
at www.ICGtesting.com
LVHW021633221223
767237LV00003B/127